MW01598313

ECONOMICS BEYOND THE MILLENNIUM

The ASSET Series

This is a book in the ASSET Series. ASSET is the Association of Southern European Economic Theorists, which exists to encourage the development among participating centres of programmes of research into economic problems. The group has from its beginnings enjoyed the support of several national governments and also the European Union in order to promote exchanges of researchers and ideas among institutions that are all based in Southern Europe. The group also distributes its own discussion papers. The books in this series are all derived from work carried out in an ASSET centre.

Participating centres are: Departament d'Economia e Historia Economica, Universitat Autonoma de Barcelona, Spain; Instituto de Economia Publica and Departmento de Fundamentos del Analisis Economico, Facultad de Ciencias Economicas y Empresariales, Universidad del Pais Vasco–Euskal Herriko Unibersitatea, Bilbao, Spain; Departamento de Fundamentos del Analisis Economico, Universidad de Alicante, Spain; Facultat de Ciencies Economiques I Empresarials, Universitat Pompeu Fabra, Barcelona, Spain; Groupe de Recherche en Economie Mathématique et Quantitative, Centre National de la Recherche Scientifique, Ecole des Hautes Etudes en Sciences Sociales et Université des Sciences Sociales de Toulouse, France; Groupement de Recherche en Economie Quantitative d'Aix-Marseille, Centre National de la Recherche Scientifique, Ecole des Hautes Etudes en Sciences Sociales et Universités d'Aix-Marseill II et III, Aix-en-Provence et Marseille, France; Department of Economics, European University Institute, Firenze, Italy; Dipartimento di Scienza Economiche, Universita degli Studi di Bologna, Italy; Department of Economics, Athens University of Economics and Business, Greece; Faculdade de Economia, Universidade Nova de Lisboa, Portugal; Faculdade de Ciencias Economicas e Empresariais, Universidade Catòlica Portuguesa, Lisboa, Portugal; Centre for Economic Design, Boğaziçi University, Istanbul, Turkey; Eitan Berglas School, Faculty of Social Sciences, Tel Aviv University, Israel.

The screening committee for the series consists of S. Barbera, Universitat Autonoma de Barcelona, Spain; L. Cabral, Universidade Nova Liboa, Portugal; J. Crémer, Groupe de Recherche en Economie Mathématique et Quantitative, Toulouse, France; R. Davidson, Groupement de Recherche en Economie Quantitative d'Aix-Marseille, Marseille, France; J. P. Florens, Groupe de Recherche en Economie Mathématique et Quantitative, Toulouse, France; L. A. Gérard-Varet, Groupement de Recherche en Economie Quantitative d'Aix-Marseille, Marseille, France; A. P. Kirman, Groupement de Recherche en Economie Quantitative d'Aix-Marseille, Marseille, France; T. Kollintzas, Athens University of Economics and Business, Greece; A. Mas Colell, Universitat Pompeu Fabra, Barcelona, Spain.

Economics Beyond the Millennium

Edited by
ALAN KIRMAN
and
LOUIS-ANDRÉ GÉRARD-VARET

OXFORD
UNIVERSITY PRESS

OXFORD

UNIVERSITY PRESS

Great Clarendon Street, Oxford OX2 6DP
Oxford University Press is a department of the University of Oxford.
It furthers the University's objective of excellence in research, scholarship,
and education by publishing worldwide in

Oxford New York

Athens Auckland Bangkok Bogotá Buenos Aires Calcutta
Cape Town Chennai Dar es Salaam Delhi Florence Hong Kong Istanbul
Karachi Kuala Lumpur Madrid Melbourne Mexico City Mumbai
Nairobi Paris São Paulo Singapore Taipei Tokyo Toronto Warsaw
and associated companies in Berlin Ibadan

Oxford is a registered trade mark of Oxford University Press
in the UK and certain other countries

Published in the United States
by Oxford University Press Inc., New York

© Oxford University Press 1999

The moral rights of the author have been asserted
Database right Oxford University Press (maker)

First published 1999

All rights reserved. No part of this publication may be reproduced,
stored in a retrieval system, or transmitted, in any form or by any means,
without the prior permission in writing of Oxford University Press,
or as expressly permitted by law, or under terms agreed with the appropriate
reprographics rights organizations. Enquiries concerning reproduction
outside the scope of the above should be sent to the Rights Department,
Oxford University Press, at the address above

You must not circulate this book in any other binding or cover
and you must impose the same condition on any acquirer

British Library Cataloguing in Publication Data
Data available

Library of Congress Cataloging in Publication Data
Economics beyond the millennium / edited by Alan P. Kirman and Louis
-André Gérard-Varet.
p. cm. — (The ASSET series)
Includes bibliographical references and index.
1. Economic forecasting. 2. Econometric models. 3. Twenty-first
century—Forecasts. I. Kirman, A. P. II. Gérard-Varet, L.-A.
(Louis-André) III. Association of Southern European Economic
Theorists. IV. Series.
HB3730.E25 1998
330'.01'12—dc21 98–17369
ISBN 0–19–829211–2

1 3 5 7 9 10 8 6 4 2

Typeset by Graphicraft Ltd, Hong Kong
Printed in Great Britain
on acid-free paper by
Biddles Ltd, Guildford & King's Lynn

Contents

Contents

III. ISSUES IN ECONOMETRICS

Contributors

Patrick Artus	Caisse des Dépôts et Consignations, Paris
Luc Bauwens	CORE, Université Catholique de Louvain, Louvain-La-Neuve, Belgium
Richard Blundell	University College, London; Institute for Fiscal Studies
Claude d'Aspremont	CORE, Université Catholique de Louvain, Louvain-La-Neuve, Belgium
Russell Davidson	GREQAM, EHESS, Marseille
Jacques Drèze	CORE, Université Catholique de Louvain, Louvain-La-Neuve, Belgium
Rodolphe Dos Santos Ferreira	BETA, Université Louis Pasteur Strasbourg, Strasbourg
Jean Gabszewicz	CORE, Université Catholique de Louvain, Louvain-La-Neuve, Belgium
Louis André Gérard-Varet	EHESS, Marseille
Christian Gourieroux	CREST, CEPREMAP, Malakoff, France
Werner Hildenbrand	Rheinishce Friedrich-Wilhelms Universität Bonn
Alan Kirman	Université Aix-Marseille III; GREQAM, EHESS, Marseille
Michel Lubrano	GREQAM, CNRS, EHESS, Marseille
Edmond Malinvaud	CREST, CEPREMAP, Malakoff, France
Agustín Maravall	Banco de Espana, Suboficina de Informacion y Methodos de Calculo, Servicio de Estudios, Madrid
Philippe Michel	GREQAM, Université d'Aix-Marseille II; IUF, EHESS, Marseille
Heracles Polemarchakis	CORE, Université Catholique de Louvain, Louvain-La-Neuve, Belgium
Jean-Pierre Ponssard	CNRS, Laboratoire d'Econométrie de l'Ecole Polytechnique, Paris
Suzanne Scotchmer	Graduate School of Public Policy, University of California, Berkeley
Margaret E. Slade	Department of Economics, The University of British Columbia, Vancouver; GREQAM, EHESS, Marseille
Hervé Tanguy	INRA, Laboratoire d'Econométrie de l'Ecole Polytechnique, Paris
Jacques-Francois Thisse	CORE, Université Catholique de Louvain, Louvain-La-Neuve, Belgium
Eric van Damme	Center for Economic Research, Tilburg University, Tilburg, The Netherlands

Introduction

Alan P. Kirman, Louis-André Gérard-Varet, and Michèle Ruggiero

Economists are notoriously bad at predicting, and therefore one might suspect that they would not do a very good job of forecasting how their own discipline will evolve as it passes the next millenium. Nevertheless, this was the task set for the authors of this book, who met on the occasion of the tenth anniversary of the GREQE (which has now become the GREQAM, Groupe de recherche en economie quantitative et econometrie d'Aix-Marseille). Whether the forecasts turn out to be accurate or not, the vision of the contributors sheds interesting light on the different areas covered. Furthermore, their different attitudes concerning the direction that economics will take reveal that, at least within the economics profession, there is no obvious convergence of expectations. Despite this, there are several common threads that can be picked out in the various chapters, and while the introductions to the three parts of the book give a clear picture of the contents of each section and how the various components fit together within each part, the purpose of this brief introduction is to try identify those points on which there is some common accord.

Perhaps the first of these common themes is the shift that many authors detect from the construction of rigorous and self-contained theoretical models towards models that are more descriptive and possibly, in consequence, more realistic. Van Damme and Ponsard, in rather different ways, both take this point of view. For the former, the road of endowing agents with super-rationality and concentrating on equilibrium refinements is not the one to take. Rather, he suggests that empirical relevance will occupy a greater place in the future. This should lead one away from the current frustrating situation in which 'anything can happen' in game-theoretical models into one in which outcomes are more specific. The position that Ponsard adopts is that the firm cannot be taken as the almost vacuous entity of standard theory: rather, one should consider the way in which the firm is organized and the resultant role of strategic analysis. Rationality in its strongest form is sacrificed in order to obtain more testable propositons.

At its peak, the period of 'high theory' in economics was preoccupied with internal consistency rather than with empirical relevance, as Malinvaud clearly explains. Indeed, as he says, a standard part of the intellectual game became the proving of the possibility of counterintuitive results without the need to worry about their empirical relevance. That this has changed is amply illustrated in the various chapters of this book. Even in those areas that adopt a traditional approach to economic theory, using, for example, the representative consumer, there is the feeling, which is expressed here by Artus, that there has been insufficient empirical testing of the propositions generated by the theory. Again, Slade's emphasis on the idea that the owners of firms may choose the objectives for managers strategically and that this may lead them away from the profit maximization of standard theory is motivated by a concern for greater realism.

Econometrics has not been free from this sort of precoccupation, as Davidson points out. The availability of new and sometimes very large data sets, such as the panel data that Blundell discusses, has called for appropriate statistical tools for their analysis. The same applies to high-frequency data from financial markets. The richness of these data sets allows for the use of non-parametric and semi-parametric methods which were previously inappropriate in examining economic data. Of course, as Gourieroux indicates, the very richness of the data may mean that any theoretical model would have to be unduly complicated to fit it. There is a way round this that does not resort to the use of non-parametric methods, which is to use a simpler but misspecified model and then, using simulation, to adjust the estimates to the 'true model'.

While all this reflects an increasing concern with empirical facts, the gulf between those concerned with 'explanation' and analysis and those, such as Maravall, concerned with the practical problem of forecasting is still considerable. Maravall's insistence on the need to generate good forecasts is sometimes regarded by econometricians as misplaced. Yet if economists and econometricians are not prepared to take on this task, it is likely to be confined to the realm of 'technical' or 'engineering' problems with all the obvious associated dangers. In fact, forecasting plays an important role in theory. One cannot talk of 'rational expectations' without at least invoking an implicit theory of forecasting. The same thing applies to the study of learning in game theory and economic theory in general, as pointed out by both van Damme and Kirman. Here, however, there is a natural bridge, the Bayesian approach discussed by Bauwens and Lubrano. Although it has fallen somewhat from favour in modern econometrics, Davidson suggests that it finds its natural place in forecasting, for he argues that the econometrician is concerned principally with dealing with observed data and not with trying to extrapolate from them. (This, incidentally, is not a positon with which Malinvaud agrees: he sees forecasting as part and parcel of the economist's activity.) However, to return to the place of Bayesian analysis, one could go a step further and mention that this approach has been widely used in studying adaptive behaviour in economic models. Curiously, in this context, there has been a move away from the Bayesian approach towards less sophisticated forms of updating, such as least squares learning or the simpler forms of reinforcement learning involved in using classifier systems, for example.

This is a reflection of a tendency in the theoretical literature to move away from full-blown rationality towards a more adaptive approach to modelling the behaviour of economic agents. A particular interest in the literature discussed by van Damme is the extent to which learning of this type leads to a situation corresponding to an equilibrium of the underlying game. However, as Kirman emphasizes, the very process of learning may change the environment about which agents are learning and thus may modify the evolution of the model. There may be, for example, no convergence, and the dynamics may become very complex. Nevertheless, the study of learning and adaptive behaviour will undoubtedly play an increasing role in economic analysis in the future.

Another theme that permeates the book is that of the heterogeneity of an economic agent's characteristics. Macroeconomic models in which sectors of the economy are characterized by some single 'representative' agent will continue to be widely used, as they are in endogenous growth theory discussed here by Artus. Indeed, Malinvaud argues that this is normal until we find an alternative that will serve us better. Yet there is a growing dissatisfaction with this type of approach. Perhaps the most direct answer is to continue to use the general equilibrium approach, which makes no concessions to aggregation and considers the characteristics of all the agents in the economy. The disadvantage of this is, as mentioned earlier, that almost no restrictions are placed on aggregate outcomes. Nevertheless, such an approach is that used by most studies of incomplete markets such as those by Dreze and Polemarchkis. As Michel remarks, one of the most challenging questions here is to explain why certain markets are, in fact, missing.

D'Aspremont, Dos Santos Ferreira, and Gerard-Varet (DDG) also use the general equilibrium approach to study the impact of imperfect competition, and Gabzewicz surveys the literature on this subject. DDG introduce a new solution concept which subsumes a number of standard ones. Although Kirman argues that the full general equilibrium approach does not provide enough structure to yield predictable results, he rejects the idea of subsuming the aggregate activity of the economy and suggests that we have to look at the, possibly limited, interaction between agents and to preserve their diversity. He argues that taking account of direct interaction will yield more restrictions on aggregate outcomes, although as Malinvaud says this has yet to be proved on a large scale. Hildenbrand argues, in this respect, that the full individualistic description of general equilibrium analysis is too burdensome and furthermore does not yield useful restrictions on aggregate behaviour. He suggests that properties of empirical distributions of behaviour may be very important and more relevant in generating aggregate properties. He adopts an approach that some economists find heretical, which is to start from an empirically established regularity of the *distribution* of agents' choices and to deduce from this, if it holds in general, that then certain properties such as the 'Law of Demand' must hold. The importance of this approach is the idea that 'nice behaviour' at the aggregate level may result from aggregation, and that it is heterogeneity that plays an important role in this.

Two other contributions also emphasize the role of heterogeneity. Blundell is concerned with the capacity that we now have to follow individual behaviour empirically and suggests that the use of this panel type of data, which previously used to be available only through some specific parameters such as the mean, will become increasingly important. Once again, the argument here is that many characteristics of the distribution of agents' behaviour may be important and that the availability of detailed data sets will enable us to take account of them. Scotchmer and Thisse, in emphasizing the role of space in economic theory, are going in the same direction. The distribution of characteristics and behaviour in space may play an important role in determining aggregate outcomes. This is particularly the case when interaction is local. One interesting aspect of this analysis is the extent to which spatial distribution is the result of individual choices as opposed to being exogenously given. In the former case, the evolution over time bcomes considerably more complex.

There is then, in this book, a wealth of points of view regarding the future evolution of our subject. It might be suggested that the changing emphasis in theory, moving away from super-rationality to more rule-based approaches and to more emphasis on learning and adaptation, might undermine the importance of the analytical and formal approaches that have characterized the work of groups such as the GREQAM. Thus, one might be tempted to argue, as Hahn has done, that in the future we will have to content ourselves with 'softer analysis'. Yet, as Malinvaud cogently argues, there is nothing intrinsic in this sort of shift that should make us abandon rigorous analysis. It would be a mistake to identify rigour with one particular mathematical approach. Rather, we should be capaable of developing new types of reasoning and models without ever abandoning our criteria for rigour. Indeed, the future offers the interesting challenge of determining how to move towards more empirical relevance, and as Malinvaud suggests more a normative approach, without compromising our standards. If empirical work is to move back to the forefront, econometricians will play an increasingly important role, and both they and their economic theorist colleagues will be faced with what the Chinese regard as a curse—an eventful furture.

I

Microeconomic Foundations of Macroeconomics

Introduction to Part I

Philippe Michel

How many 'representative consumers'?

I shall build my brief presentation of the five papers that make up the first part of the book around this question. Each paper has its own viewpoint, from the 'evolutionary' view taken by A. P. Kirman to the 'prophetic' view by E. Malinvaud, the 'aggregate' approach of W. Hildenbrand, the 'monetary' view of J. Dreze and H. Polemarchakis, and the 'endogenous' vision of P. Artus. This is not a synthesis of, or even an orderly overview of, these articles. I mix my own personal considerations with those ideas presented by the various authors. All of them I find very interesting, if somewhat eclectic and even sometimes contradictory. Nevertheless, in order to give some structure to my presentation, I shall start with the representative consumer when he is on his own, as does P. Artus, shall then move on to consider the future of economics (Malinvaud and Kirman), dip into the foundations of aggregation (Hildenbrand), and then leave all this to come back to general equilibrium (Dreze and Polemarchakis). In so doing I shall pose my question and come up with the following answer: at least two representative consumers, but not too many.

In the theory of *endogenous growth* as presented and discussed by Patrick Artus, the assumption of the infinitely lived representative agent is spelled out in all its glory. The summary representation of the demand for consumption goods and of labour supply which is exogenous and somewhat radically assumed to be constant is in stark contrast to the precise and varied analysis of production. The explicit spelling out of research and development technology, the analysis of how this is financed, and the behaviour of the firms that are protected by patents are at the heart of this theory, which is based essentially on technological considerations with the assumption of returns to scale, which are constant only with respect to reproducible factors and on the role of externalities. The principal weakness of this theory, as emphasized by Patrick Artus, is the scarcity of empirical papers on the subject, which contrasts with the extensive development of its theoretical analysis. Artus concludes by proposing several directions for future exploration and suggests the use of econometric techniques for this.

This indifference to empirical data is hardly something of which those who have developed another recent theory, that of the real business cycle, can be accused. This theory, which started with the pioneering article by Kydland and Prescott (1982) and which has met with considerable success, is curiously overlooked in this book. Is this because the principle on which the theory is based is so simple? Its proponents construct a theoretical model, simulate it, and then calibrate it using empirical data. But here again, the infinitely lived representative consumer reigns supreme. One can only hope that his reign will not last for ever. Since the early 1980s, he has been the object of severe criticism which has not, in my view, had the impact that it deserves.[1] Perhaps this will happen early in the 21st century. A highly revelant criticism is that which points out that basing a structural model on the assumption of the representative consumer does not avoid the 'Lucas critique' (Lucas 1976). It is not the estimated behavioural coefficients that change with a change in economic policy, but rather the representative consumer himself (who is used simplistically to match the emipirical data), who is transformed into another representative consumer (whose behaviour is consistent with the new data) when economic policy is modified. This of course damns any normative prescription derived from a representative consumer model.[2]

In his essay in which he forecasts the evolution of economic theory, Edmond Malinvaud predicts a return to the normative approach which he identifies with one of the two poles between which economic theory has oscillated. He associates one pole, with its focus on production and normative and operational issues, with the work of Allais, Boiteux, Koopmans, and Kantorovich. The other pole focuses on exchange economies and on a positive approach and has developed since the 1960s.[3] The theory of incomplete markets, which does not appear in this book, seems to Malinvaud more promising than game theory and the theory of imperfect competition, which are given extensive converage in Part II. Malinvaud challenges the view that economists will move away from abstract mathematics towards softer approaches, and he expects that 'hard mathematics' will remain useful. In line with my view that one representative consumer is not enough, I think that a possible extension of the analysis of incomplete markets would be to study which particular markets are missing. Indeed, adding additional markets which cannot be used by all agents may create more distortions than those that they eliminate.

Alan Kirman suggests that highly formalized economic theory has forced itself into an impasse and that the time is ripe for a 'regime shift'. He criticizes the static, perhaps even inert, nature of the equilibrium approaches that have envolved, for both historical and technical reasons, without leaving any room for a 'genuinely dynamic approach'. The stability and uniqueness of equilibrium are more or less assumed unless they are obtained through the use of such unrealistic assumptions as gross substitutability of all goods, or the existence of a

---

[1] See e.g. Geweke (1985); Stoker (1986). A recent survey of the criticisms of this approach is given in Kirman (1992).

[2] In my opinion, this use of the representative consumer has given rise to considerable confusion between the normative and positive approaches: see Michel (1994).

[3] The infinitely lived representative consumer was 'born' a little later as a reinterpretation of the optimal growth model with the assumption of rational expectations.

single representative consumer. Kirman foresees an evolution, or rather a break in the development of economics, which will lead to an analysis of convergence to equilibria or, better still, the evolution over time of the equilibrium itself. He sees the study of interactions as being the most promising route. Global interaction sheds lights on two important economic questions: the aggregation process, and the way in which organizations are formed. Local interactions constitute the other face of the dynamic analysis of market structures and processes. It is the way in which these local interactions develop endogenously that we have to try to understand.

Werner Hildenbrand makes a rigorous analysis of the more specific problem of aggregation and tests his assumptions against household data for France and Great Britain. The thorny problem of the aggregation of economic behaviour has been neglected by the profession since the impressive negative results obtained by Sonnerschein, Debreu, and Mantel. Hildenbrand (1983, 1989, 1994) and Grandmont (1987, 1992) developed a new approach, which focuses not on the details of individual behaviour but rather on the distribution of individual characteristics, income distribution (Hildenbrand), or distribution of preferences (Grandmont). This removes, in the strict sense, the 'microeconomic foundations of macroeconomics' and shifts to an analysis of interactions and structural assumptions. This provides testable assumptions, and Hildenbrand successfully undertakes such tests. To return to my theme, I wonder whether it is not worth considering an economy with two 'laws of demand', where such a law does not hold for the economy as a whole. In fact, one cannot avoid the difficulties involved in data analysis—which data can we reasonably hope to aggregate; which aggregates should we define?

The theorist may well reply that one should not aggregate, that all consumers should be modelled, and that the relevant framework for macroeconomic analysis is that provided by general equilibrium theory. Indeed, Jacques Dreze and H. Polemarchakis use this framework to study money and monetary policy. Their abstract model involves an exchange economy with several time periods, with or without uncertainty, with a finite number of agents, periods, and states of the world. Banks emit one or several monies against bonds and make profits which are distributed as dividends. Monetary equilibria are indeterminate, and when there is a positive interest rate they are sub-optimal. Numerous examples are given of the different approaches to monetary theory (cash in-advance, Baumol–Tobin, $IS-LM$).

This is an impressive attempt to provide the 'micro-foundations for macroeconomics'. Yet it is not the first attempt to tackle macroeconomics through general equilibrium. The theory of fixed-price equilibria with quantity rationing was very popular in the 1970s after the appearance of the work of Benassy, Dreze, and Malinvaud. It seemed that this was the key to providing micro-foundations for Keynesian macroeconomics. Since that time this approach has been more or less abandoned, although it has left concepts which have been absorbed into economic theory, such as the distinction between classical and Keynesian unemployment.

P. Michel

It seems to me that general equilibrium is necessarily a limited approach to macroeconomic questions. The general equilibrium world is, in a certain sense, just as poor a socioeconomic structure as that of the representative consumer. Since all the individuals communicate only though the price system, each pursuing his own interests, each of these agents is strangely like the others. The macroeconomist cannot, however, aviod the problems of conflicts of interest or of making common cause. The overlapping generations model, which distinguishes those who work from those who live off their previous earnings, brings out this sort of phenomenon. Many other categories of agent with which we are familiar, such as skilled and unskilled workers, the unemployed, and those who have become excluded from society, merit this kind of analysis. But to choose the appropriate aggregate class and the corresponding representative consumer is, and has to be, more or less explicitly an ideological choice. The apparent neutrality of settling for one of the two extreme cases—either that of the representative consumer or that of considering all the individuals separately—explains why these choices have enjoyed a certain success. Yet we know that even the failure to choose is, in fact, a particular choice, and if such a choice is inevitable then it is better to make it clear. This would allow us to develop theories in which several representative agents who do not share the same interests coexist, and I hope that as we enter the next millennium this will give rise to some fascinating ideological debates.

REFERENCES

Benassy, J-P. (1975), 'Neo-Keynesian Disequilibrium Theory in a Monetary Economy', *Review of Economic Studies*, 42: 503–24.

Dreze, J. H. (1975), 'Existence of an Equilibrium under Price Rigidity and Quantity Rationing', *International Economic Review*, 16: 301–20.

Geweke, J. (1985), 'Macroeconomic Modeling and the Theory of the Representative Agent', *American Economic Review*, 00: 206–10.

Grandmont, J-M. (1987), 'Distributions of Preferences and the Law of Demand', *Econometrica*, 55: 155–62.

—— (1992), 'Transformations of the Commodity Space, Behavioural Heterogeneity, and the Aggregation Problem', *Journal of Economic Theory*, 57: 1–35.

Hildenbrand, W. (1983), 'On the Law of Demand', *Econometrica*, 51: 997–1019.

—— (1989), 'Facts and Ideas in Microeconomic Theory', *European Economic Review*, 33: 251–76.

—— (1994), *Market Demand: Theory and Empirical Evidence*. Princeton: Princeton University Press.

Kirman, A. P. (1992), 'Whom or What Does the Representative Individual Represent?' *Journal of Economic Perspectives*, 6: 117–36.

Kydland, F. E., and Prescott, E. C. (1982), 'Time to Build and Aggregate Fluctuations', *Econometrica*, 50: 1345–70.

Lucas, R. E., Jr (1976), 'Econometric Policy Evaluation: a Critique', in K. Brunner, and A. H. Meltzer (eds.), *The Phillips Curve and Labor Markets*, Carnegie–Rochester Conferences on Public Policy, Vol. 1, *Journal of Monetary Economics*, Suppl.: 19–46.

Malinvaud, E. (1977), *The Theory of Unemployment Reconsidered*, Oxford: Basil Blackwell.

Michel, P. (1994), 'Point de vue: la croissance optimale', GREQAM, *Lettre d'Information*, no. 1, May.

Stoker, T. M. (1986), 'Simple Tests of Distributional Effects on Macroeconomic Equations', *Journal of Political Economy*, 94: 763–95.

1

The Future of Economic Theory

Alan P. Kirman

A new scientific truth does not triumph by convincing its opponents and
making them see the light, but rather because its opponents generally die
and a new generation grows up that is familiar with it.

Max Planck

1.1. Introduction

In this paper I will suggest that we are at a turning point in economic theory.
Much of the elegant theoretical structure that has been constructed over the last
one hundred years in economics will be seen over the next decade to have
provided a wrong focus and a misleading and ephemeral idea of what constitutes
an equilibrium. If we consider the two standard criteria for a scientific theory—
prediction and explanation—economic theory has proved, to say the least, inadequate. On the first count, almost no one contests the poor predictive performance of economic theory. The justifications given are many, but the conclusion
is not even the subject for debate. On the second count, there are many economists who would argue that our understanding of how economies work has
improved and is improving and would therefore contest the assertion that economic theory, in this respect, has proved inadequate. The evidence is not reas-
suring, however. The almost pathological aversion to facing economic theory
with empirical data at anything other than the most aggregate level is indicative
of the extent to which 'explanation' is regarded as being a self-contained rather
than a testable concept.

There have been so many Cassandra-like predictions about the future of 'standard economic theory' over recent years that readers would be perfectly justified
in asking why they should give any more credence to this than to the others.

My argument can be summarized as follows. Economic theory has taught us
much, but the organizing structure of that theory has proved more and more
stultifying. Using two analogies from the preoccupations of economic theory
itself, I would suggest that, first, economic theory has become 'locked in' to a
technology that has resisted challenges from potentially interesting alternatives
which have not received sufficient investment to develop a competitive formal
structure; and second, that nevertheless, partly because of developments in other
sciences, economic theory is now ready for a 'regime change'.

I will cite as evidence for this last assertion the steadily increasing body of research in which an economy is viewed as a complex adaptive system, in which agents interact with each other actively and not just passively through the price system, and in which there is no necessary convergence to some sort of stationary equilibrium.

Let me first turn to these analogies with recent preoccupations of economists which may be useful in situating the current state of economic theory. Economists have recently become interested again in explaining 'turning points' and 'regime changes' in economics. The idea is a simple one. A certain structure, or rather set of structural relationships, may prevail over a period of time and then in the course of a relatively short interval be replaced by another structure. There are different ways of analysing such changes, and one approach is to suggest that there is an underlying system which exhibits multiple equilibria and one is simply observing a switch from one equilibrium to another. An alternative is to suggest that the system itself is changing over time and is characterized by the passage from one period of relatively little internal change to another. Thus, econometricians might be able, for example, to estimate the parameters of a structure that had a particular, possibly stochastic, lifetime and then to re-estimate the relation if a significant change in some of the underlying structural relationships occurred.[1]

A second focus of attention is that of technological innovation. The specific approach that interests me here is that adopted by Arthur (1988), David (1985), and their various collaborators. These authors argue that, when various technologies are available and when there are externalities from choosing a technology that others have already adopted, what happens early on will have great significance in determining which technology predominates in the long run. Thus, the choice of a particular technique by a few firms early on may be enough to develop a momentum which results in the widespread adoption of that technique, even though everyone would have been better off had some other technique become the standard.

Why are these two analogies relevant to the present discussion? Let me start with the last one. Many economists have suggested that a particular difficulty with economic theory in general, and with general equilibrium theory in particular, it that it has developed and become trapped in a highly specific formalism from which it cannot escape without great difficulty. Here the parallel with the idea of getting 'locked in' to a particular technology is obvious. Thus, the particular formalization that has been adopted in economics has influenced and, many would argue, severely constrained the development of our discipline. This point is made with particular force by Ingrao and Israel (1990), for example. Mirowski (1989) goes further and, incidentally, provides the simplest explanation for the fact that economic theory is so frequently compared with physics. For he goes beyond the suggestion that the mathematical framework that is the basis of the neoclassical paradigm is the same as that of physics in the nineteenth

---

[1] A standard example of such an approach is that of Hamilton (1989).

century, and that it is simply this that has kept economics in a straitjacket. His argument is rather that economics took over lock stock and barrel the framework of theoretical physics. Indeed, he says:

The dominant school of economic theory in the West, which we shall call 'neo-classical economics', has in the past often been praised and damned by being held up to the standard of physics. However, in my little epiphany, I realised that no one had ever seriously examined the historical parallels. Once one starts down that road, one rapidly discovers that the resemblances of the theories are uncanny, and one reason they are uncanny is because the progenitors of neo-classical economic theory boldly copied the reigning physical theories in the 1870s. The further one digs, the greater the realisation that those neo-classicals did not imitate physics in a desultory or superficial manner; no, they copied their models mostly term for term and symbol for symbol, and said so. (Mirowski 1989)

The way in which economics has remained trapped in this framework becomes very clear when one looks at the notion of equilibrium, which derives naturally from the mathematical structure within which economic theory was developed at the turn of the century. This concept of equilibrium is still central to the standard theoretical model in economics. The problems that have arisen with this notion are a result of the increasing rigour used in economic analysis and the consequent separation of the traditional stories about how equilibrium is achieved from the results that can actually be proved. This account yields two lessons. First, without formal analysis the limitations of the standard model would not have become so clear. Second, the severe constraints imposed by the mathematical framework within which equilibrium is defined have become all too apparent.

With appropriate assumptions on the characteristics of agents, preferences, and production technologies, the existence of such an equilibrium can be guaranteed. Although this classic notion of equilibrium is well defined and amounts to no more than finding a solution of a set of equations, it leaves much to be desired. In particular, it leaves no room for truly dynamic evolution. Dynamics are introduced either by simply dating the commodities in the standard model, or by discussing the conditions under which the economy will converge to a static or stationary equilibrium.

Despite various efforts such as Hahn and Negishi's to examine non-*tâtonnement* processes and the discussion of convergence in rationed economics (see e.g. Herings *et al.* 1994), for the most part the changes in the economy are considered as taking place in virtual time and the basic path of the economy is considered the equilibrium one. The idea that the economy may spend a considerable part of its time off its 'equilibrium path' is one that is difficult to incorporate into the general equilibrium framework and has, in consequence, been generally overlooked.

Perhaps most importantly, the notion that the structure of the economy, rather than just the parameters of the structural relationship, might be substantially modified over time has received little formal attention.

The basic problem is historical. From Walras onwards, the tradition in general economics has been to maintain that such an equilibrium is one to which a market economy would gravitate. Prices would adjust in such a way as to bring about equilibrium. This notion, captured formally in the *tâtonnement* process, for example, and frequently referred to as the 'invisible hand', conveys the idea that economic equilibrium should be thought of as the resting point of a process, and that this process should be stable. The presumption has tended to be that the market equilibrium is intrinsically stable. Where this is not directly assumed, some strong hypothesis which generates stability, such as all goods being gross substitutes, is generally introduced. However, such hypotheses cannot be imposed by making assumptions on individual characteristics. Without prolonging the discussion too much, two things have to be noted here. What I am asserting is that an equilibrium notion is unacceptable if there is no plausible account as to how it might be attained. However, one might well ask whether the problem does not lie with the choice of adjustment process and whether some alternative process might not make Walrasian equilibria stable. The answer to this is mixed. On the one hand, Saari and Simon (1978) have shown that an arbitrarily large 'amount of information' is required to ensure global stability of a process; on the other hand, Kamiya (1990) and Herings (1994) have developed universally stable adjustment processes. However, these processes depend structurally on the particular price at any moment, and some have argued that this is not economically plausible.

A second problem arises in that, if analysis of the change in the equilibrium that results from a discrete change in the parameters of the model is to be possible, one should require that equilibrium to be unique. Yet once again, there are no natural assumptions on the individual level that guarantee this. Stability depends on the particular adjustment process involved, while obviously, uniqueness is independent of this. The two problems are separate, but in economics the two have often been considered together. This is probably because the standard, economically interpretable, conditions that guarantee one also guarantee the other.

Where does this leave us? Formal analysis has succeeded in showing under very general conditions that equilibrium does exist. The particular merit of this result is seen as being that such aggregate or macro consistency is obtained from underlying 'rational' or optimizing behaviour at the micro level. However, as I have already emphasized, to obtain *stability* of the equilibrium under a reasonable adjustment process or *uniqueness*, we know from the results of Sonnenschein, Mantel, and Debreu that more structure must be imposed on the system than is obtained from assumptions of the characteristics of the isolated individuals in the economy. Such assumptions can, of course, simply be made on the aggregate relations directly. To use them, however, would invalidate the economist's claim that aggregate analysis was based on underlying individual 'rationality'.

Hence, ever since the results just referred to showed how little structure is imposed on macro behaviour by the standard assumptions on individual economic agents, efforts to derive more macro structure from micro characteristics have increased. This is a reflection of the, probably mistaken, desire to derive macroeconomic results directly from the underlying individual behaviour. The relationship between micro and macro behaviour is far from simple, however. The standard way of circumventing this problem has a long tradition in economics and consists of considering the aggregate behaviour of the economy as though it were the behaviour of a single 'representative agent'.[2] This approach ensures that the problems of existence, uniqueness, and stability are solved simultaneously. However, although analytically convenient, this approach is conceptually unsatisfactory and theoretically unsound (see e.g. Kirman 1992). Nevertheless, the length of this tradition will, no doubt, prevent its rapid disappearance.

My argument here is that economic theory has indeed provided us with valuable insights into the functioning of economies and the behaviour of economic agents, and that it would be quite unthinkable to reject all of this out of hand. Yet much of current theorizing continues as if no real challenge to the intrinsic value of the standard notion of equilibrium had occurred. The result of this is that the pursuit of standard general equilibrium analysis is becoming increasingly esoteric and further removed from the aim of understanding economic phenomena. The theory is becoming self-contained and self-sustaining. While there is no a priori reason for ceasing this kind of activity, it is also not unreasonable to question its value.

This does not, of course mean that efforts have not been made by some economic theorists to face these problems. Remaining within the general equilibrium framework, for example, one possible approach is to argue that to rescue the equilibrium notion we have to go beyond simple assumptions on the characteristics of individual agents and that we must also make assumptions on the *distribution* of those characteristics. The representative agent approach is, of course, a special case of this since it consists of concentrating the distribution on one point. However, taking the opposite point of view, and therefore refusing the unnatural idea of representing the whole economy as if it were a single individual, a number of authors have pursued a research programme involving the idea that heterogeneity and a dispersion of agents' characteristics may lead to regularity in aggregate behaviour. This idea of focusing on the distribution of agents' characteristics with a large support can be traced back to Cournot (1838) and has been developed with considerable success by, for example, Hildenbrand (1983, 1989, 1994) and Grandmont (1987, 1992).

The aim of some of this type of work was precisely to rescue economic theory in its standard form from the trap into which it naturally fell, as a result of its mathematical framework. The problem is a fundamental one, since a theory that, under standard assumptions, can be shown to be intrinsically incapable of producing empirically refutable results is, at best, of limited value. However, whether or not the theory can be saved by the type of approach just mentioned, it is important to understand that what is put in question by recent destructive results is not formalization in general, but rather the particular formalization generally employed in economic theory. That a paradigm should be shown to be deficient does not

---

[2] Reference to such a concept can be found in Edgeworth (1881), for example.

imply that one should cease to search for a paradigm. Whether progress will be made by the advancers, to use Kuhn's terminology, who will add to or modify the existing paradigm, or by the revolutionaries who will change the paradigm itself, remains an open question. My argument here is that we are about to see, in terms of my second analogy, a 'regime shift'. There are several economists who have made distinguished contributions to the field of general equilibrium but whose view is that we have come to the end of the equilibrium road and that we are ready for a radical change. This attitude is epitomized by Werner Hildenbrand when he says,

> I had the naive illusion that the microeconomic foundation of the general equilibrium model, which I admired so much, does not only allow us to prove that the model and the concept of equilibrium are logically consistent (existence of equilibria), but also allows us to show that the equilibrium is well determined. This illusion, or should I say rather, this hope, was destroyed, once and for all, at least for the traditional model of exchange economies.
>
> I was tempted to repress this insight and to continue to find satisfaction in proving existence of equilibria for more general models under still weaker assumptions. However, I did not succeed in repressing the newly gained insight because I believe that a theory of economic equilibrium is incomplete if the equilibrium is not well determined. (Hildenbrand 1994)

All of this is simply a reflection of the fact that a formal theoretical structure can, as it is developed, show itself to be either empty or self-contradictory. While the difficulties encountered by what is too frequently referred to as the 'neo-classical paradigm' may comfort those who criticize the formal approach to economics, it would be wrong to infer that it is the idea of an analytical framework itself that is defective. Again, the criticism of some modern theoretical work in economics as consisting of uninteresting, even if sophisticated, generalizations of existing results is often justified. However, once more, this does not justify the rejection of the use of formal models in economics. As yet, no one has advanced any convincing argument to sustain the idea that the subject matter of economics is intrinsically incapable of being expressed as a series of relationships between well defined variables. Indeed, the great majority of economists not only believe that this is so but also believe that the 'basic laws' which define the basic relations are known and reasonably well understood. The essential core is, in the standard view, equilibrium theory in some form. It is, as I have emphasized, with this that I quarrel, not with the idea that a well articulated economic theory can be specified and rigorously analysed. Indeed, the probability of success of a new paradigm is low, unless it is susceptible to rigorous analysis.

1.2. The Way Forward

If economic theory is to make sense, it must be capable of evaluation in terms of the two criteria used to judge any science: prediction and explanation. It is difficult to find economists who believe that theoretical economic models have enhanced our ability to predict. Indeed, there is a long tradition of showing that simple mechanical extrapolation predicts better than more sophisticated reduced-form models whose structure is derived from theoretical considerations. This then leads to the second question: has economic theory led us to a better understanding or explanation of observable economic phenomena? A view that was current for a long while and is still reflected by many economists is that economic theory is a satisfactory simplification of reality. This is the view advanced by Koopmans, when he says:

Whether the postulates are placed beyond doubt (as in Robbins), or whether doubts concerning their realism are suppressed by the assertion that verification can and should be confined to the hard-to-unravel more distant effects (as in Friedman)—in either case the argument surrounds and shields received economic theory with an appearance of invulnerability which is neither fully justified nor at all needed. The theories that have become dear to us can very well stand by themselves as an impressive and highly valuable system of deductive thought, erected on a few premises that seem to be well-chosen first approximations to a complicated reality. They exhibit in a striking manner the power of deductive reasoning in drawing conclusions which, to the extent one accepts their premises, are highly relevant to questions of economic policy. In many cases the knowledge these deductions yield is the best we have, either because better approximations have not been secured at the level of the premises, or because comparable reasoning from premises recognised as more realistic has not been completed or has not yet been found possible. Is any stronger defense needed, or even desirable? (Koopmans 1957)

Unfortunately, this approach does not withstand critical examination. In asserting that the premises on which economic theory is based are 'well-chosen approximations', Koopmans begs the whole logical question, for this very phrase implies that we understand underlying reality and therefore are able to judge what a good approximation of it consists of. However, if we were to accept this, there would be no need for any empirical test of any of our assertions, since any proposition derived correctly from the premises would have to be accepted.

My basic point is that we are far from understanding the nature of economic reality and that we need to develop models that are more likely to enable us to do so. One of the fundamental difficulties with standard theory is that, in trying to establish rigorous foundations for individual behaviour from which to derive aggregate relations, we are obliged to use notions that are intrinsically unobservable, such as preferences. The way out of this dilemma is to use 'introspection', as Hildenbrand points out, and he cites Koopmans and Malinvaud, who argue that our capacity to use introspection to justify hypotheses about the behaviour of economic agents is a distinct advantage. However, he also cites Hutchison, who says:

No scientist can rely on introspection alone if he want results of general applicability, while he can only communicate the results of his introspection . . . by his behaviour or his written or spoken words. Though, on the other hand, he could *conceivably*, if scarcely in practice, dispense with introspection entirely, it is certainly an invaluable and in fact practically indispensable method for the forming of general hypotheses about one's fellow human beings to observe, first, from a peculiarly intimate but not necessarily more trustworthy or accurate position, oneself—though all such hypotheses must afterwards be tested by empirical investigation. (Hutchison 1938)

Hildenbrand himself goes on to say:

Everybody who ever tried to model individual behavior knows that it is impossible to avoid a priori assumptions completely. Only some economic methodologists—who, as a matter of fact, perform no modelling themselves, but give prescriptions on how to do so—advise the profession not to use a priori assumptions at all. The best one can do, in my opinion, is to be flexible, to be a methodological pluralist. One should minimize the use of a priori assumptions as far as possible. If, however, they cannot be avoided, one should state them explicitly rather than try to cover them with some pseudoscientific justification. (Hildenbrand 1994)

Now the question is, how should we set about tackling economic theory if we are to discard the basic notion of the isolated maximizing agent? One approach is to simply move from observable facts through deductive reasoning to general conclusions. Thus, if we take Hildenbrand (1994) as the pioneering example, we simply have to test whether it is true that people's consumption bundles are more spread out as income increases. If this is always true, then consumption of goods will satisfy the 'Law of Demand'. There are two things to note here. First, there is no behavioural assumption made to justify the choices of consumers; that is, no underlying maximizing behaviour is assumed. Second, the hypothesis tested is one about the distribution of behaviour and not one about the individuals themselves. Thus, one arrives at an important conclusion without any real model of the individual. This does not mean that we should eschew any reflection on the purposeful behaviour of individuals, but it does mean that we can make substantial progress without necessarily using the elaborate introspection which typifies standard economic theory. In the Hildenbrand example, the regularity at the aggregate level is obtained as a *result of aggregation* and is not a feature of the individual behaviour itself. Thus, the relationship between micro and macro behaviour is very different from that generally assumed.

I would like to go further and suggest that, if we take specific account of the direct interaction between economic agents, the relation between the aggregate and the individual level becomes more complicated but even more interesting. As in many physical and biological systems, aggregate behaviour may be quite regular but it cannot be deduced directly from the behaviour of the components in isolation. Once again, 'good behaviour' can be the result of aggregation.

Perhaps the most radical reaction to the 'methodological individualism' that is built into the general equilibrium model in its pure form has been the widespread reintroduction of non-cooperative game theory into economics. Let me take a step back for a moment and recall the notion of equilibrium in the normal economic model, which is simple and well defined. Agents independently make choices as a function of market signals. An equilibrium signal is one that engenders choices that satisfy some rule of consistency. In the market framework, the signal is the price vector and the consistency condition is that markets clear. In a system where there is interaction, the idea must be modified.

Now consider the opposite extreme to the model with isolated decision makers —that in which every individual reacts to every other one. This is the situation in a non-cooperative game: every individual takes account of the strategies of every other player and, what is more, knows that the other does so, and knows that he knows, and so forth. Despite the complexity of the reasoning imputed to the individuals, the basic equilibrium notion, the Nash equilibrium, is also clear and well defined. It is a strategy for each player which cannot be improved upon, given the strategies of the others. It is clear that market equilibrium can be recast in this way; no agent given the market rules could make a better choice (see Debreu 1952).

However, it seems clear to me that Nash equilibrium and the full-blown game-theoretic model do not point the way to satisfactory economic research in the future. This approach, although a healthy reaction to the idea of the isolated individual, shares fundamental defects with the market model. Such equilibria are not, in general, unique, and there is no obvious way in which they would be arrived at. What is worse, perhaps, is that the complexity of these games and the reasoning involved means that they not only rely even more heavily on intro-spective 'rationality' than the standard model, but they do so to the point where they pose problems of logical consistency (see Binmore 1990). The consequence is that only very simple examples are analytically tractable, and this deprives the approach of much of its appeal for the ordinary economist.

What I would like to suggest as the most fruitful way forward is to analyse models in which the interaction between agents is between the two extremes I have just described. Agents may, for example, interact without restriction with any other agents (global interaction), even though they may actually do so only with some randomly drawn sample from the population. Alternatively, they may meet only with their neighbours (local interaction), and thus the consequences of their behaviour may take some time to have an effect on agents with whom they are not directly linked. In this case one may see influences or changes 'percolat-ing' through the economy or market. Although a static equilibrium notion can be defined, it is more interesting to study the dynamic evolution of the systems I have in mind. Thus, the idea is to look at the changes over time in the economy resulting from the interaction between agents. In this case one is interested in knowing how the state of the system evolves over time and whether it settles down to what might be thought of as some sort of equilibrium.

There are a number of ways of doing this, some of which are now widely used. One can think of a repeated series of markets or games, for example, each of which is the same as its predecessor and in which the payoffs in the current game are not directly affected by the players' actions in previous rounds. If the game is repeated infinitely often one might look, for example, at a stationary equilibrium which would be just a sequence of identical equilibria for each round. Of course, even if current payoffs only reflect current strategies, the latter will and should take into account histories of play to date. This simple consid-eration leads to the 'folk theorem' sort of results with a large class of equilibria. Here an equilibrium would be the occurrence of one, but not necessarily the same, outcome in each of the sequences of identical games. An interesting problem here, and one that has been widely investigated, is under what circumstances players, by learning, will converge to some particular equilibrium. This will depend crucially on what information they have at each point and, in the context here, who they play against in each period.

Perhaps it is worth making a general point at this stage. There is a natural tendency for economists to want systems to converge to some, usually static, equilibrium. Thus, a typical question would be, does behaviour that is not fully calculating lead to an outcome that corresponds to an equilibrium that would have resulted had the players been 'fully rational'? The problem with this is that one is starting with an a priori idea of what the resting point of the system should be and is not allowing this to be determined by the natural evolution of the system itself. In other words, one tends to select those models in which convergence to a standard equilibrium does occur as being interesting and to devote less attention to others.

There are various examples of analysis that does not insist on the evolution of the system towards some equilibrium of some corresponding static model. One is the pioneering work on the diffusion of information done by Allen (1982). Another is the adoption of technological innovations as agents profit from the externalities of others having already adopted a particular technique (see Arthur 1989 and David 1985). Yet another is the sort of herd behaviour that may arise as agents are influenced by what other agents do (see e.g. Kirman 1993; Sharfsterin and Stein 1990; Topol 1991; Orléan 1990), and indeed a number of phenomena corresponding to Keynes's 'beauty queen' contest can arise. The idea that individuals may infer things from the actions of others is also important, and a number of authors such as Banerjee (1992) and Bikhchandi *et al.* (1992) have shown that 'informational cascades' can occur in which, once a mass movement starts, all individuals will have a tendency to ignore their own information in favour of that conveyed by the others. This will lead, with positive probability, to an inefficient outcome from the point of view of social welfare.

One can also think of the evolutionary games literature in this light. The number of agents who are identified with successful strategies expands over time. Agents are typically matched randomly with others in this sort of model, but it is by no means always true that stable patterns will develop, or that even if they do they will correspond to socially optimal outcome. Perhaps the most interesting contribution to this literature is that of Lindgren (1991). In most of the literature on games such as the 'repeated prisoners' dilemma', the strategy space is fixed and hence notions of equilibrium are well defined. However, Lindgren allows new strategies to develop, and these have an important effect on the behaviour of the system over time. Thus, although the system starts out with strategies with a fixed memory length, other strategies with different memory lengths enter the population. The evolution of the system is complicated, with periods in which strategies of increasing memory length dominate and then undergo periods of extinction. There are also periods in which the average payoff is low as a new mutant exploits the existing species. Such an open-ended system can exhibit a number of interesting features which are very different from those of a more closed model.

Another approach is that adopted by Stanley *et al.* (1993, 1994), who consider a repeated prisoners' dilemma model in which players can choose to refuse to play against other players on the basis of updated expected payoffs. This can lead to the emergence and persistence of multiple payoff bands. Once again, the important feature is that the dynamics of the interaction between agents can lead to results that could not occur in a model in which the evolution of the relationships between individuals was not allowed for.

Up to this point, I have focused on models in which interaction is taken into account directly but in which no specific relationship between economic agents is assumed, and I have suggested, as does Lesourne (1992), that if such models are considered in a dynamic setting many interesting properties may arise. In particular, one can observe the emergence of 'organization', recalling the notions of 'self-organization' used in a number of disciplines. An obvious parallel is with Williamson's (1975) theory of the firm, although his approach is essentially a comparative-statics one. However, in that sort of model the agents who link up with each other to form a firm are far from being chosen at random.

This brings me naturally to models with local interaction. These are interesting, for they give concrete form to the idea that agents are limited to a set of neighbours with whom they interact and their calculations and arrangements are made within this local environment. Furthermore, as a result, changes will not affect all agents simultaneously but rather will diffuse across the economy. Typically, in such models agents are thought of as being placed on a lattice and interacting with their neighbours (see Durlauf 1990; Benabou 1992; Blume 1993; and Ellison 1993). In this case one is interested to know whether pockets or clusters with certain behaviour or characteristics may form. The spatial connotation is by no means necessary, however, and alternative structures of links can be considered (see Kirman *et al.* 1986; Ioannides 1990; and Gilles *et al.* 1994). Indeed, in many problems in economics links are created as a result of a community of interest or relationship between characteristics rather than mere geographical proximity.

In all these models, the important feature, from an economic point of view, of the graph representing the links between agents is how connected it is. This will determine how fast information diffuses and how quickly an epidemic of opinion or behaviour will occur. Stochastic graphs become surprisingly highly connected as the number of agents increases, provided that the probability that any two individuals are connected does not go to zero too fast. The dynamic evolution of the state of the individuals linked in a graph-like structure is particularly interesting, and some of the results from other disciplines (see Weisbuch 1990) can be evoked in the context of economic models.

Another interesting approach is to examine what happens when, although agents modify their behaviour in the light of their own and their neighbours' experience, the consequences of their behaviour may affect other agents further afield. Weisbuch *et al.* (1995), for example, show how agents may choose polluting or non-polluting devices from local experience, but their choice may result in pollution that diffuses widely. The consequences of this may be a rather sharp division into areas in which all the agents have adopted one type of device while in another area the alternative device will be used.

Although such models represent a significant step forward, they still have the defect that the communication structure is exogenous. My own view is that one of the most promising avenues of research that will open up from this approach is the *endogenous* formation of market structure. What I am suggesting is that the most interesting challenge in this area is to study not just the behaviour or 'states' of individuals who interact in a general or local way, but also the evolution of the communications graph itself. While what I have in mind here is the evolution of links within a certain type of market organization, a more ambitious task would be to consider the evolution of the market type itself.

To return to the less ambitious, but already daunting, task, Durlauf (1990) introduces something of this sort when he considers not that the network itself is changing, but rather that agents may choose when to place themselves in the network, and this recalls an older model of neighbourhood preferences due to Schelling.

More directly, Vriend's (1994) contribution presents a first step to simulating a model in which either the links themselves or the probability that they will be used over time evolve. He constructs a market in which buyers learn when to shop and firms learn, from experience, how much to supply. In this model, firms sell indivisible units of a homogeneous good, the price of this good is fixed, and agents demand at most one unit. Nevertheless, it is particularly interesting to note the development and persistence of a non-degenerate size distribution of firms, even though all firms are identical to start with. Furthermore, some buyers always return to the same store while others continue to search. There is empirical evidence for this sort of division of activity both on product and in financial markets.

This model has been generalized to include price-setting in a multi-period framework in Kirman and Vriend (1995). In another model (Weisbuch *et al.* 1995), one in which much more 'rationality' is attributed to agents, the transition from a highly organized market in which buyers regularly visit the same sellers to one in which buyers basically search at random is shown to be surprisingly abrupt as the actors' sensitivity to their experience changes. This corresponds to a well known phenomenon in physics.

These are efforts to address the problems I have mentioned, but there are rather few other theoretical economic models that consider the evolution of the network itself. One example already mentioned is that of Stanley *et al.* (1994). These authors develop an evolutionary model of the repeated prisoners' dilemma in which, as agents learn from experience, they may refuse to play with certain others, and where one can examine the distribution and local concentration of communication links and the strategies that develop.

An interesting contribution is that of Albin and Foley (1992), who look at the problem of geographically dispersed agents who trade with each other but face communication costs and have only limited rationality. They find that decentralized trading results in a significant improvement over random allocations. However, in contrast with the Walrasian mechanism, agents who start out with the same endowments may end up with very unequal wealth even if inequalities in utility are reduced. Interestingly, neighbourhood price effects appear as a consequence of the cost of communication.

A step in the direction of the more difficult problem, that of looking at the emergence of the market structure itself, has been made by van Raalte and Gilles (1995), who show how a general market may break up into local ones. The idea is that certain agents are paid to fill the role of market-marker or Walrasian auctioneer. The equilibrium distribution of market-makers and consumers across local markets is then studied. Although interesting, the problem with this approach is that no indication is given as to how precisely agents actually do manage to organize and clear markets.

All of these examples are intellectual straws in the wind, but they indicate how many possibilities there are of incorporating the sort of features that I have suggested as being fundamental to the approach I have outlined.

1.3. Conclusion

In conclusion, it seems clear that there is much to be gained in relaxing the constraints that economic theory has imposed upon itself and to develop models that take account of the direct interaction between agents. These allow us to provide an account of macro phenomena which are caused by this interaction at the micro level but are no longer a blown-up version of that activity. Furthermore, the sort of behaviour that may occur at the aggregate level is much richer than in standard models. Bubble-like phenomena in financial markets, persistence of inferior technologies, and spatial distributions of activities or of income levels are among the phenomena that arise naturally in this sort of model. The mathematical tools for this type of analysis are available (see e.g. Blume 1993 and Aoki 1995), and there is no need to argue, as some have done, that progress in this direction must be at the expense of rigour.

Such an approach will enable us to escape from the sterile notion of static equilibrium and allow us to develop a richer and more complete account of the relationship between macro- and microeconomic phenomena. However, perhaps the most interesting of all is the avenue opened up by this type of analysis towards an understanding of how market structure may emerge endogenously in an economy.

REFERENCES

Albin, P., and Foley, D. K. (1992), 'Decentralized, Dispersed Exchange without an Auctioneer', *Journal of Economic Behavior and Organization*, 18: 27–51.

Allen, B. (1982), 'Some Stochastic Processes of Interdependent Demand and Techno-logical Diffusion of an Innovation Exhibiting Externalities among Adopters', *International Economic Review*, 23: 595–608.

Aoki, M. (1995), *A New Approach to Macroeconomic Modelling*. New York: Cambridge University Press.

Arthur, W. B. (1988), 'Self-Reinforcing Mechanisms in Economics' in P. W. Anderson, K. J. Arrow, and D. Pines (eds.), *The Economy as an Evolving Complex System*. Redwood City, Calif.: Addison-Wesley, pp. 9–32.

—— (1989), 'Competing Technologies, Increasing Returns and Lock-in by Historical Events', *Economic Journal*, 99: 116–31.

Banerjee, A. (1992), 'A Simple Model of Herd Behaviour', *Quarterly Journal of Economics*, 108: 797–817.

Bikhchandani, S., Hirschleifer, D., and Welch, I. (1992), 'A Theory of Fads, Fashion, Custom and Cultural Change as Informational Cascades', *Journal of Political Economy*, 100: 992–1026.

Binmore, K. (1990), *Essays on the Foundations of Game Theory*. Oxford: Blackwell.

Blume, L. (1993), 'The Statistical Mechanics of Social Interaction', in *Games and Economic Behaviour*.

Cournot, A. (1838), *Recherches sur les principes mathémathiques de la théorie des richesses*. English edition: *Researches into the Mathematical Principles of the Theory of Wealth*, ed. N. Bacon. London: Macmillan, 1897.

David, P. (1985), 'Clio and the Economics of QWERTY', *American Economic Review*, 75: 332–7.

Debreu, G. (1952), 'A Social Equilibrium Existence Theorem', *Proceedings of the National Academy of Sciences of the USA*, 38: 886–93.

Gilles, R., Haller, H., and Ruys, P. (1994), 'Modelling of Economies with Relational Constraints on Coalition Formation', in R. Gilles, and P. Ruys (eds.), *Imperfections and Behaviour in Economic Organizations*. Dordrecht: Kluwer.

Grandmont, J-M. (1987), 'Distributions of Preferences and the Law of Demand', *Econometrica*, 55: 155–62.

—— (1992), 'Transformations of the Commodity Space, Behavioural Heterogeneity, and the Aggregation Problem', *Journal of Economic Theory*, 57: 1–35.

Hamilton, J. D. (1989), 'A New Approach to the Economic Analysis of Non-Stationary Time Series and the Business Cycle', *Econometrica*, 57: 357–84.

Herings, P. J. J. (1994), 'A Globally and Unicersally Stable Price Adjustment Process', CentER Discussion Paper 9452, CentER, University of Tilburg.

Hildenbrand, W. (1983), 'On the Law of Demand', *Econometrica*, 51: 997–1019.

—— (1989), 'Facts and Ideas in Microeconomic Theory', *European Economic Review*, 33: 251–76.

—— (1994), *Market Demand: Theory and Empirical Evidence*. Princeton: Princeton University Press.

Hutchison, T. W. (1938), *The Significance and Basic Postulates of Economic Theory*. New York: Augustus M. Kelley.

Ingrao, B., and Israel, G. (1990), *The Invisible Hand*, Cambridge, Mass.: MIT Press.

Kamiya, K. (1990), 'A Globally Stable Price Adjustment Process', *Econometrica*, 58: 1481–5.

Kirman, A. P. (1992), 'What or Whom Does the Representative Individual Represent?' *Journal of Economic Perspectives*, 6: 117–36.

Kirman, A. P. (1993), 'Ants, Rationality and Recruitment', *Quarterly Journal of Economics*, 108: 137–56.

—— and Vriend, N. (1995), 'Evolving Market Structure: A Model of Price Dispersion and Loyalty', mimeo, European University Institute, Florence.

Lesourne, J. (1992), *The Economics of Order and Disorder*. Oxford: Clarendon Press.

Lindgren, K. (1991), 'Evolutionary Phenomena in Simple Dynamics', in C. G. Langton, C. Taylor, J. D. Farmer, and S. Rasmussen (eds.), *Artificial Life II*. Redwood City, Calif.: Addison-Wesley.

Mirowski, P. (1990), *More Heat than Light*. Cambridge: Cambridge University Press.

Orléan, A. (1990), 'Le Rôle des influences interpersonelles dans la détermination des cours boursiers', *Revue Economique*, 5: 839–68.

Sharfsterin, D. S., and Stein, J. C. (1990), 'Herd Behaviour and Investment', *American Economic Review*, 80: 465–79.

Stanley, E. A., Ashlock, D., and Tesfatsion, L. (1993), 'Iterated Prisoner's Dilemma with Choice and Refusal of Partners', Economic Report no. 30, Iowa State University, Ames, Iowa.

—— —— and —— (1994), 'Iterated Prisoner's Dilemma with Choice and Refusal of Partners', in C. G. Langton (ed.), *Artificial Life III*. Santa Fe Institute Studies in the Sciences of Complexity, Proceedings, xvii. Redwood City, Calif.: Addison-Wesley.

Topol, R. (1991), 'Bubbles and Volatility of Stock Prices: Effects of Mimetic Contagion', *Economic Journal*, 101: 786–800.

van Raalte, C., and Gilles, R. (1995), 'Endogenous Formation of Local Economies', mimeo, CentER for Economic Research, University of Tilburg.

Weisbuch G. Kirman, A. P., and Herreiner, D. (1995), 'Market Organisation', mimeo, Laboratoire de Physique Statistique, Ecole Normale Superieure, Paris.

Williamson, O. E. (1975), *Markets and Hierarchies: Analysis and Antitrust Application*. New York: Free Press.

2

The Theory of Prices and
Resource Allocation

Edmond Malinvaud

2.1. Introduction

How will the theory of prices and resource allocation evolve during the next ten years? Before trying to answer, one should be clear on both the nature of the prediction and the scope of the theory under discussion.

A forecast can only be based on a diagnosis about current trends if it is to be based on something other than wishful thinking. This is why I was never a strong supporter of the distinction between forecasts and projections: our best forecasts are intelligent projections. Moreover, it turns out that learning about the diagnosis that underlies a forecast is often much more rewarding than learning about the forecast itself. This paper then aims at diagnosing current trends in a branch of economic theory. Clearly the diagnosis, as well as the selection of significant trends, will be somewhat subjective and will reflect my own sense of priorities.

Trends of a scientific discipline concern three interrelated evolutions that have all to be considered. First, the set of problems, or at least the viewpoints from which these problems are perceived, evolves. Second, the methods change, usually progressing so as to be more efficient or more adequate for the current concerns. Third, the discipline experiences the effects of an uncontrolled inner dynamics of theory-building or fact-finding: each result suggests a new conjecture or the need for a deeper investigation of an abstract or empirical nature.

Current trends in the scientific field, moreover, concern evolution combining various components, in the same way as they do in other fields. A kind of time-series analysis may more particularly distinguish cycles and long-run trends. This dimension also must be kept in mind, since a good extrapolation into the future may have to be more sophisticated than a linear projection. The microeconomic theory of prices and resource allocation has a long past; hence one may well try and detect in its historical development more than a linear trajectory.

Beyond the knowledge of specific subject matters, this theory also has a special function in economics, namely that of providing foundations for all other theories dealing with different phenomena in market economies. Such foundations are partial, incomplete, and specific to each theory, because the prospect of ever being able to achieve a grand unified explanation of all economic phenomena is a useless dream. However, the theory of prices has so central a place in our discipline that its evolution cannot be well grasped without some reference to the broader changing concerns to which economists have to pay particular attention.

In the first part of this paper I am going to argue the thesis that one can identify a cycle in the history of the theory of resource allocation, and that the present position of the pendulum will now lead this theory to give weight again to the analysis of production, to predictive purposes, and to normative issues. The second part, dealing with long-run trends, will consider how research during the next ten years is likely to react to the present explosion at the boundaries of the theory from which a myriad of diverging sky-rockets emanate. Section 2.4 will discuss methodology, in particular the role of mathematics in this branch of economics.

In order to avoid misunderstandings, I should stress that, when considering these various points, one ought to accept a broad definition of the theory under discussion. Dealing with the determination of relative prices and remuneration rates, of production, exchanges and consumption, this theory does not boil down to the study of the general competitive equilibrium and of related side issues. Besides providing foundations for the study of many aspects of market economies, it also has to serve within its own field in explaining observed phenomena and in guiding decisions. It does not deal with all economic factors that contribute to the explanation of its object. But the exceptions must be spelled out. They seem to concern two main topics: (i) the generation and impact of the macroeconomic environment, i.e. of tension or slack on various markets with their implications for the degree of utilization of resources and for the general trend of prices; (ii) the generation and impact of institutions ruling particular markets such as the labour market, the housing market, and so on.

2.2. The Recurring Cycle

Within this broad theory of prices, tensions between alternative purposes have always been present, different priorities being chosen by various scientists or schools of scientists. Three such tensions seem to matter for our prospective exercise. (i) Should one stress the analysis of exchange or that of production? (ii) Should theory aim only at a positive explanation or also at a study of normative rules for organizing resource allocation? (iii) When it aims at explaining, is it in order to predict the effects of exogenous changes, or in order to clarify ideas, to examine the full range of possibilities and to classify them (in other words, to provide what F. Hahn has called a 'filing cabinet')? When referring to this last question, I shall speak for short of the 'operational' purpose versus the 'analytical' purpose.

I am proposing here the thesis of the past occurrence of a cycle, or rather of a to-and-fro movement, with, at the peak or the right end, preference for exchange, for being positive only, and for being analytical, and, at the trough or the left end, the preference on the contrary for production, for being normative also, and in any case for being operational.

1. In this century I identify two cycles, beginning from the left in the first decade of this century and in the 1950s. How to take correct account of the main features of production was an obvious concern in the writings of such authors as Pareto (1906), Colson (1901–7), and Wicksell (1901, 1923). At the same time, the planning aspect of resource allocation was motivating those engineers that turned their attention to the economic impact of public decision criteria. (As is well known, engineers of that type were particularly present in this country; Colson was one of them.) Similarly, a large place was given to efficiency and optimality in the writings of Pareto (a former engineer). The celebrated article of Barone (1908) on a possible organization of socialist planning was written in this intellectual environment.

A similar environment prevailed when I was a young economist. The theory of general equilibrium as elaborated by Allais (1943) was considered to be in direct interaction with the work of such engineers as Massé (1946). Its perceived operational relevance is also apparent in the paper written by Boiteux (1956) and in the early work of Debreu (1951).

The situation was not special to France. The three main features that I identified were much more generally apparent. Production was not only the main object of activity analysis as promoted by Kantorovich (1939) and Koopmans (1951); it also played the dominant role in capital theory and in the reflections of the Cambridge group around Sraffa (1960). In those days public economics and the theory of planning were flourishing, in close contact with the theory of prices and resource allocation. One important output of equilibrium models, which were built to fit various aspects of the price system and of its role, was considered to be their comparative-statics results; those were meant to be relevant and useful for the prediction of the effects to be expected from exogenous changes. Reading the many writings of P. A. Samuelson will convince anyone that this was often presented as the main ultimate aim.

2. Starting in the 1960s, a change in common wisdom occurred. Interest in the work on production and activity analysis faded away, coming to be left aside more and more for a few isolated specialists or for Russian mathematical economists. The exchange economy became the almost exclusive object of reflection in the theory of general equilibrium; one became less and less credible when arguing that this polarization was to be explained by a pedagogical purpose or by the concern to simplify analysis in a first phase of exploration.

A similar trend occurred for the normative objectives of the theory of resource allocation. One might deny that the fate of the literature on planning has to do with our present subject; one might argue that this literature was a temporary fashion whose disappearance was predictable and has no more general meaning.

But the same trend appears with all concerns for resource allocation in public economics.

This last field deserves attention here because it remained the object of active research; but it progressively became more conceptual and fundamental, its substantive implications for practitioners being less and less clear. Certainly, the issues were better specified, as they were approached with the tools of modern theoretical microeconomics. In his thought-provocating EEA presidential address, Guesnerie (1995) convincingly shows that a 'second-best culture' is now emerging, one that is suited for reflection about the problems of public economics. But he has to grant that firm references for applications are so far lacking and that development of a sound 'second-best doctrine' providing these references is a major challenge.

Thus, it is legitimate to write that economists have their share of responsibility in the fact that hardly anyone now complains when seeing that actual decisions on tax systems and on public investment projects are left to administrators and politicians with less and less influence of economic considerations. One reason for this fact seems to be that, when closely examining the issues, economists have realized how complex they are, that hardly any applicable rule could be given that could be proved right under all conditions.

This may be seen as a consequence of the exclusive use of the hypothetico–deductive method in the microeconomic theory of prices. Looking for properties that would apply in full generality within the now common frameworks leads to disappointment. Only very few trivial properties can hold no matter what the primary resources of the economy and their ownership, the technological feasibilities, the wants and fancies of the individuals. The message that 'anything could conceivably be true' is unfortunately interpreted as 'anything can go'.

The same reason explains the progressive withdrawal of claims concerning the search for comparative-statics results from the largest part of price theory. Not only are the objectives of the theory then considered almost exclusively positive, but also they appear to be just analytical, with no predictive aspiration. One seems to be satisfied after having built a model and having proved the existence of an equilibrium. Extra satisfaction accrues when one can prove that the effect of an exogenous change that naive people would think to be positive could also be negative.

3. The situation I have just described shows that the pendulum went far to the right. I am now forecasting that its movement will reverse in the next ten years. This prevision is based on more than a purely mechanical extrapolation relying on a disputable thesis about past cycles. There will be a return of the pendulum because it went too far in one direction.

Economists cannot be satisfied if the outcome of their work is just a fine-wrought filing cabinet for some detached philosophers. Dust will tend to fall on the cabinet if it has no other use. Hahn (1991) himself predicts that 'theorizing of the pure sort will become both less enjoyable and *less possible*' (my italics). His reasons, he does say, are 'all internal to pure theory'. But he is dismissing too easily the contention that this pure theory 'will wither under the scorn of practical men or women'. There will be such 'practical' people among economic theorists, namely all those who will value again the operational purpose of our theory.

There are already signs that this purpose cannot be neglected. All recent developments at the fringe of the theory of prices and resource allocation aim at deriving comparative-statics results, most often in an economy with production. This is true of competitive growth theory, with its two modern avatars, real business cycles and endogenous growth. This is true of the product differentiation model that became familiar for the analysis of monopolistic competition, of production location, and of international trade (see Dixit and Stiglitz 1977). This is true of asset pricing theory. Of course, these developments raise important questions about the generality of the results obtained. Pure theorists can have serious suspicion about them. But my point is simply that the theory of prices can no longer ignore the appeal of such operational purposes. If the theory were to stand in a purely hostile posture, then it would indeed wither.

Neither can the theory long sustain the ambiguous position it now has about normative issues of resource allocation. People may today invoke it, depending on their tastes, either for advocating *laissez-faire* and its implementation by a simple programme of privatization and deregulation, or for announcing, like Cassandras, the many market failures we are exposed to and the evils they will eventually bring. Can we scientists accept such an ambiguous situation? Similarly, can we accept the idea that the second-best literature will never be able to give more precise conclusions than the ones now available?

2.3. Long-Term Trends

Twenty years ago, when Arrow and Hahn (1971) was published, I would have made a poor forecast of the progress that was to be realized since then. I did not anticipate that so much would come from the serious consideration of uncertainties, of restricted market structures (fixed prices and incomplete markets), and of asymmetric information. I did not expect either the new role of the theory of games for the analysis of imperfect competition and incentives, after two decades during which it did not seem very promising. I should now be careful when attempting to detect what the future of this branch of economics will be. But a too guarded anticipation would not help our thinking. I must accept the risk of being wrong once more.

I am first going to grant that something remains to be done, and that something will be done, within the now-traditional research programme of general equilibrium theory. But I shall also argue that a new research line offers more relevant prospects, namely the one combining data analysis with the rigorous thinking to which we are used. I shall then consider the progress still likely to be made in the study of resource allocation under asymmetric information. Finally, I shall explain why I remain fairly pessimistic about the outcome of the present infatuation for game-theoretic problems.

1. The theory of capital asset pricing is an impressive development of the last twenty years, all the more so as it results in precise formulas taught to many students. What seems to be still not so clear is how robust these comparative-statics formulas are with respect to deviations from the hypotheses used in their derivation, particularly when the underlying decision problem is dynamic. I expect that attention will be brought to the robustness issue, in the same way as the origin of this modern literature was discussed twenty years ago (Cass and Stiglitz 1970; Ross 1978). Since the decision problems are now more complex, the theoretical challenge is greater. But it is precisely this that may stimulate research from bright young people.

The case of incomplete markets is the domain in which the theory of the general competitive equilibrium is now being extended the most actively along traditional lines. I cannot pretend to be perfectly informed of its latest stage of development. But I would guess that it is not yet complete and that new inter-esting problems are still to be discovered. Thus, I believe this will be a subject of active research for at least a decade or so. At present it seems to me that the characterization of the inefficiencies resulting from incomplete markets are worth exploring further, as is the role of limited liability.

A natural side issue of this branch of economics is to know which markets are open in a modern economy. The question is likely to be first usefully approached for financial assets. But it ought later to be extended to other objects, such as labour contracts. One may anticipate that incentive questions will attract attention in such a framework and that perhaps a fruitful bridge will then be made with another line of research.

The most urgent challenge would be to face seriously the issues arising from the presence and importance of production in economies with a developed mar-ket system. It is clearly not satisfactory to assume that the random returns on financial assets are exogenously given. Many other questions are also raised as soon as one thinks about production issues, as Drèze (1989) does.

I am conscious of the fact that the above list is only a sample of the topics that will be studied during the next ten years within the confines of the general equilibrium research programme as broadly understood. But this sample may suffice to give an idea of what can be imagined at present.

2. I previously argued that the theory of prices is now facing the obligation to give increasing attention to its operational purposes. This has some implica-tions for research behaviour and research priorities. Indeed, it forces theoreti-cians to come closer to practitioners and to better understand the latter's needs when they have to explain, predict, or decide. Sharing such concerns may lead us to revise for particular purposes the set of assumptions on which the theory is based, thus agreeing to make this theory less unified, and hence less beautiful. It may lead us to look more intensely for affirmative results about the validity of

comparative-statics properties that are frequently assumed to hold by practitioners. It may lead us to look for revised and more valid rules of operation to be used in applications.

For all this work, there is, I believe, no alternative but to complement the hypothetico-deductive method that was more and more exclusively used during the past decades. One has to look at data in order to reach specific conclusions, either positive or negative. The kind of statement one should aim at providing may proceed along the following lines. 'Considering available empirical evidence, it is safe (dangerous) to assume such or such property of such or such market demand or supply function.' A statement like this is not a theorem, which might give to the property the appearance of being absolutely true. (Of course, it would be true only on the assumptions of the theorem.) Some may fear that searching for such statements would imply a lower degree of rigour than has been now achieved in mathematical economics. I shall consider this point in the last section of this paper. Here, let me simply state that aiming at relevance is an important aspect of scientific rigour.

The theory of prices has to combine modelling and data analysis in order to consider in particular the characteristics of mean behaviour, which plays a significant role not only in the construction of macroeconomics, but also in many applications. This is the typical aggregation problem, which is well known as challenging. When one has to say, for instance, how savers and investors will react, in the aggregate, to a given change in their economic environment, it is usually the case that pure data analysis says too little to be useful, and pure theory also too little to be useful; the solution is to combine the two. The first approach to this combination neglects aggregation problems and derives the econometric model from the analysis of the rational behaviour of two representative agents, an individual saver and an individual investor.[1] It belongs to price theory to identify when it is safe to so neglect aggregation difficulties; it also belongs to price theory to provide a workable solution for the macroeconomist or econometrician when, unfortunately, these difficulties are substantial. In order to meet this request, price theory itself must look at data. The need is so obvious and so important that I cannot imagine that our profession will ignore it and prefer to go on producing negative results for the abstract world that it itself built.

---

[1] In a provocative article, Kirman (1992) declares that 'the representative agent deserves a decent burial'. I suggest that, before killing him, we ought to consider whether anyone is prepared to offer services superior to the ones he is modestly providing. More seriously, I agree with Kirman on a number of detailed points, but not with the general spirit of his article. In the first place, he is confusing issues when associating the use of a representative agent with a particular kind of macroeconomic model. ('. . . treat the economy as a maximizing representative individual' are the last words of his article.) In the second place, he puts great emphasis on theoretical possibilities, whose domain of relevance is far from being universal, and great confidence in an alternative approach, which so far has been experimented with on only a quite limited domain. Although I too think the approach is promising, I believe that a lot of work is still to be performed before it becomes operational for all practitioners.

In fact, the required development is already well initiated by a few economists who are facing the challenge of working on data sets, after having carefully defined the questions to which factual answers are seeked. The research project of W. Hildenbrand has already brought a number of significant results (see e.g. Hildenbrand 1989, 1994). Others have taken similar routes (Lewbel 1991). One may reasonably predict that these pioneers will inspire a flow of emulators.

Testing the implications derived from the most disputable hypotheses used in modern microeconomic theory is also a challenge. One knows that extreme forms of rationality are unrealistic, and this will be further confirmed by laboratory experiments; but there often does not seem to be any clearly superior assumption to make for building the theory. In such cases, it is a minimum requirement to test whether the results are nevertheless approximately true, i.e. whether the determination of prices, of productions, and of consumptions, operates more or less as if firms were run by perfectly rational and informed owners, as if everybody made rational expectations, and so on. Testing of the same kind ought also to bear on simplified macroeconomic models used to represent the outcome of resource allocation by markets: growth models, models aiming at taking monopolistic competition into account, and so on.

3. Among the achievements of the last decades, we must not overlook what was learned about the treatment of asymmetric information. Research concerning this broad subject was buoyant and enlightening; it is unlikely to have reached a rest-point. In which direction ought it to develop during the next decade? I cannot avoid this question, although my unfamiliarity with some of the new results is a serious handicap. The best service I can provide to the reader is probably to provide my own brief survey of recent progress and to stress a difficulty, which looks troublesome to me and might deserve widespread discussion.

In its initial phase, research clarified the distinction between problems coming from hidden characteristics (adverse selection) and from hidden actions (moral hazard); later it turned towards contracts that were more complex than a simple exchange at a given market price. (The premium of an insurance contract may be non-proportional to the degree of coverage; the remuneration of an agent may depend on a verifiable outcome.) In order to determine which contracts are likely to emerge, the notion of incentive compatibility was borrowed from the theory of allocation mechanisms, which initially was introduced for planning procedures and the provision of public goods. A fruitful advance was the discovery of the revelation principle, according to which one will not miss any incentive-compatible contract by limiting attention to 'revelation mechanisms', to which agents react by spontaneously revealing the private information at their disposal.

This theoretical advance permitted us to deal with a wide array of relevant problems. However, even putting aside recent developments to be mentioned below, it seems that the contract theory so reached is not unified: in each context a particular model has to be found, specific incentive constraints to be introduced into the formalization. This lack of unity may be natural and well accepted in particular fields such as labour economics, where incentive problems have long been faced. But it is disturbing for a theoretician who aims at providing a well-defined framework for the treatment of new problems. For lack of a general theory, would it be possible to work out a clear typology of situations that would be easily identified, a direct approach applying to each one of them?

Moreover, in thinking about contracts in modern societies, one naturally has to view many of them as ruling long-term relationships. Having invested sunk costs in such a relationship, the parties have to face new contingencies without relying on outside competition to decide on the sharing of benefits or costs arising from these contingencies. With long-term contracts a number of new issues appear, some of which were for a long time deliberately left aside because they did not fit the simple notion of market economies, such as the role of authority in the execution of contracts or the possibility of renegotiating agreed terms of contracts. Recent research had good reason for aiming to deal with these largely unexplored issues.

But then, 'a methodological divide may have developed . . . between some who advocate pragmatism and build simple models that capture aspects of reality, and others who wonder about the foundations and robustness of these models and are concerned by the absence of a modeling consensus similar to the one that developed around the moral hazard and adverse selection paradigms in the 1970s' (Tirole 1994: 1). Tirole claims to have sympathy for both viewpoints. Certainly, the pragmatic attitude cannot be held exclusively and for ever in theoretical research. Pragmatism is advisable in applications, and it may be unavoidable at the exploratory stage of a research; but there is no theory without some degree of robustness and generality. Again, the challenge now seems to be to unify the new developments.

4. The most difficult question for predicting the future of the theory of prices and resource allocation is to know where the present abundance of works applying the theory of games for imperfect competition, for industrial organization, for contract theory and for the decentralization of decisions in resource allocation will lead. On the one hand, one can easily see in each case why the decisions to be analysed are truly interactive and why the problems belong so decidedly to the group of those that the theory of games is designed to solve. On the other hand, the study of each case seems to raise at least as many questions as it answers. One then has to wonder whether this state of affairs is just a transitory phase whose outcome will be a useful reorganization of important branches of theory, with the result of new insights and new procedures for dealing with applications. If not, the future may be gloomy because people may lose interest in a research activity that does not appear to be sufficiently rewarding.

If we are lucid, we must admit that economic activity in our times is tremendously complex and that, confronted with this complexity, our present theory of prices and resource allocation grossly simplifies. The new investigations with a game-theoretic approach attempt to bring us closer to various parts of the actual complexity and often succeed in doing so. Unfortunately, it often also leads to the conclusion that minor changes in the specification of the case have strong implications for its treatment and for propositions applying to it. In other words, a close analysis of the complex world blurs the picture that we had seen when standing at a distance.

An obvious positive result of these investigations will be in the teaching of economics, since they much enrich the set of tools available for the analysis of various problems. This is already found useful for applications in the fields of management, of industrial relations, of public regulation, and so on. During the coming decades, academic research will have to devote part of its activity to finding how best to integrate this game-theoretic dimension in the teaching of microeconomics. (The textbook of Kreps (1990) is clearly not the final solution.) But the question remains to know whether theory will benefit more fundamentally.

At present I am rather pessimistic, perhaps because of a lack of imagination. Consider in particular how to take account of imperfect competition in our theory. We have the traditional monopoly model with its convenient concept of degree of monopoly. We know how to represent monopolistic competition, particularly with the help of the product differentiation model. We have, for large atomless economies, the equivalence principle between the set of competitive equilibria and various solution concepts for cooperative and non-cooperative games of resource allocation. Can we get anything more, for instance from the present studies of bargaining and market games? I may also refer to the incentive problem in an economy with public goods. Can we expect the new game-theoretic research to permit us to understand this problem better and to evaluate its consequences for various public decision procedures?

2.4. Methodology

The January 1991 issue of the *Economic Journal* (which seriously pretends to deal with the next *hundred* years!) contains a number of complaints about the present methodology of our discipline, particularly about its over-reliance on mathematics. The criticism ought to concern first and foremost the subject matter of this paper, since for no other branch of economic theory have axiomatization and rigorous mathematical reasoning been as prevalent and as advanced. We must face the question here because this dissatisfaction, if it were to be shared more and more widely, might lead to a change of methodology. But it seems to me that, to a large extent, dissatisfaction really concerns two side issues: the academic evaluation of research, and the spontaneous evolution of research programmes in economics.

1. When I was young, we mathematical economists made a very lively group within which research was strongly stimulated. But nowhere was academic recognition easy to get, not even in the United States. For economics faculties or departments, our work was unduly formal and esoteric; in order to be excused for it, we had to show that we could also perform in economics as it was then

practised. The situation has changed a great deal since then. Our colleagues may grumble, but *de facto* mathematical performance is highly valued in appointments and promotions. One reason of course applies much more generally in our societies: mathematical expertise is correlated with other abilities and can be much more objectively evaluated. But the achievements of mathematical economics also has to be recognized. These two reasons created the background for the star system within our profession to revise its values and to put on top whoever either proved 'deep theorems' or used advanced mathematical tools, or at least behaved cleverly enough to induce his colleagues to believe that he could. This evolution went too far, no doubt. Some kinds of achievement in mathematics may be useless for economists, and some achievements in economics require very little use, if any, of mathematics. Here too the pendulum will have to come back somewhat, but the movement will have no real meaning for our methodology.

2. As a discipline becomes better formalized, hence more rigorous in its deductive or inductive arguments, new problems are brought to light. Side hypotheses have to be introduced in order to validate a property often asserted before; going deeper into the analysis, can one prove that these hypotheses must hold, or may be dispensed with. A problem that was formerly loosely defined appears really to split into two or several problems; can they all be solved? And so on. Moreover, going one step upstream seldom is the end: the new problem usually reveals still another problem, or several others. So research embarks on a chain of investigations into questions that are successively raised. Sooner or later one may have to wonder whether to stop or to go on, because the *raison d'être* of the investigations is more and more remote.

Such an autogeneration of research topics occurs in all advanced sciences, and it raises the same question everywhere. Many physicists complain about the self-development of theoretical physics and its undue abstraction. Every now and then a reconsideration occurs; people realize that the interesting problems have been neglected. Then the most lively research starts anew, leaving the old programmes to belated specialists.

Reconsiderations also occur in mathematical economics. But many economists are not yet used to viewing as a natural phenomenon not only the renewal of research programmes but also the scholastic phase that precedes such a renewal. They may be right in identifying scholastic deviations within mathematical economics; but they are wrong in hinting that the use of advanced mathematics in our discipline has no other outcome. In other words, dissatisfaction should concern not the principles of the methods now common, but the way in which these methods are sometimes applied.

Since I thought it necessary to make this rectification, I may add that I also happen to feel serious qualms about the ultimate relevance of some research developments that were born within the theory of prices and resource allocation but now appear to me to have become too scholastic. Here I am thinking not about the study of the game-theoretic problems previously discussed; at present this study stands quite close to the real phenomena it aims to explain. But there are other lines of research about which I feel the same cannot be said, and about which claims to realism or applicability seem to me to be unsubstantiated.

3. Well aware of the above two side issues, Hahn (1991) nevertheless forecasts an important change in our methodology, and this for reasons arising from the inner evolution of the science. He writes:

none of the [next crucial questions] can be answered by the old procedures. Instead of theorems we shall need simulations. Instead of simple transparent axioms there looms the likelihood of psychological, sociological and historical postulates . . . it is unlikely that those with the temperament of mid-twentieth-century theorists will find this a congenial road. There will be a change of personnel and economics will become a 'softer' subject than it now is. (Hahn 1991: 47)

I find it difficult to accept this vision. I agree that simulations will sometimes be useful, but perhaps no more than now. I agree that postulates will have to be borrowed, more than now, from psychology or sociology. But I do not see why this would imply a softer methodology than the one now used. Behind Hahn's intuition probably lies the realization that economic theory will have to work on less well integrated systems: we shall no longer indefinitely extend the consequences of rational behaviour. (What, for instance, about the study of an economic system in which agents are rationally learning how to reach rational expectations?) But the change in the type of system to be studied does not imply that hard mathematics will become less useful. Neither the study of market disequilibria nor that of incomplete markets seems to announce such a change of method.

The useful mathematics will of course evolve. For instance, the systematic use of data that I anticipated in Section 2.3 above will require other kinds of analysis than the ones now taught in an economics department. One will have to borrow from statistics departments, but also to proceed to original mathematical investigations for solving some of the inference problems appearing in the economic context.

4. My methodological discussion thus far was polarized on mathematics, because I believe prevision of its future role is particularly difficult and debatable. But I do not wish to be misunderstood. The theory of prices and resource allocation was built and will be further developed with other tools as well. I am short on them, simply because I have nothing more to say than to signal their presence.

The theory of prices was first built from the partial analysis of a single ideal market. It then made frequent reference to experience of what happened on concrete markets, either in their day-to-day operations or under exceptional circumstances. Literary descriptions and historical reports were the main sources here. Later they were supplemented by reference to data on prices, on quantities traded, and on related variables. Still later econometric estimations and tests made the reference more rigorous. But each new stage did not make the methods used in the previous stages obsolete. Even now we find it appropriate on occasions to use the full range, as for instance with the symposium on bubbles introduced by Stiglitz (1990). I see no reason for announcing a change in this eclecticism.

Resource allocation problems similarly require more than abstract thinking on very general models. For groups of applications, one has to make the models more specific, particularly as they concern productive activity or natural resources. Technical information has to be considered, even though it is hardly ever econometrically processed. Again, I do not see why a change of approach ought to occur. Theory will be challenged to contribute to the solution of the problems perceived as becoming more pressing. In principle, theory ought to know how to do it.

REFERENCES

Allais, M. (1943), *Traité d'économie pure*. Paris: Imprimerie Nationale, 1953.

Arrow, K., and Hahn, F. (1971), *General Competitive Analysis*. San Francisco: Holden Day.

Barone, E. (1908), 'The Ministry of Production in the Collectivist State', Eng. trans. in F. Hayek (ed.), *Collectivist Economic Planning*. London: Routledge, 1935.

Boiteux, M. (1956), 'Sur la gestion des monopoles publics astreints à l'équilibre budgétaire', *Econometrica*, 24: 22–40.

Cass, D., and Stiglitz, J. (1970), 'The Structure of Investor Preference and Asset Returns, and Separability in Portfolio Allocation', *Journal of Economic Theory*, 2: 122–60.

Colson, L. (1901–7), *Cours d'économie politique*, 3 vols. Paris: Gauthier-Villars.

Debreu, G. (1951), 'The Coefficient of Resource Utilization', *Econometrica*, 19: 273–92.

Dixit, A., and Stiglitz, J. (1977), 'Monopolistic Competition and Optimum Product Diversity', *American Economic Review*, 67: 297–308.

Drèze, J. (1989), *Labour Management, Contracts and Capital Markets*. Oxford: Basil Blackwell.

Guesnerie, R. (1995), 'The Genealogy of Modern Theoretical Public Economics: From First Best to Second Best', *European Economic Review*, 39: 353–81.

Hahn, F. (1991), 'The Next Hundred Years', *Economic Journal*, 101: 47–50.

Hildenbrand, W. (1989), 'Facts and Ideas in Microeconomic Theory', *European Economic Review*, 33: 251–76.

——— (1994), *Market Demand: Theory and Empirical Evidence*. Princeton: Princeton University Press.

Kantorovich, L. (1939), 'Mathematical Methods of Organizing and Planning Production', Eng. trans. in *Management Science*, 6 (1960): 363–422.

Kirman, A. (1992), 'Whom or What Does the Representative Individual Represent?' *Journal of Economic Perspectives*, 6 (2): 117–36.

Koopmans, T. (ed.) (1951), *Activity Analysis of Production and Allocation*. New York: John Wiley.

Kreps, D. (1990), *A Course in Microeconomic Theory*. Princeton: Princeton University Press.

Lewbel, A. (1991), 'The Rank of Demand Systems: Theory and Nonparametric Estimation', *Econometrica*, 59: 711–30.

Massé, P. (1946), *Les réserves et la régulation de l'avenir*. Paris: Hermann.

Pareto, W. (1906), *Manuale d'economia politica*. Milan: Societa Editrice Libraria.

Ross, S. A. (1978), 'Mutual Fund Separation in Financial Theory: the Separating Distributions', *Journal of Economic Theory*, 17: 254–86.

Sraffa, P. (1960), *Production of Commodities by Means of Commodities*. Cambridge: Cambridge University Press.

Stiglitz, J. (1990), 'Symposium on Bubbles', *Journal of Economic Perspectives*, 4(2): 13–18.

Tirole, J. (1994), 'Incomplete Contracts: Where Do We Stand? Walras–Bowley lecture delivered at the 1994 North American Summer Meeting of the Econometric Society in Quebec City.

Wicksell, K. (1901), *Lectures on Political Economy*, i, *General Theory*. Eng. trans. London: Routledge and Kegan Paul, 1934.

—— (1923), 'Real Capital and Interest', English trans. included in the translation of Wicksell (1901).

3

On the Empirical Content
of Economic Theories

Werner Hildenbrand

Inflation, the evolution of price indices, interest rates, the level of unemployment —all these indicators of economic activity directly affect the living standards of many individuals. Even more abstract measures, such as the balance of payments or a worsening deficit in the public sector, can raise fears in the general public. Since such indicators of economic activity are studied in economics, it is not surprising that most individuals consider the work of economists both important and significant. At any rate, there can be no doubt that the general public expects much from the economics profession.

However, on various occasions prominent economists have warned the public not to ask too much from economics. Since the state of knowledge in this field is not yet sufficiently advanced to respond properly to all the demands put upon it, an economist often finds himself in a serious dilemma:

One must either refuse to answer questions which are nevertheless both urgent and directly relevant to one's domain of specialisation, or one must advance propositions which are poorly supported, trusting in one's own intuition or extending beyond what has been legitimately established. (Malinvaud 1988: 5)

Should we answer, or should we abstain from answering? The economics profession is divided on this question. In fact, the most competent economists are often among those who abstain from answering. I am sure that their reluctance is due neither to an unwillingness to face the challenge nor to fear of direct action. Rather, I believe that there is a lack of confidence in economic theories.

Naturally, it is not the internal logic of economic theories that is questioned. In fact, nowadays most economic theories are presented in an axiomatic form which allows any reader to check the logical deduction of the propositions. Instead, the source of doubts is in the nature of the hypotheses on which economic theories are built. Of course, these doubts are not shared by all economists. For example, Lionel Robbins wrote:

This chapter draws largely on my inaugural lecture at the College de France which was presented in French in 1993.

The efforts of economists during the last hundred and fifty years have resulted in the establishment of a body of generalisations whose substantial accuracy and importance are open to question only by the ignorant or the perverse. (Robbins 1953: 1)

As I doubt this substantial accuracy and importance, and since I do not consider myself ignorant, according to Robbins I must be animated by a spirit of contradiction if I am correctly interpreting the term 'perverse'. Admittedly, as we often hear from those who defend an established position, criticism is useless unless it implies an alternative. Thus, in what follows I will first be quite critical and will then try to propose an alternative in the framework of a particular theory: the theory of market demand.

3.1. Every Theory has an Objective

As with all scientific theories, an economic theory concerns either a real phenomenon or a real problem, and usually both. As an intellectual construct, a theory justifies its existence only in so far as it is either a means of comprehension of the phenomenon or an aid in the solution of the problem. Although most economic theories are represented by a model, the theory is not just the model, as there can be different models for the same theory. More importantly, any economic theory must specify the correspondence between the abstract entities in the model and their counterparts in the real world. *Without such a correspondence, a theory is immune to any empirical falsification.* In addition, an economic theory must make some assertions on the functional form of some of its relations, and in some cases must specify the order of magnitude of certain parameters in the model. *Without this degree of specificity, a theory may turn out to be empty.* In fact, a theory always implies a limitation on what is possible. Finally, an economic theory must specify the key to reading the model and the instructions on how to use it.

All this is well known, and I believe that I have only stated what is generally accepted. However, I have taken the trouble to repeat this because, during methodological discussion of the hypothesis in economic theory, we sometimes forget that any theory should have an objective.

3.2. The Nature of the Hypotheses

Economics consists of a multiplicity of specialized theories. For example, we speak of microeconomic or macroeconomic theories, of partial or general theories, and of dynamic or static theories. More specific examples would be the theory of value, price theory, growth theory, business cycle theory, etc. Consequently, the hypotheses underlying the various theories can be very different. Generally, the fundamental hypotheses concern the following:

- The structure and organization of markets
  - Are prices flexible or sticky in the short run?
  - Is there a complete set of contingent markets?

- The individual behaviour of economic agents
  — To what degree is individual behaviour characterized by internal coherence or even some form of rationality?
  — What capacity do individuals have for processing complex information?
- The nature of equilibria
- The rôle of time
  — is the environment stationary or does it change over time?

A complete list of the fundamental hypotheses would be very long, and of course I cannot deal with them all. In the following, I will concentrate on those hypotheses concerning individual behaviour.

Fundamental hypotheses in economics have long been taken a priori as self-evident—and perhaps even today some economists consider them as such. For example, John Neville Keynes, father of the great John Maynard Keynes, wrote that hypotheses in economics 'involve little more than the reflective contemplation of certain of the most familiar of every-day facts (Keynes 1891). Or, to cite once more from Robbins,

The propositions of economic theory, like all scientific theory, are obviously deductions from a series of postulates. And the chief of these postulates are all assumptions involving in some way simple and indisputable facts of experience . . . These are not postulates the existence of whose counterpart in reality admits of extensive dispute once their nature is fully realised. We do not need controlled experiments to establish their validity: they are so much stuff of our everyday experience that they have only to be stated to be recognised as obvious. (Robbins 1932: 78–9)

Although there have always been those animated by a spirit of contradiction, the vast majority in the academic economics profession still shares the optimistic point of view that these fundamental hypotheses can be immediately accepted. For example, Koopmans, one of the great mathematical economists and econometricians of the 1950s and 1960s, has repeated, more or less in the same words, the point of view taken by Robbins:

The facts of economic life are all around us. Hence much of the factual background of economics can be presupposed without extensive examination or discussion. (Koopmans 1957: 131)

These quotations, which express an astonishing confidence in the foundations of economics, seem in contradiction with the dilemma of which I spoke earlier.

We shall see that there is no contradiction. In fact, even if the doubts about the fundamental hypotheses were put aside, the conclusions—that is to say the propositions following from these hypotheses—are too general; they are not sufficiently specific either to allow a rejection of the hypotheses or to make interesting predictions.

Of course, the lack of structure (in a purely qualitative sense) of models in pure economic theory has always been recognized. This lack of structure is due to the purely qualitative nature of the fundamental hypotheses. The abstract models of economic theory are not sufficiently specific to accomplish their task.

An economic theory, represented by such a model, can be only partial and insufficient as an instrument of comprehension of the phenomena or as an aid in the solution of the problem. Here are some examples:

- Even under the simplest circumstances, the hypothesis of rational behaviour does not imply a unique course of action.
- The equilibria of the various models of price theory are not well determined. While the fundamental hypotheses allow us to prove the *existence* of an equilibrium, they do not imply *uniqueness*. If a theory with no equilibrium can be considered incoherent, then a theory with several equilibria is incomplete, since the levels of the endogenous variables which constitute an equilibria are not precisely determined. This represents a serious problem in applications: economists often want to compare the equilibria resulting under different exogenous conditions—what is known as comparative statics. If there is a multiplicity of equilibria, this comparison is undefined.
- Even in a stationary environment, the simplest price adjustment process does not necessarily converge unless the fundamental hypotheses are substantially strengthened.

A possible way of overcoming this lack of specificity (structure) of pure economic theories may lie in *econometrics*. By exploiting empirical data using the methods of mathematical statistics, econometricians claim to be able to specify and even quantify abstract models. According to econometricians, it is up to pure economic theory to provide the abstract models. However, this division of labour within economic research between pure theory on the one hand and econometrics on the other does not seem to me to be the appropriate approach. In any event, it has not proved very fruitful.

To be able to apply the methods of mathematical statistics, the econometrician needs models that are quite specific and simple. Often the analytical form of the functions involved must be known, the model itself must be specified up to certain parameters, and it is these unknown parameters that econometrics will be used to estimate. However, this is exactly the sort of model that economic theory cannot provide! Thus, in his day-to-day work, the applied econometrician must specify the model more or less *ad hoc*, without the help of economic theory or of other sources. This makes the risk of misspecification very great and can jeopardize the results of the econometrician's statistical estimations.

Economic modelling, which is the day-to-day work of the theoreticians, cannot be separated from the systematic observation of economic reality. Many economists have pointed out that a dialogue is missing between the design of models and the empirical analysis of data. This dialogue could guide the theoretician in the formulation of hypotheses and show which of many alternative hypotheses are plausible in reality. While many economists have stressed the importance of this dialogue, few have undertaken it seriously. Rather than remain on the general level, I have chosen to explain my point of view in greater detail using a specific case: the theory of market demand.

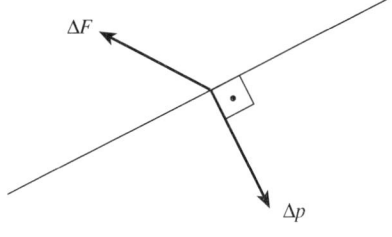

$$\Delta p \cdot \Delta F < 0$$

Fig. 3.1.

3.3. The Law of Market Demand

The simplest version of the law of market demand says that the demand for a given good or a given service will fall as its price increases. This claim seems obvious, but it cannot be valid without specifying the circumstances. In fact, most consumer goods are substitutable. Therefore, the claim is not plausible except for the case in which all prices of other goods that are substitutes and income remain unchanged. But a law that depends on such a restrictive clause is hardly interesting nor useful. On the other hand, if all prices change simultaneously, then we can say nothing conclusive about how demand will change for individual goods.

The law of market demand states that the *vector of changes in prices*, Δp, and the *vector of changes in market demand*, ΔF, must point in opposite directions (i.e. $\Delta p \cdot \Delta F < 0$) (see Fig. 3.1). In order to assert this, we must specify:

- the nature of goods and services (the level of aggregation);
- the nature of changes in prices and demand (actual or hypothetical).

In fact, the law of market demand may be interpreted in two ways:

1. as an assertion about the movement of market demand and prices (in time), i.e.

$$(p_{t+1} - p_t) \cdot (F_{t+1}(p_{t+1}) - F_t(p_t)) < 0;$$

2. as an assertion about market demand as a function of hypothetical (conditional) prices, i.e.

$$(q_t - p_t)[F_t(q_t) - F_t(p_t)] < 0.$$

The two interpretations of the law of market demand are obviously different. The first, certainly the most natural at first glance, can be tested using empirical data. This is surprising, but to my knowledge it has never been done.

However, in economic theory we need the second interpretation, which is less simple because of its hypothetical nature. It assumes that market demand is modelled by a function defined over all conceivable prices. The economic concept of demand is thus an hypothetical concept. Obviously, the two interpretations are related if we admit the auxiliary hypothesis that the market demand function does not change over time. This hypothesis is often accepted without justification. Is a justification needed for the second interpretation of the hypothesis of the law of market demand? Do we need a deductive or an inductive validation?

It seems to me that a direct falsification of the law of market demand is impossible. This is for two reasons: the hypothetical nature of the concept of market demand, and the very nature of empirical data. Even if we accept the hypothesis that, at least in the medium term, demand functions do not change over time, a precise knowledge of the form of the demand function is necessary to test the law because the data, that is to say the time-series of prices and quantities demanded, do not vary enough. In a recent book, Malinvaud discusses the fundamental difficulties in using observable data to explore economic phenomena. 'At the aggregate level, economists can only passively observe a changing reality; as a result, data remains very poor once we account for the complexity and variability of the phenomena' (Malinvaud 1991: 22).

Faced with these difficulties in the attempt to justify their hypotheses empirically, economists appeal to *introspection*. Market demand is by definition the sum of individual demands, and to understand individual behaviour, it has been claimed, *introspection can serve as a source of evidence*! I can give two quotations which advance this point of view. Koopmans wrote:

If, in comparison with some other sciences, economics is handicapped by severe and possibly unsurmountable obstacles to meaningful experimentation, the opportunities for direct introspection by . . . individual decision makers are a much needed source of evidence which in some degree offsets the handicap. (Koopmans 1957: 140)

And in *Voies de la recherche macroéconomique*, Malinvaud wrote:

Despite this . . . handicap concerning the origin of the data and the phenomena that generate them, economists still have an advantage compared to those scientists who apply induction in the physical world. Economic activity consists of the actions of men and women . . . it takes place within a framework we define ourselves. Thus, the scientist has a direct knowledge of the world he observes. A knowledge which can be trustworthy despite the reservations which may be held by psychologists or sociologists. (Malinvaud 1991: 23).

Introspection as a source of evidence in favour of hypotheses was never unanimously accepted. The most radical criticism came from Terence Hutchison, who was influenced (possibly too much) by Popper and the positivist approach of the Vienna circle. In Hutchison (1938), he argued that a discipline founded on introspection could not be scientific.

I have no wish to engage in this methodological discussion because it would be quite useless for the problem that concerns me here, i.e. a validation of the law of market demand. With this aim in mind, the relevant question must be, what model of individual behaviour is suggested by introspection? The traditional answer to this question has been that the model of individual behaviour should reveal a certain degree of 'coherence'. We also often talk of 'rationality', but I want to avoid this word, which is too loaded with other meanings.

One strong version of coherent behaviour is 'maximizing behaviour'. In the simplest case, the hypothesis of maximizing behaviour means that the vector of goods demanded by a household can be considered that vector of goods which is most desired by the household. This implies that the individual demand function —defined on prices and incomes—represents the solution to the maximization, subject to a budget constraint, of an ordinal utility function. Of course, the hypothesis of maximizing behaviour implies some much discussed restrictions on the individual demand functions, but it does not imply the law of demand. Therefore, the hypothesis of maximizing behaviour alone does not imply the law of *market* demand. In order to prove this law by a deductive argument, the hypothesis must be strengthened.

In microeconomic theory, this is done by postulating *ad hoc* some convenient properties of the utility function—which, I stress, determine the demand function with the help of the maximizing hypothesis. In Slutzsky's terminology, this means that the substitution effect, which is always negative semi-definite, must be sufficiently strong to compensate for the income effect, which is undetermined.

Unfortunately, we can also derive some extremely negative results from the hypothesis of maximizing behaviour: even if all the households adopt maximizing behaviour, the *market* demand function of a *population of households* can be practically arbitrary. Thus, the maximizing behaviour hypothesis alone—that is to say, without reinforcing it with other hypotheses—does not supply a justification for the law of market demand.

Must we conclude from these negative results that the law of market demand is an illusion that must be abandoned? The consequences of such a decision would be quite serious for economic theory. Such a pessimistic conclusion seems to me misguided. Rather, I believe that the aggregation problem is badly framed. In the literature, the aggregation problem is defined as the step from the laws established for individual behaviour to the laws holding between aggregate variables. Thus, the question has always been expressed: what properties are *preserved* by aggregation, or which property of market demand is *inherited* from individual demands?

On the contrary, should we not expect that aggregate demand possesses properties that are *not* shared with individual demands? Aggregation should *create* properties; market demand—being the sum of a large number of individual demands—should be better behaved than individual demand. Obviously, simply taking a sum of individual demands does not create new properties in the average demand. To obtain a positive aggregation effect, the population whose average is being taken must be suitably heterogeneous. This, I am sure, will seem both simple and completely natural. But, paradoxically, economists have always preferred to analyse homogeneous populations instead of exploiting the hetero-geneity that is apparent in the real world.

3.4. Heterogeneity in Household Populations

If our aim consists of justifying the law of market demand by the heterogeneity of household populations, I must first specify in what sense the household popu-lations are effectively heterogeneous—through the dialogue between model design and analysis of empirical data—and then I must show that the form of heterogeneity observed is really useful for the theory of market demand. In particular, I must show that heterogeneity implies the law of market demand.

Heterogeneity of household demand is reflected in the data on household expenditures and incomes collected by national statistical offices; for example, by the Enquête Budget de la Famille (EBF) of the Institut National de la Statis-tique in France, and by the Family Expenditure Survey (FES) of the Department of Employment in the UK. For a representative household sample (about 10,000 households in France and 7,000 in the UK), data are collected for disposable income and annual expenditure, at current prices, in different categories of con-sumption (see Fig. 3.2).

These data are illustrated in the 'sunflower' diagram in Fig. 3.2, for the case of two consumption categories, food and housing. For other years and other

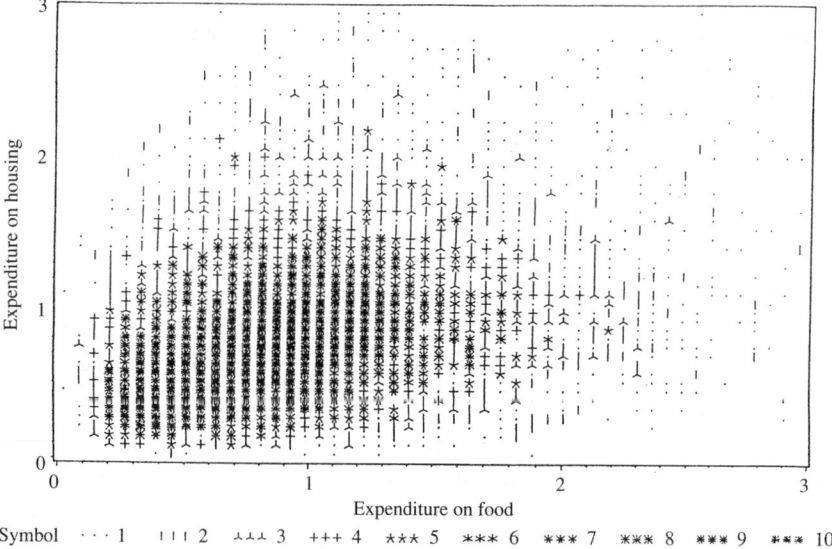

Symbol   · · · 1   ı ı ı 2   ⅄⅄⅄ 3   +++ 4   *** 5   *** 6   *** 7   *** 8   *** 9   *** 10

Fig. 3.2. Food and Housing Expenditure, 1973
Source: Family Expenditure Survey

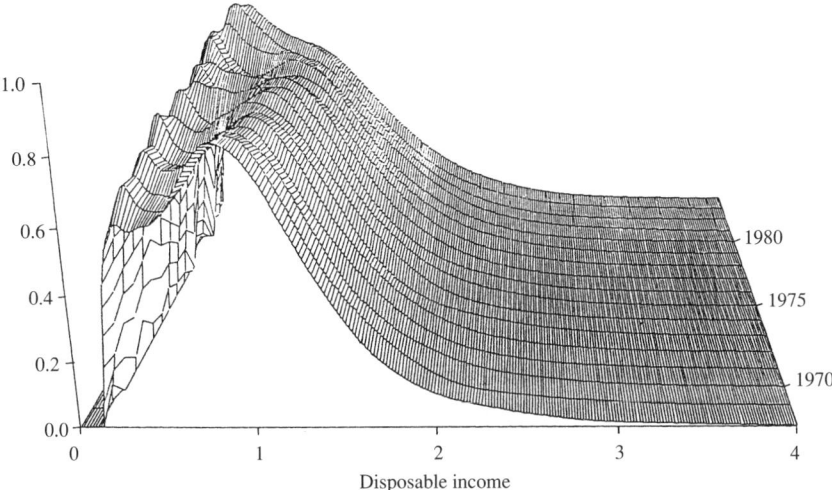

Fig. 3.3. Disposable Income (Normalized), Non-parametric Estimation, 1968–1984
Source: Family Expenditure Survey

expenditure categories, the diagrams are quite similar. One of the sources of this wide diversity of expenditures is certainly the great dispersion of incomes.

The non-parametric estimates of the distribution of normalized income (individual income divided by average income) are presented for different years in Figs. 3.3 and 3.4. Note that the normalized distribution of incomes is basically stable. In particular, although the dispersion of income is quite pronounced, the normalized income distribution varies little across the years in question.

As we may expect, income dispersion alone cannot explain the heterogeneity of data on expenditures. For example, by taking food expenditure as a function of income, we get the diagram shown in Fig. 3.5. The abscissa represents incomes and the ordinate represents expenditures on food. Fig. 3.5 still displays a great dispersion of food expenditures at each level of income. The diagrams arc similar for other categories of expenditure. The dispersion of expenditures across all households with the same level of income may be quantified by the variance of the distribution of these expenditures.

However, Fig. 3.6 shows that this conditional variance with respect to income is growing with the level of income across all categories of expenditure. Simply analysing the dispersion of expenditures for different expenditure categories does not give sufficient information. In fact, for each household with income x we should consider the *vector of expenditures*; the coordinates of this vector correspond to the different expenditure categories. For the French data, EBF, I divided total expenditure into fourteen categories, resulting in a cloud of points in $\mathfrak{R}^{14}$ space. This cloud consists of as many points as there are households with expenditure level x. Let $v(x)$ denote the distribution of this cloud of points in $\mathfrak{R}^{14}$.

W. Hildenbrand

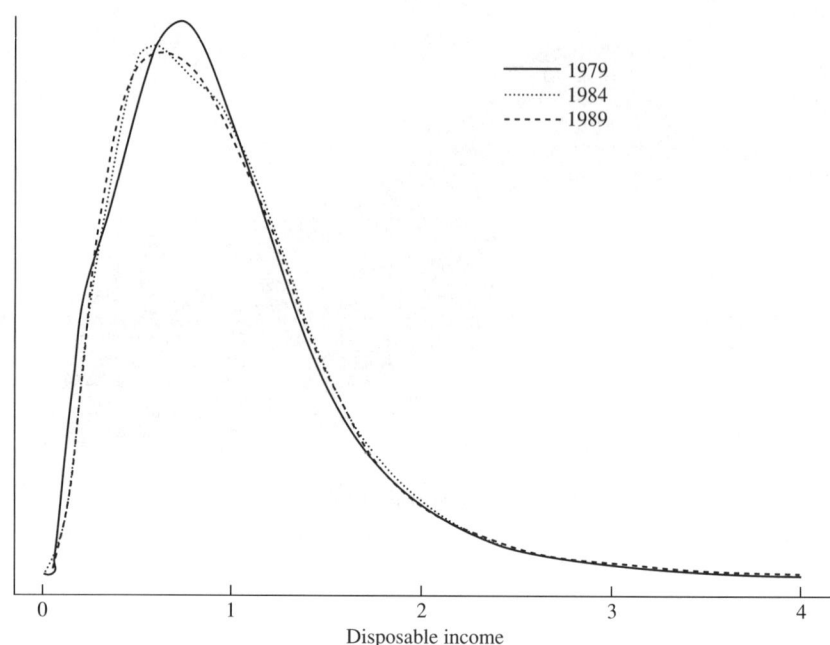

Fig. 3.4. Disposable Income (Normalized), Non-parametric Estimation, 1979, 1984, and 1989

Source: EBF

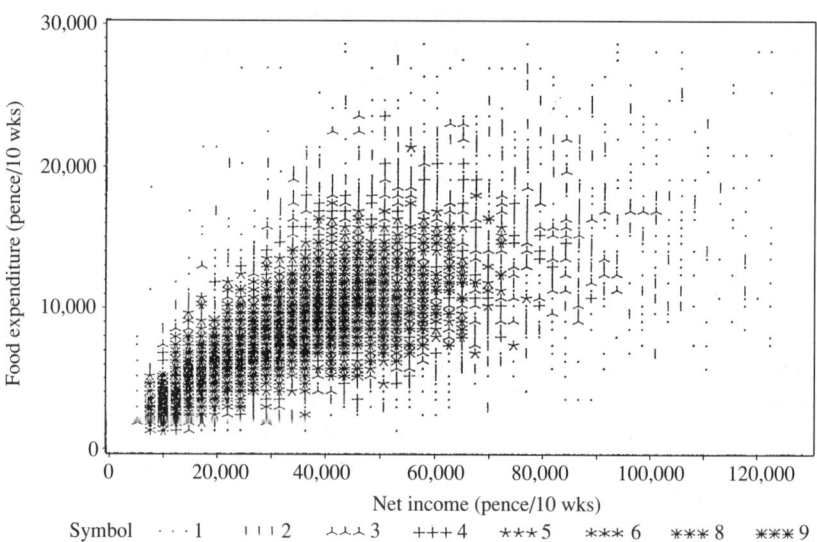

Fig. 3.5. Food Expenditure versus Net Income, 1973
Source: Family Expenditure Survey

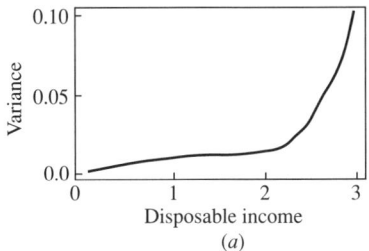

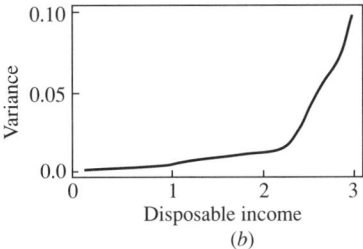

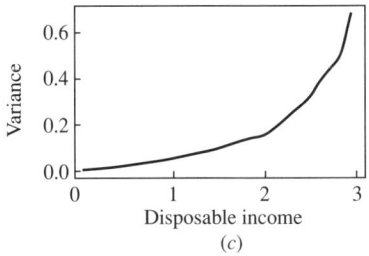

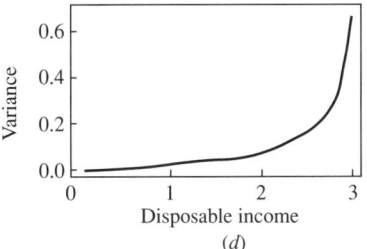

Fig. 3.6. (*a*) Food
     (*b*) Clothing
     (*c*) Transport
     (*d*) Housing

For the English data, FES, I chose nine expenditure categories; $v(x)$ denoting a distribution in $\mathcal{R}^9$. Now I want to compare the heterogeneity of the expenditure distribution $v(x)$ with the heterogeneity of the distribution $v(x+\Delta)$ when the level of income is increased by $\Delta > 0$. For example, is it true that the distribution $v(x+\Delta)$ is 'more dispersed' than the distribution $v(x)$?

One way to specify the 'more dispersed' relation is by the following definition. A distribution $v(x+\Delta)$ is more dispersed than the distribution $v(x)$ if the matrix

$$\text{cov}\,[v(x+\Delta)] - \text{cov}\,[v(x)]$$

is positive semi-definite, where cov [v] is the variance–covariance matrix of the distribution v. If we define the *concentration ellipse* of a distribution v on R^1,

$$\text{Ell}(v) := \{z \in R^1 \mid z\,(\text{cov}[v])^{-1} \le 1\},$$

then it can easily be shown that the distribution $v(x+\Delta)$ is more dispersed than the distribution $v(x)$ if and only if the ellipse $\text{Ell}(v(x))$ is contained in the ellipse $\text{Ell}(v(x+\Delta))$. For each set of two expenditure categories, we can then draw the concentration ellipse $\text{Ell}(v(x))$ for different values of income, for example $0.5\bar{x}$, $\bar{x}$, and $1.5\bar{x}$, where $\bar{x}$ is average income. The estimates of the ellipses for these three values are presented in Figs. 3.7 and 3.8.

The magnitude of the increase in dispersion of expenditures depends on the level of income. Analysis of empirical data has shown that we cannot conclude that the distribution $v(x + \Delta)$ is always more dispersed than the distribution $v(x)$ for any given value of x and of Δ. For this reason, I formulate the *hypothesis of increasing dispersion of household demand*: the matrix $C\rho$ is positive semi-definite where

$$C\rho := \int \partial_x \text{cov}[v(x)]\, \rho(x)\, dx$$

This hypothesis seems plausible, but surely has no obvious microeconomic justification. Of course, what matters is an empirical justification.

To test this hypothesis, it is necessary to estimate the smallest eigenvalue of the matrix $C\rho$ as well as its confidence interval. Table 3.1 gives estimates for the FES and EBF data.

We can see that all the confidence intervals are positive.[1] Thus, the hypothesis that the matrix $C\rho$ is positive definite is never rejected and the opposite hypothesis that the matrix $C\rho$ is not positive definite is always rejected. Therefore, the hypothesis is well established empirically.[2]

What I have just said about empirical data explains the sense in which household populations really are heterogeneous. In fact,

- there is a significant dispersion of incomes;
- there is significant empirical evidence for the hypothesis of increasing dispersion of household demand.

If we accept these empirical results, there remains an important question for the theoretical economist: are these empirical facts useful? In particular, are they useful in justifying the law of market demand? Unfortunately, I must be brief in answering the latter question. We can prove that the two empirical facts I have just illustrated are unequivocally in favour of the law of market demand.[3] In fact, with certain supplementary hypotheses—I do not wish to present the details here—we can also prove that the hypothesis of increasing dispersion and sufficient dispersion in the income distribution together imply the law of market demand.

---

[1] For the statistical methods used, see Härdle and Stocker (1989) and Hildenbrand and Kneip (1993).

[2] For more details, see Härdle *et al.* (1991), Hildenbrand and Kneip (1993) and Hildenbrand (1994).

[3] For details see Hildenbrand (1994).

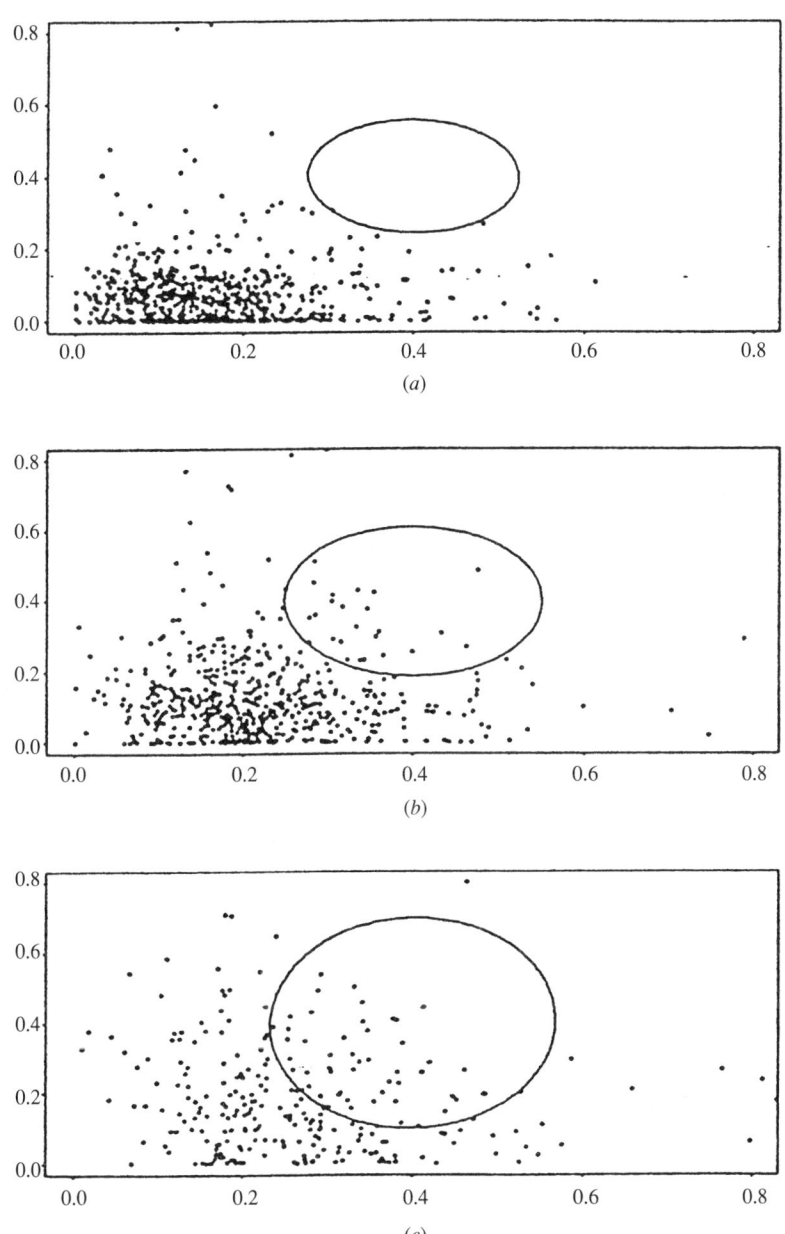

Fig. 3.7. Concentration Ellipses, Food and Housing, 1979
Source: EBF

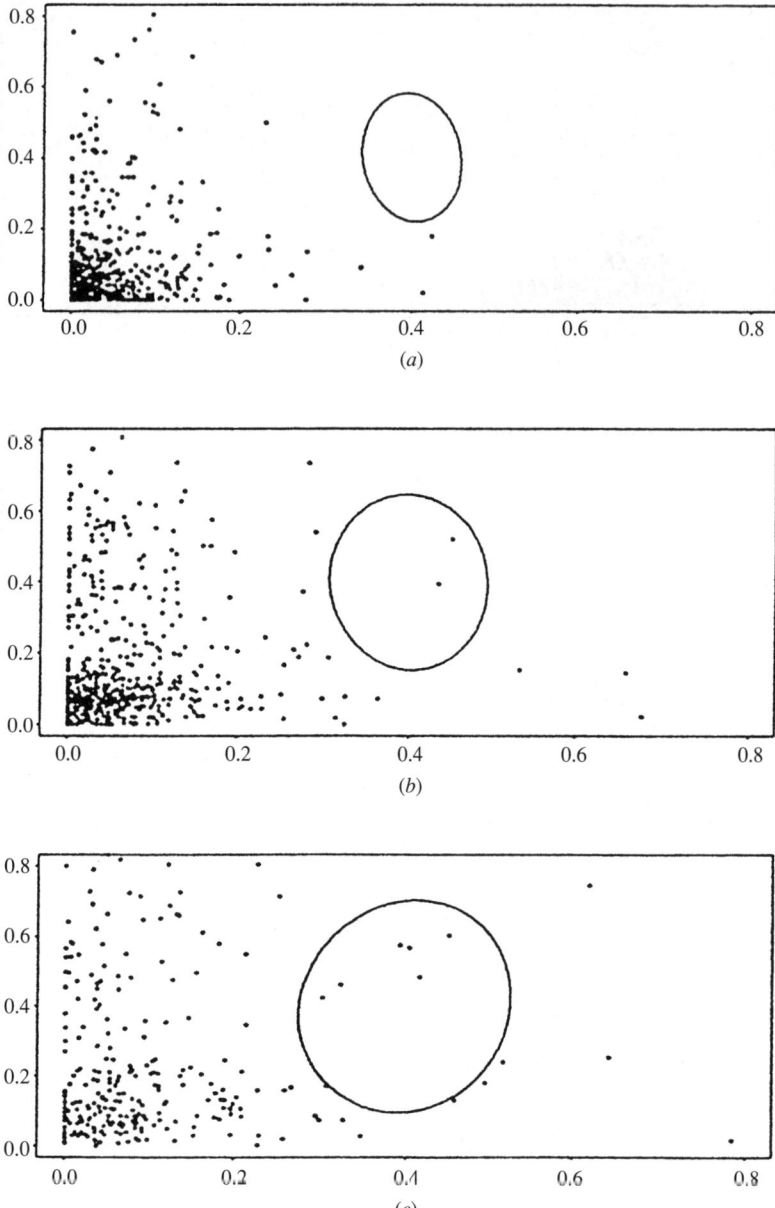

Fig. 3.8. Concentration Ellipses, Clothing and Transport, 1979
Source: EBF

Table 3.1. Smallest Eigenvalue of Cp: Estimates and Confidence Interval*

	Conf. interval, lower bound	Smallest eigenvalue	Conf. interval, upper bound	Largest eigenvalue	Sample size
(a) FES data					
1969	2.2	2.7	3.2	40	7,098
1968	2.7	3.2	3.8	42	6,954
1970	1.9	2.4	2.8	39	6,331
1971	2.3	2.8	3.3	43	7,171
1972	1.8	2.5	3.2	47	6,963
1973	1.7	2.3	3.0	43	7,059
1974	1.9	2.7	3.5	43	6,626
1975	2.2	2.8	3.5	38	7,139
1976	2.0	2.7	3.3	39	7,133
1977	1.4	1.9	2.3	43	7,124
1978	1.3	1.7	2.1	38	6,950
1979	1.0	1.3	1.6	42	6,712
1980	1.3	2.2	2.9	42	6,889
1981	1.4	1.8	2.2	43	7,415
1982	1.4	1.9	2.3	42	7,358
1983	1.0	1.3	1.5	40	6,915
1984	1.5	2.2	2.9	41	7,009
(b) EBF data					
1979	1.1	1.4	1.9	473	8,501
1984	0.7	0.8	1.0	609	11,024
1989	0.5	0.7	0.8	695	8,458

* times $10^3/\bar{x}_t$ for FES and $10^4/\bar{x}_t$ for EBF.

3.5. The Space of Engel Curves

Market demand is defined as the average demand of a household population. If we first take the average demand of the sub-sample of households at the level of income x and then take the mean with respect to the income distribution, we obtain the market demand

$$F(p) = \int \bar{f}(p, x)\, \rho(x)\, dx,$$

where ρ is the density of the income distribution and $\bar{f}(p, x)$ is average demand across all households with the income level x. The graph of the function $x \rightarrow \bar{f}_h(p, x)$ is known as the Engel curve for consumption good h after the statistician Ernst Engel. Therefore, a satisfactory model of market demand requires knowledge of the 'form' of the density ρ of income and of the Engel curves $\bar{f}_h(p, \cdot)$.

The form of the income distribution is well researched in the literature; for example, Figs. 3.3 and 3.4 suggest possibile forms. But what can one say of the form of the Engel curve of a heterogeneous population? For example, can one compose the Engel curve from some elementary functions with a simple, analytical expression?

It is clear that pure microeconomic theory cannot provide answers to these questions. In fact, hypotheses about individual behaviour—even if they are very restrictive—are not sufficient if the household population is heterogeneous. On the other hand, explicit knowledge of the Engel curves of a heterogeneous population does not entail any implication about the individual behaviour of households.

In such a situation, it seems natural to me to turn once more to the empirical data. For each category of expenditure in the study, denoted h, define $y_t^h(x)$ as the average expenditure in period t of all households with income x. It will often be more convenient to consider the relationship between expenditures and income, that is to say the expression $y_t^h/x =: g_t^h(x)$. The graph of the function $x \to g_t^h(x)$ is also known as the Engel curve.

Fig. 3.9 shows the estimated Engel curves $g_t^h(\cdot)$ for four expenditure categories (food, clothing, housing and services), $t = 1983$, FES. We can see that the Engel curve is decreasing for food expenditure; this is the original law discovered by Engel.

The Engel curves for different years are not defined on the same domain of income because this domain changes from one year to the next. For this reason, we normalize the Engel curves:

$$\zeta \to g_t^{-h}(\zeta) := g_t^h(\bar{x}_t \zeta)$$

where $\bar{x}_t$ is average income in year t.

For the EBF data this gives 42 curves (14 expenditure categories and 3 years) and for the FES data 144 curves (9 expenditure categories and 16 years). All these curves are defined across an interval; for example, we may choose $I = [0.25, 2.5]$.

In both cases, we now consider the linear space of functions on the interval I generated by these Engel curves. In the first case the linear space is generated by 42 functions, in the second case by 144 functions. A base of this linear space constitutes a parametric model of the Engel curves. So we need the dimension and a base of this space of Engel curves. Kneip has developed statistical methods to test the hypothesis that the dimension of a space is equal to $n = 1, 2, \ldots$ (Kneip 1994). For the EBF and FES data, the hypothesis that n is less than 4 is rejected, but for $n \geq 4$ the hypothesis is not rejected! To identify the base of the space, we must look for the set of transformations with respect to which the space is invariant. We can identify two such sets of transformations. More specifically, the hypothesis that the space is invariant with respect to these two sets of transformations is not rejected.[4]

---

[4] For a precise formulation and details, see Kneip (1994).

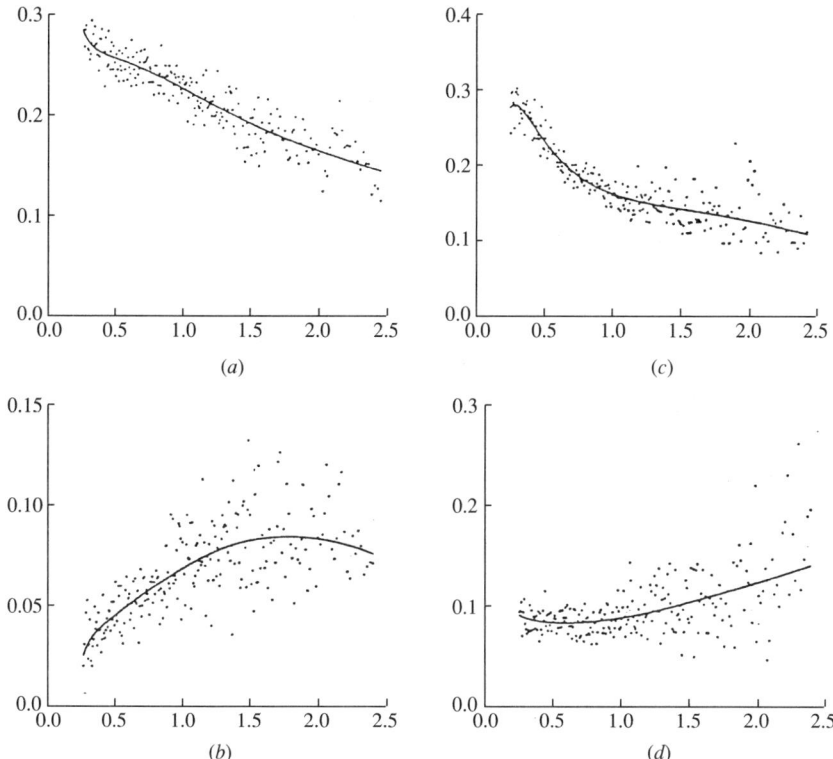

Fig. 3.9. Estimated Engel Curves for Four Expenditure Categories, 1983
    (*a*) Food
    (*b*) Clothing
    (*c*) Housing
    (*d*) Services

Source: Family Expenditure Survey

If we accept this invariance of the space $\mathcal{L}$, then we can prove that the base of the space $\mathcal{L}$ is given by the following four functions:

$$1,\ \log x,\ (\log x)^2 \text{ and } (\log x)^3$$

This result is both very strong and also surprising. It is remarkable that a *non-parametric analysis* of the data leads to a *parametric model* of the Engel curves:

$$g_t^h(x) = a_t^h + b_t^h \log x + c_t^h (\log x)^2 + d_t^h (\log x)^3.$$

3.6. Conclusion

In conclusion, I am well aware that some theoreticians in my profession will not accept this empirical approach. They will accuse me of explaining nothing and of proving nothing more than the existence of some 'empirical regularities'. I have modelled heterogeneity in a household population through the hypothesis of increasing dispersion and I have modelled Engel curves using invariant transformations. These models do not consist of a deductive validation departing from simple postulates of microeconomics, that is to say from hypotheses on individual behaviour.

I will be criticized for lack of elegance because inductive validation requires non-parametric statistical analysis, which relies on rather heavy numerical calculations. But economic theory is not a branch of mathematics and will never have the elegance of mathematical theories. If we claim that economics is a positive science, then we cannot ignore the empirical data in the choice of hypotheses.

I want to conclude by expressing my hope that in the future economic theory will be less speculative, that empirical data analysis will be given a more important role to play, and that the GREQAM will play an important role in achieving this. Once more, I would like to quote Malinvaud:

systematic observation plays a crucial role in showing which of many conceivable alternative specifications are plausible. The purely microeconomic approach too often nurtures the illusion that we can do without this comparison with data, even though negative results actually constitute evidence that one cannot reach conclusions without appealing to observation. (Malinvaud 1991: 147)

REFERENCES

Härdle, W. and Stocker, T. (1989), 'Investigating Smooth Multiple Regression by the Method of Average Derivatives', *Journal of the American Statistical Association*, 84: 986–95.

—— Hildenbrand, W., and Jericson, M. (1991), 'Empirical Evidence on the Law of Demand', *Econometrica*, 59: 1525–49.

Hildenbrand, W. (1994), *Market Demand: Theory and Empirical Evidence*. Princeton: Princeton University Press.

—— and Kneip, A. (1993), 'Family Expenditure Data, Heteroscedasticity and the Law of Demand', *Ricerche Economiche*, 47: 137–65.

Hutchinson, T. W. (1938), *The Significance and Basic Postulates of Economic Theory*. New York: Augustus M. Kelley.

Keynes, J. N. (1891), *The Scope and Method of Political Economy*. New York: Kelley & Millman, 1955.

Koopmans, T. C. (1957), *Three Essays on the State of Economic Science*. New York: McGraw-Hill.

Kneip, A. (1994), 'Nonparametric Estimation of Common Regressors for Similar Curve Data', *Annals of Statistics*, 22: 1386–1427.

Malinvaud, E. (1991), *Voies de la recherche macroéconomique*. Paris: Editions Odile Jacob.

—— (1988), *Inaugural Lecture at the Collège de France*.

Robbins, L. (1932), *An Essay on the Nature and Significance of Economic Science*, 3rd edn. London: Macmillan, 1984.

4

Money and Monetary Policy in General Equilibrium

Jacques Drèze
Heracles Polemarchakis

4.1

The introduction of banks that issue and supply balances and pay out their profits as dividends is the natural modification of the model developed by Arrow (1951, 1953), Debreu (1951, 1960, 1970), and McKenzie (1954), which encompasses monetary economies.[1]

The consistent accounting imposed by the balance sheets of banks implies that all money is 'inside': initial gross holdings are matched by liabilities, which overcomes the 'Hahn problem' (Hahn 1965; Dubey and Geanakoplos 1989*b*).

Equilibria in which money serves as a medium of exchange, and possibly only as such, exist. But they are, typically, suboptimal and indeterminate.

There is an optimal monetary policy, which in some case formalizes an earlier argument (see Friedman 1969; Vickrey 1959).

4.2

We adopt a flexible specification which allows for constraints on transactions, such as 'cash-in-advance' constraints (Clower 1965) or, alternatively, for costly transactions (Baumol 1952; Tobin 1956); we do this by introducing balances, prices, and transactions as arguments of the preferences of individuals or of the technologies of firms.

This text presents research results of the Belgian programme on Inter-University Poles of Attraction initiated by the Belgian Prime Minister's Office, Science Policy Programming. The scientific responsibility is assumed by its authors. The Commission of the European Union provided additional support through the HCM grant ERBCHRX CT-940458. The text was prepared for presentation at the international conference on Recent Developments in the Macroeconomics of Imperfect Competition organized by ADRES and CEPREMAP in Paris on 6–8 January 1994. A much earlier version was presented at the GREQE 10th anniversary conference held in Marseille on 8–10 September 1992.

[1] See also Arrow and Debreu (1954).

We consider, in sequence, economies that extend over one or more periods, with one or more currencies, under certainty or uncertainty. Subsequently, we outline a model of an abstract economy which encompasses all specifications. For clearer understanding, we contrast the model we propose here with other models of monetary economies. We conclude with a particular case of the general model which generates the *IS–LM* framework (Keynes 1936; Hicks 1937) at equilibrium.

We do not consider adjustment towards equilibrium or price adjustment (Drèze 1993a). We do not allow for non-convexities, which a realistic, detailed treatment of the transactions technology should. Most importantly, we do not explain why most transactions take the form of exchanges of goods for money (Kiyotaki and Wright 1989; Ostroy and Starr 1974). For our purposes, it is sufficient to take this common-place observation as a factual starting point. We do not pay attention to the day-to-day profile of money demand (Grossman and Weiss 1983; Hellwig 1993) and overnight rates of interest. We work with a finite number of elementary periods, of individuals, and of commodities, so that aggregate valuation is always possible. For purposes of interpretation, the length of a period is non-trivial but short; within each period, prices and rates of interest are constant; the precise timing of transactions and the resulting flow of consumption and production do not affect preferences or production possibilities, while they do affect balances and interest accounting, and the banks accommodate money demand.

4.3

A detailed illustration of the flows of transactions and accounting gives substance to the abstract formulation which we develop in subsequent sections.

An exchange economy extends over a single period (of unit length) under certainty. A bank issues aggregate balances, m, and pays out its profit, v, as dividend. An individual, h, is endowed with a bundle of commodities, $\bar{x}^h$, and a fraction, θ^h, of the shares of the bank. He consumes commodities, x^h, and uses money balances, m^h. The individual's transaction in a commodity is $z_l^h = x_l^h - \bar{x}_l^h$, and $(z_l^h)_+ = \max\{0, z_l^h\}$ is the net purchase of the commodity, while $(z_l^h)_- = \max\{0, -z_l^h\}$ is the net sale: $z_l^h = (z_l^h)_+ - (z_l^h)_-$: across commodities, $z^h = z_+^h - z_-^h$.

Flows within the single period are constant, and interest is accounted for at the end of the period. Individuals have bank accounts, to which the proceeds of their sales, for instance their salaries, are credited *ex post* n times per period. Individuals pay for their purchases with banknotes, balances, obtained from the bank. This is a stylized representation of a process of exchange through intermediaries implicitly present in the background. Each morning, farmers and craftsmen bring supplies to shopkeepers, who sell these supplies to households and deposit proceeds of the sales in the accounts of the farmers and craftsmen in the evening or after $1/n$ units of time. Finally, balances do not affect utility directly, but 'trips to the bank' affect utility adversely, through a reduction of leisure time.

EXAMPLE. Loans take the form of an overdraft facility, with interest calculated on positive and negative balances at the same rate, r.[2]

At time 0, an individual withdraws an amount m^h, $pz_+^h \geq m^h \geq 0$, which he spends at the flow rate pz_+^h. Cash balances are depleted at time m^h/pz_+^h, when a new withdrawal occurs, unless that time is 1. Because the rate of interest on positive and negative balances is the same, the timing of receipts does not affect the pattern of withdrawals, which is always of the Baumol–Tobin type: each withdrawal is in the same amount, m^h.

A time 1, the account balance is $-pz^h$. A simple calculation reveals that the interest due, $\lessgtr 0$, is

$$\frac{r}{2}\left(m^h + pz^h + \frac{pz_-^h}{n}\right).$$

This is illustrated in Fig. 4.1, for the case $n = \infty$, with $pz_+^h/m^h = 3$. The budget constraint then takes the form

$$pz^h\left(1 + \frac{r}{2}\right) + m^h \frac{r}{2} \leq \theta^h v.$$

Imposing equality and aggregating over individuals yields

$$m\frac{r}{2} = v.$$

Writing ρ for $(r/2)(1 + r/2)$ and ω for $v/(1 + r/2)$,[3] these relations become

$$pz^h + m^h\rho = \theta^h\omega = \theta^h m\rho.$$

We proceed with an analytical illustration.

Commodities are $l = 1, 2$. Individuals are $h = 1, 2$. An individual has utility function $u^h(x, m, p, \rho) = x_1 x_2[l - p(x - \bar{x}^h)_+/m]$, over the consumption–exchange set $X^h(p, \rho) = \{(x, m, p, r) : (x, m) \geq 0, \ l - p(x - \bar{x}^h)_+/m \geq 0\}$,[4] and ownership share in the bank $\theta^h = 1/2$. Individuals differ only in their endowment of commodities, with $\bar{x}^1 = (1, 0)$ and $\bar{x}^2 = (0, 1)$.

Writing k for pz_+/m, the number of 'trips to the bank', the utility function and budget constraint of individual 1 are

$$u^1 = x_1^1 x_2^1(l - k^1), \quad px^1 + m^1\rho \leq p\bar{x}_1^1 + \frac{1}{2}\omega,$$

with $m^1 = p_2 x_2^1/k^1$. Maximizing utility subject to the budget constraint for fixed k yields the first-order conditions and utility .

---

[2] Alternatively, loans may take the form of promissory notes or bonds, no interest is paid on bank accounts, and balances on bank accounts are non-negative. A single formalism encompasses both institutional settings.

[3] Throughout this paper, the greek letters π, ρ, ω are used for transformations of p, r, v.

[4] The cash-in-advance specification imposes the stronger condition $p(x - \bar{x}^h)_+ \leq m$.

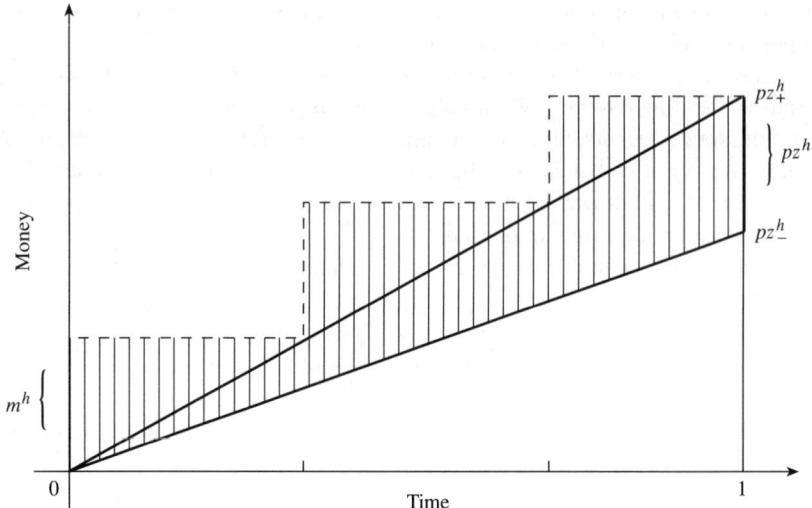

Fig. 4.1. Interest Calculation

The striped area corresponds to the overdraft amount over which interest is due, when $n = \infty$. The area above the line pz^h_+ is equal to $m^h/2$; the area between the lines pz^h_+ and pz^h_- is equal to $pz^h/2$. For $n < \infty$ the striped (overdrafts) area is enlarged by n rectangular triangles, with non-overlapping hypotenuses covering the line $0\text{-}pz^h_-$.

$$x^1_1 = \frac{p_1 + \omega/2}{2p_1(1 + \rho/k)}, \quad x^1_2 = \frac{p_1 + \omega/2}{2p_2},$$

$$u^1 = \frac{(p_1 + \omega/2)^2(l - k)}{4p_1p_2(1 + \rho/k)}.$$

The optimal value of k can be found by grid search over the positive integers. It will be close[5] to the unconstrained maximizer $k^* = (\rho l + \rho^2)^{1/2} - \rho$, which satisfies $(\rho l)^{1/2} \geq k^* \geq (\rho l)^{1/2} - \rho$.[6]

---

[5] Because u^1 is concave in k.

[6] In order to illustrate the application of the Baumol–Tobin formula, consider more general preferences described by the utility function

$$u^h = u^h(x^h, l^h) = u^h\left(\bar{x}^h + z^h, \bar{l}^h - \frac{pz^h_+}{m^h}\right),$$

where l^h is leisure time, of which each trip to the bank uses up one unit. The first-order conditions for an optimum are

$$\frac{\partial u^h}{\partial l^h}\frac{pz^h_+}{(m^h)^2} - \lambda r = 0, \quad \text{and} \quad m^h = \left(\frac{\partial u^h}{\partial l^h}\frac{pz^h_+}{\lambda r}\right)^{1/2},$$

which is precisely the Baumol–Tobin formula with λ the marginal utility of 'income', $\frac{\partial u^h}{\partial l^h}\big/\lambda$ the cost of one transaction, the marginal rate to substitution between leisure and 'income', and pz^h_+ the aggregate nominal spending per period.

Exploiting the symmetry of the example, $p_1^* = p_2^*$ and $x_1^{1*} = 1 - x_1^{2*} = x_2^{2*} = 1 - x_2^{1*}$, with

$$x^{1*} = \left(\frac{1+\rho/k}{2+\rho/k}, \frac{1}{2+\rho/k}\right), \quad \frac{m^{*1}}{p.} = \frac{1}{2k+\rho},$$

$$x^{2*} = \left(\frac{1}{2+\rho/k}, \frac{1+\rho/k}{2+\rho/k}\right), \quad \frac{m^{*2}}{p.} = \frac{1}{2k+\rho},$$

$$u^{1*} = u^{2*} = \left(1+\frac{\rho}{k}\right)\left(2+\frac{\rho}{k}\right)^{-2}(l-k).$$

When $\theta^1 \neq \theta^2$, the algebra is more complicated, because the symmtry of the problem is lost. In particular,

$$\frac{p_1^*}{p_2^*} = \frac{1+2\rho/k+\theta^1(\rho/k)^2}{2+2\rho/k+(1-\theta^1)(\rho/k)^2}.$$

A positive interest rate entails distributive effects. By way of illustration, when $\theta^1 = 1$, then

$$u^{1*} = \frac{1}{2}\left(1+\frac{\rho}{k}\right)^2\left[1+\left(1+\frac{\rho}{k}\right)^2\right]^{-1}(l-k)$$

$$u^{2*} = \frac{1}{2}\left[1+\left(1+\frac{\rho}{k}\right)^2\right]^{-1}(l-k).$$

In this case, u^{1*} is increasing in ρ *for fixed k*. The property may be lost when the adjustment of k is taken into account. For instance, the approximation $\tilde{k} = (\rho l)^{1/2}$ would make u^{1*} a decreasing function of r.

4.4

We now treat formally an exchange economy which extends over one period under certainty. This limiting case has no substantive interest but is useful to clarify the sequel.

Bundles of all commodities or services, other than balances, are $x = (\ldots , x_l, \ldots)$, and the associated prices of commodities are $p = (\ldots , p_l, \ldots)$. There is a single currency, balances are m, and the rate of interest is $r \geq 0$. The non-negativity of r reflects free disposal and absence of holding costs.

The accounting for transactions is best understood as follows. In the beginning of the period, balances are exchanged for bonds; at the end of the period, bonds and balances are redeemed and exchanged for commodities; the rate of interest within the period is r, the prices of commodities are p, and the exchange price of money is 1.

A bank issues and supplies money balances, $m \geq 0$, in exchange for bonds, d, according to the accounting or budget constraint,

$$d + m = 0.$$

The bank realizes, and distributes as dividend, profit:

$$v = -[(1 + r)d + m].$$

By substitution from the accounting constraint, it follows that

$$v = rm \geq 0.$$

In standard terminology, v is 'seignorage'.

An individual, h, is endowed with commodities, $\bar{x}^h$, shares in the bank, $\theta^h \geq 0$, $\sum_h \theta^h = 1$, and with initial balances, $\bar{m}^h \geq 0$, or debt (bonds), $\bar{d}^h \leq 0$, with $\sum_h (\bar{d}^h + \bar{m}^h) = 0$. In standard terminology, this last condition means that all the money is 'inside money'. The case where $\bar{m}^h = 0$ for all individuals is of special interest.

The individual demands balances, $m \geq 0$, in exchange for bonds, d, subject to the budget constraint

$$d + m \leq 0.$$

He demands commodities, x, subject to the budget constraint

$$px \leq p\bar{x}^h + \bar{d}^h + \bar{m}^h + (1 + r)d + m + \theta^h v.$$

The domain of preferences of the individual over commodity bundles and balances, (x, m), is the consumption–exchange set $X^h(\bar{x}^h, p, r)$. The preferences of the individual over the consumption–exchange set are represented by the utility function $u^h(x, m; \bar{x}^h, p, r)$. The possible dependence of the consumption–exchange set, or of the utility function on the initial endowment of the individual, the prices of commodities, and the rate of interest, reflects the technology of transactions and, in particular, the role of money as a medium of exchange. (The example above is an illustration.)

The absence of money illusion is captured by the homogeneity of the dependence of the consumption–exchange set and of the utility function on the prices of commodities: for $\lambda > 0$, $(x, m) \in X^h(\bar{x}^h, p, r) \Rightarrow (x, \lambda m) \in X^h(\bar{x}^h, \lambda p, r)$, and $u^h(x, m; \bar{x}^h, p, r) \geq u^h(x', m'; \bar{x}^h, p, r) \Rightarrow u^h(x, \lambda m; \bar{x}^h, \lambda p, r) \geq u^h(x', \lambda m'; \bar{x}^h, \lambda p, r)$.

The budget constraints under which the individual optimizes reduce to

$$px + rm \leq p\bar{x}^h + \bar{d}^h + \bar{m}^h + \theta^h v.$$

If (x^h, m^h) is a solution to the individual optimization problem, and since $\sum_h \theta^h = 1$, aggregate demand, (x^a, m^a), satisfies Walras's law:

$$p(x^a - \bar{x}^a) + r(m^a - m) = 0.$$

A state of the economy is an array, $(p, r, m, \ldots (x^h, m^h), \ldots)$, of prices of commodities, a rate of interest, a supply of money balances, and a bundle of commodities and balances in the consumption–exchange set of each individual. Extrapolating tradition, we do not include the initial endowments of commodities, $(\ldots \bar{x}^{h} \ldots)$, explicitly in the description of the state—but they belong implicitly as determinants of the consumption–exchange sets. In the definitions of the following three paragraphs, these physical endowments are kept fixed.

A state of the economy is feasible if and only if the markets for commodities and balances clear, i.e. if

$$\sum_{h} x^{h} = \sum_{h} \bar{x}^{h}, \quad \text{and} \quad \sum_{h} m^{h} = m.$$

Equilibrium prices of commodities, a rate of interest, and a supply of money balances, (p^{*}, r^{*}, m^{*}), are such that there exists a feasible state of the economy, $(p^{*}, r^{*}, m^{*}, \ldots, (x^{h*}, m^{h*}), \ldots)$, with the commodity bundle and balances of each individual a solution to his optimization problem.

A state of the economy, $(p^{*}, r^{*}, m^{*}, \ldots (x^{h*}, m^{h*}), \ldots)$, Pareto-dominates another, $(p^{**}, r^{**}, m^{**}, \ldots (x^{h**}, m^{h**}), \ldots)$, if and only if

$$u^{h}(x^{h*}, m^{h*}; \bar{x}^{h}, p^{*}, r^{*}) \geq u^{h}(x^{h**}, m^{h**}; \bar{x}^{h}, p^{**}, r^{**})$$

for each individual, with some strict inequality. The endowments of individuals in commodities are not allowed to vary. A state is Pareto-optimal if and only if no state Pareto-dominates it, allowing for lump-sum transfers of revenue (initial bonds and balances) across individuals.

Under standard continuity and convexity assumptions, equilibrium prices of commodities, a rate of interest, and money balances, (p^{*}, r^{*}, m^{*}), exist.

Equilibrium states of the economy are, nevertheless, indeterminate. For a fixed rate of interest and balances $(\bar{r}, \bar{m}) \geq 0$, there exist prices of commodities $\bar{p}$ such that $(\bar{p}, \bar{r}, \bar{m})$ are in equilibrium. Equilibrium states are essentially distinct if and only if the associated levels of utility are distinct for some individuals. The degree of real indeterminacy, the dimension of the set of essentially distinct equilibrium states of the economy, is, typically, 2.

It is suggestive to think about nominal variables as being the general level of nominal prices, say $\sum_{l} p_{l} = p1$, the nominal rate of interest r and the quantity of money m. Any two of these are free parameters, with the third determined (at equilibrium) by the demand for money.

In the special case where $\bar{m}^{h} = 0$ for all h, there is a single degree of real indeterminacy. In that case, it follows from the absence of money illusion and homogeneity that, if $(p^{*}, r^{*}, m^{*}, \ldots (x^{h*}, m^{h*}), \ldots)$ is a competitive equilibrium state, then $(\lambda p^{*}, r^{*}, \lambda m^{*}, \ldots (x^{h*}, \lambda m^{h*}), \ldots)$ is also a competitive equilibrium state, for any $\lambda > 0$. For $\lambda \neq 1$, these two states are 'nominally distinct', but they are not 'essentially distinct', in the sense that each individual's utility is the same. The degree of nominal indeterminacy, complementary to the degree of real indeterminacy, is then, typically, 1. In standard terminology, this nominal indeterminacy is 'neutrality'. Variations in the rate of interest, typically, yield essentially distinct equilibrium states.

The example illustrates the three ways in which the rate of interest has real consequences:

1. A higher rate of interest induces households to economize on balances, say by making more 'trips to the bank'. This effect is often labelled 'shoeleather cost'. It is represented in the example by the leisure argument, $(l - k)$, in the utility function.
2. A positive rate of interest drives a wedge between the marginal rates of substitution between two goods for two agents operating on different sides of either market. This effect may be labelled a 'liquidity cost'. It is represented in the example by the inequality

$$\frac{\partial u^1/\partial x_1^*}{\partial u^1/\partial x_2^*} = \frac{x_2^{1*}}{x_1^{1*}} = \frac{1}{1+\rho/k} < \frac{x_2^{2*}}{x_1^{2*}} = 1 + \frac{\rho}{k} = \frac{\partial u^2/\partial x_1^{2*}}{\partial u^2/\partial x_2^{2*}}.$$

3. Outside of degenerate symmetric cases, a positive rate of interest induces income transfers, from agents whose share in bank dividends falls short of interest payments to agents for whom the opposite is true. This is a 'distributive effect'. It is illustrated in the example by the case where $\theta^1 = 1$, $\theta^2 = 0$, resulting in $u^{1*} = (1 + \rho/k)^2 u^{2*}$—whereas $u^{1*} = u^{2*}$ when $\theta^1 = \theta^2$ (because of symmetry of tastes and endowments) or again when $\rho = 0$.

In general, each of these three effects influences prices and quantities; i.e., the effects are 'real'. This is illustrated in the example by the fact that the quantities consumed x^{1*}, x^{2*} and leisure all depend upon ρ, and by the fact that $p_1^* \neq p_2^*$ when $\rho \neq 0$ and $\theta^1 \neq \theta^2$.

When $\bar{m}^h \neq 0$ for some individual, the purchasing power of initial balances depends upon p, and in particular upon the general level of nominal prices. Replacing p by λp, $\lambda > 0$, entails distributive effects with real consequences.

An equilibrium state of the economy with a positive rate of interest is, typically, not Pareto-optimal. It suffices to set the rate of interest at 0 and the balances of individuals at their satiation level, and to employ transfers to compensate individuals for losses or gains of revenue as the prices of commodities adjust to maintain market-clearing.

In this trivial one-period model, interest rates do not affect intertemporal allocative decisions. As we shall see, intertemporal arbitrages reduce indeterminacy. We therefore postpone comments on that issue until the next section.

An extension of the economy that allows for production is straightforward. Technologies of firms, sets of production plans of commodities, and balances, which depend on the prices of commodities and the rate of interest, reflect the technology of transactions.

In the sections immediately following, we consider economies that extend over multiple periods, economies with multiple currencies, and economies under uncertainty. In each case, and in order to avoid repetition, we spell out only the aspects of the specification that may not be evident.

4.5

Consider an exchange economy that extends over finite, discrete time, $t = 1$ ... T, under certainty.

In period t, a commodity bundle is x_t, and the associated spot prices of commodities are p_t. Across time, a commodity bundle is $x = (\ldots , x_t , \ldots)$, and the associated spot prices of commodities are $p = (\ldots , p_t , \ldots)$. One-period bonds serve, along with balances, to transfer purchasing power across time; holdings of bonds are d_t, and the associated rate of interest is r_t. Across time, rates of interest are $r = (\ldots , r_t , \ldots)$. There is a single currency, and balances are m_t. Across time, holdings of balances are $m = (\ldots , m_t , \ldots)$.

With multiple periods, it is natural to identify the end of period t with the beginning of period $t + 1$. Thus, in period t, period t commodities are exchanged for period t balances, with surpluses (negative or positive) carried forward as period $(t + 1)$ bonds and balances. Interest and profit accounting occur at the end of the period.

Each period, a bank issues and supplies balances, $m_t \geq 0$, in exchange for bonds, d_t, according to the accounting or budget constraint,

$$d_t + m_t = 0,$$

and realizes profit

$$v_t = -[(1 + r_t)d_t + m_t],$$

which it distributes as dividends. Evidently,

$$v_t = r_t m_t \geq 0.$$

An individual optimizes under the sequence of budget constraints

$$d_1 + m_1 \leq \bar{d}^h + \bar{m}^h,$$

$$p_t x_t + d_{t+1} + m_{t+1} \leq p_t \bar{x}_t^h + (1 + r_t)d_t + m_t + \theta_t^h v_t,$$

where $\bar{x}^h = (\ldots , \bar{x}_t^h , \ldots)$ is his endowment of commodities, $(\bar{d}^h, \bar{m}^h)$ his endowment of bonds and balances, and $\theta^h = (\ldots , \theta_t^h , \ldots)$ his shares in the bank.

For $\pi = (\ldots , \pi_t = p_t[(1 + r_1) \ldots (1 + r_t)]^{-1}, \ldots)$, $\rho = (\ldots , \rho_t = r_t[(1 + r_1) \ldots (1 + r_t)]^{-1}, \ldots)$, and $\omega = (\ldots , \omega_t = v_t[(1 + r_1) \ldots (1 + r_t)]^{-1}, \ldots)$, the sequence of budget constraints under which an individual optimizes reduce to

$$\pi x + \rho m \leq \pi \bar{x}^h + \bar{d}^h + \bar{m}^h + \theta^h \omega.$$

The dependence of the effective prices of commodities, π_t, and rates of interest, ρ_t, on the underlying rates of interest, r_t, account for the possible dependence of the preferences of individuals on the rates of interest in addition to the prices of commodities.

Equilibrium prices of commodities, rates of interest and supply of balances
(π^*, ρ^*, m^*) exist.

Equilibrium states of the economy are nevertheless indeterminate. The 2
degrees of indeterminacy of the single-period model in the previous section do
not, however, become $2T$ in the T-period model. This is due to the relationships
between nominal interest rates, inflation rates and real interest rates known as
the 'Fisher conditions' (Fisher 1907).

Formally, the rate of inflation $\phi_{t,t+1}$ between periods t and $t+1$ is defined by

$$p_{t+1}\mathbf{1} = p_t\mathbf{1}(1 + \phi_{t,t+1}).$$

The real rate of interest, $R_{t,t+1}$, between periods t and $t+1$ is defined through
the return on an indexed bond which pays at the beginning of period $t+1$ an
amount $(1 + \phi_{t,t+1})(1 + R_{t,t+1})$ per unit of money invested at the beginning of
period t. Arbitrage-free pricing imposes equality between this redemption value
and that of the corresponding nominal bond,[7]

$$1 + r_t \equiv (1 + \phi_{t,t+1})(1 + R_{t,t+1}) \simeq 1 + \phi_{t,t+1} + R_{t,t+1}, \quad t = 1\ldots, T-1.$$

These Fisher conditions 'absorb' $T-1$ out of $2T$ degrees of indeterminacy—
leaving $2T - (T-1) = T+1$ degrees in the T-period model. For $T = 1$, there are
thus 2 degrees, as verified in the previous section.

One interpretation of this conclusion is that, if T nominal rates of interest are
set by the bank, there remains indeterminacy of the general price level; if the
price level in any one period is set, the remaining $T-1$ price levels are determined through the Fisher conditions. The T quantities of money are then determined through the money demand of agents (given nominal prices and interest
rates). Having set the interest rates, the bank must accommodate money demand,
at equilibrium. Alternatively, the bank could have set the level of the money
supply, and let interest rates adjust to clear the money market, conditionally on
the general price level. (With an indeterminate price level, clearing of the money
market is not well-defined; there always exists a price level low enough for a
given money supply to exceed demand at zero interest rates.)

This interpretation remains valid if the number of periods is increased—either
by extending the horizon or by subdividing more finely a given horizon. Also,
in a continuous-time formulation (limit of the subdivision process), if the rate of
interest r_t is set for all t, it still remains to determine the general price level.

An alternative interpretation is that, if the T price levels are exogenously
determined, there remains a single degree of indeterminacy; the bank could then
set one interest rate (directly or through the money supply), the remaining ones
being implied by equilibrium. Because the Fisher conditions refer to forward
arbitrages, the free interest rate is that of the last period.

---

[7] Inside period t, both instruments are valued by discounting redemption values at the same
nominal rate r_t.

The general conclusion is that there exists a single degree of indeterminacy per period, with two of the three nominal variables (price level, money supply, nominal interest rate) determined (from the real side and arbitrage-free conditions) once the third is set. There is one, single, additional degree of indeterminacy, corresponding to either the overall price level or the terminal interest rate. If initial endowments of bonds and balances are zero, the overall price level is inessential. For large T, the incidence of the terminal interest rate on the allocation and welfare becomes negligible.

The welfare cost of inflation is entirely due to the associated nominal rates, with real effects as described in the previous section. Indeed, the Fisher conditions embody the well-known property that the nominal rate is equal to the real rate plus the inflation rate. Equilibrium states with positive nominal rates of interest are typically not Pareto-optimal.

It should be noted in this connection that zero nominal rates require negative inflation when real rates are positive but positive inflation when real rates are negative. Negative real rates are neither pathological nor a theoretical curiosum. They reflect an increase over time of scarcity of resources, which is entirely possible for non-storable resources such as labour services or productive capacities. With negative real rates, the marginal cost of inflation is negative at rates of inflation below the absolute value of the real rates.

The implications of inflation for seignorage are clear. Absence of money illusion means that money demand at t is homogeneous of degree 1 in the price level at t. Write $m_t(p_t; \cdot) = p_t^1 m_t(p_t/p_t^1; \cdot)$. The period 1 purchasing power of seignorage revenue is then

$$\frac{1}{p_1 1} \sum_{t=1}^{T} \frac{r_t m_t}{\prod_{\tau=1}^{t-1}(1+r_\tau)} = \sum_{t=1}^{T} \frac{r_t m_t(p_t/p_t 1; \cdot)\prod_{\tau=1}^{t-1}(1+\phi_{\tau,\tau+1})}{\prod_{\tau=1}^{t-1}(1+r_\tau)}$$

$$= \sum_{t=1}^{T} \frac{r_t m_t(p_t/p_t 1; \cdot)}{\prod_{\tau=1}^{t-1}(1+R_{\tau,\tau+1})},$$

which is homogeneous of degree 1 in $(\ldots, r_t, \ldots)$. This corresponds to the known feature that nominal interest rates define the cost of real balances.

In this model, long rates are defined from short rates in the ususal fashion (by compounding one-period discount factors).

Our theoretical analysis is helpful for characterizing equilibria and exhibiting the degrees of nominal indeterminacy. It does not explain how the indeterminacy is lifted—for instance, by an exogenous real process of inflation determining price levels, or by monetary policy (say, bank-set nominal rates)? In other words, our theoretical analysis says nothing about the impact of monetary policy on inflation—it only spells out equilibrium relations (the Fisher conditions once again). A theory of price formation is needed to study the impact of monetary policy, and to give a substantive content to monetary theory. Alternative theories, like the quantity theory (Friedman 1969) or the Phillips curve (Phillips 1958), vest the degrees of freedom associated with indeterminacy in different hands, the central bank or wage bargainers. One should however realize that a study of monetary policy in real economies is apt to require a disequilibrium framework; typically, interest rates are raised to fight inflation, whereas at equilibrium higher nominal rates are associated with higher inflation.

4.6

Consider an exchange economy which extends over a single period under certainty.

There are multiple currencies, n, holdings of balances are $m = (\ldots, m_n, \ldots)$, and the associated rates of interest are $r = (\ldots, r_n, \ldots)$.

A bank, n, issues and supplies balances, $m_n > 0$, in exchange for bonds, d_n, according to the accounting or budget constraint

$$d_n + m_n = 0.$$

That bank realizes, and distributes as dividends, profit,

$$v_n = -[(1 + r_n)d_n + m_n].$$

Evidently,

$$v_n = r_n m_n \geq 0.$$

In addition to his endowment in commodities, an individual is endowed with shares in banks, $\theta^h = (\ldots, \theta_n^h, \ldots) \geq 0$. (For simplicity, we disregard initial balances.)

The prices of commodities in terms of currency n are p_n. The rates of exchange of currencies are e_n in the prior markets in which balances are exchanged for bonds, and e_n' in the subsequent markets in which commodities are exchanged for balances.

The individual demands balances, $m_n > 0$, in exchange for bonds, d_n, subject to the budget constraint

$$\sum_n e_n d_n + \sum_n e_n m_n \leq 0.$$

He demands commodities, x_n, against balances of currency n, according to the budget constraint

$$\sum_n e_n' p_n x_n \leq \sum_n e_n' p_n \bar{x}_n + \sum_n e_n'(1 + r_n) d_n + \sum_n e_n' m_n + \sum_n \theta_n^h e_n' v_n,$$

where

$$\sum_n \bar{x}_n^h = \bar{x}^h.$$

Individuals face budget constraints across currencies because currencies are freely exchangeable: there are no currency or capital controls. It implies that a necessary property for equilibrium rates of interest is interest rate parity,

$$\frac{e'_{n1}(1 + r_{n1})}{e_{n1}} = \frac{e'_{n2}(1 + r_{n2})}{e_{n2}}.$$

Since commodities exchanged against distinct currencies are perfect substitutes for individuals, whose preferences are defined over $x = \sum_n x_n$, a necessary property of equilibrium prices of commodities is purchasing power parity,

$$e'_{n1} p_{n1} = e'_{n2} p_{n2}.$$

Without loss of generality, $e_n = 1$.

For $\pi = e'_n p_n$, $\rho = (\ldots, \rho_n = [e'_1(1 + r_1) r_n]/(1 + r_n) = e'_n r_n, \ldots)$, and $\omega = (\ldots, \omega_n = \rho_n m_n, \ldots)$, the sequence of budget constraints under which the individual optimizes reduces to

$$\pi x + \rho m \le \pi \bar{x}^h + 0^h \omega.$$

With this reduction, the properties of equilibrium states are straightforward, and their derivation is not spelled out.

In a T-period model, there are $T + 1$ degrees of indeterminacy per currency, or $N(T + 1)$ altogether with N currencies. All exchange rates are determined by the purchasing power parity conditions. Real interest rates are unique. If the Fisher conditions are satisfied in terms of one currency, they are satisfied in terms of all currencies, and interest rate parity holds.

If currency n is the fiat money (legal tender) of a nation, then market-clearing for goods, $x_n = \bar{x}_n$, implies a balance-of-payments equilibrium (a single, intertemporal constraint).

Constancy over time of exchange rates between two currencies obtains if and only if nominal rates and inflation rates are the same for both currencies: inflation convergence is necessary and sufficient for monetary union.

Inflation convergence may reflect convergence of either price formation or monetary policy, as the case may be.

4.7

Consider an economy that extends over time under uncertainty described by an 'event tree', with as many nodes for each period as there are elements to the information partition for that period. The states correspond to the terminal nodes of the tree. There are N nodes, $n = 1, \ldots, N$, and S states, $s = 1, \ldots, S$. The set of nodes is $\mathbb{N}$ and the set of states is Σ.

If n is a node at time t, $\mathcal{N}(n)$ denotes the set of nodes n' at time $t + 1$ such that n' implies n (such that n is an immediate antecedent of n' in the event tree). Clearly, $n \in \Sigma$ implies $\mathcal{N}(n) = \emptyset$.

These definitions are illustrated for three periods in Fig. 4.2, where

$N = 10$, $\quad S = 6$, $\quad \mathbb{N} = \{1, \ldots, 10\}$, $\quad \Sigma = \{5, \ldots, 10\}$, $\quad \mathcal{N}(1) = \{2, 3, 4\}$,
$\mathcal{N}(2) = \{5, 6\}$, $\quad\quad \mathcal{N}(3) = \{7\}$, $\quad\quad \mathcal{N}(4) = \{8, 9, 10\}$.

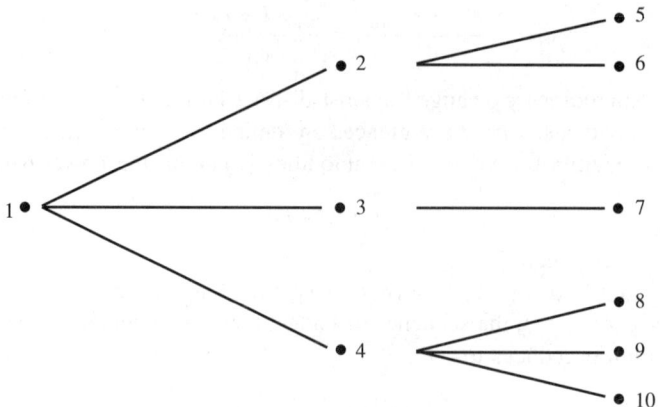

Fig. 4.2. An event tree

At node n, a commodity bundle is x_n and the associated prices of commodities are p_n. Across nodes, a commodity bundle is $x = (\ldots, x_n, \ldots)$ and the associated spot prices of commodities are $p = (\ldots, p_n, \ldots)$. At each node n in $\mathbb{N}\backslash\Sigma$, elementary securities serve to transfer revenue across nodes n' in $\mathcal{N}(n)$. Holdings of the elementary security which yields a unit of nominal revenue at node n' in $\mathbb{N}\backslash\{1\}$ are $f_{n'}$ and the associated price at node n is $q_{n'}$, where 'at node n' means 'at the beginning of the period where n is verified'. (Each n' in $\mathbb{N}\backslash\{1\}$ has a unique immediate antecedent.) At each node, there is a single currency, balances are m_n, and the rate of interest is r_n. Across nodes, holdings of balances are $m = (\ldots, m_n, \ldots)$, and the associated rates of interest are $r = (\ldots, r_n, \ldots)$.

At each node, a bank issues and supplies balances, $m_n > 0$, in exchange for bonds, d_n, according to the accounting or budget constraint,

$$d_n + m_n = 0,$$

and realizes profit,

$$v_n = -[(1 + r_n)d_n + m_n],$$

which it distributes as dividends. Evidently,

$$v_n = r_n m_n \geq 0.$$

An individual optimizes under the sequence of budget constraints

$$f_1 = \bar{d}^h + \bar{m}^h$$

$$p_n x_n + \sum_{n' \in \mathcal{N}(n)} q_{n'} f_{n'} \leq p_n \bar{x}_n^h + (1 + r_n)d_n + m_n + f_n + \theta^h v_n,$$

where $\bar{x}^h = (\ldots, \bar{x}_n^h, \ldots)$ is his endowment of commodities and θ^h his shares in the bank.

Defining recursively $Q_1 = 1$, $Q_n = q_n$ for $n \in \mathcal{N}(1)$, $Q_{n'} = q_{n'}Q_n$ for $n' \in \mathcal{N}(n)$, we may write $\pi = (\ldots, \pi_n = Q_n p_n, \ldots)$, $\rho = (\ldots, \rho_n = Q_n r_n, \ldots)$, and $\omega = (\ldots, \omega_n = Q_n v_n, \ldots)$. The sequence of budget constraints under which the individual optimizes reduce to

$$\pi x + \rho m \leq \pi \bar{x}^h + \theta^h \omega + \bar{d}^h + \bar{m}^h.$$

With this reduction, the properties of equilibrium states can be spelled out. Equilibrium states exist, and are typically sub-optimal when $r_n > 0$ at some node. With N nodes, there are potentially $2N$ degrees of indeterminacy (Section 4.4), but $N - S$ no-arbitrage conditions generalizing the Fisher conditions of Section 4.5—leaving $2N - (N - S) = N + S$ degrees of indeterminacy. The generalization of the Fisher conditions recognizes that, at each non-terminal node n, the prices of elementary securities $q_{n'}$ must satisfy $\sum_{n' \in \mathcal{N}(n)} q_{n'}(1 + r_n) = 1$. This is because a set of holdings of elementary securities $f_{n'} = 1 + r_n$ for each $n' \in \mathcal{N}(n)$ is equivalent to a unitary one-period risk-free bond, with nominal interest r_n, acquired at node n. When the above property holds, the definitions of the reduced commodity prices π_n embody a counterpart of the Fisher conditions.

There is then one degree of indeterminacy at each node, plus one more at each terminal node, resulting from the absence there of forward contracts. This agrees with the results of Section 4.5 (where $N = T$ and $S = 1$). One interpretation is that, if all rates of interest are set by the bank, there remain S degrees of price-level indeterminacy, one per path along the event-tree. Another interpretation is that, if all price levels are determined, there remains indeterminacy of interest rates at the terminal nodes.

Among the $N + S$ degrees of indeterminacy, S or $S - 1$ are inessential; that is, S if $\sum_n \bar{d}^h = \sum_n \bar{m}^h = 0$, $S - 1$ otherwise (owing to redistributive effects of the overall price level). In the most transparent two-period case, where $N = S + 1$, one sees readily that the S second-period price levels may be chosen freely and independently of all interest rates; the initial price level is then determined by the generalized Fisher condition. Alternative price levels in state s are reflected in the price of elementary security q_s but have no real effects. This also implies that variability of price levels across states, or inflation uncertainty, has no welfare costs in this complete-markets setup.

As before, a substantive theory is needed to select an interpretation (and hence to conclude about the latitudes of monetary policy). Yet, one could argue that any uncertainty about the formation of prices, hence about the impact of monetary policy on inflation, should be modelled in terms comparable to other uncertainties, i.e. through the states of the world (Drèze 1993b). (For instance, union militancy in wage bargaining belongs naturally in the definition of the states, on a par with consumer tastes.) If that sensible argument were accepted, each node corresponding to a 'real' occurrence would need to be replicated as many times as there are relevant monetary theories. The number of paths along the event tree would be multiplied, but price levels at all nodes would be uniquely determined. One should however realize that markets for claims contingent on evidence about competing monetary theories are notoriously non-existent. An incomplete-markets framework is thus indispensible for discussing monetary policy in a realistic setting.

4.8

A model of an abstract economy encompasses the above as particular cases.

There are distinct currencies, n. Holdings of balances are $m = (\ldots, m_n, \ldots)$, and the associated rates of interest are $\rho = (\ldots, \rho_n, \ldots)$.

A bank, n, issues balances, $m_n > 0$. It realizes, and distributes as dividends, profit

$$\omega_n = \rho_n m_n \geq 0.$$

Across banks, $\omega = (\ldots, \omega_n, \ldots)$.

An individual's endowment in shares in banks is $\theta^h = (\ldots, \theta_n^h, \ldots)$. He optimizes subject to the budget constraint

$$\pi x + \rho m \leq \pi \bar{x}^h + \theta^h \omega.$$

Equilibrium prices of commodities, rates of interest, and supply of money balances exist.

Competitive equilibrium states of the economy are typically indeterminate. The degree of indeterminacy is at least $N + 1$. The degree of nominal indeterminacy in an underlying model may be higher.

Equilibrium states of the economy with positive rates of interest for some currencies are typically not Pareto-optimal. Any optimal monetary policy, implementing a Pareto-optimal equilibrium state of the economy, should thus entail zero nominal rates, if that is compatible with the price formation process.

4.9

In order to allow for money at equilibrium, alternative modelling approaches are possible.

Most simply, balances are treated like any other commodity. Evidently, the consumption of balances is then a proxy for future consumption, which accounts for the adoption of this approach in models of temporary equilibrium (Grandmont 1974). But this eschews the transaction demand for money, except for the dependence of the preferences of individuals on the prices of commodities.

The modification that permits interest payments effectively to tax away the outstanding balances is a wedge between the aggregate supply of balances and the balances in the aggregate endowment of individuals. But the determination of the rate of interest becomes naive: it is simply equal to the ratio of the additional balances to the balances in the aggregate endowment of individuals (Dubey and Geanakoplos 1989b).

It is instructive to see how and whether alternative specifications allow for equilibria. If balances are not issued by a bank but are instead part of the initial endowment of individuals, $\bar{m}^h$, with $\bar{m}^a > 0$, individuals optimize under the budget constraints

$$d + m \le \bar{m}^h$$

and

$$px \le p\bar{x}^h + (1+r)d + m,$$

or, equivalently,

$$\pi x + \rho m^h \le \pi \bar{x}^h + (1+\rho)\bar{m}^h.$$

Aggregate demand satisfies

$$\pi(x^a - \bar{x}^a) = \bar{m}^a;$$

thus, Walras's law is satisfied and equilibrium is possible only if

$$\bar{m}^a = 0.$$

If, alternatively, the supply of balances, m, exceeds the aggregate endowment of individuals, $\bar{m}^a$, in an economy extending over a single period, say, an interest rate

$$\rho = \frac{\bar{m}^a}{m} < 1$$

does indeed restore Walras's law and equilibria do exist. But the equilibrium rate of interest is dictated by income accounting and does not reflect the role of money in transactions.

4.10

A model of a simple economy allows for standard macroeconomic analysis and indicates the effects of monetary and fiscal policy.

Economic activity extends over periods 1 and 2, under certainty. In the first period, factors of production, a capital good, k, and labour, l, are employed to produce, in the second period, output, y, according to the production function

$$y = \xi k^\kappa l^\lambda, \quad \xi > 0, \kappa > 0, \lambda > 0, k + \lambda < 1,$$

where ξ is a productivity parameter and κ and λ are the shares of capital and labor, respectively.

A consumption good coincides in the first period, with the capital good and in the second, c_2, with the output. The prices of the consumption good in the two periods are p_1 and p_2, respectively. The wage in the first period is w. Bonds, d, serve, along with balances, m, to transfer revenue across periods. The rate of interest is r.

The rate of inflation is $\pi = (p_2/p_1) - 1$, the real rate of interest is $\rho = [(1+r)/(1+\pi)] - 1$, and the real wage is $\omega = (w/p_1)$. Agents in the economy are a bank, a firm, and a representative consumer.

The bank issues balances in exchange for bonds in the first period, according to the accounting constraint

$$d + m = 0.$$

It realizes and distributes as dividends to the consumer, in the second period, profit

$$v^b = -[(1 + r)d + m].$$

The firm exchanges bonds against balances, in the first period, according to the budget constraint

$$d + m = 0,$$

and then exchanges the balances against inputs to production according to the cash-in-advance constraint

$$m \geq p_1 k + wl.$$

It realizes and distributes as dividends to the consumer, in the second period, profit $v^f = p_2 y + (1 + r)d + m$ or, equivalently,

$$\frac{1}{p_2} v^f = y - (1 + \rho)k - \omega(1 + \rho)l,$$

which it maximizes.

The consumer, in addition to his shares in the bank and the firm, is endowed with $\bar{l}$ units of labour, which he supplies inelastically, and $\bar{c} > 0$ units of the consumption good in the first period. In the first period, he exchanges cash balances against the consumption good and labour subject to the budget constraint

$$m + p_1 c_1 \leq p_1 \bar{c} + w\bar{l}.$$

In the second period he redeems his balances and shares against the consumption good according to the budget constraint

$$p_2 c_2 \leq m + v^b + v^f.$$

The sequence of budget constraints reduces to $p_1 c_1 + p_2 c_2 = p_1 \bar{c} + w\bar{l} + v^b + v^f$ or, equivalently,

$$c_1 + \frac{1}{1+\rho} c_2 = \bar{c} + \omega\bar{l} + \frac{1}{1+\rho}\left(\frac{1}{p_2}v^b + \frac{1}{p_2}v^f\right).$$

The intertemporal utility function of the individual is

$$ln c_1 + \delta ln c_2, \quad \delta > 0,$$

which he maximizes.

From the optimization of the firm, it follows that the demand for factors in the first period is

$$k^f = \kappa(1+\rho)^{-1}y,$$

$$l^f = \lambda(\omega(1+\rho))^{-1}y,$$

and

$$\frac{m^f}{p_1} = (1+\rho)^{-1}(\kappa+\lambda)y$$

$$y = \zeta(1+\rho)^{[-\mu/(1-\mu)]}\omega^{[-\lambda/(1-\mu)]}$$

where $\zeta = (\xi\kappa^\kappa\lambda^\lambda)^{1/(1-\mu)}$ and $\mu = \kappa + \lambda$, and the real dividend of the firm is

$$\frac{1}{p_2}v^f = (1-\mu)y.$$

The real dividend of the bank is

$$\frac{1}{p_2}v^b = r\frac{p_1}{p_2}(k+wl) = \frac{r}{1+r}(1+\rho)(k+\omega l) = \frac{r}{1+r}\mu y.$$

From the optimization of the individual, it follows that the demand for the consumption good in the first period is

$$c_1 = \frac{1}{1+\delta}\left[\bar{c} + \omega l + \frac{1+r}{1+\rho}\left(1-\frac{\mu}{1+r}\right)y\right] = \frac{1}{1+\delta}\left[\bar{c} + \frac{y}{1+\rho}(1+r-\kappa)\right],$$

and in the second,

$$c_2 = \delta c_1\frac{p_1}{p_2} = \frac{\delta}{1+\delta}\left[\frac{1+\rho}{1+r}\bar{c} + \frac{y}{1+r}(1+r-\kappa)\right].$$

In the first period, equilibrium requires that in the goods market $c_1 + k^f = \bar{c}$, or

$$\frac{y}{1+\rho}(1+r+\delta\kappa) = \delta\bar{c}.$$

In order to generate the *IS* curve from this, one must specify how the labour market clears. Two cases may be compared:

1. *Walras*: $l^f = \bar{l}$ or $\omega = \dfrac{\lambda y}{\bar{l}(1+l)}$,

$$y* = \zeta(1+\rho)^{-\kappa/(1-\mu)}\left(\frac{\lambda y}{\bar{l}}\right)^{-\lambda/(1-\mu)} = \left(\frac{y}{1+\rho}\right)^\kappa \zeta k^\kappa \bar{l}^\lambda = \left(\frac{y}{1+\rho}\right)^\kappa \zeta*$$

$$y^{1/\kappa}(1+r+\delta\kappa) = \delta\bar{c}\zeta*^{1/\kappa}, \text{ the } IS \text{ curve;}$$

2. *Keynes*: $w = \bar{w},\ l^f < \bar{l}$,

$$\bar{y} = \zeta(1+\rho)^{[-\mu/(1-\mu)]}\bar{w}^{[-\lambda/(1-\mu)]} = \left(\frac{y}{1+\rho}\right)^\mu \zeta k^\kappa\left(\frac{\lambda}{\bar{w}}\right)^\lambda = \left(\frac{y}{1+\rho}\right)^\mu \bar{\zeta}$$

$$y^{1/\mu}(1+r+\delta\kappa) = \delta\bar{c}\bar{\zeta}^{1/\mu}, \text{ the } IS, \text{ curve.}$$

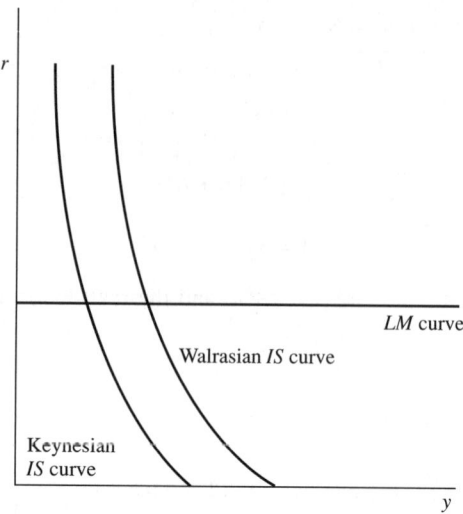

Fig. 4.3. IS–LM diagram

The Walrasian *IS* curve is defined with flexible wages and equilibrium in the labour market, while the Keynesian *IS* curve is defined with fixed wages and excess supply of labour.

The fact that the Keynesian curve lies inside the Walrasian curve ($\bar{y} < y*$ identically in r) is readily verified:

$$\frac{\bar{y}}{y*} = \left(\frac{l^f(\bar{w})}{\bar{l}}\right)^\lambda < 1.$$

The *LM* curve in this oversimplified illustration is horizontal at the rate r chosen by the bank. A higher r results in lower output, because c_1 is increasing in r:

$$c_1 = \frac{\bar{c}(1+r)}{1+r+\delta\kappa}.$$

Utility is diminishing in r, owing to the induced intertemporal substitution, compounded in the Keynesian case by underutilization of labour:

$$\frac{du}{dr} = \begin{cases} \dfrac{-r\delta\kappa}{(1+r)(1+r+\delta\kappa)}, & \text{at } y*, \\[3mm] \dfrac{-r\delta\kappa - (1+r)\delta\lambda}{(1+r)(1+r+\delta\kappa)}, & \text{at } \bar{y}. \end{cases}$$

Given $r > 0$, the first-best could be restored through policies reducing c_1 to its first-best level $\bar{c}/(1+\delta\kappa)$. We do not pursue the matter, because the model is too special.

4.11

In a companion paper (Drèze and Polemarchakis 1994) we give proofs of the properties of competitive equilibria.

Further work should focus on

1. economies with uncertainty in which the asset market is incomplete and where monetary policy is effective, not only by modifying the interest cost of holding balances, but also by modifying the distribution of returns to nominal assets;[8]
2. economies that extend over time, preferably with an infinite horizon, which circumvents terminal period effects, where real and monetary factors jointly determine equilibrium paths (Tobin 1955);
3. economies with explicit price adjustment, which may modify the degree of indeterminacy of equilibrium states of the economy;
4. models, along the lines of the *IS–LM* framework of the last section, that provide an analytical framework for the analysis of macroeconomic and monetary policy,[9] and can be calibrated and applied to the analysis of the effects of policy in actual economies;
5. models that formalize the uncertainty about price formation and the impact of monetary policy on inflation.

REFERENCES

Arrow, K. J. (1951), 'An Extension of the Basic Theorems of Classical Welfare Economics', in J. Neyman (ed.), *Proceedings of the Second Berkeley Symposium on Mathematical Statistics and Probability.* Berkeley, Calif.: University of California Press, 507–32.

—— (1953), 'Le Rôle des valeurs boursières pour la répartition la meilleure des risques', *Econométrie*, 11: 41–8.

—— and Debreu, G. (1954), 'The Existence of Equilibria for a Competitive Economy', *Econometrica*, 22: 265–90.

Baumol, W. J. (1952), 'The Transactions Demand for Cash: an Inventory-Theoretic Approach', *Quarterly Journal of Economics*, 66: 545–56.

Chamley, C., and Polemarchakis, H. M. (1984), 'Assets, General Equilibrium and the Neutrality of Money', *Review of Economic Studies*, 51: 129–38.

Clower, R. (1965), 'A Reconsideration of the Microfoundations of Monetary Theory', *Western Economic Journal*, 5: 1–8.

Debreu, G. (1951), 'The Coefficient of Resource Utilization', *Econometrica*, 19: 273–92.

—— (1960), 'Une Économie de l'incertain', *Economie Appliquée*, 13: 111–16.

—— (1970), 'Economies with a Finite Set of Equilibria', *Econometrica*, 38: 387–92.

---

[8] Chamley and Polemarchakis (1984); Detemple *et al.* (1995); Dubey and Geanakoplos (1989*a*); Magill and Quinzii (1992).

[9] Gagey *et al.* (1986); Geanakoplos and Polemarchakis (1986); Grandmont and Laroque (1975, 1976*a*, *b*).

Detemple, J., Gottardi, P., and Polemarchakis, H. M. (1995), 'The Relevance of Financial Policy', *European Economic Review*, 39, 1133–54.

Drèze, J. H. (1993a), *Money and Uncertainty: Inflation, Interest, Indexation*. Rome: Editions Elefanti.

—— (1993b), 'The Formulation of Uncertainty: Prices and States', Discussion Paper no. 9347, CORE, Université Catholique de Louvain.

—— and Polemarchakis, H. M. (1994), 'Monetary Equilibria', Discussion Paper no. 9400, CORE, Université Catholique de Louvain.

Dubey, P. and Geanakoplos, J. D. (1989a), 'Liquidity and bankruptcy with incomplete markets: exchange', Discussion Paper no. 950, Cowles Foundation, Yale University.

—— and —— (1989b), 'The Value of Money in a Finite Horizon Economy: a Role for Banks', in P. S. Dasgupta, D. Gall, O. D. Hart and E. Maskin (eds), *Economic Analysis of Markets and Games: Essays in Honor of F. H. Hahn*, MIT Press, 407–44.

Fisher, I. (1907), *The Rate of Interest*, New York: Macmillan.

Friedman, M. (1969), 'The Quantity Theory of Money: a Restatement', in M. Friedman (ed.), *Studies in the Quantity Theory of Money*. Chicago: University of Chicago Press.

Gagey, F., Laroque, G., and Lollivier, S. (1986), 'Monetary and Fiscal Policy in a General Equilibrium Model', *Journal of Economic Theory*, 39: 329–57.

Geanakoplos, J. D., and Polemarchakis, H. M. (1986), 'Walrasian Indeterminacy and Keynesian Macro-economics', *Review of Economic Studies*, 53: 755–79.

Grandmont, J.-M. (1974), 'On the Short Run Equilibrium in a Monetary Economy', in J. H. Drèze (ed.), *Allocations under Uncertainty: Equilibrium and Optimality*. London: Macmillan.

—— and Laroque, G. (1975), 'On Money and Banking', *Review of Economic Studies*, 42: 207–36.

—— and —— (1976a), 'The Liquidity Trap', *Econometrica*, 44: 129–35.

—— and —— (1976b), 'Temporary Keynesian Equilibria', *Review of Economic Studies*, 43: 53–67.

Grossman, S., and Weiss, L. (1983), 'A Transactions Based Model of the Monetary Transmission Mechanism', *American Economic Review*, 73: 871–80.

Hahn, F. H. (1965), 'On some Problems in Proving the Existence of an Equilibrium in a Monetary Economy', in F. H. Hahn and F. P. R. Brechling (eds.), *The Theory of Interest Rates*. London: Macmillan.

Hellwig, M. (1993), 'The Challenge of Monetary Theory', *European Economic Review*, 37: 215–42.

Hicks, J. R. (1937), 'Mr. Keynes and the Classics', *Econometrica*, 5: 147–59.

Keynes, J. M. (1936), *The General Theory of Employment, Interest and Money*. London: Macmillan.

Kiyotaki, N., and Wright, R. (1989), 'On Money as a Medium of Exchange', *Journal of Political Economy*, 97: 927–54.

Magill, M. G., and Quinzii, M. (1992), 'Real Effects of Money in General Equilibrium', *Journal of Mathematical Economics*, 21: 301–41.

McKenzie, L. (1954), 'On Equilibrium in Graham's Model of World Trade and Other Competitive Systems', *Econometrica*, 22: 147–61.

Ostroy, J. M., and Starr, R. M. (1974), 'Money and the Decentralization of Exchange', *Econometrica*, 42: 1093–1113.

Patinkin, D. (1965), *Money, Interest and Prices*. New York: Harper and Row.

Phillips, A. W. (1958), 'The Relation between Unemployment and the Rate of Change in Money Wage Rates in the United Kingdom, 1861–1957', *Economica*, 25: 283–99.

Tobin, J. (1955), 'A Dynamic Aggregative Model', *Journal of Political Economy*, 63: 103–15.

—— (1956), 'The Interest Elasticity of Transactions Demand for Cash', *Review of Economics and Statistics*, 38: 241–7.

Vickrey, W. (1959), 'The Optimum Trend of Prices', *Southern Economic Journal*, 25: 315–26.

5

Endogenous Growth: Which are the Important Factors?

Patrick Artus

5.1. A Brief Survey of Recent Theoretical Developments

The endogenous growth theory has been developed because of various un-satifactory features of the neo-classical growth model. In the usual model, the longterm growth rate is exogenous and depends neither on agents' behaviour (consumption, investment, etc.) nor on economic policy (Romer (1987b)). More-over, the neo-classical model does not explain the evolution of income differences between countries or regions (Barro, Sala-i-Martin (1990a); Quah (1990)), or the fact that capital does not move towards poorer countries where the marginal productivity of capital should be larger than in richer countries (Lucas (1990)).

In fact, it is not fully clear that sophisticating the neo-classical model does not allow us to understand better actual evolutions. The various developments of the basic growth model that have been proposed and go in that direction are the intro-duction of transition dynamic between two steady state equilibria (Barro (1987); King, Rebelo (1989)); the growth paths actually observed would result from the fact that countries converge towards a similar long-term equilibrium but starting from different initial conditions; the introduction of multiple equilibria or thresh-old effects (Murphy, Shleifer, Vishny (1989)); the multiplication of the different types of capital (Baily, Schultze (1990), Krueger, Osmund (1990)) or of labour (Leamer (1984)) or, finally the specification of a production function with a lower bound for the marginal productivity of capital (Jones, Manuelli (1990a); Sala-i-Martin (1990)).

However, endogenous growth theory proves richer, more promising, and more able to explain, as will be seen below in empirical studies, the significant differ-ences between various groups of countries. Two groups of endogenous growth models emerge:

The first group consists in models with a growth factor with an accumulation process showing increasing returns to scale. The second group includes models with total constant returns to scale with respect to the capital stock, avoiding

Paper prepared for the conference 'Economics: Beyond the Millennium' at GREQE, Marseille, September 7, 8, 9th 1992.

thus the effects of decreasing returns to scale (stationnary long term equilibrium). We will first present the contents and functionning of the two types of models.

5.1.1. MODELS WITH A 'GROWTH FACTOR'

There is in fact a great diversity of such endogenous growth models, although most of them can be summarized as follows. Production Y_t of goods requires one (or more) production factor available in limited quantity (land, labour, etc.) N_t, one (or more) standard fixed factor (capital) K_t, and one special growth factor H_t, the meaning and contents of which will be discussed below, for instance:

$$Y_t = N_t^a K_t^b H_t^c \quad a, b, c, \text{ being positive constants.} \tag{1}$$

Production is shared between consumption C_t and investment I_t in fixed capital:

$$Y_t = C_t + I_t$$

with $K_{t+1} = K_t(1 - \delta) + I_t \quad (\delta: \text{depreciation rate}) \tag{2}$

Finally, the growth factor accumulates according to a dynamic process incorporating a non-convexity, for instance:

$$H_{t+1} - H_t = dH_t(\overline{N} - N_t) \quad (d > 0) \tag{3}$$

$\overline{N}$ is the total available quantity of the variable factor N, $\overline{N} - N_t$ the quantity of that factor not used in the production Y of the commodity; the larger the initial stock of the growth factor H_t, the larger the increase $H_{t+1} - H_t$ corresponding to a given allocation of the variable factor $(\overline{N} - N_t)$. The existing models differ with respect to the interpretation given to the growth factor H. We present below some of the most usual ones. H can be interpreted as: the existing number of inputs in the production process; the number of consumption goods available; the quality of products; human capital.

a-Increase in the number of production inputs:

Technical progress consists in the diversification of inputs used in the production of the consumption good (Romer (1990b, 1990c); Grossman, Helpman (1989b, 1990b, 1989e)). In equation (1) above one has:

$$H_t^c = \int_0^{A_t} x_t(i)^{1-a} \, di \tag{4}$$

$x(i)$ is the quantity used of input i; at time t, the 'number' of inputs is A_t with:

$$A_{t+1} - A_t = dA_t(\overline{N} - N_t) \quad \text{(which replaces (3))} \tag{5}$$

All inputs are similar as far as their role in production is concerned; hence: $x_t(i) = x_t$; the production of the input i requires β unit of fixed capital per unit of input, hence:

$$K_t = \beta A_t x_t \tag{6}$$

The production function (1) can therefore be written as:

$$Y_t = N_t^a A_t x_t^{1-a} = N_t^a \left(\frac{K_t}{\beta}\right)^{1-a} A_t^a \tag{7}$$

and the model is equivalent to (1) (2) (3) with $H = A$, which defines the growth factor.

The development of a new input means an increase in A_t, and according to (5), an externality benefitting all firms involved in developing new inputs (Romer (1986)). The member of available goods can be defined in terms of outputs and not in term of inputs, which we now examine.

b-Increase in the number of consumption goods:

Consumption is defined by:

$$C_t = \left[\int_0^{A_t} (x_t(i)^a \, di)\right]^{1/a} \tag{8}$$

where $x_t(i)$ is the consumption of differentiated good number i at time t, A_t is the number of available varieties of goods (Grossman, Helpman (1989d)); the dynamics of A_t is given by (5).

The production of one unit of $x_t(i)$ requires a_N unit of factor N, hence:

$$N_t = a_N \int_0^{A_t} x_t(i) \, di = a_N A_t x_t$$

(in equilibrium consumption levels are identical, and $x_t(i) = x_t$)   (9)

Therefore, for aggregate consumption:

$$C_t = A_t^{1/a} x_t = \frac{N_t}{a_N} A_t^{\frac{1-a}{a}} = Y_t \tag{10}$$

which identifies production function (1) with $H = A^{\frac{1-a}{a}}$ for the growth factor. A different idea is to expand not the number of goods, but their quality.

c-Increase in the quality of products:

Grossman, Helpman (1989a, 1989c) assume that consumption is:

$$C_t = q_{jt} C_{jt} \tag{11}$$

where q_{jt} is the quality of the consumption good at time t, C_{jt} the quantity consumed of quality q_{jt}, and is assumed constant ($\bar{C}_{jt} = c$).

Quality is given by:

$$q_{jt} = \lambda^j \quad \text{where } \lambda > 1 \tag{12}$$

If Research and Development effort is i, the quantity of labor used in R & D is $a_N i$; and the probability that an innovation is obtained during the next period is i; an innovation is represented by an increase by 1 of q in (12).

To produce c units of consumption, $a_c c$ units of labour are required. One has therefore:

$$\overline{N} = a_c c + a_N i \quad \text{where } N \text{ is the total supply of factor } N \text{ (labour)} \quad (13)$$

since:

$$q_{t+1} + i(q_t + 1) + (1 - i)q_t \quad (14)$$

One has:

$$q_{t+1} - q_t = \frac{\overline{N} - N_t}{a_N} \quad \text{where } N_t = a_c c \quad (15)$$

which replaces (3) in the representative model with:

$$Y_t = C_t = cq_t = \frac{N_t}{a_c} q_t \quad (16)$$

which replaces (1) with quality q playing the role of the growth factor.

d-Learning by doing:

In this case, the increase in human capital is an automatic byproduct of the fact that labour is used to produce goods (Lucas (1988), Romer (1989)).

If one simply has:

$$H_{t+1} - H_t = d H_t N_t, \quad \text{with (1),} \quad (17)$$

there is no allocation of labour problem; such a problem appears if one introduces two sectors with different learning by doing processes.

e-Human capital:

Increasing human capital is intentional, which makes it very different from learning by doing.

The basic model is exactly (1) (2) (3), where increasing human capital H_t requires one to subtract a part of labour supply from goods producing activities (King, Rebelo (1990), Prescott, Boyd (1987), Rebelo (1990), Romer (1986), Stokey (1991)).

In all these cases, finally, one defines a growth factor (H in our notations), the accumulation of which is made easier if the initial existing stock is larger hence the increasing returns to scale. We now turn to the second group of models, with respect to the usual capital stock, and no specific growth factor.

5.1.2. CONSTANT RETURNS TO SCALE WITH RESPECT TO CAPITAL

The basic model is a model *with external returns to scale*, based on the aggregate capital stock level. For each firm i, the production function is:

$$Y_{it} = N_{it}^a K_{it}^b K_t^{1-b} \quad (18)$$

where N_i is employment in firm i; K_i captiral in firm i, K aggregate capital (in the economy, in the industry, etc.).

$$K = \sum_i K_i; \quad N = \sum_i N_i \quad \text{(aggregate employment)} \tag{19}$$

These are M identical firms; the aggregate production function is therefore:

$$Y_t = MY_{it} = N_t^a K_t M^{1-a-b} \tag{20}$$

and shows constant returns to scale with respect to capital.

In steady state equilibrium, Y_t and K_t grow at the same rate, N_t is constant, and the growth rate is not determined by (20), which would be the case with diminishing returns to scale. Investment is given by:

$$I_t = sY_t \quad \text{where } s \text{ is the savings rate.} \tag{21}$$

The growth rate of the economy is therefore:

$$\frac{\dot{Y}_t}{Y_t} = \frac{\dot{K}_t}{K_t} = s\frac{Y_t}{K_t} - \delta \quad \text{where } \delta \text{ is the depreciation rate of capital.} \tag{22}$$

(20) could also in fact be obtained from (1) if one assumes that productive capital itself carries new ideas and is the growth factor (King, Robson (1989)). With external returns to scale, long-term growth is determined by the saving rate. It has also been proposed to introduce an aditionnal type of capital, public investment.

b-Public investment:

Public investment (in infrastructures, education, etc.) is often considered as an important production factor (Barro, Sala-i-Martin (1990*b*)). One has for instance:

$$Y_t = N_t^a K_t^b G_t^{1-b} \tag{23}$$

where G is public spending which has to be financed by a tax on production at rate $t = G/Y$.

Efficiency implies that $Y_t - G_t$ is maximized, hence:

$$\frac{\partial Y_t}{\partial G_t} = 1 \quad \text{and} \quad \frac{G_t}{Y_t} = 1 - b \tag{24}$$

The production function therefore becomes:

$$Y_t - N_t^{a/b} K_i (1-b)^{\frac{1-b}{b}} \tag{25}$$

with constant returns to scale with respect to the capital stock, because of the link between the optimal level of public capital and production.

c-Financial factors of growth:

These models have been developed by Levine (1990, 1991), Bencivenga, Smith (1991), Greenwood, Jovanovic (1990), Saint-Paul (1992). The basic idea is the following: the existence of developed financial intermediaries or financial markets leads to an increase in investment, hence in growth. The reasons are the same as those that have been put forward to justify the existence of banks. In all cases, the ratio of investment in firms' capital to income increases, which increases growth if one assumes constant returns to scale with respect to capital (see (22)).

Another interesting idea is the following: growth is reduced when households divert a part of their savings from productive investment (which stimulates growth). Possible examples (obtained in an overlapping generations growth model) are public debt (Alogoskoufis, Van der Ploeg (1990)) or speculative bubbles (Yanagawa, Grossman (1992)); bubbles are sustainable if they do not exceed the size of the savings of the younger generation, i.e. if the interest rate is less than the growth rate (Tirole (1985)). This is much easier to obtain in an endogenous growth model where the growth rate depends on behavioural parameters.

It is therefore unfavourable that individual investors find that financial assets which do not contribute to the financing of growth are appealing.

All the endogenous growth models have two common features, which we now describe briefly: the decentralized equilibrium is not an optimum because of the various externalities; a stable long-term growth rate is obtained only for very specific salves of the parameters.

5.1.3. TWO COMMENTS ON ENDOGENOUS GROWTH MODELS

a-Decentralized equilibrium and optimum:

Whatever the kind of model chosen, an important feature is the difference between equilibrium and Pareto optimum. We show this using simple versions of the two types of models described above.

(i) Let us first take a very simple model with a growth factor:

Y: production
C: consumption
N: labor
H: technical progress (growth factor)
$\overline{N}$: total available labour

$$\begin{cases} Y_t = N_t^a H_t = C_t \\ H_{t+1} - H_t = dH_t(\overline{N} - N_t) \end{cases} \tag{26}$$

Consumers are assumed to maximize a time separable exponential utility-function:

$$\text{Max} \sum_{t=0}^{\infty} \frac{1}{(1+\rho)^t} \frac{C_t^{1-\sigma} - 1}{1-\sigma} \tag{27}$$

where ρ is the degree of time preference, which implies that:

$$\frac{C_t}{C_{t-1}} = 1 + g = \left(\frac{1+\rho}{1+r}\right)^{-1/\sigma} \tag{28}$$

where g is the growth rate, r the real interest rate. (28) shows a positive relationship between the growth rate and the real interest rate. When the social planner maximizes (27), he takes into account the dynamic externality appearing in the accumulation process of H_t. This means that the *social marginal return of employment in the production sector* is given by:

$$\frac{\partial\left(\frac{N_{t+1}^a H_{t+1}}{1+r} + N_t^a H_t\right)}{\partial N_t} = \frac{\partial(N_{t+1}^a H_t(1 + d(\bar{N} - N_t)) + N_t^a H_t)}{1+r}$$

$$= -\frac{d N_{t+1}^a H_t}{1+r} + a N_t^{a-1} H_t \tag{29}$$

whereas the *private marginal return of employment* is simply:

$$a N_t^{a-1} H_t \quad \text{and is larger.} \tag{30}$$

Decentralized firms hire too many people in order to produce consumption goods; less labour can be devoted to the production of technical progress than would be efficient.

(ii) Let us now consider a model with *external returns to scale*. (28) is still valid. The production function is given by (20). The *social marginal productivity of capital* is:

$$N_t^a M^{1-a-b} \tag{31}$$

The *aggregate private marginal productivity of capital* is:

$$b N_t^a M^{1-a-b} \tag{32}$$

and is smaller than the social one since the externality is not taken into account by individual firms.

The differences between the social and private rates of return of the various production factors give a role to economic policy. As we shall see below, the authorities may subsidize investment and employment in research and development to bring the private marginal return on the growth factor closer to its social level. We now turn to the second systematic feature of endogenous growth models.

b-Robustness of the models:

As is clear in equations (3) or (18), the model parameters must obey very strict constraints if one wants to be able to generate a steady state path. If (3) was transformed into:

$$H_{t+1} - H_t = d H_t^e(\bar{N} - N_t) \quad \text{where } e \neq 1 \tag{3'}$$

or (18) into:

$$Y_{it} = N_{it}^a K_{it}^b K_t^{1-c} \quad \text{where } c \neq b \tag{18'}$$

One would get explosive growth ($e > 1$ or $c < b$) or zero growth in the long-run ($e < 1$, $c > b$).

Having a steady state growth path is appealing, but the necessary constraints can certainly not be verified in empirical work. Estimation will always lead to $e \neq 1$ and $c \neq b$, and it seems very difficult to imagine an econometric version of an endogenous growth model. Future research will perhaps be able to propose models with the same kind of externalities but with less restrictive conditions on the specifications. Even though econometric estimates are therefore difficult to obtain in the strict context of the theoretical growth models, a number of attemps at estimating endogenous growth effects have been described in the literature.

5.2. Survey of Empirical Results

Many authors have tried to document the endogenous growth model and to discover which were the important factors in explaining growth rates, or growth rates differentials between countries. We are going to discuss briefly the results obtained for the different possible factors: investment and convergence towards the situation of the high-income countries; research and development; public investment accumulation of human capital; income distribution; financial factors of growth; and finally economic openness.

5.2.1. INVESTMENT, INITIAL INCOME AND CONVERGENCE

As has been said in the introduction, the neo-classical growth model implies that the levels of real income per head converge in the long-run (Barro, Sala-i-Martin (1990a) and distinguish between β convergence (poor countries have larger growth rates) and σ convergence (the dispersion of the levels of income diminishes)). Most of the papers show that convergence actually occurs between industrialized countries (Dowrick, Nguyen (1989), Baumol (1986)), but not between industrialized and developing countries (Baumol, Wolff (1988), Baumol, Blackman, Wolff (1988), Chenery, Robinson, Syrquin (1986), Abramovitz (1986), Summers, Heston (1988)). Many tests are based on the database built by Heston and Summers (1988) and Summers, Heston (1991) and on the convergence equation derived by Mankiw, Romer, and Weil (1990):

$$\ln(y(t)) - \ln(y(0)) = (1 - e^{-\lambda t}) \frac{a}{1 - a - \beta} \ln \frac{I}{Y} + (1 - e^{-\lambda t}) \frac{\beta}{1 - a - \beta} \frac{I_H}{Y}$$
$$- (1 - e^{-\lambda t}) \frac{a + \beta}{1 - a - \beta} \ln(n + g + \delta) \tag{33}$$

where $\lambda = (n + g + \delta)(1 - a - \beta)$ is the speed of convergence, $y(t)$ is income per head at time t, I investment in productive capital, Y production, I_H investment in human capital, n the growth rate of population, g the growth rate of technology, δ the depreciation rate, a the elasticity of production with respect to capital, β with respect to human capital.

Let us show some results from the literature (see also Barro (1989*a*, *b*), Dervis, Petri (1987), Levine, Renelt (1990)). Helliwell, Chung (1992) estimate the model for four groups of countries (OECD, Africa, Asia, Latin America). They find very different results for these four groups. The results confirm the role of productive investment (see also Khan, Reinhart (1990)) and the absence of convergence between groups of countries. Dowrick (1992) separates rich, middle-income and poor countries. He finds that convergence does not appear for middle-income countries; the effect of investment on growth is also limited in those countries. Dowrick, Gemmell (1991) separate the economies in two sectors (agriculture and the rest) and take into account spillovers effects from the rest of the world. They find a significant spillover effect for the manufacturing sector in the case of middle-income countries, and not of poor countries. Copying or importing technology makes convergence possible for middle-income countries. Poorer countries probably don't have the technical capacity of absorbing new technologies (Abramovitz (1986)). Durlauf, Johnson (1992) confirm that the estimated parameters for equation (33) differ very much between countries; they build homogenous groups of countries for which convergence occurs depending on the initial income/head level and on the degree of literacy.

The existence of local and not global convergence is consistent with the literature exhibiting multiple equilibria or threshold effects (Azariadis, Drazen (1990), Murphy, Schleifer, Vishny (1989)). The fraction of the population enrolled in primary school proves very important to explain growth in countries with a low literacy rate. De Long, Summers (1991) estimate the same kind of equation but stress the effect of investment in equipment.

5.2.2. RESEARCH AND DEVELOPMENT

The capital in Research and Development (R&D) is a natural candidate for representing the growth factor in endogenous growth models. However, numerous studies have examined the effect of R&D in neo-classical growth models.

The estimated elasticity of production with respect to the capital in R&D varies from 0.02 to 1.26 in the different papers (Griliches (1981) or see a survey in Mairesse, Mohnen (1990) or Mairesse, Sassenou (1991)); time series estimates for the manufacturing sector vary from 0.06 (France, UK) to 0.08 (US), 0.27 (Germany) and 0.33 (Japan) (Soete, Patel (1985)); Hall, Mairesse (1992) show that an estimate between 0.05 and 0.25 seems quite robust.

However, endogenous growth effects are often obtained. A number of studies find spillover effects between firms or industries of investment in R&D (Jaffe

(1986); Griliches (1984); Goto, Suzuki (1989); Geroski (1989); Bernstein, Nadiri (1988)). Guellec, Ralle (1991) find a link between the number of patents (y), representing the number of available products, and the number of researchers on time series for the US:

However, estimations on time series prove very difficult because of the very long lags between R&D and production (up to 20 or 30 years according to Adams (1990)).

On a cross section of 24 OECD countries for the period 1980–1989, Artus and Kaabi (1991) find a significant link between growth, the number of patents, R&D expenditures and employment in R&D. An important result is the fact that the absolute level of R&D expenditures or employment gives much better results than the relative level (per dollar of GDP or per head), which confirms the positive size effect appearing in endogenous growth models.

The relationships between physical investment and investment in R&D have been analyzed in a number of papers. Hall, Hayashi (1989) and Lach, Schankerman (1989) show that the volatility of physical investment is much larger than the volatility of R&D investment. This result can be rationalized taking into account the fact that R&D investment *causes* physical investment (which is found on panel data for French firms, Crepon, Dureau (1991)), and on time series for the US as well (Lach and Rob (1992)). This causality result is very important because it shows that growth factors can be interrelated: both R&D and (later) investment are necessary to growth.

5.2.3. PUBLIC EXPENDITURES AND PUBLIC INVESTMENT

The effect of public investment on private productivity has been demonstrated in a number of studies (for instance Aschauer (1989)). The best results are obtained when public capital is restricted to 'core infrastructure' such as highways, airports, electricities, water supply, or public transportation. Aschauer finds no effect of public consumption (Ram (1986) finds a positive effect, but a negative coefficient of public investment in buildings, of military expenditures is most of the time obtained; see Barro (1990, 1991)).

Morrison, Schwartz (1992) estimate generalized Leontieff cost functions including private and public capital, energy, productive and non-productive labour. They estimate the relative reduction in production cost associated to public capital. They find estimates between 30% and 100% for the different US regions. It appears therefore that public investment is almost as important as private investment in explaining private productivity.

5.2.4. HUMAN CAPITAL

Rather crude measures of human capital have been introduced in a number of empirical studies (see for instance Baumol (1990); Otani, Villanueva (1980)).

According to Barro (1991) and Romer (1989), the proportion of children going to primary or secondary school plays a significant role. Murphy, Schleifer, Vishny (1991) illustrate a model showing that if talented people act as entrepreneurs, they stimulate growth, whereas if they act as rent-seeking people, they slow it down.

Clearly the notion of human capital has to be sophisticated, and more precise estimates of the effects of the various skills and levels of education have to be obtained.

5.2.5. INCOME DISTRIBUTION

The basic theory has been developed by Alesina, Rodrick (1991). They assume that each consumer in the economy owns a different share of capital. They show that the welfare of capitalists depends on the growth rate (maximizing their welfare is equivalent to maximizing growth), but that wage-earners favour a slower growth. In a democracy, majority vote is equivalent to median vote. If the distribution of wealth is unequal, the median voter owns a low share of capital, which means that the vote is favourable to wage earners and that growth is reduced. Income inequality should therefore be negatively correlated with growth, particularly in democracies, which is confirmed by their estimation.

Berg, Sachs (1988) and Persson, Tabellini (1991) (who use the Gini index of income distribution) find similar results. Saint-Paul and Verdier (1992) show that, in a democracy, inequality leads to slower growth if it implies the taxation of capital income, but not if redistribution is made through education subsidies. If education increases grow, people accept taxation to finance education even through they do not themselves benefit from education (Creedy, Francois (1990), Johnson (1984), Perotti (1990)). Buiter (1991), Alogoskoufis, Van der Ploeg (1990), Saint-Paul (1990) analyse intergenerational transfers. If income is redistributed from the young to the old, the young save less and growth is reduced.

5.2.6. FINANCIAL FACTORS OF GROWTH

The basic idea, consistent with one of the theoretical models described above, is the fact that a positive relationship exists between growth and financial liberalization and development. Positive real interest rates are often considered as a signal of the existence of organized intermediaries and markets, able to collect savings, whereas negative real interest rates are a result of financial distortions and lead to capital flight.

World Development Report (1989), Polak (1989), Khan, Villanueva (1991) and Dornbusch (1990) get similar results, i.e. the fact that high real rates are correlated with more long-term growth. Roubini, Sala-i-Martin (1991) also find that financial distortions measured both by too low real interest rates and too high reserves of the banking system, depress growth. Jappelli, Pagano (1992) use a completely different type of argument to show that some kinds of financial imperfections can stimulate growth. They show that liquidity constraints facing consumers (credit ceilings for instance) lead to an increase in savings and hence in growth. Finally, Villanueva, Mirakhor (1990) show that bank supervision and control by the monetary authorities is favourable to growth.

Crucially, however, no test of the link between the structure of savings (stocks, bonds, liquidity, etc.) and growth is presently available, where theory seems to indicate that the existence of financial assets which do not contribute to the financing of investment leads to a reduction in growth.

5.2.7. ECONOMIC INTEGRATION, FREE TRADE

The overall effect of international economic integration on growth is ambiguous from a theoretical point of view. Rivera-Batiz and Romer (1991*a*) point out several favorable effects: ideas are available in all countries, with trade relations implying an access to world technology (see also Grossman, Helpman (1990); Parente, Prescott (1991)); if integration occurs, markets are larger, which increases the return on research and development (Romer (1990*c*)). Finally, international specialization in production leads to international specialization in research and to less redundancy; it also leads to delocalization of production, which makes resources available for research and development (see Grossman, Helpman (1989*a*–1989*e*)).

However, integration might be unfavourable for less developed countries, since it implies that they abandon the production of more advanced goods for which developed countries have a comparative advantage, and since the production of those goods is a source of growth through learning by doing or spillover effects (Young (1991)). It might also reduce growth because of allocation effects, for instance if specialization leads to a development of production and hence to a reduction of resources devoted to research and development or to the modern sector (Matsuyama (1991), Grossman, Helpman (1990*b*)).

Unfortunately, no precise empirical evaluation of the above-described ideas is available in the context of the 'growth factor' models. The situation is different as far as the returns to scale model is concerned. External economies of scale have been obtained at the firm and industry levels (Cabarello, Lyons (1989, 1990)). Using those results, Baldwin (1989) obtains very strong estimates of the supplementary growth permitted by the European economic integration. Finally, increased competition and the suppression of non-tariff barriers can impose efficiency and stimulate growth (Porter (1990), Jacquemin, Sapir (1988, 1990), Neven, Röller (1990)).

5.2.8. OTHER POSSIBLE EXPLANATIONS OF GROWTH

A major difficulty in assessing empirically the role of the various factors in the determination of growth is the fact that growth rates depend on a large number of variables representing structural situations or economic policies pursued, which might be very difficult to distinguish from the basic growth factors or to introduce in a theoretical endogenous growth model. A very large number of factors or variables having a significant effect on growth has been displayed in the literature. A list of those factors with the corresponding references is given in the *Annex*. The negative role of inflation of various price distorsions, and of all inefficient public sectors are clearly demonstrated.

5.2.9. SYNTHESIS

Finally as has been stressed by Stern (1991), it is difficult to estimate the endogenous growth model. Many variables are found to have a significant effect on growth rate differentials: investment, education, R&D expenditures, public investment in infrastructures, political stability, income distribution, interest rates, financial imperfections, and various aspects of economic policy (export strategy, protection, taxes, foreign debt, exchange rates . . .). However, all this empirical evidence contains little support for the endogenous growth model, except in the cases of the estimated link between the level of R&D expenditures (or employment) and growth rates, and of the external returns to scale put in evidence in European industries.

In the other cases, the estimations suffer from various shortcomings. First, they could as well apply to the neo-classical growth model, assuming a variety of production factors is introduced (R&D capital, quality of labour . . .); in no case, the dynamic equation characteristic of the endogenous growth model is estimated, and only the production function is introduced. This is due to the fact that the estimations are almost always done on a cross-section of countries, and not on time-series due to the fact that very long series would be necessary to estimate the dynamic processes. Moreover, the proxies used for the different variables are often rather crude. Human capital is for instance measured by the proportion of children getting various levels of education, but this might be too unprecise to be helpful for policy making, for instance for helping to design a subsidization program. Another example is financial development, which is represented by real interest rates; this provides absolutely no information on the kind of intermediaries or markets which are useful in promoting savings and growth, or on the effect of the allocation of financial wealth amongst the different available assets on growth.

Even though knowledge about the determinants of growth has improved it is not directly related to the endogenous growth model, and is not yet useful in devising precise economic reforms.

The technical shortcomings of the estimations presented are also noteworthy. For a number of variables, we don't know if the production function or a reduced form of the overall functioning of the economy is estimated. One finds indeed in the equation a mix of production factors, policy variables and structural effects. As the dynamic accumulation process for the growth factors is not estimated, we don't know if there is really a conflict for the allocation of resources to the production of goods or to the production of research, this conflict being the core of endogenous growth models. Is the same factor actually used in both productions? As the precise nature of the growth factor remains rather mysterious or is unprecisely known, the economic integration effects are difficult to assess: is there really a redundancy for the kind of research development which stimulates growth? Is there a possibility of increasing the base of knowledge by integrating the economies or is the stock of knowledge already common to all countries? As has been shown in the example of physical investment and R&D, several growth factors have to be developed simultaneously in order to stimulate growth. However, empirical studies do not test for the substitutability or complementarity between such factors as human capital, R&D, physical capital, financial markets. Promoting or subsidizing only one of these might prove very inefficient.

We are now going to illustrate these points using small theoretical models representing the different versions of the endogenous growth model or the different issues discussed above. Our goal here is to show that the *policy implications might be very clearcut if we had a precise idea of the relevant growth model.*

5.3. Policy Implications

We present here some examples of policy advice based on endogenous growth models, and show to which extent they depend on the exact structure of the model and on the precise knowledge of the relevant growth factors. We will be examining a number of different models: a model with a growth factor, a model with a second kind of capital, and a model of economic integration between two groups of countries.

5.3.1. HUMAN CAPITAL OR TECHNOLOGY

The basic model has been described above in Section 5.1. Let us write it as:

$$\begin{cases} Y_t = AN_t^a H_t^{1-a} = C_t \\ H_{t+1} - H_t = dH_t(\bar{N} - N_t) \\ \text{Max} \sum_{t=0}^{\infty} \ln(C_t) \dfrac{1}{(1+\rho)^t} \end{cases} \qquad (34)$$

Y is production; N, the factor available in the limited amount $\bar{N}$ (labour and land); H, the growth factor (education, capital in R&D, financial intermediaries, etc.); C is consumption, and ρ the degree of time preference. Let us analyse the effects on the equilibrium in that model of several policies.

(i) Subsidizing labour (factor N) in both sectors

We assume here that the authorities subsidize labour in both the goods-producing and technology producing sectors. The wage rate (or, more generally speaking, the price of factor N) paid by firms becomes $w(1 - \tau)$, where τ is the rate of subsidy and w the wage. The subsidy is financed by a lump-sum tax levied on consumers. It is easy to see that this policy has no effect whatsoever; the real wage increases, so that $w(1 - \tau)$ remains constant. The growth rate is unaffected as well as the welfare of consumers.

(ii) Subsidizing labour only in the technology producing sector

Growth is stimulated since the price of technology (factor H) is reduced. The subsidy implies a reallocation of factor N from the goods-producing sector to the technology producing sector.

(iii) A tax on the production of goods

This is equivalent to a decrease in A. It does not affect growth, since it changes in the same proportion the marginal productivity of labour (N) and the marginal productivity of technology (H).

(iv) A tax on labour in the good producing sector

Growth is stimulated since the demand for labour N is reduced, and labour is shifted to the technology producing sector; moreover, the tax can be redistributed to wage-earners.

The foundations of policy in this case are very simple: all the measures that favour the traditional (goods-producing) sector are unfavourable; all those that favour the sector developing technology lead to a shift in resources towards that sector and increase welfare. It is therefore very important for policy makers to know exactly which factors (which precise kind of skilled labour, of infrastructures, etc.) can actually be used in both sectors (and are fully utilized), and which are sector-specific (or under-utilized). Subsidizing the use in the traditional industries of a factor which can contribute to production in both sectors, which seems a reasonable policy, has very unfavorable consequences according to the endogenous growth model.

The question of the explicative incentives for the production of the growth factor can also be asked (Cohen and Levin (1989)). Does investment in R&D or in human capital respond mostly to technological opportunities, to the appropriation of innovation revenues (if rents can be extracted from the ownership of partly excludable technology), or to shifts in demand. Knowing the determinants of the production of the growth factor is important in order to implement the right type of incentive.

The second kind of model generating endogenous growth is a model with both private and public capital stocks.

5.3.2. PUBLIC INFRASTRUCTURES

Barro, Sala-i-Martin (1990*b*) discusses the effect of investment in public infrastructures on growth according to the nature of those infrastructures and on the
way they are financed. Let us start from a very simple model:

$$
\begin{cases}
Y_t = K_t^{1-a}G_t^a;\ G_t = hY_t \quad or \quad Y_t = K_t h^{\frac{a}{1-a}} \\
Y_t = C_t + G_t + I_t \quad or \quad Y_t(1-h) = C_t + K_{t+1} - K_t \\
\text{Max} \sum_{t=0}^{\infty} \frac{\ln (C_t)}{(1+\rho)^t}
\end{cases}
\tag{35}
$$

where Y_t represents production; K_t, private capital; G_t, public expenditures; I_t,
investment in private capital; C_t, consumption.

We introduce two possibilities to finance public expenditures: a lump-sum tax
on income, $T_t = G_t = hY_t$, paid by consumers, or a tax on production, at rate h,
paid by firms.

If a lump-sum tax on consumers is chosen, the equilibrium growth rate is too
large: firms ignore the fact that more capital means more public expenditures,
and hence more taxes are paid.

This is not the case if a tax on production is chosen, since firms internalize
the fact that more investment leads to more taxes. The empirical research available certainly shows that production grows with public capital. However, the
task for policy makers is not easy. Clearly, the various kinds of public expenditures have very different effects on private productivity; the simple model above
shows that the level of each investment should be proportional to the elasticity
of production with respect to that investment. Measuring the extent to which
public expenditures (infrastructures, education, public services) are productive
or not may prove very difficult. The usual classification between consumption
and investment may well be completely irrelevant. Moreover, increasing public
expenditures can be the source of distortions between the social and private rates
of return if the way expenditures are financed is not carefully designed.

The taxes put in place must be non distortionary; in our example, they must
be such that firms choose capital taking into account taxes in the same way as
the social planner; if public expenditures were assumed to have a direct effect
on consumers' welfare, the same precaution would apply on the household's
side.

5.3.3. GROWTH AND EMPLOYMENT

Bertola (1990) and Aghion, Howitt (1989, 1990) show that more growth can
imply a cost in the labour market; modern techniques replace obsolete ones,

which leads to adjustment costs or to unemployment for wage-earners who have to swith from a traditional to a modern industry.

Indeed, the general side effects of growth must not be ignored. In particular, accelerating the rhythm of technical progress by subsidizing research can prove inefficient if the labour force does not have the necessary skills; complementarity between production techniques and human capital implies that copying or importing technology can be a source of large unexpected costs. Let us turn to the effects on welfare of economic integration.

5.3.4. ECONOMIC INTEGRATION

We examine the effects on growth and welfare of economic integration between two countries. Integration means that knowledge, technology, and human capital can circulate more freely between the two countries, and that consumption goods can be exported or imported. We must distinguish between the two possible sources of increased growth: more powerful external returns to scale and better use of technology (human capital, etc.).

EXTERNAL RETURNS TO SCALE. The basic idea is the following: In each country, the production of each firm (all firms are identical) depends on its own capital and on the aggregate capital in the country, for instance in country 1 for firm i:

$$Y_{1i} = K_{1i}^a \bar{K}_1^{1-a} \quad (Y_i: \text{production of firm } i, K: \text{capital of firm } i) \quad (36)$$

where:

$$\bar{K}_1 = \sum_{i=1}^{N_1} K_{1i}, \quad \text{where } N_1 \text{ is the number of firms in country 1.}$$

Hence:

$$
\begin{cases}
Y_1 = \sum_i Y_{1i} = N_2^{1-a}\bar{K}_1 & \text{since all firms are identical} \\
Y_2 = N_2^{1-a}\bar{K}_2 & \text{for county 2.}
\end{cases}
\quad (37)
$$

After economic integration, the total capital in both countries exerts a positive influence on each firm's production.

$$Y_{1i} = K_{1i}^a (\bar{K}_1 + \bar{K}_2)^{1-a} \quad \left(\bar{K}_2 = \frac{N_2}{N_1}\bar{K}_1\right) \quad (38)$$

Hence:

$$Y_1 + Y_2 = (\bar{K}_1 + \bar{K}_2)(N_1 + N_2)^{1-a} \quad (39)$$

If the savings rates is the same in both countries, the growth rate before integration is:

$$\frac{d(\bar{K}_1)}{\bar{K}_1} = \frac{sY_1}{\bar{K}_1} = sN_1^{1-a} \quad (sN_2^{1-a} \text{ in country 2}) \tag{40}$$

after integration, it becomes:

$$\frac{d(\bar{K}_1 + \bar{K}_2)}{\bar{K}_1 + \bar{K}_2} = s(N_1 + N_2)^{1-a} \tag{41}$$

and is larger: integration increases growth through external economies of scale.

However, this result can be criticized on various grounds. Technology was perhaps mobile before economic integration (patents could be purchased, multinational firms used the same techniques in all countries). If (38) was already valid, no gains in terms of growth can be expected from integration.

If capital is mobile, the situation described before integration is not a stable one. Assume $N_1 > N_2$ (country 1 is larger); in that case,

$$\frac{\partial Y_1}{\partial \bar{K}_1} = N_1^{1-a} > \frac{\partial Y_2}{\partial \bar{K}_2}:$$

all capital flows to country 1; owners of immobile production factors are ruined, and compensatory transfers have to be put in place (Bertola (1992)). This means that a situation like (37) is very unlikely, which reduces the probability of an acceleration of growth.

Let us now assume that even before integration, one observed a (weak) link between production and the capital in the other country (as is assumed by Bertola (1992) and by Grossman, Helpman (1991) at the sectoral level). If, after integration, perfect symetry prevails and (38) becomes valid, total production is given by (39) which implies an increase in the growth rate.

The preceding examples show that the size of the gains in growth to be expected after economic integration depend heavily on the nature and importance of the spillover effects between the countries before and after integration, and the degree of capital mobility before integration. If a sizeable spillover effect already exists, or if capital has already flown towards the more efficient country, no significant growth effect of economic integration is likely to appear.

Economic integration can also be examined using a model with a specific growth factor.

ECONOMIC INTEGRATION AND THE GROWTH FACTOR. We use the same model as in 5.3.1.

Let us first show some effects of opening the economies which can't appear in the model as it is designed. We have up to now assumed perfect competition and free entry in the market of the production of technology. Let us now assume that in each country, a monopolist produces technology, and that the monopolist knows the demand function for technology. The demand of technology increases with the market size, and with the profitability. If economic integration increases the potential sales, or leads to an increase in profit margins, more technology will be produced and growth will be faster. Most of the existing papers show that the positive market effect is at work (Baldwin (1992)), while one might expect a negative profitability effects, since free trade implies more import competition, and thus a decrease in profitability in the incentive to innovate (Feenstra (1990)).

Let us go back to our basic model of 5.3.1. Two countries are assumed to grow separately, as described by system (34). At time $t = 0$, the two economies merge. In some papers, it is assumed that the total stock of technology of the unified country becomes $H_0 = H_{10} + H_{20}$. For a given allocation of the rare factor N (labour), the growth rate increases considerably since the initial level of productivity increases (in (34), d becomes $2d$).

However, this seems a much too unprecise and unrealistic assumption. Let us distinguish several cases, according to the initial state of technology in the different countries and to the feasibility of the transmission of technology to the other country after integration.

CASE A. THE TECHNOLOGY IS INITIALLY THE SAME IN THE TWO COUNTRIES
The benefit from the same patents, (the same human capital). The effect of integration is therefore *to eliminate duplications in research*, which of course is profitable. After unification, the common technology grows according to:

$$H_{t+1} - H_t = dH_t(\bar{N}_1 + \bar{N}_2 - N_{1t} - N_{2t}) \tag{42}$$

and is used in the two production sectors:

$$\begin{cases} Y_{1t} = N_{1t}^a H_{1t}^{1-a} \\ Y_{2t} = N_{2t}^a H_{2t}^{1-a} \end{cases} \tag{43}$$

The optimal employment (factor N) devoted to research is larger than its level in each of the countries before unification. It is also larger than the total employment in research in both countries before unification. This is due to the fact that the social planner knows that research increases production in both countries, hence there is a much larger marginal productivity of research. The suppression of redundancy in research stimulates growth.

CASE B. DIFFERENT TECHNOLOGIES WITH INTERNATIONAL TRANSFER POSSIBLE
We assume now that the two countries have developed different technologies, the one available in country 1 being more efficient. We have before integration:

$$\begin{cases} H_{1t+1} - H_{1t} = d_1 H_{1t}(\bar{N} - N_{1t}) & \text{(country 1)} \\ H_{2t+1} - H_{2t} = d_2 H_{2t}(\bar{N} - N_{2t}) & \text{(country 2)} \end{cases} \quad (d_1 > d_2) \tag{44}$$

After integration, the authorities have to maximize welfare and have the choice of the technology they use, since it is transferable to one country to the other. They will clearly use the technology H_1 of country 1 for both countries, hence shut down research firms in country 2.

CASE C. DIFFERENT TECHNOLOGIES, WITH NO POSSIBLE TRANSFER

After integration, the choice is to keep different production techniques in the two countries or to close all firms in country 2, and make production for the consumers of both countries with the technology and firms of country 1. If labour is immobile, this solution will certainly not be chosen. Assume labour is mobile.

This second solution will be chosen if the initial level of technology in country 1 is sufficiently large.

These example show that economic integration and pooling of the stock of knowledge can stimulate growth if it is possible to eliminate duplications in research, or if it is possible to transfer without a substantial cost the technology (human capital, stock of knowledge) of the more advanced country, or if it is possible to move labour to the firms of the more advanced country if technology is not transferrable. The increase in market size also increases the incentive to innovate (find new products, new production techniques).

However, if increased competition means lower profitability, it is more likely that growth will diminish; if neither technology nor labour can be exported, economic integration will not bring much change compared with autarky.

These various examples have shown that, whatever the model of endogenous growth used, the links between growth and economic policy (subsidization, public investment, international economic integration) or between growth and welfare depend heavily on the precise nature of the factors determining growth. The most important questions to be answered at the empirical level are as follows: Can production factors be devoted without restrictions or adjustment costs to the production of research or of consumption goods, or to industries with traditional or modern production techniques? What is the relative importance of their effect on private productivity or welfare? How is their production financed? What are the externalities (spillover effects) generated by these factors between countries, between industries? What are the links between these externalities and the liberalization of trade, of capital movements, of labour migration? What is the market structure of the sector producing technology (knowledge)? Do increased profits stimulate research? What are the main incentives of the production of knowledge? (rents, demand, etc.) To what extent can technology (or knowledge) be imported, copied, adapted to existing productive capital or to the available labour force?

One has to recognize that existing empirical work gives limited answers to those crucial issues, if the research on endogenous growth models is to play a role in the design of policies.

5.4. Conclusion

Endogenous growth models brought a considerable improvement to the theory of growth; the 'residual' of the usual growth accounting could find new explanations; a link could be made between growth, agents' behaviour and economic policy; innovative policy advice could be formulated (concerning allocation incentives of rare resources; public expenditures policies, tariffs and protection; subsidization of research, etc.); size and economic integration effects could be discussed; the relationships between employment, growth and innovation could be discussed.

However, the enormous quantity of theoretical research contrasts with the limited useful empirical work available. As we have mentioned above, econometric estimations seem insufficient, particularly due to the following difficulties:

THE TEST OF THE PRECISE DEFINITION OF GROWTH FACTORS. It would be very useful in order to promote growth to know exactly which type of education (primary, secondary, university, in which fields) is the most necessary for the different groups of countries; in particular because it corresponds to their production technology; which kind of public infrastructures (roads, telecommunications) are first to be developed; which financial markets or intermediaries or financial assets prove most useful; which kind of research (fundamental, applied in firms, in the public sector) has the largest effect on the effective stock of knowledge.

THE USE OF TIME-SERIES DATA INSTEAD OF CROSS-SECTIONS OF COUNTRIES. It might be different to analyse the past causes of the growth rate differentials and the explanatory elements of national growth for a given country; the question of time-lags in particular seems very important.

THE ANALYSIS OF THE DETERMINANTS OF THE QUANTITY OF TECHNOLOGY PRODUCED AND OF THE MARKET STRUCTURE OF THE CORRESPONDING SECTOR. In particular, which is the most common behaviour of the agents who produce research, patents, etc.? Which incentives are therefore most likely to stimulate growth?

THE ANALYSIS OF THE SUBSTITUTABILITY OR COMPLEMENTARITY BETWEEN VARIOUS GROWTH FACTORS. It seems obvious that research, new products, and new technologies are useless without physical investment which allows implementation of new ideas in the productive sectors, without the human capital necessary to put into operation the new technologies and perhaps without the financial markets or intermediaries which provide the funds necessary to invest.

However, few studies examine how these various factors are interrelated: most concentrate only on one, or simply let them play independent roles.

ANNEX

Additional factors having a significant effect on growth:

- nutrition (Dasgupta (1991)): basic minimal nutrition need must be covered before any other work effort is done.

- allocation of production between the various sectors (Chenery, Robinson, Syrquin (1986)).
- existence of a inefficient bureaucracy, lack of clear property rights (Reynolds (1983)).
- real exchange rate; Heston, Summers (1988*a*) find a positive correlation between the real exchange rate and income per head for OECD and Asian countries, not for poorer or more inflationnist countries.
- exports (Rivera-Batz and Romer (1991*a*, 1991*b*); export-oriented strategies lead consistently to quicker growth (De Long, Summers (1991)), because of the necessary imports of high-tech equipment goods, and of learning by doing effects (Feder (1983), Balassa (1978), Tyler (1981)).
- price distortions which reduce growth; De Long, Summers (1991) measure distortions by the level of tariffs or of protections.
- exchange rate distortions; Easterly (1991) estimates the multiple equilibria model first developed by Rebelo (1991); low growth appears when the marginal return on capital is low, which has a disincentive effect on savings. A probit model is built, that shows that large black exchange rate market premia (exchange rate distortions) increase the probability of remaining in the low growth equilibrium. Fischer (1991) finds a similar effect for black market premia.
- inflation which is most of the time found to reduce growth (Dornbusch, Reynoso (1989), Villanueva (1990), Grier, Tullock (1989), Fischer (1991)).
- taxes which reduce growth (King, Rebelo (1990)).
- foreign debt. It deters investment and slows down growth (Borensztein (1990)), a result which is not confirmed by Cohen (1991) on a cross-section of 81 developing countries.

REFERENCES

M. Abramovitz (1986), 'Catching up, forging ahead and falling behind', *Journal of Economic History*, 46: 385–406.

J. Adams (1990), 'Fundamental stocks of knowledge and productivity growth', *Journal of Political Economy* 98 (4): 673–702.

P. Aghion, P. Howitt (1989), 'A model of growth through creative destruction', Mimeo. MIT.

——, —— (1990), 'Unemployment: a symptom of stagnation or a side effect of growth?, Working paper, Delta Paris.

A. Alesina, D. Rodrik (1991), 'Distributive politics and economic growth', CEPR Discussion Paper 565.

G. S. Alogoskoufis, F. Van der Ploeg (1990*a*), 'On budgetary policies and economic growth', CEPR Discussion Paper 496.

——, —— (1990*b*), 'Endogenous growth and overlapping generations', Discussion Paper 90/26. Birkbeck College, London.

P. Artus, M. Kaabi (1993), 'Dépenses publiques, progrès technique et croissance', *Revue Economique*, forthcoming.

D. A. Aschauer (1989), 'Is public expenditure productive?', *Journal of Monetary Economics*, 23 (2): 177–200.

C. Azariadis, A. Drazen (1990), 'Threshold externalities in economic development', *Quarterly journal of Economics*, CV: 501–26.

M. N. Baily, C. L. Schultze (1990), 'The productivity of capital in a period of slower growth', *Microeconomics Annual*, 369–408.

B. Balassa (1978), 'Exports and economic growth: further evidence', *Journal of Development Economics*, June 5: 181–9.

R. Baldwin (1989a), 'The growth effect of 1992', *Economic Policy*, 9: 248–81.

—— (1989b), 'On the growth effect of 1992', NBER Working Paper 3119.

—— (1992), 'On the growth effect of import competition', NBER Working Paper 4045.

R. J. Barro (1987), *Macroeconomics*. John Wiley, New York.

—— (1989), 'A cross-country study of growth, saving and government', NBER Working Paper 2855.

—— (1990), 'Government spending in a simple model of endogenous growth', *Journal of Political Economy*, XCVIII: S103–S125.

—— (1991), 'Economic growth in a cross section of countries', *Quarterly Journal of Economics*, May: 407–44 and NBER Working paper 3120, September, (1989b).

—— X. Sala i Martin (1990a), 'Economic growth and convergence across the United States', NBER Working Paper, July.

——, —— (1990b), 'Public finance in models of economic growth', NBER Working Paper 3362.

W. J. Baumol (1986), 'Productivity growth convergence and welfare: what the long run data show', *American Economic Review*, 76: 1072–85.

—— (1990), 'Entrepreneurship: productive, unproductive and destructive', *Journal of Political Economy*, XCVIII: 893–921.

—— E. N. Wolff (1988), 'Productivity growth, convergence and welfare: reply', *American Economic Review*, 78: 1155–9.

—— S. Blackman, E. N. Wolff (1989), *Productivity and American leadership: the long view*. MIT Press, Cambridge MA.

V. Bencivenga, B. D. Smith (1991), 'Financial intermediation and endogenous growth', *Review of Economic Studies*, 58 (2): 195–209.

A. Berg, J. Sachs (1988), 'The debt crisis: structural explanations of countries' performance', NBER Working Paper 2607.

J. Bernstein, I. Nadiri (1988), 'Interindustry spillovers, rates of return and production in high-tech industries', *American Economic Review*, 78 (2): 429–34.

G. Bertola (1990), 'Flexibility, investment and growth', CEPR Discussion Paper 422.

—— (1992), 'Models of economic integration and localized growth', CEPR Discussion Paper 651.

E. Borensztein (1990), 'Debt overhang, credit rationing and investment', *Journal of Development Economics*, 32: 315–35.

J. A. Brander, S. Dowrick (1990), 'The role of fertility and population in economic growth: new results from aggregate cross-national data', CEPR Discussion Paper 232.

W. H. Buiter (1991), 'Saving and endogenous growth: a survey of theory and policy', CEPR Discussion Paper 606.

R. J. Cabarello, R. K. Lyons (1989), 'Increasing returns and imperfect competition in European Industry', Columbia University Working Paper.

——, —— (1990), 'Internal versus external economies in European industries', *European Economic Review*, 34: 805–30.

H. Chenery, S. Robinson, M. Syrquin (1986), *Industrialization and growth: a comparative study*, Washington, The World Bank.

D. Cohen (1991), 'Slow growth and large LDC debt in the eighties: an empirical analysis', CEPR Discussion Paper 46.

W. Cohen, R. Levine (1989), 'Empirical studies of innovation and market structure', in *Handbook of Industrial Organisation*, R. Schmalensee, R. D. Willig (eds), Elsevier.

J. Creedy, P. Francois (1990), 'Financing higher education and majority voting', *Journal of Public Economics*, 43: 181–200.

B. Crepon, G. Dureau (1991), 'Investment in research and development: a causality analysis in a generalized accelerator model', Document de travail 9112–INSEE, Paris.

P. Dasgupta (1991), 'Nutrition, non-convexities and redistributive policies', *Economic Journal*, 101: 22–6.

J. B. De Long, L. H. Summers (1991), 'Equipment investment and economic growth', *Quarterly Journal of Economics*, 106: 445–502.

K. Dervis, P. Petri (1987), 'The macroeconomics of successful development: what are the lessons?', NBER Macroeconomics Annual, 211–55.

R. Dornbusch (1990), 'Policies to move from stabilization to growth', CEPR Discussion Paper 456, September.

—— A. Reynoso (1989), 'Financial factors in economic development', *American Economic Review*, 79 May: 204–9.

S. Dowrick (1992), 'Technological catch up and diverging incomes: patterns of economic growth 1960–88', *Economic Journal*, May, 600–10.

—— D. T. Nguyen (1989), 'OECD Comparative economic growth 1950–85: catch-up and convergence', *American Economic Review*, 79 (5): 1010–30.

—— N. Gemmell (1991), 'Industrialization catching up and economic growth: a comparative study across the world's capitalist economies', *Economic Journal*, 101: 263–75.

S. N. Durlauf, P. A. Johnson (1992), 'Local versus global convergence across national economies', NBER Working Paper 3996.

W. Easterly (1990), 'Endogenous growth in developing countries with government induced distorsions', NBER Working Paper 3214.

—— (1991), 'Economic stagnation, fixed factors and policy thresholds', Mimeo, World Bank.

G. Feder (1983), 'On exports and economic growth', *Journal of Development Economics*, 12 February–April: 59–73.

R. Feenstra (1990), 'Trade and uneven growth', NBER Working Paper 3276.

S. Fischer (1991), 'Growth, macroeconomics and development', NBER Working Paper 3702.

P. Geroski (1989), 'Entry, innovation and productivity growth', *Review of Economics and Statistics*, XXI (4): 572–8.

A. Goto, K. Suzuki (1989), 'R&D capital, rate on return on R&D investment and spillover of R&D in japanese manufacturing industries', *Review of Economics and Statistics*, LXXI (4): 555–64.

J. Greenwood, B. Johanovic (1990), 'Financial development, growth and the distribution of income', *Journal of Political Economy*, 98 (5): 1076–107.

K. Grier, G. Tullock (1989), 'An empirical analysis of cross-national economic growth 1951–80', *Journal of Monetary Economics*, 24: 259–76.

Z. Griliches (1984), *R&D, Patents and Productivity*, University of Chicago Press, Chicago.

—— (1990), 'Patent statistics is economic indicators', *Journal of Economic Literature*, XXVIII (4): 1661–707.

G. M. Grossman, E. H. Helpman (1989*a*), 'Quality ladders and product cycles', NBER Working Paper 3201, and *Quarterly Journal of Economics*, May: 557–86.

——, —— (1989*b*), 'Product development and international trade', *Journal of Political Economy*, December: 1261–83.

——, —— (1989*c*), 'Quality ladders in the theory of growth', NBER Working Paper 3099.

——, —— (1989*d*), 'Endogenous product cycles', NBER Working Paper 2913.

——, —— (1989*e*), 'Growth and welfare in a small open economy', NBER Working Paper 2970.

——, —— (1990*a*), 'Trade innovation and growth', *American Economic Review*, 80: 86–91.

——, —— (1990*b*), 'Comparative advantage and long run growth', *American Economic Review*, 80: 796–815.

——, —— (1990*c*), 'Trade, knowledge, spillovers and growth', NBER Working Paper 3845.

——, —— (1991), *Innovation and growth in the global economy*. MIT Press, Cambridge, MA.

D. Guellec, P. Ralle (1991), 'Endogenous growth and product innovation', Mimeo, INSEE, Commissariat Géneral du Plan, Paris.

B. Hall, F. Hayashi (1989), 'Research and Development as an Investment', NBER Working Paper 2973.

—— J. Mairesse (1992), 'Exploring the relationship between R&D and productivity in French manufacturing firms', NBER Working Paper 3956.

J. Helliwell, A. Chung (1990), 'Macroeconomic convergence: international transmission of growth and technical progress', NBER Working Paper 3264.

——, —— (1992), 'Convergence and growth linkages between North and South', NBER Working Paper 3948.

E. Helpman (1991), 'Endogenous macroeconomic growth theory', NBER Working Paper 3869.

A. Heston, R. Summers (1988*a*), 'A new set of international comparisons of real product and price levels: estimates for 130 countries', *Review Income and Wealth*, March: 1–25.

——, —— (1988*b*), 'What have we learned about prices and quantities from international comparisons: 1987', *American Economic Review*, 78 (2): 467–73.

A. Jacquemin, A. Sapir (1988), 'International trade and integration of the European Community', *European Economic Review*, 32: 57.

——, —— (1990), 'Competition and imports in the European Market', CEPR Discussion Paper 474.

A. B. Jaffe (1986), 'Technological opportunity and spillovers of R&D: evidence from firms' patents, profits and market value', *American Economic Review*, December: 984–1001.

T. Jappelli, M. Pagano (1992), 'Saving, growth and liquidity constraints', CEPR Discussion Paper 662.

G. Johnson (1984), 'Subsidies for higher education', *Journal of Labor Economics*, 2: 303–18.

L. E. Jones, R. Manuelli (1990*a*), 'Finite lifetimes and growth', NBER Working Paper 3469.

——, —— (1990*b*), 'A convex model of equilibrium growth', *Journal of Political Economy*, October: 1008–38.

M. S. Khan, C. Reinhart (1990), 'Private investment and economic growth in developing countries', *World Development*, January: 19–27.

—— D. Villanueva (1991), 'Macroeconomic policies and long-term growth: a conceptual and empirical review', Mimeo, International Monetary Fund.

R. G. King, S. Rebelo (1989), 'Transitionnal dynamics and economic growth in the neo-classical model', NBER Working Paper 3185.

——, —— (1990), 'Public policy and economic growth: developing neo classical implications', *Journal of Political Economy*, 98, October: S126–S150.

—— C. Plosser, C. Rebelo (1988), 'Production growth and business cycles; II: new directions', *Journal of Monetary Economics*, May.

M. A. King, M. Robson (1989), 'Endogenous growth and the role of history', LSE Financial Markets Group Discussion Paper 63.

A. Krueger, D. Osmond (1990), 'Impact of government on growth and trade', NBER Working Paper 3185.

S. Lach, R. Rob (1992), 'R&D, investment and industry dynamics', NBER Working Paper 4060.

—— M. Schankerman (1989), 'Dynamics of R&D and investment in the scientific sector', *Journal of Political Economy*, August: 880–904.

E. Leamer (1984), *Sources of international comparative advantage*. MIT Press, Cambridge, MA.

R. Levine (1990), 'Financial structure and economic development', Board of Governors of the Federal Reserve System International Finance Discussion Paper 381.

—— (1991), 'Stock markets, growth and tax policy', *Journal of Finance*, September: 1445–65.

—— D. Renelt (1990), 'Cross country studies of growth and policy: methodological conceptual and statistical problems', Mimeo, World Bank.

R. E. J. Lucas (1988), 'On the mechanics of economic development', *Journal of Monetary, Economics*, 22: 3–32.

—— (1990), 'Why doesn't capital flow from rich to poor countries?', American Economic Review Papers and Proceedings, May: 92–6.

J. Mairesse, P. Mohnen (1990), 'Recherche-développement et productivité: un survol de la littérature économétrique', *Economie et Statistique*, 237–338: 99–108.

—— N. Sassenou (1991), 'R&D and productivity: a survey of econometric studies at the firm level', *Science-Technology-Industry Review*, 8: 317–48. OCDE, Paris.

N. G. Mankiw, D. Romer, D. N. Weil (1990), 'A contribution to the empirics of economic growth', NBER Working paper 354, and *Quarterly Journal of Economics*, May: 407–38.

K. Matsuyama (1991), 'Agricultural productivity, comparative advantage and economic growth', NBER Working Paper 3606.

C. J. Morrison, A. E. Schwartz (1992), 'State infrastructure and productive performance', NBER Working Paper 3891.

K. Murphy, A. Shleifer, R. Vishny (1989), 'Industrialization and the big push', *Journal of Political Economy*, 97: 1003–26.

——, ——, —— (1991), 'The allocation of talent: implications for growth', *Quarterly Journal of Economics*, May: 503–30.

D. J. Neven, L. H. Röller (1990), 'European integration and trade flows', CEPR Discussion Paper 367.

I. Otani, D. Villanueva (1989), 'Theoretical aspects of growth in developing countries: external debt dynamics and the role of human capital', IMF Staff Papers, June: 307–42.

S. L. Parente, E. G. Prescott (1991), 'Technology adoption and growth', NBER Working Paper 3733.

R. Perotti (1990), 'Political equilibrium, income distribution and growth', Mimeo, MIT.

T. Persson, G. Tabellini (1991), 'Is inequality harmful for growth? Theory and evidence', CEPR Discussion Paper 581.

J. Polak (1989), *Financial policies and development.* OECD, Paris.

M. E. Porter (1990), *The comparative advantage of nations.* Macmillan, London.

E. Prescott, J. H. Boyd (1987), 'Dynamic coalitions: engines of growth', *American Economic Review, Papers and Proceedings*, May: 63–7.

D. Quah (1990), 'Galton's fallacy and tests of the convergence hypothesis', Working Paper, MIT, May.

R. Ram (1986), 'Government size and economic growth: a new framework and some evidence from cross section and time series data', *American Economic Review*, March: 191–203.

S. Rebelo (1990), 'Long run policy analysis and long run growth', NBER Working Paper 3325.

—— (1991), 'Growth in open economies', Mimeo, World Bank.

L. A. Rivera-Batz, P. M. Romer (1991*a*), 'International trade and endogenous technological change', NBER Working Paper 3594.

——, —— (1991*b*), 'Economic integration with endogenous growth', *Quarterly Journal of Economics*, 106: 531–6.

P. M. Romer (1986), 'Increasing returns and long run growth', *Journal of Political Economy*, 94: 1002–37.

—— (1987*a*), 'Growth based on increasing returns due to specialization', *American Economic Review*, May: 56–62.

—— (1987*b*), 'Crazy explanations for the productivity slowdown', NBER Macroeconomics Annual, MIT Press, Cambridge, MA.

—— (1989), 'Human capital and growth: theory and evidence', NBER Working Paper 3173.

—— (1990*a*), 'Are nonconvexities important for understanding growth?', *American Economic Review*, 80 (2): 97–103.

—— (1990*b*), 'Endogenous technological change', *Journal of Political Economy*, 98: S71–S102.

—— (1990*c*), 'Capital labor and productivity', Brookings papers on Economic Activity, Brookings Institution, 337–67.

N. Roubini, X. Sala-i-Martin (1991*a*), 'The relation between trade regime, financial development and economic growth', NBER Fourth Annual Interamerican Seminar on Economics.

——, —— (1991*b*), 'Financial development, the trade regime and economic growth', NBER Working Paper 3876.

G. Saint-Paul (1990), 'Fiscal policy in an endogenous growth model', Delta, Document 91–04.

—— (1992), 'Technological choice, financial markets and economic development', *European Economic Review*, May: 763–81.

—— Th. Verdier (1992), 'Education, democracy and growth', CEPR Discussion Paper 613.

X. Sala-i-Martin (1990), 'Lecture notes on economic growth, II', NBER Working Paper.

L. Soete, P. Patel (1985), 'Recherche développement, importations de technologie et croissance économique', *Revue Economique*, 36 (5): 975–1000.

N. Stern (1991), 'The determinants of growth', *Economic Journal*, January: 122–33.

N. Stokey (1991), 'Human capital product quality and growth', *Quarterly Journal of Economics*, May: 587–616.

R. Summers, A. Heston (1988), 'A new set of industrial comparisons of real product and prices: estimates for 130 countries', *Review of Income and Wealth*, 34: 1–26.

—— A. Heston (1991), 'The Penn World Table (Mark 5): an expanded set of international comparisons, 1950–88', *Quarterly Journal of Economics*, 106: 327–68.

J. Tirole (1985), 'Asset bubbles and overlapping generations', *Econometrica*, 53: 1499–1528.

W. Tyler (1981), 'Growth and export expansion in developing countries: some empirical evidence', *Journal of Development Economics*, August: 121–30.

D. Villanueva, A. Mirakhor (1990), 'Strategies for financial reforms: interest rate policies, stabilization and bank supervision in developing countries', IMF Staff Papers, September: 509–36.

World Development Report (1989), World Bank.

N. Yanagawa, G. M. Grossman (1992), 'Asset bubbles and endogenous growth', NBER Working Paper 4004.

A. Young (1991), 'Learning by doing and the dynamic effects of international trade', *Quarterly Journal of Economics*, May: 369–406.

II

Markets and Organization

Introduction to Part II

Margaret E. Slade

In 1992, a number of well-known economists were asked to present their views on the past, present, and future of their subject. The occasion was the tenth anniversary of GREQE, the research institute that had been founded in Marseille a decade earlier. It is interesting to see what subjects researchers might choose when given such a broad mandate. Two considerations would of necessity enter into their choice of topic: their area should be important, and it should be one that they knew intimately. These considerations clearly played a role in the selection that occurred.

The papers in the middle section of this book are organized around the theme of markets and organizations, a heading that is broad enough to include most of microeconomics. Indeed, the papers range from the very micro level to the interface between micro and macroeconomics. In particular, there are two papers that deal with individual decision-makers; one of these (van Damme) looks at strategic interactions among individuals, whereas the other (Ponssard and Tanguy) looks at the organization of individuals into firms. At the second level of aggregation, there is a paper that considers the provision of private and public goods in local markets (Scotchmer and Thisse). Finally, there are two papers that deal with the economy in a general equilibrium context (Gabszewitz, and d'Aspremont, Dos Santos Ferreira, and Gérard-Varet).

The two papers that focus on the extremely micro level have a number of features in common. Specifically, each author considers a subject that has received a great deal of attention in the last decade and analyses its evolution—its successes, failures, and future directions. In contrast, the authors of the other three papers consider subjects that have been to some extent neglected and suggest ways in which this situation might be remedied.

In Chapter 10, van Damme traces the development of non-cooperative game theory from the mid-1940s to the present and stresses how it has gradually changed from a pure deductive science into one that is more descriptive. In his chapter we are shown both the strengths and the weaknesses of the discipline. In particular, we observe the disillusionment that the refinements programme, under which stronger and stronger rationality requirements were placed on the notion of Nash equilibrium, has met with. In addition, the currently more fashionable notions of learning, where players have only limited rationality, and evolution, where they have even less, are developed.

One frustration that applied as well as theoretical researchers often experience with game theory is its ability to explain virtually any behaviour pattern as an equilibrium of a game played by rational agents who are making optimal choices. In explaining everything, does it explain nothing? van Damme is more optimistic. In particular, he stresses the increased role that empirical relevance will play in the development of the discipline and predicts that future extensions will focus more on imagination and less on logic.

In Chapter 9, Ponssard and Tanguy open the firm's black box and investigate what lies within these walls. Like game theory, managerial economics has undergone radical changes since the 1980s. Moreover, these changes have taken the subject from a point where optimization and forecasting assumed centre-stage to one where more qualitative strategic analysis has taken the dominant role. Indeed, many business schools have introduced or expanded their management strategy groups while at the same time de-emphasizing or abandoning the more traditional management science.

The recent textbook on organization theory by Milgrom and Roberts (1992) illustrates this trend. The authors stress incentive problems within the firm, the role of coordination, flexibility, and job design, and the desirability of structuring a firm around a set of complementary activities. The more traditional techniques of management science, such as optimal control and statistical forecasting, are mentioned only in passing.

We see, therefore, that both game theory and managerial economics have evolved from disciplines that emphasized optimization, super-rationality, and predictability to ones that are more strongly grounded in a context or environment in which flexibility and adaptation take the forefront.

Chapter 8, by Scotchmer and Thisse, lies in the middle ground between individual decision-making and the economy as a whole. Here, the authors attempt to unify two strands of the microeconomics literature that deal with local-market phenomena: the first emphasizes the choice of spatial location by firms, whereas the second considers the provision of local public goods by municipalities. The unifying feature of these two areas is space or the notion that competition is local. However, the two subdisciplines—one from industrial organization and the other from public finance—treat space in very different ways. Indeed, in the Hotelling (1929) model of firm location, the spatial location of consumers is exogenous, and there is therefore no land market. In contrast, in the Tiebout (1956) model of local public-good provision, consumers choose where they will live, and their location decisions, which affect land values, are instrumental in allocating scarce facilities.

Unfortunately, very little work has been done that integrates these two literatures. One hopes that future collaboration between these two authors, one from the Hotelling and the other from the Tiebout tradition, will bear fruit, and that the interesting ideas that they propose in their chapter will be developed in ways that further our understanding of space in different contexts.

Finally, the two papers on imperfect competition in a general equilibrium context, which take distinct approaches to the subject, complement one another nicely. In particular, Chapter 6 by Gabszewicz provides a more historical perspective, whereas Chapter 7 by d'Aspremont, Dos Santos Ferreira, and Gerard-Varet (hereafter DDG) proposes a relatively new solution concept.

In the first of these papers, Gabszewicz describes the two major approaches that have historically dominated the subject: one, which is related to the competitive paradigm, substitutes a strategic mechanism for an auctioneer but leads to competitive prices when agents are sufficiently numerous. The second, in contrast, allows some agents to exercise market power, even in the limit, while others behave passively.

After describing his subject's past, Gabszewicz lists some of the problems that these lines of research have uncovered. These include the non-existence of equilibria when there are nonconvexities arising from, for example, increasing returns, the difficulties associated with defining a product group (i.e. a group of close substitutes) when prices are endogenous, and the appropriateness of non-cooperative solution concepts when agents can form powerful coalitions.

Gabszewicz's discussion sets the stage for the DDG paper, which summarizes some of the authors' recent work in the general equilibrium area. Their line of research, which has appeared in a series of papers, derives much of its tractability from its strong partial equilibrium flavour.

There are two simplifying features that characterize the DDG work. First, the rational expectations requirement that is implicit in all games is weakened. Specifically, strategic agents make plans with respect to the parts of the economy where they have market power but behave passively with respect to the others. In other words, they take into account the feedbacks from their choices to only a limited set of markets. Second, the notion of a price schedule, which eliminates the need to invert a complete system of demand equations, is introduced. These two simplifications make possible a consideration of a wide variety of games. In particular, DDG show how Walras, Cournot, and monopolistically competitive equilibria can be special cases of their equilibrium solution concept. In other words, when specific restrictions are imposed, familiar games result.

This collection of papers thus deals with individuals, organizations, markets, and economies. Moreover, much of the analysis involves overlaps between two or more economic phenomena. For example, there are discussions of how strategic interactions among individuals within a firm affect that firm's performance, and of how strategic interactions among firms in markets affect the functioning of the economy. In concluding, I would like to suggest yet another overlap that seems to me to be a fruitful area for future research—the interaction between the internal organization of firms and the external organization of product markets.

Much has been written about the internal organization of firms, the conflicts that are generated by diverse objectives, and the feedbacks from these conflicts to firm performance, where by internal organization I mean both ownership (e.g.

entrepreneurial versus managerial) and control structure (e.g. hierarchical versus lateral). In particular, we know that, with the exception of small entrepreneurial firms where owner, manager, and worker are one and the same, it is unrealistic to expect that firms maximize profits.

Much of the literature in this area deals with the problem of aligning the interests among shareholders (owners), managers (decision-makers), and workers who implement decisions. For example, one tool that can be used to achieve some degree of alignment is the design of compensation schemes (profit-sharing, stock options, etc.). Indeed, when managers and workers are given more entrepreneurial incentives, they will be more likely to minimize production costs and to choose the profit-maximizing level of output. However, the use of high-powered incentives inevitably conflicts with the need to insure risk-averse agents and to insulate them from the undiversifiable risk of job loss. Moreover, uninsured agents may adopt strategies that are too conservative from the owners' points of view, or may attempt to diversify inefficiently by choosing projects that are not complementary. An optimal contract therefore must balance these conflicts.

Even more has been written about product market competition. For example, nearly two-thirds of the chapters in Tirole's (1989) industrial organization textbook are devoted to this subject. Moreover, the way in which market outcomes depend on the type of game that firms engage in is well understood, where by type of game I mean the number and size distribution of firms in the market, the choice variables available to these firms (price, quantity, advertising, R&D, etc.), the nature of the products that they produce (homogeneous, imperfect substitutes, complements, etc.), the dynamic structure of the game, and the equilibrium solution concept.

Much less has been written about the interface between internal organization issues and the nature of product market competition. This interface works both ways—the degree of competition in the product market affects the incentives that managers and workers face, and agent-incentive schemes affect product market competition.

Consider first the feedback from product market competition to agent incentives. Our level of ignorance in this area is truly surprising. In particular, economists traditionally assume that, whereas there may be managerial slack in imperfectly competitive firms (owing to, say, discretionary profits), competitive firms must maximize profits if they are to survive. However, this link is far from well understood. For example, is it the number of firms in the market that causes managers to be efficient? Clearly not, since all of the above mentioned problems are found in atomistic price-taking firms; indeed, if there are n firms in a market and $n - 1$ of them are not minimizing costs, there is little competitive pressure on the nth manager to be efficient. Perhaps instead it is the number of entrepreneurial firms relative to managerial firms that causes managers to minimize costs. This route, however, was taken by Hart (1983), who shows that the link is tenuous at best.

The second feedback, from internal organization to product market competition, is somewhat better understood. For example, there have been several papers analysing how managerial compensation schemes affect the game that is played in the product market (e.g. Fershtman and Judd 1987). Nevertheless, many unresolved problems remain.

For example, researchers who attempt to bridge this gap usually neglect the more traditional incentive or motivational aspects of compensation packages. Indeed, it is standard to assume that there exists a first-best contract that solves the traditional agency problem so that the product market game can be analysed in a straightforward fashion. However, with more realistic models, game- and agency-theoretic motives can easily conflict. To illustrate, from a game-theoretic point a view, it might be optimal for owners to endow their managers with aggressive objectives so that they will be tough with their product market rivals. However, increased agent aggression might easily conflict with agent insurance motives.

In addition, it is possible that when owners choose agent objectives strategically they drive yet another nail in the coffin of the 'firms-maximize-profits' hypothesis. For example, one way of ensuring that managers will be more aggressive might be to base their compensation at least partly on the basis of the revenue or sales rather than on the profits that they generate.

These are only a few examples of some of the ideas that surface in this literature. Space limitations inhibit a more comprehensive treatment. Nevertheless, I hope that readers have acquired some idea of the possibilities for further research.

REFERENCES

Fershtman, C., and Judd, K. L. (1987), 'Equilibrium Incentives in Oligopoly', *American Economic Review*, 77: 927–40.

Hart, O. (1983), 'The Market Mechanism as an Incentive Scheme', *Bell Journal of Economics*, 74: 366–82.

Hotelling, H. (1929), 'Stability in Competition', *Economic Journal*, 39: 41–57.

Milgrom, P., and Roberts, J. (1992), *Economics, Organization, and Management*. Englewood Cliffs, NJ: Prentice-Hall.

Tiebout, M. (1956), 'A Pure Theory of Local Expenditure', *Journal of Political* Economy, 64: 416–24.

Tirole, J. (1989), *The Theory of Industrial Organization*. Cambridge, Mass.: MIT Press.

6

GeneRal EQuilibrium Economics: Allowing for Imperfect Competition

Jean J. Gabszewicz

Even in the country of Madame Soleil, it is difficult to predict the way in which the future will evolve. And when we look back, the past rarely appears as we had imagined it would. Who could have imagined, back in 1982, when GREQE was located in the second storey of a *maison borgne* in the centre of Marseilles, that the 1992 conference celebrating its tenth birthday would be held in the 'Hospice de la Vieille Charité' with magnificent views over the Mediterranean? Similarly, science develops along uncertain paths, and extrapolations about the 'hot' topics of the future based on current research activity are a hazardous game to play. Who could have guessed at the end of the Second World War the impending explosion in mathematical economics? Who could have guessed at the beginning of the 1960s the tremendous influence that game theory would have on micro-economics, and in particular on industrial economics? Transitory fashions often make obscure the deeper developments of a science. But the organizers of this conference have asked us to play this dangerous game of prediction, and I shall not escape my duties: I have chosen to talk about the future of general equilibrium theory in its relationship to imperfect competition.

Let me, to begin with, justify the choice, which may be surprising since the topic has been dormant for so long. First, I think that there is no microeconomic theory if it is not eventually cast in a general equilibrium framework. Of course, partial models give insights, and also serve as natural starting points. But, in its very essence, the economy is a system of interrelated markets where the influence of what happens at some point is unavoidably propagated throughout the system, via the chain of markets, through the possible substitutions and complementarities between goods that are due to tastes and technologies. Any micro theory that would enclose itself in a partial approach would be self-defeating, for it would miss the essence of the functioning of markets. And, in some sense, economic theory did regress when Marshall set the clock back to the partial approach, from the general equilibrium approach where Walras had guided it.

Something of the same kind happened in the 1970s and 1980s. After the blossoming of general equilibrium in the 1950s and 1960s, a gang of microeconomists —and I was one of them—disowned the gods they had adored, and substituted for the works of Arrow, Debreu, Aumann, and others a kind of 'Mickey Mouse economics', as it was labelled by Professor Hildenbrand. A good example of this phenomenon is the approach in the recent book by Professor Tirole, *The Theory of Industrial Organization* (1988). It provides a convincing patchwork of specific models, which undoubtedly shed some light on important economic issues. But one is invaded with a feeling of frustration upon closing this book: where is the unified framework that links all the questions and answers considered through the chapters? How do these issues make up a whole economic system? Of course, one should not imagine that a comprehensive view of the functioning of the economy under imperfect competition can be realized by a *coup de baguette magique*. Nevertheless, Walras did succeed in giving this comprehensive view when all markets behave competitively. The time has come to attempt a similar integration when the economy does not work in the frictionless manner imagined by our predecessors.

Happily, there are some building blocks, inherited from the past, that can serve as cornerstones in this attempt. And, since the future has its roots in the past, let me briefly remind readers what we have inherited from the pioneers of both theories: imperfect competition and general equilibrium. With respect to imperfect competition, five great names, in my opinion, occupy the forefront. The first, and greatest, is Cournot. His contribution to economic theory goes far beyond the discovery of the notion of 'non-cooperative equilibrium'. In fact, Cournot discovered the theory of monopoly, the theory of oligopoly, and the theory of competition as the limiting case of oligopoly. He settled all the important questions relating to market structure and the importance of demand—*la loi de débit*, as he called it—in the explanation of price formation. He would have constructed the complete foundations for micro theory had he also considered the role of supply, as derived from the technological conditions of production, and the need for a general equilibrium approach, a task assigned to Walras some fifty years later. At any rate, he was the first to suggest that the lack of cooperation between the agents operating in a market must guide the market towards a non-cooperative equilibrium, a concept reinvented by Nash in the abstract framework of game theory.

The second name is Edgeworth. The profound work of Edgeworth on bilateral monopoly and the contract curve received little attention from the economics profession before it was rediscovered by game theorists, in the light of the work on cooperative games initiated by von Neumann and Morgenstern. In contrast with Cournot, Edgeworth based his approach to imperfect competition on an assumption of cooperation between agents leading to Pareto-optimal outcomes. He also introduced the role of collusion, via the distinction he made between a *coalition* of economic agents—which can always dissolve before the outcome is settled—and a *combination* of traders, which is an institutional collusive agreement between agents, and which cannot dissolve before the outcome is reached (see Edgeworth 1881). This distinction forms the basis of the idea of a syndicate, viewed as a group of agents which does not enter into a broader coalition, except in unison.

As for Hotelling (1929), he appears as the forerunner of the 'Monopolistic Competition Revolution', as labelled by Samuelson (1968) and reformulated a little later by Chamberlin (1965). He was also the first to use the notion of subgame-perfect equilibrium, in his famous paper 'Stability in Competition', where the choice of location and prices is presented as strategies in the sequential game of spatial competition.

All of the above authors were interested in the role of demand in determining the market outcome under imperfectly competitive conditions; but none of them was aware of the role of supply in the process. The first who drew the attention of the profession on this feature is P. Sraffa. As formulated by Samuelson (1968), 'Increasing returns to scale is the prime case of deviations from perfect competition.' Increasing returns lead firms to become large relative to the market demand size, making the price-taking assumption absolutely untenable. Strangely enough, little has been done along the avenue opened by Sraffa's remarks. With the exception of the literature related to limit pricing theory—a good example of which is the famous paper by Modigliani (1958), 'New Developments on the Oligopoly Front'—little attention has been devoted to the role of supply and technological conditions on the market outcome in an imperfectly competitive environment.

The last name on my list is von Neumann. The reason why I feel that he should appear on this list is that he provided the methodological framework in which the basic ideas of economic theorists about cooperation and non-cooperation could be precisely formulated and expanded. What could be a better example of scientific cross-fertilization than the interplay between game theory and economics over the last twenty-five years? This would not have been possible without von Neumann.

A common feature of all the theorists I have listed above is that none of them has ever considered perfect competition as an adequate model of the real world. On the contrary, they took as a postulate that market imperfections and the search for power by economic agents are the rules that govern the market mechanism. Perfect competition, when considered, was viewed only as an ideal version of the functioning of markets, and a reference point to which market outcomes in an imperfect environment could be compared.

This should be contrasted with the developments in general equilibrium theory, as they evolved in the 1950s. These developments were centred entirely around the competitive paradigm, and, with the exception of my colleague R. Triffin (1940), no one thought of mixing general equilibrium and imperfect competition. This was perfectly understandable, since the Walrasian model was built for analysing the interplay of competitive markets, and since important questions such as the existence of a competitive equilibrium and the welfare properties of the competitive equilibrium had not yet been solved completely. What is perhaps more surprising, however, is that the first emergence of game theory into general equilibrium was also oriented entirely towards the competitive paradigm, the basic objective being to study the relationship between the cooperative concept of core and the set of competitive allocations in economies with many agents. This approach culminated in Aumann's equivalence theorem, showing that, in economies with an atomless continuum of traders, these concepts coincide. This is surprising, because game theory was especially tailored for analysing the outcomes of situations with strategically interacting agents, while perfect competition excludes, by definition, such interactions. Nevertheless, the work of Debreu and Scarf (1963), Aumann (1964), and Hildenbrand (1974) about the cooperative concept of core opened the door of general equilibrium to game theory, and Aumann's version of the model spontaneously invited game theory to a variant of it, which had been suggested earlier by Shapley (1961) in a paper entitled 'Values of Large Games: A Corporation with Two Large Stockholders'. This variant proposes a mixed version of the exchange model, including both a competitive sector, represented by an atomless continuum of traders, and a sector consisting of 'significant' traders, represented in the model by atoms. To quote from Aumann:

of course, to the extent that individual consumers or merchants are in fact not anonymous (think of General Motors), the continuous model is inappropriate, and our results do not apply to such a situation. But in that case, perfect competition does not obtain either. In many real markets the competition is indeed far from perfect; such markets are probably best represented by a mixed model, in which some of the traders are points in a continuum, and others are individually significant. (Aumann 1964: 41)

Since a considerable amount of research work was performed in the 1970s around this model, and since I view this work as the first real attempt to integrate imperfect competition into general equilibrium theory, I will spend some time re-examining the main results obtained, and interpretating the mixed model.

First, the results. In exchange situations involving both non-negligible and negligible agents, one should not generally expect equivalence between the core and the set of competitive allocations to hold. For instance, when a collusive agreement is signed between the traders in a non-null subset of an atomless economy, it eliminates all coalitions including a proper subset of this set. As a consequence, the core may be enlarged to those exchange allocations that could have been improved upon otherwise via some of these excluded coalitions, thereby possibly destroying the equivalence of the core and the set of competitive allocations. The first group of results identifies situations in which, in spite of the existence of large traders, the equivalence is not destroyed. This is true in particular when the large traders are similar to each other in terms of preferences and endowments—a result due to Shitovitz (1973)—or when to each such large trader there corresponds a set of small traders that are similar to him—a result due to Gabszewicz and Mertens (1971). These circumstances suggest that, to large traders, competitors similar to them in the economy may well imply the dilution of their market power, a property that is reminiscent of Bertand price competition in a non-cooperative context. But this property is now established in a general equilibrium model. By the equivalence theorem, all core allocations can be decentralized through the competitive price mechanism when the economy is atomless: this is the equivalence result. When there are atoms, this is no longer guaranteed. Does this mean that core allocations can no longer be characterized via *some* price mechanism? Another important result obtained by Shitovitz in the framework of the mixed model is that core allocations can still be supported by a price system that, although not carrying all the properties of a competitive price system, shares with it some interesting features. In particular, at this price system no small trader (in the atomless part) can, with the value of his initial endowment, buy a commodity bundle that he prefers to the bundle obtained at the core allocation. *But this restriction does not apply to atoms.* Accordingly, small traders can be budgetarily exploited at those prices that support a core allocation.

So much for the results. Now I'll comment on the interpretation of the mixed model. What does an atom mean in the exchange model? A proposal was made by Gabszewicz and Drèze (1971) interpreting an atom as a set of traders who have organized a collusive agreement among them. Assume that (T, τ, m) is an atomless measure space where the set T is the set of traders, and τ is the set of possible coalitions of traders. Imagine that, for any reason whatsoever, all traders in some non-null subset A in T decide to act only 'in unison', for instance by delegating to a single decision unit the task of representing their economic interests in the trade. Whenever effective, such a binding agreement definitely prevents the formation of any coalition of traders including a *proper* subset of A: while such coalitions were allowed before the collusive agreement, they are henceforth forbidden. Formally, the σ-field τ no longer represents the class of acceptable coalitions: this class is now reduced to a 'smaller' σ-field, in which the set A constitutes an atom. The actions of the syndicate of traders in A are no longer mathematically negligible.

I must confess that this possible interpretation of an atom has not met with unanimity; and out of fairness, I would like to quote the opinion of Professor Hildenbrand:

From a formal point of view one might also consider a measure space $(A, \mathcal{Q}, \nu)$ with atoms and an atomless part. In terms of the interpretation given earlier, one could consider an atom as a syndicate of traders, that is a group of agents which cannot be split up; either all of them join a coalition or none does so. Note, however, that the mapping ε, and also every allocation f, must be constant on an atom. This means that all agents in the atom must have identical characteristics and must all receive the same bundle in an allocation. This is so special a case that it makes the interpretation of atoms as syndicates of little economic significance.

An alternative approach is to consider an atom as a 'big' agent. In the framework of the model under consideration 'big' can only mean 'big' in terms of endowment. Thus, an atom would be an agent who has infinitely more endowment than any agent in the atomless part. Now the measure $\nu(S)$ has a different interpretation. Formerly it expressed the relative number of agents in the coalition S, here it expresses something like the relative size of the endowment of S. Moreover the allocation $f(a)$ and the preferences $\succ_a$ must be reinterpreted. The net result is far from clear.

No doubt a rigorous interpretation of a model with 'big' and 'small' traders is possible. However, in a model with pure exchange, where there is no production, where all goods have to be consumed, and where there is no accumulation, it is difficult to see the economic content of such an interpretation. (Hildenbrand 1974: 126–7)

Of course, I disagree with Professor Hildenbrand's criticism of the syndicate interpretation of an atom: it is not because one treats a 'special case' that the whole interpretation is 'of little economic significance'. By contrast, I agree with him that the alternative interpretation—considering an atom as a 'big' agent—needs further clarification. I also agree that production should enter into the picture for giving shape to the distinction between a 'big' and 'small' agent. I will come back to this later. In any case, the study of the core in imperfectly competitive economies constitutes the first formal attempt to integrate imperfect competition and general equilibrium, and in this respect could be expected to attain prominence again in the future, for those who are interested in extending 'Mickey Mouse economics' to a true general system of markets.

The above theory was in line with the work of Edgeworth, founded on the idea of cooperating agents. Now, what can be said about non-cooperative theory and general equilibrium? The non-cooperative approach to general equilibrium has developed along two major lines. The first has been defined by Shapley as 'an essay to throw some light into the shadowy transition between "many" and "few"'. This calls for building a model that treats all agents symmetrically and allows them individually to manipulate the price structure. Then it is shown that this possibility vanishes when the number of traders grows indefinitely: the price constellation at the non-cooperative equilibrium approaches the competitive prices because they result from vanishing responsiveness to the traders' buy/sell decisions. The main object of this research is again related to the competitive paradigm: it aims at substituting for the auctioneer who quotes prices a strategic mechanism which would lead to the same competitive prices when agents are sufficiently numerous. It is along this line of research that several recent developments in the non-cooperative theory of exchange were developed (see Shapley 1977; Shapley and Shubik 1977; Dubey and Shubik 1978). But this theory, although of the general equilibrium type, does *not* cover situations of imperfect competition, because all agents are symmetric and because the problem is again related to the competitive paradigm.

The second development of non-cooperative theory in general equilibrium aims at explaining the outcome to be expected in an economy in which there is an inherent asymmetry in the 'market power' of strategic agents: there are 'significant' agents who individually manipulate the price structure, while some anonymous traders possibly behave as price-takers. Gabszewicz and Vial (1972) have written a paper along this line in which strategic agents are firms, while consumers behave as price-takers. Unfortunately, there are some difficulties with this approach, to which I shall return. More recently there has been a revival of interest in this type of model, with, I think, a substantial conceptual progress, to the extent that some of the difficulties met in my paper with Vial have now disappeared. Furthermore, the new equilibrium concept that is proposed also covers situations in which all agents act strategically, while the Gabszewicz–Vial paper assumed the existence of a competitive sector including some agents behaving as price-takers. Formally, the new concept also covers situations of product differentiation, in which some agents can influence several markets simultaneously.

The basic idea is as follows. In a competitive economy each trader comes with his total initial endowment in each good to a central market-place, where the sum of these endowments is supplied for trade. A price vector is announced, which determines the income of each trader as the scalar product of the price vector with the vector of his initial endowment. Then each utility-maximizing competitive trader buys back a bundle of commodities, the value of which does not exceed his income. When a trader perceives that his supply can influence exchange prices—as under imperfect competition—he may prefer to supply one or several markets with only a restricted share of his initial holdings of the corresponding commodity, keeping for later consumption the remaining share. Then this remaining share does not transit through the market and, accordingly, does not influence the market-clearing process. The interest of restricting his supply of one or several goods comes from the fact that the resulting equilibrium prices can give the trader better overall market opportunities than the equilibrium prices that would obtain, should he supply the market with his total initial endowment, as in perfect competition. But the influence of each non-competitive trader on equilibrium prices is only partial; indeed, he may find other non-competitive traders competing with him in the same manner and on the same markets. Accordingly, the equilibrium notion must reflect this complex system of rivalry among the non-competitive traders on the various markets. The non-cooperative equilibrium notion some of us have recently studied does exactly this.

Having made a reasonably full report of the past and present work on general equilibrium theory and imperfect competition, let me now address the future. The first need is to integrate production into the general equilibrium model with imperfect competition. Although there have been some attempts to do this in the theory of the core (the work of Böhm, Sondermann, and others), no satisfactory treatment of production has been given that relates production to the concepts provided by game theory. The whole work I was referring to above was cast into an exchange model, except for the case of my paper with Vial, and this, unfortunately, has revealed two major difficulties in using the usual framework for treating production with strategic firms. First, there may be situations in which the maximization of profits cannot be regarded as a rational decision criterion for the firms that are able to manipulate equilibrium prices. By choosing an output vector so as to maximize the wealth of the firm's owners, the firm may neglect alternative strategies which would yield higher utility levels for its shareholders, a point confirmed in a recent paper with P. Michel (Gabszewicz and Michel 1997). Second, the non-cooperative equilibrium is not invariant with respect to the normalization rule used for defining the absolute prices. An example is provided in my paper with Vial (Gabszewicz and Vial 1972), in which the equilibrium is different when two different normalization rules are used.

How can these difficulties be circumvented? The first one can be logically circumvented if firms are owned by single individuals, simply because one can replace the profit criterion by the owner's utility criterion. Furthermore, this assumption of firms owned by single individuals also solves the second difficulty, because the resulting definition of non-cooperative equilibrium, using utilities as payoffs, no longer depends on the normalization rule used to define absolute prices, as was shown in Gabszewicz and Michel (1997). But this does not really solve the problem, not only because firms are generally not owned by single individuals, but also, and mainly, because of the reason why the difficulty arises in the first place. The goods produced by an oligopolistic firm enter as arguments in the utility functions of its owners. Since the choice of the level of production serves simultaneously as an instrument both in influencing prices via quantities and in meeting the desired level of consumption of these goods by the owners, it is impossible to separate, as under perfect competition, consumption and production decisions via the profit criterion. However, firms do not generally take into account, in their production decisions, the level of consumption of the goods they produce that is desired by their owners. A firm producing toothpaste, even if it is owned by thousands of individuals who brush their teeth every morning and evening, does not choose the quantity of toothpaste to produce by taking into account the owners' desired consumption of toothpaste. The natural model of a firm could however require this, to the extent that private consumption of toothpaste by the owners of the firm influences the relative price of toothpaste. This is clearly absurd, and some device should be found to circumvent this difficulty. But this is not easy, because it opens the door to arbitrariness. This problem of course disappears for a profit-maximizing firm when it takes the price as given; then profit maximization leads to owners' wealth maximization, which in turn implies utility maximization. Hopefully, research in the coming years could lead to satisfactory decision criteria of firms in an imperfect environment.

But this is clearly not the sole problem that is met when production is introduced into the general equilibrium model with an imperfectly competitive environment. In particular, the main deviation from perfect competition comes from the existence of increasing returns to scale. As stated before, the problem has never been seriously tackled in the past. Nevertheless, the paper by Sraffa (1926), which should be re-read carefully by all those who are interested in the field, gives some hints on the way in which this question could be precisely formulated in a general equilibrium model. Hopefully, between now and 2002 someone will propose a solution that will meet with unanimity in the profession.

Beyond the problem of production, there are still many unsolved problems in the framework of the exchange model. The first is the existence of an oligopoly equilibrium. I am referring here to the existence of *pure* strategy equilibria. I am among those who do not give credit to mixed strategy equilibria, which I regard as a clever trick borrowed from mathematicians to create something where something does not exist. Let me say to begin with that there is no hope of proving a general existence theorem for an oligopoly equilibrium. Even in partial equilibrium analysis, there are so many identified and reasonable situations in which no equilibrium in price strategies can exist that the hope of building a general equilibrium model providing the existence of a solution under mild conditions would be presumptuous. Moreover, if a situation leads to the absence of a non-cooperative equilibrium, it should be interpreted as a situation where the players will prefer to coordinate their decisions, rather than to play non-cooperatively. At any rate, a more promising avenue to follow lies in examining the asymptotic behaviour of oligopoly equilibria when the number of oligopolists increases indefinitely. When the sequence of oligopoly equilibria converges to a regular competitive equilibrium, one may find an oligopoly equilibrium in the neighbourhood of this competitive equilibrium. This method was successfully applied by Roberts to my model with Vial (Gabszewicz and Vial 1972). There too, one should expect progress in the coming years for the more recent versions of the model.

Another promising avenue with respect to the same problem of existence lies in applying the recent work of Grandmont on aggregation to imperfectly competitive markets. In a recent paper, he has shown that enough heterogeneity in demand behaviour may lead to a well-behaved aggregate market demand and to revenue for firms that display attractive concavity properties, which, when applied to Cournot partial equilibrium models, imply the existence and uniqueness of an equilibrium. The extension of this approach to the general equilibrium framework could be fruitful in finding sufficient conditions for existence related to the behavioural heterogeneity of agents.

Let me now consider the matter of product differentiation. The problem of product diversity in a given industry clearly calls for further study. In most models of value theory, the list of commodities constitutes a 'primitive' of the model. It turns out, however, that a basic decision of firms in an imperfect market concerns the choice of the product itself, or the line of products, the firm is willing to market. According to Chamberlin (1965), this is even the essence of monopolistic competition, as opposed to pure competition:

under pure competition a producer may, of course, shift from one field of activity to another, but his volume of sales never depends, as under monopolistic competition, upon the product or the variety of products he chooses, for he is always a part of a market in which many others are producing the identical good. Where the possibility of differentiation exists, however, sales depend upon the skill with which the good is distinguished from others and made to appeal to a particular group of buyers. When both prices and 'products' may be varied, complete equilibrium must involve stability with respect to both. (Chamberlin 1965: 71, 72)

The existence of more or less close substitutes to each good plays a crucial role in defining the optimal choice of product variety by the firm. The usual

definition of substitution between commodities, however, relies on price relationships, which makes it useless in analysing the choice of product variety by
firms: prices cannot be pre-existent to the products themselves. To be operational
in describing this choice, an alternative definition of 'proximity' between products is needed. If potential products appear as points in a space of characteristics, substitution between two goods in a given group can be measured in terms
of the differences between the amounts of each attribute they embody.

I think that the introduction of the 'characteristics approach' in general equilibrium is an important challenge for those interested in properly treating the
problem of product differentiation. But this is not an easy task, to the extent that
it implies the existence of a continuum of potential products and, thus, postulates
an infinite-dimensional commodity space. This is another problem to be tackled
as we enter the next millennium.

Finally, as I have stressed above, a major topic in imperfect competition
theory deals with the possibility open to a set of initially negligible economic
agents of moulding themselves into a powerful group decision-making unit. This
is the problem of collusion. We have seen that the beginning of a theory is
available, which deals with this problem in the framework of a mixed model '*à
la* Shitovitz'. However, much remains to be done to transform this starting essay
into a consistent body of analysis. Some particular questions are: how can we
extend the notion of a syndicate when all the participants do not share the same
characteristics? How is it possible to integrate firms in the mixed model? What
is an atom if the members of the syndicates have productive activities? The
answer to such questions could help our understanding of the reasons why
market power does not come as God's gift, but follows from the decisions of the
agents.

REFERENCES

Aumann, R. J. (1964), 'Markets with a Continuum of Traders', *Econometrica*, 32: 39–50.
Chamberlin, E. H. (1965), *The Theory of Monopolistic Competition*, 8th edn. Cambridge,
    Mass.: Harvard University Press.
Debreu, G., and Scarf, H. (1963), 'A Limit Theorem on the Core of an Economy',
    International Economic Review, 4: 235–46.
Dubey, P., and Shubik, M. (1978), 'A Theory of Money and Institutional Institutions',
    28: The Non-cooperative Equilibria of a Closed Trading Economy with Market Supply
    and Bidding Strategies', *Journal of Economic Theory*, 17: 1–20.
Edgeworth, F. Y. (1881), *Mathematical Psychics*. London, Paul Kegan.
Gabszewicz, J. J., and Drèze, J. H. (1971), 'Syndicates of Traders in an Exchange Economy',
    in H. W. Kuhn and G. Szegö (eds.), *Differential Games and Related Topics*. Amster-
    dam: North-Holland.
—— and Mertens, J.-F. (1971), 'An Equivalence Theorem for the Core of an Economy
    whose Atoms Are Not "Too" Big', *Econometrica*, 39: 713–21.

—— and Michel, P. (1997), 'Oligopoly Equilibrium in Exchange Economies', in B. C. Eaton and R. G. Harris (eds.), *Trade, Technology and Economics: Essays in Honour of Richard G. Lipsey.* Cheltenham, Edward Elgar.

Gabszewicz, J. J., and Vial, J.-Ph. (1972), 'Oligopoly "*à la* Cournot" in General Equilibrium Analysis', *Journal of Economic Theory*, 4: 381–400.

Hildenbrand, W. (1974), *Core and Equilibria of a Large Economy.* Princeton, NJ: Princeton University Press.

Hotelling, H. (1929), 'Stability in Competition', *Economic Journal*, 39: 41–57.

Modigliani, F. (1958), 'New Developments on the Oligopoly Front', *Journal of Political Economy*, 66: 215–32.

Samuelson, P. (1968), 'The Monopolistic Competition Revolution', in R. E. Kuenne (ed.), *Monopolistic Competition Theories: Studies in Impact (Essays in Honour of E. H. Chamberlin).* New York: John Wiley, pp. 105–44.

Shapley, L. S. (1961), 'Values of Large Games, III: A Corporation with Two Large Stockholders', *R-M 2650.* Santa Monica, Calif.: Rand Corporation.

—— (1977), 'Non-cooperative General Exchange', in S. A. Lin (ed.), *Theory and Measurement of Economic Externalities.* New York, Academic Press.

—— and Shubik, M. (1977), 'Trade Using One Commodity as a Means of Payment', *Journal of Political Economy*, 85: 937–78.

Shitovitz, B. (1973), 'Oligopoly in Markets with a Continuum of Traders', *Econometrica*, 41: 467–505.

Sraffa, P. (1926), 'The Lax of Returns under Competitive Conditions', *Economic Journal*, 36: 540–92.

Tirole, T. (1988), *The Theory of Industrial Organization.* Cambridge, Mass.: MIT Press.

Triffin, R. (1940), *Monopolistic Competition and General Equilibrium Theory.* Cambridge, Mass.: Harvard University Press.

7

Imperfect Competition and General Equilibrium: Elements for a New Approach

Claude d'Aspremont
Rodolphe Dos Santos Ferreira and
Louis-André Gérard-Varet

7.1. Introduction

When analysing an economy in terms of an equilibrium concept, we look for some consistency, over time and space, resulting from actions taken by the economic agents. Any equilibrium concept can be defined with respect to three general principles.[1] The first principle states how actions taken by individual agents are *coordinated*, and the global feasibility constraints that are satisfied. The second principle, that of *individual rationality*, deals with the internal consistency of individual choices. The third principle, concerning individual *expectations* (*conjectures* or *beliefs*), asserts what consistency is required between the representation of the environment, the plans, and the current actions of individuals.

The pure competitive approach as initiated by Walras (1874), and as incorporated into the Arrow–Debreu model,[2] provides an elegant and integrated treatment of the three principles, which allows us to deal with many different economic issues by relying on assumptions about the individual agents' characteristics. However, the simplicity of the Walrasian analysis is all due to a single behavioural assumption, namely, the hypothesis that *all agents take the price system as given when selecting optimal trades, while conjecturing that their plans will be fulfilled*. This hypothesis, which allows for a transparent notion of individual rationality (trades are individual best replies to the price system), is altogether a postulate on expectations (expectations are rigid) and about some exogenous form of coordination (the auctioneer).

The same methodology has appeared useful to study alternative institutional restrictions, e.g. in the fix-price literature.[3] But what about agents who are not

---

[1] See d'Aspremont *et al.* (1994). Walras can be associated with the first principle, and Cournot and Marshall with the second and the third, respectively.

[2] See Arrow and Debreu (1954); Debreu (1959).

[3] See Bénassy (1982) for a comprehensive treatment of the fix-price literature in that perspective.

price-takers and who realize that their decisions may affect their environment? Following non-cooperative game theory, any theory that predicts or prescribes the behaviour of all agents when there are strategic interactions must designate a Nash equilibrium if it is to be understood by all, and is not to impute irrational behaviour to any participant. As shown by the literature on market games,[4] the Walrasian equilibrium can be formulated as a Nash equilibrium of a properly defined game.[5] However, once the price-taking assumption is discarded, one also wants to allow for strategic agents taking into account the influence of their choices on (part of) the institutional framework of the economy, on the price system, and possibly also on the environments of other participants in the economy. The foundations of an equilibrium concept in terms of coordination, individual rationality, and expectations have to be reconsidered accordingly.

In recent years, many insights have been obtained on strategic behaviour in partial equilibrium models.[6] The problem that we consider here arises because we want to analyse the entire economy. The interdependencies that are the core of general equilibrium now appear not only when considering the parametric adjustments of prices at their equilibrium values at the observer's level, i.e. as a part of a coordination or consistency principle, but also as an individual rationality and planning issue, at the level of agents deciding on the strategies optimal for them.

In general equilibrium, with a multi-market and multi-product economy, complex structures of interactions are present. There are cross-market interactions arising because agents consume not only their own endowments, or their own product, but may also consume on several markets with various degrees of substitutability. There are demand linkages, in that demand for a commodity in a market depends on the incomes generated in other sectors. If all goods are normal, there will be positive spillover effects, with expansion in one sector benefiting other sectors via demand. Quoting Arrow (1986: 207–8), 'From a general equilibrium point of view . . . the demand curve relevant to the monopolist must be understood *mutatis mutandis*, not *ceteris paribus*.' The parameters of the demands that monopolists or oligopolists are facing, such as prices of other commodities, and consumers' incomes, which are ignored in a partial equilibrium approach by appealing to the *ceteris paribus* argument, can no longer be left out. There is actually more, as is observed by Nikaido (1975: 7): 'Demand for goods must be effective demand coming from the incomes earned by agents in the national economy . . . Suppose the maximum monopoly profit is distributed among certain agents. The distributed profit will be spent and will result in the effective demand for goods. Thus, *the demand function may have profit as one of its arguments*.' This circularity between demand, price/quantity decisions, and

---

[4] See e.g. Shapley and Shubik (1977), Schmeidler (1980), Dubey (1982), Simon (1984), Bénassy (1986).

[5] There should be some 'common knowledge of rationality'. In fact, Nash's concept is not the weakest in that respect. For a discussion see ch. 4 (with A. Brandenburger) in Binmore (1990).

[6] See the survey by Tirole (1988).

income (dividends and wage bills), sometimes called 'income feedback effects',[7] raises the question of the general equilibrium foundations of the demand that strategic agents are facing.

The difficulty was already recognized by Cournot (1838), in chapter XI, 'On the Social Income':

So far we have studied how, for each commodity by itself, the law of demand, in connection with the conditions of production of that commodity, determines the price of it and regulates the income of its producers. We considered as given and invariable the prices of other commodities and the income of other producers; but in reality the economic system is a whole of which all the parts are connected and react on each other . . . It seems, therefore, as if, for a complete and rigorous solution of the problems relative to some parts of the economic system, it were indispensable to take the entire system into consideration. But this would surpass the powers of mathematical analysis and of our practical methods of calculations, even if the values of all the constants could be assigned to them numerically . . . (Cournot 1838: 127)

The research programme on imperfect competition in general equilibrium that we consider here is an attempt to deal with the issues raised by Cournot, while staying as close as possible to a Cournotian treatment of market power. As observed by Mas-Colell (1982), 'it cannot be expected that the same level of institutional parsimoniousness as in Walrasian theory can be reached' (p. 183). *The Walrasian principle of coordination among individual actions has to be redefined to integrate a new individual rationality principle and a correspondence between plans and actions allowing for strategic behaviour.* Meanwhile, we have to look for a compromise between assumptions on the primitives—the agents' characteristics—and the models of strategic behaviour, in particular in relation with general equilibrium effects of individual actions through prices and incomes.

In the first part of this chapter we give an overview of the attempts in the literature to take into account market powers through some notion of how a system of markets reacts to strategic behaviour, with the outcomes of the markets as a function of profiles of strategic agents, through some 'market reaction function'. In a perfectly competitive universe, agents need to know only the relevant prices in order to choose an optimal action. When there is imperfect competition, strategic agents are eventually assumed to 'conjecture' (the subjective approach) or to 'know' (the objective approach) a full general equilibrium model of the economy. However, this is requiring heavy informational or computational capabilities from the part of the strategic agents.

In the second part of the chapter we take a different point of view, remaining close to a 'Cournotian approach' of oligopolistic markets. Following the advice of Hart (1985), we give to our general treatment of market powers a 'strong partial equilibrium flavour' and assume, as it is the case for competitive markets, that agents take a large number of variables as given.

---

[7] This is the terminology used by Hart (1985). To recognize Henry Ford's intuition, these phenomena may also be called 'Ford effects': see d'Aspremont *et al.* (1989).

7.2. Price-Making and Market Reaction Functions

Price-making agents do not fit easily with the idea of 'decentralization' which is at the heart of general equilibrium. To discuss that matter, we shall consider an economy in which there is a set $H = \{0, 1, \ldots, h, \ldots, l\}$ of $l+1$ *goods*, a set $I = \{1, \ldots, i, \ldots, m\}$ of *consumers*, and a set $J = \{1, \ldots, j, \ldots, n\}$ of *firms*. Good 0, also called money, will be taken as a *numéraire*. A price *system* is a vector in $\mathbb{R}_+^H$ of the form $p = (1, p_1, \ldots, p_h, \ldots, p_l)$. With each consumer $i \in I$ is associated a consumption set $X_i \subset \mathbb{R}^H$, a vector of initial resources $\omega_i \in X_i$ and a real-valued utility function $U_i(x_i)$ defined on X_i. For each firm $j \in J$ there is a production set $Y_j \subset \mathbb{R}^H$. An *allocation* is a pair (x, y) with x a vector of *consumption plans* in $\times_{i \in I} X_i$ and y a vector of *production plans* in $\times_{j \in J} Y_j$. Feasibility requires: $\sum_{i=1}^{m} (x_i - \omega_i) - \sum_{j=1}^{n} y_j = 0$. The *profit* of firm j at a price system p is written $p y_j = \sum_{h=0}^{l} p_h y_{jh}$. The profit of each firm j is distributed among all consumers according to some given vector of shares $(\theta_{ji})_{i \in I}$, $\theta_{ji} \geq 0$, such that $\sum_{i=1}^{n} \theta_{ji} = 1$. Assumptions on the agents' characteristics will be given later (although standard ones will remain implicit).

When all firms and consumers take all prices as given, and with a complete set of markets, a *Walrasian equilibrium* is a well-defined solution. First, it is a feasible allocation (x^*, y^*) and a price system p^w such that, for all firms $j \in J$, y_j^* maximizes over $y_j \in Y_j$ the profit $p^w y_j$ measured in p^w. Second, for all consumers $i \in I$, x_i^* maximizes $U_i(x_i)$ over the budget set determined by the wealth $W_i(p^w) \overset{\text{def}}{=} p^w \cdot (\omega_i + \sum_{j=1}^{m} \theta_{ji} y_j^*)$. Then, defining

$$\zeta_j(p) \overset{\text{def}}{=} -\arg\max_{y_j \in Y_j} p y_j, \quad \text{and} \quad \zeta_i(p) \overset{\text{def}}{=} \arg\max_{\{x_i \in X_i : p\, x_i \leq W_i(p)\}} U_i(x_i) - \omega_i$$

to be the net demand functions of firm j and consumer i respectively at price p, denoting $A \overset{\text{def}}{=} I \cup J$ as the set of agents (consumers and firms), a Walrasian equilibrium is characterized by prices $p^W \in \mathbb{R}_+^H$ such that

$$\sum_{a \in A} \zeta_a(p^W) = 0. \tag{1}$$

In a Walrasian equilibrium only the relative prices are determined; the normalization of the price system cannot have real effects. There is no loss of generality to take a numeraire. Also, in a Walrasian equilibrium, where it is known that firms maximizing profits at given prices select an efficient outcome, the shareholders, who take the same price system as given when choosing a consumption plan, agree that maximizing profit is a relevant criterium for firms' management. Actually, any production plan of a firm that does not maximize profit makes some shareholder of that firm strictly worse off. Furthermore, the 'value' of a firm is, at a Walrasian equilibrium, identical to the maximum profit it can obtain, and with complete commodity markets there is no need to trade assets in the firms.

To model imperfect competition, we partition $A = I \cup J$ into two groups of agents: a set A^* of *strategic agents*, and a set $\hat{A} = A \backslash A^*$ of *competitive agents*. Competitive agents select their best replies (whether consumption plans or production plans) at given prices in all markets, and behave, as in a Walrasian environment, under the assumption that their plans will be fulfilled. Strategic agents are assumed capable of exercising some monopolistic (possibly monopsonistic) power over certain markets, by choosing strategically a price or a quantity (or both) in those markets. We take as given the set $H_a \subset H$ of markets in which an agent $a \in A^*$ has some monopoly power. Thus, there is a set $H^* = \cup_{a \in A} H_a$ of *strategic goods* and a set $\hat{H} = H \backslash H^*$ of *competitive goods*, with the numeraire always being a competitive good ($0 \in \hat{H}$). We also denote A_h^* the set of agents who are strategic in market $h \in H^*$, so that $A^* = \cup_{h \in H^*} A_h$.

To model strategic agents, we need to consider interactions among these agents, as well as their behaviour in markets outside of their control, and the conjectures with respect to which their plans are designed. An advantage of the 'subjective model' initiated by Negishi (1961) is to stay close to the Walrasian approach of decentralized markets in general equilibrium. Each price-maker is assumed to behave with respect to a 'subjective' perception about how markets react to his actions, i.e. a *subjective demand model* which will be 'correct' at equilibrium, although possibly inconsistent when out of equilibrium. The problem with this approach is that the conjectured market reactions are not determined within the model. The obtain a more 'objective' concept,[8] one has to consider how to relate these conjectures in more detail to the 'true' underlying model. However, as we will see, there is no such thing as a true model independently of how competition is organized and how strategic agents take into account their influence on the price system, or on the actions of other participants in the economy, in particular through expectations about responses to their own actions.

We discuss first the subjective demand model. We then turn towards issues raised in designing an objective demand model, both in the case of a pure exchange economy and in the case of an economy with a productive sector, in order to consider specific difficulties which are related to the foundations of the firm's objectives.

7.2.1. THE SUBJECTIVE DEMAND MODEL

To make the analysis as simple as possible, assume that only firms are price-makers. The set of strategic agents is a subset $A^* \subseteq J$ of the set of firms. Following Negishi (1961), we denote[9] $\tilde{p}_j(y_j, y_j^*, p^*) \in \mathbb{R}_+^H$ the *conjecture* of firm

---

[8] The distinction between the subjective and the objective models has been emphasized by Hart (1985), but was already made by Triffin (1940).

[9] Negishi (1961: 197) credits Bushaw and Clower (1957) for the idea. Triffin (1940) had already suggested tackling imperfect competition in general equilibrium along similar lines. Usually one sticks to monopolistic competition, i.e. $H_i \cap H_j = \varnothing$ with $i \neq j$, ruling out oligopolistic competition and bilateral monopoly. This is not required here, although there may be reasons to exclude bilateral monopolies.

$j \in A^*$ about how markets react to a choice of $y_j \in Y_j$, given that $y_j^* \in Y_j$ and $p^* \in \mathbb{R}_+^H$ are respectively the prevailing net output of the firm and the prevailing price vector. Actually, we could have $\tilde{p}_j$ depending upon supplies and demands elsewhere in the economy at the prevailing prices p^*. We neglect this point here. A conjecture is an 'individual theory' of an agent about how markets, including all feedbacks, would react in response to a change by the agent from y_j^* to y_j. The conjectures are assumed continuous, homogeneous of degree one in p, and satisfying a *consistency* condition,

$$\tilde{p}_j\,(y_j,\,y_j,\,p) = p.$$

If the firms retain the prevailing production plan, then they must conjecture that prices are unchanged. Clearly, it is assumed that in every market there is some 'market price', with different firms charging the same price for the same good, as in a Cournot model. Strategic agents act given these conjectures about how market prices in the economy react to changes in their plans. But this is the main departure from the Walrasian model. For the rest, competitive agents act with rigid expectations. Of course, both the individual rationality and the coordination principles have to be redefined accordingly.

Let us assume that all firms maximize profits, with competitive firms acting as price-takers and strategic firms maximizing conjectured profits. Let the conjectural net supply of firm $j \in A^*$ at prevailing net output y_j^* and price p^* be a production plan $-\tilde{\zeta}_j\,(y_j^*,\,p^*) \in Y_j$ such that

$$\forall y_j \in Y_j, \quad \tilde{p}_j(y_j,\,y_j^*,\,p^*)\,y_j \leq \tilde{p}_j\,[-\tilde{\zeta}_j(y_j^*,\,p^*),\,y_j^*,\,p^*]\,[-\tilde{\zeta}_j\,(y_j^*,\,p^*)].$$

Under standard assumptions on the production sets, and assuming strict quasi-concavity of the conjectural profits with respect to strategic variables, supply functions $-\tilde{\zeta}_j$ of strategic firms are well-defined and continuous. A *conjectural equilibrium* at given conjectures $(\tilde{p}_j)_{j \in A^*}$ is obtained at net output $y^N \in (\mathbb{R}^H)^{A^*}$ and prices $p^N \in \mathbb{R}_+^H$, subject to

$$\forall j \in A^*, \quad y_j^N = -\tilde{\zeta}_j(y_j^N,\,p^N) \quad \text{and}$$

$$\sum_{a \in A\backslash A^*} \zeta_a(p^N) + \sum_{a \in A^*} \tilde{\zeta}_a(y_a^N,\,p^N) = 0, \tag{2}$$

where $\zeta_a(p)$, $a \in A/A^*$, are the competitive net demands. Markets clear at equilibrium, with the values of the market variables conjectured by the strategic agents equal to their equilibrium values. The Walrasian coordination principle is extended to encompass the parametric adjustment, giving the required consistency between conjectured and realized values of market prices for strategic firms. Existence of a conjectural equilibrium is then obtained by classical arguments.

The approach is quite general. It allows for a large number of market structures in a decentralized framework, and appears as a generalization of the competitive model. Actually, price-taking is equivalent to conjecturing perfectly elastic market reactions. Furthermore, relying on a *tâtonnement* with respect to all prices (including conjectured prices) allows for all feedback effects and market interactions among agents. However, the achievement relies on strong assumptions, such as quasi-concavity of conjectural profits. Silvestre (1977*a*) has shown that it is possible to weaken this assumption and to introduce some form of increasing returns.

More fundamentally, the model itself is questionable. It supports an equilibrium at given conjectures, but nothing is said about how these conjectures are generated. The conjectures may sustain some monopoly powers independently of any objective characteristics. An agent, negligible in the economy, may get some rent only because it is (rationally) conjectured that the market is inelastic to his choice. As shown by Gary-Bobo (1989*b*), any feasible allocation in the economy can be supported as a conjectural equilibrium by appropriate conjectures. Moreover, imposing that conjectured prices and market prices coincide only at equilibrium is a weak rationality requirement. Following Hahn (1977) or Silvestre (1977*b*), a stronger condition is that the first derivatives of conjectural and realized market reaction functions coincide at equilibrium. But this requires a model of what are the 'true' or 'objective' market reactions.

Taking firms to be the only strategic agents, we have maintained from competitive analysis the principle that profits are maximized. This criterium, which has well-defined foundations in a Walrasian environment where firms act at given prices, is no longer necessarily consistent with the owners' interests when the firms can influence the price system, or rationally conjecture that they can. A firm is interested in monetary profits and behaves on the basis of prices in absolute values, whereas its shareholders are concerned about what they can get from dividends, and hence about relative prices. To avoid these difficulties, Arrow and Hahn (1971) and Silvestre (1977*b*) have suggested directly introducing the firms' reaction functions, independently of what the specific individual objectives are. This however leads to assumptions or notions far from the primitives.

We shall consider the issues raised by the construction of an objective demand model, first by considering the case of an exchange economy. In a second step a productive sector will be reintroduced to deal with the question of the foundation of the objectives of strategic firms.

7.2.2. THE OBJECTIVE DEMAND MODEL: THE CASE OF AN EXCHANGE ECONOMY

Take a pure exchange economy where some consumers are strategic agents.[10] A possible foundation for an objective model with strategic agents acting on the basis of the 'true' market reaction function is to assume Cournot behaviour, with

---

[10] This can be considered as a particular case of a production economy where each consumer owns a firm ($I = J$) and, for every $i \in I$, the individual production possibility set is $Y_i = \{y_i : 0 \leq y_i \leq \omega_i\}$.

perfect information about the underlying structure of the economy. However, the Cournot story is not that easy to fit into a general equilibrium setup.

Assume that *all* agents in the economy are strategic, acting *à la* Cournot, with the net demands being the individual strategies. At a feasible allocation (the sum of net demands equal to zero), no individual agent can modify his net demand while maintaining market-clearing. Thus, if each strategic agent behaves while accepting market-clearing as an a priori requirement, any feasible allocation will be an equilibrium. A traditional way to circumvent the difficulty is to assume that there is in the economy a competitive sector (i.e. $A \backslash A^* \neq \emptyset$) with the strategic agents selecting their net demands while contemplating how this competitive sector adapts to the resulting change in the price system. This leads to the *Cournot–Walras approach*, first introduced by Gabszewicz and Vial (1972), and recently reconsidered in the case of an exchange economy by Codognato and Gabszewicz (1991) and by Gabszewicz and Michel (1992).

The Cournot–Walras model belongs to a tradition in oligopoly theory, attributed to Cournot (1838), where quantity-setting and price coordination are put forward. Another approach, as considered by Marschak and Selten (1974) or Nikaido (1975) and recently reconsidered by Bénassy (1988), more in the tradition of Edgeworth and Chamberlin, stresses prices as strategic variables in a monopolistic competitive environment. Quantities now have to be adjusted to prices, in order to define an 'effective demand'. The *monopolistic competition* approach shares with the Cournot–Walras some common methodological features. The two approaches introduce two coordination mechanisms, one for competitive agents and another for strategic agents, both interrelated through a two-stage procedure. At the first stage strategic agents act (through prices or quantities), while at the second stage market variables adjust competitively to clear the markets (possibly with rationing). With the market-clearing values at the second stage being uniquely defined, there is a mapping from stategies to market outcomes which is the 'objective market reaction function' on which first-stage strategic choices are based. For the first stage, the solution concept is a Nash equilibrium, with strategic agents planning on the basis of 'rational conjectures' with respect to the competitive part of the economy (at the second stage) and on the basis of Nash conjectures with respect to their competitors (at the first stage).

Let $A^* \subset I$ be the set of strategic agents and for every $i \in A^*$, $Q_i \subset R^H$ be the set of admissible vectors signalling the quantities of each good h in H_i that the agent i wants to offer ($q_{ih} > 0$) or to bid for ($q_{ih} < 0$) in the markets where he has some monopoly power (q_{ih} is restricted to be zero for $h \in H \backslash H_i$). For every vector $q_i \in Q_i$ and every consumer $i \in I$ there is, associated with any $p \in \mathbb{R}_+^H \backslash \{0\}$, a *net demand*:

$$\zeta_i(p, q_i) + \omega_i \stackrel{\text{def}}{=} \arg \max \ \{U_i(x_i) : x_i \in X_i,\ px_i \leq p\omega_i \text{ and}$$
$$\forall h \in H,\ q_{ih}(\omega_{ih} - q_{ih} - x_{ih}) \leq 0\}.$$

For a competitive agent $i \in \hat{A} = I \backslash A^*$, $\zeta_i(p, o)$ is simply identified to the competitive net demand $\zeta_i(p)$. Codognato and Gabszewicz (1991) and Gabszewicz and Michel (1992) do not allow for negative quantity signals. We introduce them for the sake of symmetry and also to emphasize the 'signalling' aspect of such strategic variables, in contrast to some kind of 'endowment with holding' aspect. The following assumption is needed.

ASSUMPTION 1. For all $q \in Q = \times_{i \in A^*} Q_i$, there is a unique price system $\tilde{p}(q) \in \mathbb{R}_+^H$ such that $\sum_{i \in I} \zeta_i(\tilde{p}(q), q_i) = 0$; i.e., $\tilde{p}(q)$ (uniquely) clears the markets given the vector of quantity signals.

A *Cournot–Walras equilibrium* is a pair of prices and quantities (p^{cw}, q^{cw}) in $\mathbb{R}_+^H \times Q$ such that

$$p^{cw} = \tilde{p}(q^{cw}) \text{ and } \forall i \in A^*, \quad q_i^{cw} \in \arg\max_{q_i \in Q_i} U_i \{\zeta_i[\tilde{p}(q_i, q_{-1}^{cw}), q_i] + \omega_i\},$$

where $q_{-i}^{cw} = (q_j^{cw})_{j \in A^* \setminus (i)}$. In other words, once all the functions ζ_i are well-defined and Assumption 1 holds, solving the second stage, the Cournot–Walras quantity q^{cw} is a Nash equilibrium of the first-stage game with players in $A^* \subset I$, strategies in Q, and payoffs given by $\{U_i [\zeta_i(\tilde{p}(q), q_i] + \omega_i\}_{i \in A^*}$. In the special case $H_i = \varnothing$ for all consumers i, the first stage degenerates, each net demand $\zeta_i(p, o)$ coincides with the competitive net demand $\zeta_i(p)$, and the Cournot–Walras equilibrium reduces to the Walras equilibrium.

Monopolistic competition arises when no two strategic agents control the price of the same good, i.e. when $H_i \cap H_j = \varnothing$ for all $i, j \in A^*$, $i \neq j$. Following Marschak and Selten (1974) and Nikaido (1975), one considers now a game where at the first stage each strategic agent $i \in A^*$ (unilaterally) chooses the prices that he controls while taking as given other monopolistic prices and anticipating the resulting quantities and the competitive prices which adjust to clear the markets. More precisely, we make the following assumption.

ASSUMPTION 2. For all p_{H^*} in some admissible subset $\mathcal{P}$ of $\mathbb{R}_+^{H^*}$, there is a unique vector of competitive prices $\hat{p}(p_{H^*}) \in \mathbb{R}_+^{\hat{H}}$ and a unique vector of quantities $\hat{q}(p_{H^*}) \in Q$ (with $q_{ih} \neq 0$ for $h \in H_i$) such that all markets clear: $\sum_{i \in I} \zeta_i[p_{H^*}, \hat{p}(p_{H^*}), \hat{q}_i(p_{H^*})] = 0$, and such that the constraints defining ζ are all binding.

Assumption 2 guarantees a (unique) solution to the problem of existence of an effective demand. A *monopolistic competition equilibrium* is a pair of prices and quantities (p^{MC}, q^{MC}), in $\mathbb{R}_+^H \times Q$ such that

$$q^{MC} = \hat{q}(p_{H^*}^{MC});$$

$$\forall h \in \hat{H}, \, p_h^{MC} = \hat{p}_h(p_{H^*}^{MC}); \text{ and}$$

$$\forall i \in A^*, \, p_i^{MC} \in \arg\max \, U_i \{\zeta_i[p_i, p_{-i}^{MC}, \hat{p}(p_i, p_{-i}^{MC}), \hat{q}_i(p_i, p_{-i}^{MC})] + \omega_i\}$$

with $p_i \in \mathbb{R}_+^H$, subject to $(p_i, p_{-i}^{MC}) \in \mathcal{P}$.

Once all the functions ζ_i are well-defined and Assumption 2 holds solving the second stage, the monopolistic competition equilibrium price vector p^{MC} is a (generalized) Nash equilibrium of the first-stage game with players $A^* \subset I$, strategies in $\mathscr{P}$ and payoffs given by

$$\{U_i[\zeta_i(p_{H^*}, \hat{p}(p_{H^*}), \hat{q}_i(p_{H^*})) + \omega_i]\}_{i \in A^*}.$$

For both concepts, the first stage non-cooperative game is designed with respect to a market reaction function, $\tilde{p}$ for Cournot–Walras and $(\hat{p}, \hat{q})$ for a monopolistic competition equilibrium. This is very much like a 'strategic market game', where a 'strategic outcome function', which represents the decentralized functioning of all markets, determines the transactions and trading prices of all agents in every market (under mutual consistency). Actually, the market reaction function which solves the second stage depends here upon the characteristics of the economy. This gives a 'context-dependent' market game.

The major advantage of an objective approach is to remove the arbitrariness of the conjectural equilibrium concept. However, there are serious drawbacks. To derive the functions $\tilde{p}$ and $(\hat{p}, \hat{q})$, Assumptions 1 and 2 are required to obtain the existence and uniqueness of second-stage market vectors. In the absence of uniqueness at the second stage, one would need a 'selection mechanism', reintroducing some arbitrariness. Also, for both concepts, existence requires properties of the market reaction functions themselves, far from the agents' characteristics.

The two concepts of Cournot–Walras and monopolistic competition equilibrium, although one has to do with quantities and the other prices, are not dual. In a monopolistic competition equilibrium, there are individual quantities determined at the second stage to clear the markets, together with competitive prices, given first-stage strategic prices. These quantities may not coincide with the optimal choices of the strategic agents, meaning either that some rationing must occur or else that the voluntary exchange principle is violated. This motivates the revised notion of equilibrium with price-makers introduced by Bénassy (1988), where the second stage is a fix-price equilibrium.[11] It gives a 'true' objective demand model for competition by prices in general equilibrium which comes close to being the dual of Cournot–Walras. Another advantage of the concept, as advocated by Bénassy (1988), is that global uniqueness of the fix-price equilibrium is obtained under nice conditions, namely that changes in quantity constraints 'spill over' into the other markets by less than 100 per cent in value terms.[12]

7.2.3. THE PRODUCTIVE SECTOR AND THE OBJECTIVES OF THE FIRMS

Let us reintroduce a (non-trivial) productive sector $\{Y_j : j \in J\}$ allowing firms to be strategic agents. Assume for simplicity, for the Cournot–Walras case, that the

---

[11] Stahn (1996) takes a different viewpoint, closer to that of Nikaido (1975).

[12] These conditions however are not sufficient to ensure uniqueness in economies with production; see Stahn (1996).

set of firms is the set of strategic agents,[13] i.e. $A^* = J$, each being strategic on all (non-money) markets, i.e. $\forall j \in J$, $H_j = H^*$. With any allocation $y \in Y = \times_{j \in J} Y_j$ is associated, for every consumer $i \in I$, a modified initial endowment:

$$\tilde{\omega}_i(y) = \omega_i + \sum_{j \in J} \theta_{ji} y_j. \tag{3}$$

When firm j thinks over the production plan y_j, it considers the price system emerging in the pure exchange economy defined by the consumers, each endowed with these initial resources (3), assuming that the other firms have chosen y_{-j}. Let $\mathcal{W}(y)$ be the set of Walrasian equilibrium prices in the pure exchange economy defined with respect to the modified endowments (3). In the spirit of Assumption 1, we assume that there exists[14] a selection $\tilde{p} \in \mathcal{W}$. A Cournot–Walras equilibrium for the productive economy is now a pair (p^{cw}, y^{cw}) in $\mathbb{R}_+^H \times Y$ such that

$$p^{cw} = \tilde{p}(y^{cw}) \quad \text{and} \quad \forall j \in J, \; y_j^{cw} \in \arg \max_{y_j \in Y_j} \tilde{p}(y_j, y_{-j}^{cw}) y_j.$$

It is a Nash equilibrium of a game where firms maximize profits, after having imagined the consequences of their choices through $\tilde{p} \in \mathcal{W}$.

When markets are competitive and complete, and shareholders are utility maximizers, firms take the price system as given and may be assumed to maximize profits consistently. That profit maximization may still be a plausible concept under market power is largely accepted in the literature. Tirole (1988), for example, considers profit maximization as a good proxy for utility maximization, even in a general equilibrium context. The position can be justified by the idea that revenue accruing via profits is what shareholders mostly take into account, and that adverse price effects are negligible. However, the paper by Gabszewicz and Vial (1972) has shown that, without specific assumptions, such price effects may matter.

In the literature, another possibility has been considered. Shareholders maximize the utility that they derive from trades. When there is only one shareholder in each firm, a natural objective for the firm is to maximize the indirect utility of its owner. The equilibrium is well defined (and independent of its normalization). There is also the case of many shareholders, all with the same homogeneous utility function, or with the same utility function and the same property rights. This has been recognized in the case of Cournot–Walras (e.g. Dierker and Grodal 1986), but less so in the case of price-setting under monopolistic competition (as the example in Böhm 1994 seems to imply). Moreover, when there are different shareholders (for instance with the same non-homogeneous utility

---

[13] This is the original situation contemplated by Gabszewicz and Vial (1972). Allowing for a competitive productive sector is an easy extension; see Fitzroy (1974).

[14] Notice that if $\mathcal{W}(y) \neq \emptyset$ there are in general finitely many price vectors. Only in very special cases will there be a unique price vector in $\mathcal{W}(y)$; see Debreu (1970).

function, but different shares), a coordination problem among shareholders appears[15] (Dierker and Grodal 1986, 1994; Ventura 1994).

However, there are circumstances in which the shareholders can agree upon profit maximization as the appropriate objective of the firm. This is the case when the firms produced commodities, and, more fundamentally, when the prices of the consumed goods are independent of the firms' strategic behaviour. This is what is assumed in the 'island model' of Hart (1982). Still, a problem remains, linked to the choice of normalization.

We have assumed that prices are normalized by using the first commodity as numeraire. Under perfect competition it does not matter how prices are normalized. This is no longer the case here: changing the numeraire may have real effects. The reason is rather intuitive: changing the numeraire fundamentally modifies the objective of a non-competitive firm. Indeed, a normalization rule may be written as a positive real-valued function, $v(p)$, modifying the market-reaction function to $v(\tilde{p}(y))$ and the objectives of the firms accordingly. Examples of such modifications can be found in Dierker and Grodal (1986) and Ginsburgh (1994) following Gabszewicz and Vial (1972). There is even an indeterminacy property (see Grodal 1992 in the case of Cournot–Walras, and Böhm 1990 in that of a monopoly): under imperfect competition almost all production choices by strategic firms, whether efficient or not, can be rationalized just by changing the normalization.

The dependence on the normalization rule may also have an impact at the limit, when the economy is replicated. K. Roberts (1980) has analysed the limits of Cournot–Walras equilibria, when each firm becomes small compared with the rest of the economy.[16] He shows that (for some $\tilde{p}$) the limits of Cournot–Walras equilibria satisfying a regularity property are the set of Walras equilibria, and therefore independent of normalization. However, there might be limits of Cournot–Walras equilibria that are not Walras equilibria, depending upon the normalization rule (see Grodal 1992).

In Cornwall (1977) it was also made clear that not only equilibrium outcomes, but the very existence of equilibria, might depend on the normalization. There are well-known examples by J. Roberts and Sonnenschein (1977) showing that there may not exist an equilibrium (in pure strategies) because the firms' profit functions (the normalization being given together with $\tilde{p}$) may not be quasi-concave. Dierker and Grodal (1986) go one step further, considering a situation where the (upper semi-continuous) Walrasian price correspondence does not allow for a continuous selection. They further give an example where, for some market reaction function $\tilde{p}$ and for some normalization, there does not exist an equilibrium, even in 'mixed' strategies. Existence of a pure strategy equilibrium in ensured for other normalizations.

---

[15] Ventura (1994) suggests relying on a well-known criterion by Drèze (1974) for decisions under incompleteness of markets.

[16] The sequence of economies is generated when the original economy is replicated r times, with $r \to \infty$, looking at corresponding sequences of average production plans for each type of firm.

As stressed by Dierker and Grodal, 'the reason why equilibrium allocations depend on the normalization rule is that profit functions based on different price normalizations are objectives that are generally not related to each other by monotone transformations' (1994: 2). The results show that it does not make sense for the firms to maximize profit with respect to an arbitrary normalization rule. In the set of all possible normalization rules, some have to be considered as not admissible, since they modify the balance of power among producers. One way to implement this conclusion is to have several competitive markets in which prices cannot be (consciously) affected by strategic behaviour, and to restrict normalization rules to those prices. Except in special cases, this is not possible in either the Cournot–Walras or the monopolistic competition approach, since each of these assumes that strategic agents are conscious of their influence on all markets (see Assumptions 1 and 2, respectively), except possibly for one numeraire good. The semi-competitive approach of the next section explicitly introduces such a possibility.

7.3. An Alternative Cournotian Approach: a Semi-Competitive Model

There are different possible routes to solving the difficulties faced when one wants to integrate imperfect competition in general equilibrium, while staying as close as possible to the primitive description of the economy. If one sticks to a model where there are strategic agents making first-stage calculations with respect to a competitive market system which clears at the second stage, one route is to introduce more structure on the demand side of the economy. Recent works on aggregation allow some optimism in this direction (see e.g. Grandmont 1993). Another route is to weaken the first-stage equilibrium, for instance by considering a 'local Nash equilibrium', which is a configuration of strategies at which the first-order conditions for payoff maximization are satisfied simultaneously and all strategic agents are at a local (if not global) maximum of their 'true' payoffs.[17] This, essentially, represents a compromise between a 'subjective' and an 'objective' approach.

A motivation to introduce local Nash equilibria is that, 'at any given status quo', each strategic agent 'knows only the linear approximation of its demand curve and believes it to be the demand curve it faces' (Bonanno and Zeeman 1985: 277). A 'local consistency property' then requires that at equilibrium not only do conjectural and true demand coincide, but also, the slopes of the two demands are equal. However, Gary-Bobo (1987) has shown that, under usual sufficient conditions on the demand side (leading to strong quasi-concavity of the payoff functions with respect to strategic variables), as soon as the above first-order rationality conditions are imposed on the conjectural market reaction functions, the conjectural equilibria have to coincide with the Cournot–Walras equilibria. Hence, the difficulties mentioned above remain.

---

[17] See Silvestre (1977a), Bonanno and Zeeman (1985), Gary-Bobo (1987, 1989a, b). Bonanno (1990) discusses the literature along these lines.

We take a third route, which consists in looking for an objective model by modifying the whole structure of the model. Notice first that a fully objective model would be meaningless. It would have strategic agents sharing one, and only one, 'true' theory about how markets react to their own behaviour. Any such individual theory has to specify all other agents' theories, and it has to consider how the 'real outcome' varies with these individual theories. The difficulty actually is shared with any 'rational expectation' approach (see d'Aspremont *et al.* 1994).

In the proposed framework, a non-cooperative Nash behaviour remains the individual rationality principle for strategic agents, although enlarged to allow these agents to act on prices and quantities altogether. On the other hand, the expectation principle is weakened by assuming that strategic agents make their plans not with respect to the whole economy, but only with respect to the part of the economy where their market powers are 'significant'. The coordination principle is adapted accordingly: markets clear only at equilibrium, and there are feasibility requirements to be satisfied for variables out of equilibrium.

The concept that we propose relies on a reinterpretation of Cournotian oligopolistic competition. A Cournot equilibrium may be seen as the outcome of coordinated optimal decisions of monopolists, facing some (imperfectly elastic) 'residual' demand in their sector but taking, as in the competitive model, the prices of all other sectors as given (thus neglecting the impact of their decisions outside their own sector).[18] The Cournot model for homogeneous goods is usually viewed as a model of quantity competition only. To formalize this conclusion, we introduce a concept of 'pricing scheme' to represent the coordination pricing decisions reached in an industry, which remains implicit in the use of the inverse demand function in Cournot's traditional approach.

The concept of pricing schemes is introduced first in the case of an industry for a homogeneous product (in Section 7.3.1), then extended (in Section 7.3.2) to a general equilibrium framework. This leads to a notion of equilibrium based on interrelated monopoly problems, which avoids assuming that the strategic agents are able to carry over in their computation the inversion of a complete demand system, with all cross-sectoral effects taken into account.

The proposed Cournotian model is an alternative to the Cournot–Walras approach and to the monopolistic competition approach, both of which require that strategic agents face a market function obtained by solving a whole market system. This model also incorporates suggestions by Marshak and Selten (1974) or Hart (1982, 1985), to have strategic agents take other agents incomes as independent of their own decisions, thus ignoring income feedback effects (or 'Ford effects'), and suggestions by Laffont and Laroque (1976) and Hart (1982) to have these strategic agents behave competitively in the markets where their market power is negligible. It is a 'semi-competitive' model. This leaves open the issue of the existence (and uniqueness) of market-clearing values of the

---

[18] See d'Aspremont *et al.* (1991*a*, *b*, 1995).

relevant variables. We actually require market-clearing at equilibrium only, keeping the market reaction functions closely related to the primitives of the economy (preferences, endowments, technologies). The conclusions are also usefully compared (in Section 7.3.3) to those derived from a strategic market game approach, which provides an alternative description of how decentralized market mechanisms determine transactions and trading prices of agents in every market on the basis of individual quantity and price signals.

7.3.1. P-EQUILIBRIUM: AN INTRODUCTION

Let us consider a market for a single homogeneous good where a set $J = \{1, \ldots, j, \ldots, n\}$ of firms face a real-valued demand function $\phi: \mathbb{R}_+ \to \mathbb{R}_+$. There is a well-defined and non-trivial inverse demand function $\phi^{-1}: \mathbb{R}_+ \to \mathbb{R}_+$. Each individual firm $j \in J$ can produce any quantity $y_j \geq 0$ at a non-negative cost $C_j(y_j)$. As is well-known, a *Cournot equilibrium* is a vector $y^C \in \mathbb{R}_+^n$ where, for every $j \in J$, $y_j^C \in \arg\max_{y_j \geq 0} \{y_j \, \phi^{-1}(\sum_{k \neq j} y_k^C + y_j) - C_j(y_j)\}$. However, we do not stick to that notion and consider that individual firms also choose strategically price signals $\psi_j \geq 0$. There is in the market a coordination device, or *pricing scheme*, denoted P, which associates with each vector $\psi = (\psi_1, \ldots, \psi_j, \ldots, \psi_n)$ of price signals a single market price $p = P(\psi)$. (We assume that $P = \mathbb{R}_+^n \to \mathbb{R}_+$ is non-decreasing.) Given a pricing scheme P, a demand function ϕ, and individual cost functions $(C_j)_{j \in J}$, we have a (generalised) game with the strategies of firms $j \in J$ being pairs $(y_j, \psi_j) \in \mathbb{R}_+^2$. Following d'Aspremont *et al.* (1991*a*), an equilibrium with respect to P, or *P-equilibrium*, is a vector $(y^*, \psi^*) \in \mathbb{R}_+^{2n}$ of quantities and price signals which are such that $\sum_{j \in J} y_j^* = \phi(P(\psi^*))$ and where, for every $j \in J$,

$$(y_j^*, \psi_j^*) \in \arg\max \{y_j \, P(\psi_j, \psi_{-j}^*) - C_j(y_j) : (y_j, \psi_j) \in \mathbb{R}_+^2,$$

$$y_j \leq \phi\,[P(\psi_j, \psi_{-j}^*)] - \sum_{k \neq j} y_k^*\}.$$

The notion of a pricing scheme P captures part of the coordination device which is usually incorporated into the inverse demand ϕ^{-1}. However, pricing schemes may vary according to the degree of 'manipulability' of the market price by each individual firm. A pricing scheme P which has full range (i.e. $P(\mathbb{R}_+^n) = \mathbb{R}_+$) and is strictly increasing in each variable ψ_j is *unilaterally manipulable*: that is, all firms together exercise complete control over the market price, and each individual firm has local control on that price. Actually (d'Aspremont *et al.* 1991*a*, proposition 1), if P is unilaterally manipulable and if the Cournotian profit function $(y_j \, \phi^{-1}(\sum_k y_k) - C_j(y_j))$ is strictly quasi-concave in y_j, then, given a pair $(y^*, \psi^*) \in \mathbb{R}_+^{2n}$ subject to $P(\psi^*) = \phi^{-1}(\sum_k y_k^*)$, the pair (y^*, ψ^*) is a *P*-equilibrium *if and only if* y^* is a Cournot equilibrium. The assumption of a strictly quasi-concave Cournotian profit function can be omitted if the condition on the pricing scheme is reinforced to require *full individual manipulability*, meaning that each firm $j \in J$ has complete control over the market price (i.e., at every ψ_{-j}, $P(\cdot, \psi_{-j})$ has full range). In any case, a strategic firm always saturates its residual demand. A *P*-equilibrium under that condition, or a Cournot equilibrium, can be characterized as a vector of quantities y^* and a market price $p^* = P(\psi^*)$ such that each oligopolist $j \in J$, acting as a monopolist on the residual demand $(\phi(p) - \sum_{k \neq j} y_k^*)$, selects the market price p^*.

Clearly, this is assuming very much manipulability on the part of the individual agents. As a matter of fact, there are examples of coordination devices documented by the literature on industrial organization, the so-called 'facilitating practices', or conventional norms of conduct among competitors, which lead to a market price above its competitive level. Public announcements of price changes with or without price leadership, and contractual clauses such as the 'meet-or-release' clause or the 'most-favoured-customer' clause are among these devices which allow competitors to coordinate their pricing behaviour. In particular, the combination of the two last clauses leads, under perfect information, to a specific pricing scheme: the market price is established, from the sellers' point of view, at the minimum of all individual price signals;[19] i.e., $P^{min}(\psi) = \min \{\psi_j; \; j \in N\}$. Clearly, such a pricing scheme has a full range, but is not strictly increasing with respect to individual price signals, and *a fortiori* is not fully individually manipulable.

The duopoly example represented by Fig. 7.1, with a linear demand and the same increasing strictly convex cost function for the two firms, illustrates a situation where, for the P^{min} pricing scheme, there is a continuum of symmetric

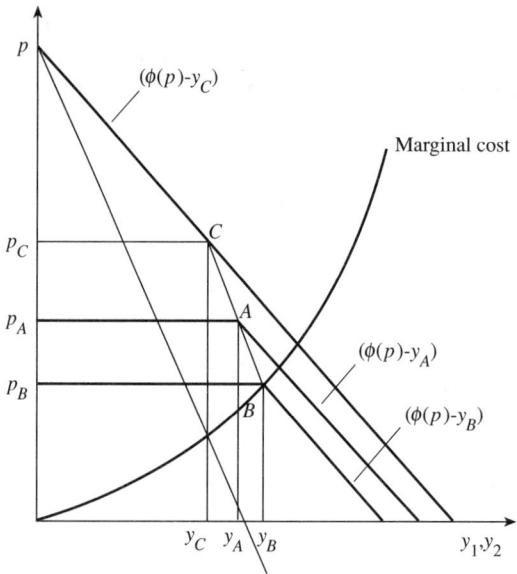

Fig. 7.1. Symmetric equilibria

equilibria, namely the segment BC. At point C we have a Cournot equilibrium, which can be characterized as a situation where at equilibrium the two firms 'fully exploit' the monopoly power on their residual demand. But there are other (symmetric) equilibria[20] where each firm produces as much as possible considering the residual demand, as long as the marginal revenue (which is discontinuous) is above the marginal cost. Each firm would prefer to increase the price, but cannot individually do so. It is as if the firms were facing 'kinked' demand curves. In particular, point B corresponds to a Bertrand equilibrium where the market price is at the marginal cost, and the two firms can be price-takers only with respect to the equilibrium price.

7.3.2. AN APPROACH TO GENERAL EQUILIBRIUM

Let us go back to general equilibrium. We allow for production with firms maximizing profits measured in the numeraire good, which is a competitive good. We also keep a strong partial equilibrium flavour by restricting market powers to a sector-by-sector formulation. Price formation is modelled as in partial equilibrium: in each 'sector', corresponding to a set of commodities, there is for each good a pricing scheme associating with any vector of individual price signals a common market price. Meanwhile transacted quantities are specified in Cournot's way, by computing for each market its residual demand. We also assume that the distribution of profits, or the vector of dividends, is considered as given by the producers and solved for the true distribution at equilibrium.[21]

A *sector* is a set of markets for which a number of agents realize their strategic interdependence and coordinate their decisions by sending price signals.[22] The set of markets H is partitioned into a set of sectors $\{S^0, S^1, \ldots, S^T\}$, where $S^0 = \hat{H}$ is the set of competitive goods. Associated with every monopolistic sector S^t, $t \geq 1$, is the set $A^t = U_{h \in S^t} A_h$ of strategic agents active in the sector. Each agent $a \in A^t$ sends a vector of price signals ψ_a^t chosen in some admissible set Ψ_a^t, and the pricing scheme P_h determines the market price $P_h(\psi^t)$, with $\psi^t \in \Psi^t = \times_{a \in A^t} \psi_a^t$. In other terms, the market price of each good $h \in S^t$ may be affected by the price signals of all the agents involved in the sector. Notice that the number of price signals per agent can actually be smaller than the cardinal of S^t. An example is when a single price signal affects the market prices of several goods similar but differentiated by some characteristic, such as its selling location, its packaging, its intrinsic quality. For commodity of notation, $P(\psi)$ denotes the vector of prices for all markets in H^*, with $\psi \in \Psi = \times_{t \geq 1} \Psi^t$.

---

[20] There are also asymmetric equilibria (see d'Aspremont *et al.* 1991*a*).

[21] We follow, in that respect, Marschak and Selten (1974). Actually, Marschak and Selten and Nikaido (1975) have also considered the case where dividends are strategic variables in the hands of monopolistic firms.

[22] One could also use the terminology, used in the industrial organization literature for antitrust purposes, of 'relevant market' (see Willig 1991).

Let us recall that, for every strategic agent $a \in A^*$, Q_a is the subset in $\mathbb{R}^H$ of admissible quantity signals: a quantity q_{ah} represents the quantity of good h that agent $a \in A^*$ is ready to offer $(q_{ah} > 0)$ or bid for $(q_{ah} < 0)$ in a market $h \in H_a$ where he is strategic. In the markets in which agent a is competitive, $q_{ah} = 0$. We denote $Q = \times_{a \in A^*} Q_a$.

Let $\pi_a \in \mathbb{R}_+$ be the total profits accruing to consumer $a \in I$, and $\pi \in \mathbb{R}_+^I$ be the vector of total profits going to all consumers. A pricing scheme P_h being fixed for every market $h \in H^*$, we may again define, for every agent $a \in A$, a net demand function $\zeta_a(p, q_a, \pi_a)$ conditional on $q_a \in Q_a$ and $p \in \mathbb{R}_+^H$, where, for every $h \in H^*$, $p_h = P_h(\psi_h)$. For a consumer $a \in I \subset A$, ζ_a is taken to satisfy

$$\zeta_a(p, q_a, \pi_a) = \arg \max \{ U_a(x_a) : x_a \in X_a, \, p(x_a - \omega_a) \le \pi_a, \text{ and}$$
$$\forall h \in H, \quad q_{ah}(\omega_{ah} - x_{ah} - q_{ah}) \le 0 \}.$$

The net demand function of a producer $a \in J \subset A$ is a function $\zeta_a(p, q_a, \pi_a) = \zeta_a(p, q_a)$ of prices and quantity signals only, which is determined by

$$\zeta_a(p, q_a) = -\arg \max \{ p \, y_a : y_a \in Y_a, \text{ and } \forall h \in H, \, q_{ah}(q_{ah} - y_{ah}) \le 0 \}.$$

A *P-equilibrium* (with *parametric dividends*) is a vector of prices, quantity signals, and dividends (p^*, q^*, π^*), with $p^* \in \mathbb{R}_+^H$, $q^* \in Q$, $\pi^* \in \mathbb{R}_+^I$, and, for every h in every monopolistic sector S^t, $p_h^* = P_h(\psi^{t*})$ for some $\psi^{t*} \in \Psi^t$, satisfying:

$\forall a \in A^*$, if $a \in I$,
$$U_a(\zeta_a(p^*, q_a^*, \pi_a^*) + \omega_a) \ge U_a(\zeta_a(P(\psi_a, \psi_{-a}^*), \hat{p}^*, q_a, \pi_a^*) + \omega_a)$$

(resp. if $a \in J$,
$$-p^*\zeta_a(p^*, q_a^*) \ge -(P(\psi_a, \psi_{-a}^*), \hat{p}^*)\zeta_a(P(\psi_a, \psi_{-a}^*), \hat{p}^*, q_a)), \qquad (4)$$

subject to

$$\forall h \in H^*, \quad \zeta_{ah}(P(\psi_a, \psi_{-a}^*), \hat{p}^*, q_a^*, \pi_a^*) \times \qquad\qquad\qquad (4')$$

$$[\zeta_{ah}(P(\psi_a, \psi_{-a}^*), \hat{p}^*, q_a, \pi_a^*) + \sum_{\alpha \ne a} \zeta_{\alpha h}(P(\psi_a, \psi_{-a}^*), \hat{p}^*, q_\alpha^*, \pi_\alpha^*)] \le 0.$$

with $\psi_a \in \Psi_a = \times_{t \ge 1} \Psi^t$ $q_a \in Q_a$, and

$$\sum_{a \in A} \zeta_a(p^*, q_a^*, \pi_a^*) = 0, \qquad\qquad\qquad (5)$$

$$\forall a \in I, \quad \pi_a^* = -\sum_{j \in J} \theta_{ja}(p^* \zeta_j(p^*, q_j^*)). \qquad\qquad\qquad (6)$$

Condition (4) requires each strategic agent a to maximize his utility (or profit) by manipulating the prices p_{ah} in the sectors where he is active ($h \in S^t$, for any t such that $a \in A_t$), sending quantity signals q_{ah} for the goods he controls ($h \in H_a$) and taking as given prices in other sectors and quantity signals of other agents. This is a generalization of Cournot's concept. Actually, (4′) are constraints on this strategic behaviour: in the markets in which an agent is strategic, the deviations are allowed only on the short (non-rationed) side. The deviating agent's net demand should have an opposite sign to, and be bounded by, the resulting total net demand by the others. This is a feasibility restriction, although not a market-clearing condition. Condition (5) goes further, by requiring market-clearing in all markets at equilibrium. Condition (6) simply says that the equilibrium profit distribution should be the true one.

To define a *P*-equilibrium, we do not need to assume the existence and uniqueness of some market-clearing configuration of market variables at the second stage of a sequential procedure. However, the equilibrium notion does rely on some pricing scheme, in fact on some class of pricing schemes, according to the degree of manipulability of particular market prices they confer to strategic agents. Assume that, for every monopolistic sector S^t and every $h \in S^t$, the pricing scheme P_h is fully individually manipulable (for any a and ψ_{-a}^t, $P_h(\cdot, \psi_{-a}^t)_{h \in S^t}$ has full range). Each strategic agent has then has a complete control on the market prices $h \in S^t$, so that it is equivalent to choose pure price signals or to choose directly the prices themselves. In that case a *P*-equilibrium reduces to an equilibrium where each strategic agent can be seen as a monopolist optimizing against a 'residual' demand so that, at equilibrium, any two agents who control the price of the same good optimally choose the same value. The equilibrium concept can be defined without explicit reference to a particular mechanism.[23]

Actually, a *P*-equilibrium is relative not only to the kind of pricing scheme, but also to the underlying sector structure. For instance, one can assume that the economy has a single competitive good (money) and a single non-competitive sector, and that all market prices (except for $p_0 = 1$), can be individually manipulated by all strategic agents. Then a *P*-equilibrium (based on fully individually manipulable pricing schemes) is a Cournot–Walras equilibrium. Clearly, if a *P*-equilibrium were not a Cournot–Walras equilibrium, a strategic agent would be able to deviate by some feasible quantity signal. But under full manipulability the resulting market price would be obtained through some price signals sent by the agent, therefore contradicting the *P*-equilibrium definition.

Since a deviation from a *P*-equilibrium need not satisfy the market-clearing condition in all markets together, the converse may not hold and, even under full individual manipulability with respect to the single non-competitive sector, a Cournot–Walras equilibrium may not be a *P*-equilibrium. However, assume that in a Cournot–Walras equilibrium an agent deviating by some price and quantity signals may start a *tâtonnement* (which is under his control because of full manipulability), leading to another deviation where all markets clear, the process being monotone, so that the agent does not get worse off along the path, and the

---

[23] This is the notion of a *Cournotian monopolistic equilibrium*, as studied in d'Aspremont *et al.* (1995).

price of good 0 remains unchanged. Then we get a P-equilibrium. In other words, with fully individually manipulable pricing schemes for the whole economy, when the net demand functions are such that there is, for every admissible vector of quantity signals, a unique Walras equilibrium which is perfectly stable for some numeraire *tâtonnement*,[24] then a Cournot–Walras equilibrium is a P-equilibrium (d'Aspremont *et al.* 1997, propositions 2.1 and 2.2). Thus, under these assumptions, the two concepts coincide. However, this seems to be an extreme use of pricing schemes, which are better thought of as manipulable by a limited number of agents, for a limited number of goods, on a multi-sector basis.

It is even more difficult to compare a P-equilibrium, which belongs to the Cournot tradition, with the monopolistic competition equilibrium concept, which is in the Bertrand–Chamberlin tradition. Assume however that we only have *unilateral monopolies*. This is a very simple sectoral partition of the economy, consisting in having a single strategic agent per sector, with, for every $a \in A^*$, $H_a = S^t$ for some $t \geq 1$. Moreover, no two strategic agents sell to each other and the money market remains the only competitive market. If there are market-clearing quantities uniquely determined for all admissible price strategies of the monopolists (see Assumption 2), so that a monopolistic competition equilibrium is well-defined, and if the pricing scheme is fully individually manipulable, then (under unilateral monopolies) any *P-equilibrium is a monopolistic competition equilibrium*.[25]

All these properties rely on fully individually manipulable pricing schemes. We have already argued that there are empirical arguments in favour of coordination mechanisms with much less manipulability available to each agent, such as having the market price set at the minimum (resp. maximum) of prices announced by sellers (resp. buyers). Of course, when all prices in the economy are non-manipulable, a Walrasian equilibrium is a P-equilibrium. The problem is to investigate the same result when there is limited manipulability, with the markets 'sufficiently' competitive. This is related to the question of Nash equilibria of strategic markets.

7.3.3. P-EQUILIBRIUM, WALRAS EQUILIBRIUM, AND STRATEGIC MARKET GAMES

A pricing scheme P is a particular case of a *price outcome function*, as considered in the literature on strategic market games. In this literature the outcome function for market h also includes[26] *a transaction outcome function* $Z_{ah}(\psi, q)$,

---

[24] Perfect global stability is implied by conditions such as gross substituability, which lead to the uniqueness of the Walras equilibrium.

[25] As above, the converse also holds under stronger assumptions and a monopolistic competition equilibrium is a P-equilibrium if the Walras equilibrium conditional to any admissible choice of a quantity orders is perfectly globally stable (d'Aspremont *et al.* 1997: propositions 3.1 and 3.2).

[26] See e.g. Dubey (1980); Dubey and Rogawski (1990); Aghion (1985); Bénassy (1986).

giving transactions allowed to any agent a on any non-competitive market h as a function of price and quantity signals. The outcome function that represents feasible trades has to satisfy, in every market h, the global feasibility requirement $\sum_a Z_{ah}(\psi, q) = 0$, for every $\psi \in \Psi$ and $q \in Q$. (One also assumes that the amount of numeraire collected by the sellers cannot exceed the quantity distributed by the buyers on the market.)

Let us take the framework of an economy with one good per sector ($S' = \{h\}$, for $t = h = 0, 1, \ldots, l$). Suppose that the outcome function is continuously differentiable. As in Bénassy (1986), we may derive, from the first-order conditions for both a Nash and a Walrasian equilibrium, a necessary condition to get a Walrasian outcome at a Nash equilibrium:

$$\frac{\partial P_h}{\partial \psi_a^h} \bigg/ \frac{\partial Z_{ah}}{\partial \psi_a^h} = 0, \quad \forall h \text{ where } a \text{ is active (the net trade is non-null).}$$

Either agent a cannot manipulate the market price or, if he can, there is a discontinuity in the transaction function with respect to the price signal. Bénassy (1986: 103) also shows that, for a strategic outcome function to have a Nash equilibrium supporting the Walrasian outcome, it is sufficient to have *voluntary exchange* in *frictionless* markets: no agent can be forced to trade more than he wants or to change the sign of his desired transaction, or to trade at a price less favourable than the one he quoted; furthermore, one cannot find a supplier and a buyer both rationed in a market when their price signals are consistent.

In our context, a transaction outcome function is obtained by letting

$$Z_{ah}(\psi, q_a) = \zeta_{ah}(P(\psi), \hat{p}, q_a), \quad a \in A^*, \quad h \in H \backslash \{0\},$$

where $\hat{p} \in \mathbb{R}_+^{\hat{H}}$ are competitive prices, $\psi \in \times_{a \in A^*} \Psi_a$ are price signals, and $q_a \in Q_a$ are quantity orders. Properties assumed on the net demands with respect to prices at equilibrium exclude to find the discontinuities in the transaction outcome function that are essential in a competitive mechanism. Thus, for fully individually manipulable pricing schemes, implying $\partial P_h / \partial \psi_a^h > 0$ for all $h \in H_a$, the Walrasian equilibrium cannot be one among the P-equilibria. This suggests the consideration of pricing schemes with limited individual manipulability. Actually, the *min* and *max pricing schemes* create those price rigidities that are required to make the Walrasian equilibrium a P-equilibrium.

The min pricing scheme and its dual, the max pricing scheme, are:

$$P_h^{\min}(\psi^h) \stackrel{\text{def}}{=} \min_{a \in A_h} \{\psi_a^h\}, \quad P_h^{\max}(\psi^h) \stackrel{\text{def}}{=} \max_{a \in A_h} \{\psi_a^h\},$$

with $\psi_a^h \in \Psi_a^h = \mathbb{R}_+$. We apply each of these pricing schemes to two different sets of agents, the 'natural sellers' and the 'natural buyers'. An agent $a \in A$ is a *natural seller* (resp. *natural buyer*) with respect to good $h \in H \backslash \{0\}$ if, for every $p \in \mathbb{R}_+^H$, $q_a \in Q_a$, $\pi_a \in \mathbb{R}_+$,

$$\zeta_{ah}(p, q_a, \pi_a) \le 0 \, (\zeta_{ah}(p, q_a, \pi_a) \ge 0).$$

We denote by A_h^{ns} (resp A_h^{nb}) the set of natural sellers (resp. buyers) with respect to good h. A natural seller (buyer) for good h is an agent who is selling (buying) good h whatever the values of the prices and other variables in its demand function. It implies restrictions on the technologies for the firms, and on tastes and endowments for the consumers.[27]

We shall limit the set of price-makers to be either natural sellers or natural buyers, as a plausible necessary condition for market power, excluding however bilateral monopolies. This allows us to apply the min pricing scheme to a market with natural sellers and, symmetrically, to apply the max pricing scheme to a market with natural buyers. The interesting fact is that, for an economy where pricing schemes are limited in this way, all Walrasian equilibria are included in the set of P-equilibria, under the condition that there are at least two strategic agents in each market.

ASSUMPTION 3. For all $h \in H^*$, either $A_h = A_h^{nb}$ or $A_h = A_h^{ns}$, but not both, and $|A_h| \geq 2$.

We have the following proposition.[28]

PROPOSITION 1. Under Assumption 3, any Walrasian equilibrium with price system p^W is obtained as a P-equilibrium for some quantity orders $q^* \in Q$, with the transactions based on the min pricing scheme $P_h^{\min}$ (resp. the max pricing scheme $P_h^{\max}$) for each market h involving strategic sellers $A_h = A_h^{nb}$ (resp. strategic buyers $A_h = A_h^{ns}$).

Proof. Suppose a Walrasian equilibrium at prices p^W cannot be obtained as a P-equilibrium as described. Then two cases can arise.

(i) There exists a consumer $i \in A^*$, $p_i \in \mathbb{R}_+^{H_i}$ and $q_i \in Q_i$, such that

$$U_i(\zeta_i(p_i, p_{-i}^W, \hat{p}^W, q_i, \pi_i^W) + \omega_i) > U_i(\zeta_i(p^W, \pi^W) + \omega_i)$$

with, for any $h \in H_i$ and some $\psi_i^h \in \mathbb{R}_+$,

$$p_{ih} = \min\{\psi_{ih}, p_h^W\} \text{ if } i \in A_h^{ns} \quad \text{and} \quad p_{ih} = \max\{\psi_i^h, p_h^W\} \text{ if } i \in A_h^{nb},$$

the other prices and profits hold at their Walrasian equilibrium value, and condition (4′) holds for all $h \in H_i$. Consumer i would however reach an even higher level of utility by disregarding constraints (4′) and neglecting q_i; i.e.,

$$U_i(\zeta_i(p_i, p_{-i}^W, \hat{p}^W, \pi_i^W) + \omega_i) \geq U_i(\zeta_i(p_i, p_{-i}^W, \hat{p}^W, q_i, \pi_i^W) + \omega_i),$$

where

$$\zeta_i(p_i, p_{-i}^W, \hat{p}^W, \pi_i^W) = \{\arg\max U_i(x_i) : x_i \in X_i, \text{ and}$$
$$(p_i, p_{-i}^W, \hat{p}^W)(x_i - \omega_i) \leq \pi_i^W\} - \omega_i$$

---

[27] In a standard textbook economy, in which consumers sell only labour and buy other goods from firms that are buying only labour, all agents are natural sellers or natural buyers for every good.
[28] This extends to a production economy proposition 4 in d'Aspremont *et al.* (1997).

Since p^W is a Walrasian equilibrium price system, we must have

$$p^W \zeta_i(p_i, p_{-i}^W, \hat{p}^W, \pi_i^W) > \pi_i^W \geq (p_i, p_{-i}^W, \hat{p}^W) \zeta_i(p_i, p_{-i}^W, \hat{p}^W, \pi_i^W).$$

Therefore we have

$$\sum_{h \in H_i} (p_h^W - p_{ih}) \zeta_{ih}(p_i, p_{-i}^W, \hat{p}^W, \pi_i^W) > 0.$$

However, if $i \in A_h^{ns}$, $\zeta_{ih}(p_i, p_{-i}^W, \hat{p}^W, \pi_i^W) \leq 0$ and $p_h^W \geq p_{ih}$; or if $i \in A_h^{nb}$, $\zeta_{ih}(p_i, p_{-i}^W, \hat{p}^W, \pi_i^W) \geq 0$ and $p_h^W \leq p_{ih}$. This leads to a contradiction.

(ii) There exists a producer $j \in A^*$, $p_j \in \mathbb{R}_+^{H_j}$ and $q_j \in Q_j$, such that

$$-(p_j, p_{-j}^W, \hat{p}^W) \zeta_j(p_j, p_{-j}^W, \hat{p}^W, q_j) > -p^W \zeta_j(p^W),$$

with, for any $h \in H_j$ and some $\psi_j^h \in \mathbb{R}_+$,

$$p_{jh} = \min\{\psi_j^h, p_h^W\} \text{ if } j \in A_h^{ns} \quad \text{and} \quad p_{jh} = \max\{\psi_j^h, p_h^W\} \text{ if } j \in A_h^{ns},$$

the other prices being held at their Walrasian equilibrium value, and condition (4') holding for all $h \in H_j$. By disregarding these constraints and neglecting q_j, producer j could reach a higher profit; i.e.,

$$-(p_j, p_{-j}^W, \hat{p}^W) \zeta_j(p_j, p_{-j}^W, \hat{p}^W) \geq -(p_j, p_{-j}^W, \hat{p}^W) \zeta_j(p_j, p_{-j}^W, \hat{p}^W, q_j),$$

where

$$-\zeta_j(p_j, p_{-j}^W, \hat{p}^W) = \arg \max_{y_j \in Y_j}(p_j, p_{-j}^W, \hat{p}^W) y_j.$$

Since we also have

$$-p^W \zeta_j(p^W) \geq -p^W \zeta_j(p_j, p_{-j}^W, \hat{p}^W),$$

we get

$$-(p_j, p_{-j}^W, \hat{p}^W) \zeta_j(p_j, p_{-j}^W, \hat{p}^W) > -p^W \zeta_j(p_j, p_{-j}^W, \hat{p}^W).$$

Therefore,

$$\sum_{h \in H_j} (p_h^W - p_{jh}) \zeta_{jh}(p_j, p_{-j}^W, \hat{p}^W) > 0.$$

This gives a contradiction, since $p_{jh} \leq p_h^W$ and $\zeta_{jh}(p_j, p_{-j}^W, \hat{p}^W) \leq 0$ when $j \in A_h^{ns}$ and $p_{jh} \geq p_h^W$ and $\zeta_{jh}(p_j, p_{-j}^W, \hat{p}^W) \geq 0$ when $j \in A_h^{nb}$.

Since in both case (i) and case (ii) we get a contradiction, the result follows.

It should be emphasized that, in an economy as described by Assumption 3, one could expect, in general, multiple P-equilibria with the $P^{\min}$ and $P^{\max}$ pricing schemes. However, by Proposition 1, whenever there exists a Walrasian equilibrium, it is one of them. In that sense, Proposition 1 leads to an existence result, under assumptions no stronger than those ensuring that there is Walrasian equilibrium.

7.4. Conclusion

The concept of P-equilibrium, which belongs to the Cournot tradition, provides a framework for modelling imperfect competition in general equilibrium, on a sector-by-sector basis, limiting strategic agents' calculations and allowing for different price manipulabilities. Because of a 'subgame-perfection' property, Cournot–Walras and other related concepts imply that strategic agents take their decisions by running a detailed general equilibrium model of the whole economy, even when their strategy spaces cover only a few markets. In this approach, non-myopic strategic agents face myopic competitive agents and act non-competitively in all markets. In our approach, a strategic agent can be a price-maker in a limited number of markets, the 'relevant markets', taking into account feedback effects over this set of markets only; in the remaining markets, the strategic agents act competitively, taking the corresponding prices as given and ignoring any constraints on the transactions over the corresponding goods. Of course, the coordination of all agents among markets then requires some parametric adjustments, with respect to prices or wealth.

However, in the extreme case where the whole economy is one sector, and if the pricing scheme is fully individually manipulable, the concept of P-equilibrium may coincide with that of the Cournot–Walras equilibrium. Also, again under full individual manipulability, the concept may even reduce to that of the monopolistic competition equilibrium, when the sector structure is limited to the unilateral monopoly case.

A pricing scheme can be seen as a formal device used by the observer to define and characterize an equilibrium concept. Equilibrium prices are those prices that each strategic agent would choose, should he have the power to manipulate them freely. This is very much like a Lindahl solution for public goods, where each consumer has to choose independently the same quantity of public goods. A pricing scheme can also be seen as a reduced form describing the equilibrium of some process of dynamic interactions among strategic agents. We have emphasized a third interpretation, *that of a coordination device with respect to which trades are organized.* Accordingly, a P-equilibrium is a specific realization of a coordination principle, designed on a sector-by-sector basis allowing for different combinations of strategic and competitive behaviours. In that respect, individual full manipulability is a limiting case, and partially manipulable pricing schemes, such as the min or max pricing schemes, express better the constraints on strategic manipulabilities coming from competitors. Indeed, under min or max pricing schemes, price manipulability is limited upwards or downwards for each individual. This captures some feature of the Walrasian equilibrium concept. Actually, for a rather general class of economies (with strategic agents limited to natural buyers or sellers) a Walrasian equilibrium is a P-equilibrium under such limited price manipulability, thus opening the possibility of an efficient P-equilibrium.

More generally, what this analysis should suggest is the advantage, while introducing strategic behaviour in general equilibrium, of maintaining at the same time many aspects of competitive behaviour. This double approach may allow us to capitalize both on the results of general competitive analysis and, thanks to its strong partial equilibrium flavour, on some elements in industrial organization. Our purpose here was simply to demonstrate the possibility of such a semi-competitive model. Obviously, many problems remain.

REFERENCES

Aghion, P. (1985), 'On the Generic Inefficiency of Differentiable Market Games,' *Journal of Economic Theory*, 37: 126–46.

Arrow, K. J. (1959), 'Towards a Theory of Price Adjustment', in A. Abramovitz (ed.), *The Allocation of Economic Resources*, Stanford: Stanford University Press.

—— (1986), 'Rationality of Self and Others in an Economic System', in R. M. Hogarth and M. W. Reder (eds.), *Rational Choice*, Chicago: University of Chicago Press, pp. 201–16.

—— and Debreu, G. (1954), 'Existence of an Equilibrium for a Competitive Economy', *Econometrica*, 22: 265–90.

—— and Hahn, F. H. (1971), *General Competitive Analysis*. San Francisco: Holden Day.

Bénassy, J. P. (1982), *The Economics of Market Disequilibrium*. New York: Academic Press.

—— (1986), 'On Competitive Market Mechanisms', *Econometrica*, 54: 95–108.

—— (1988), 'The Objective Demand Curve in General Equilibrium', *Economic Journal*, 98 (Suppl.): 37–49.

Binmore, K. (1990), *Essays on the Foundations of Game Theory*. Oxford: Basil Blackwell.

Böhm, V. (1990), 'General Equilibrium with Profit Maximizing Oligopolists', Discussion Paper no. 41, University of Mannheim.

—— (1994), 'The Foundations of the Theory of Monopolistic Competition Revisited', *Journal of Economic Theory*, 63: 208.

Bonanno, G. (1990), 'General Equilibrium with Imperfect Competition', *Journal of Economic Surveys*, 4: 297–322.

—— and Zeeman, C. E. (1985), 'Limited Knowledge of Demand and Oligopoly Equilibria', *Journal of Economic Theory*, 35: 276–83.

Bushaw, D. W., and Clower, R. W. (1957), *Introduction to Mathematical Economics*. Homewood, Ill.: Richard D. Irwin.

Codognato, G., and Gabszewicz, I. J. (1991), 'Cournot–Walras in Price Exchange Economies', CORE Discussion Paper no. 9110, Université Catholique de Louvain.

Cornwall, R. R. (1977), 'The Concept of General Equilibrium in a Market Economy with Imperfectly Competitive Producers', *Metroeconomica*, 29: 57–72.

Cournot, A. A. (1838), *Recherches sur les principes mathématiques de la théorie des richesses*. Paris; trans. N. Bacon, *Researches into the Mathematical Principles of the Theory of Wealth*. New-York, Macmillan, 1897.

d'Aspremont, C., Dos Santos Ferreira, R., and Gérard-Varet, L. A. (1989), 'Unemployment in an Extended Cournot Oligopoly Model', *Oxford Economic Papers*, 41: 490–505.

d'Aspremont, C., Dos Santos Ferreira, R., and Gérard-Varet, L. A. (1991*a*), 'Pricing Schemes and Cournotian Equilibria', *American Economic Review*, 81: 666–73.

d'Aspremont, C., Dos Santos Ferreira, R., and Gérard-Varet, L. A. (1991*b*), 'Concurrence en prix et équilibres cournotiens', *Revue Economique*, 42: 967–26.

—— —— —— (1994), 'Fondements stratégiques de l'équilibre en économie: coordination, rationalité individuelle et anticipations', in L. A. Gérard-Varet and J. C. Passeron (eds.), *Le Modèle et l'enquête*. Paris: Editions de l'EHESS, pp. 447–68.

—— —— —— (1995), 'Concurrence et coordination dans le modèle de Hotelling', *Revue d'Economie Industrielle*, Hors-Série: 287–303.

—— —— —— (1997), 'General Equilibrium Concepts under Imperfect Competition: a Cournotian Approach', *Journal of Economic Theory*, 73: 199–230.

Debreu, G. (1959), *Theory of Value*. New-York: John Wiley.

—— (1970), 'Economies with a Finite Set of Equilibria', *Econometrica*, 38: 387–92.

Dierker, H., and Grodal, B. (1986), 'Non-existence of Cournot–Walras Equilibrium in a General Equilibrium Model with Two Oligopolists', in W. Hildenbrand and A. Mas-Colell (eds.), *Contributions to Mathematical Economics in Honor of Gerard Debreu*. Amsterdam, North-Holland, pp. 167–85.

—— and —— (1994), 'Profit Maximization, Relative Prices and the Maximization of Shareholders Real Wealth'. Mimeo.

Drèze, J. (1974), 'Investment under Private Ownsership: Optimality, Equilibrium and Stability', in J. Drèze (ed.), *Allocation under Uncertainty: Equilibrium and Optimality*. New York: John Wiley.

Dubey, P. (1980), 'Nash Equilibrium of Market Games: Finiteness and Efficiency', *Journal of Economic Theory*, 22: 363–76.

—— (1982), 'Price–Quantity Strategic Market Games', *Econometrica*, 50: 111–26.

—— and Rogawski, J. D. (1990), 'Inefficiency of Smooth Market Mechanisms', *Journal of Mathematical Economics*, 19: 285–304.

Fitzroy, F. (1974), 'Monopolistic Equilibrium, Non-convexity, and Inverse Demand', *Journal of Economic Theory*, 7: 1–16.

Gabszewicz, J. J., and Michel, P. (1992), 'Oligopoly Equilibria in Exchange Economies', CORE Discussion Paper no. 9247, Université Catholique de Louvain.

—— and Vial, J. P. (1972), 'Oligopoly *à la* Cournot in a General Equilibrium Analysis', *Journal of Economic Theory*, 4: 381–400.

Gary-Bobo, R. (1987), 'Locally Consistent Oligopolistic Equilibria are Cournot–Walras Equilibria', *Economics Letters*, 23: 217–21.

—— (1989*a*), *Equilibre général et concurrence imparfaite*, Monographie d'Econometrie. Paris: Editions du CNRS.

—— (1989*b*), 'Cournot–Walras and Locally Consistent Equilibria', *Journal of Economic Theory*, 89: 10–32.

Ginsburgh, V. A. (1994), 'In the Cournot–Walras General Equilibrium Model, There May Be "More to Gain" by Changing the Numeraire than by Eliminating Imperfections: a Two-Good Economy Example', in J. Mercenier and T. W. Scrinivason (eds.), *Applied General Equilibrium and Economic Development: Present Achievements and Future Trends*. Ann Arbor: University of Michigan Press, pp. 217–24.

Grandmont, M. (1993), 'Behavioral Heterogeneity and Cournot Oligopoly Equilibrium', *Ricerche Economiche*, 47: 167–87.

Grodal, B. (1992), 'Profit Maximization and Imperfect Competition', mimeo, July.

Hahn, F. H. (1977), 'Exercises in Conjectural Equilibria', *Scandinavian Journal of Economics*, 79: 210–24.

Hart, O. D. (1982), 'A Model of Imperfect Competition with Keynesian Features', *Quarterly Journal of Economics*, 97: 109–38.

—— (1985), 'Imperfect Competition in General Equilibrium: an Overview of Recent Work', in K. J. Arrow and S. Honkapohja (eds.), *Frontiers of Economics*. Oxford: Basil Blackwell, pp. 150–69.

Laffont, J. J., and Laroque, G. (1976), 'Existence d'un équilibre de concurrence imparfaite: une introduction', *Econometrica*, 44: 283–94.

Marschak, T., and Selten, R. (1974), *General Equilibrium with Price-Making Firms*, Lecture Notes in Economics and Mathematical Systems 91. Berlin: Springer.

Mas-Colell, A. (1982), 'The Cournotian Foundations of Walrasian Equilibrium Theory: an Exposition of Recent Theory,' in W. Hildenbrand (ed.), *Advances in Economic Theory*. Cambridge: Cambridge University Press, pp. 183–224.

Negishi, T. (1961), 'Monopolistic Competition and General Equilibrium', *Review of Economic Studies*, 28: 196–201.

—— (1972), *General Equilibrium Theory and International Trade*. Amsterdam: North-Holland.

Nikaido, H. (1975), *Monopolistic Competition and Effective Demand*. Princeton: Princeton University Press.

Novshek, W., and Sonnenschein, H. (1977), 'Cournot and Walras Equilibrium', *Journal of Economic Theory*, 19: 223–66.

Roberts, J., and Sonnenschein, H. (1977), 'On the Foundations of the Theory of Monopolistic Competition', *Econometrica*, 45: 101–13.

Roberts, K. (1980), 'The Limit Points of Monopolistic Competition', *Journal of Economic Theory* (Symposium issue): 256–79.

Schmeidler, D. (1980), 'Walrasian Analysis via Strategic Outcome Functions', *Econometrica*, 48: 1585–93.

Shapley, L. S., and Shubik, M. (1977), 'Trade Using One Commodity as a Means of Payment', *Journal of Political Economy*, 85: 937–68.

Silvestre, J. (1977a), 'General Monopolistic Equilibrium under Non-convexities', *International Economic Review*, 18: 425–34.

—— (1977b), 'A Model of General Equilibrium with Monopolistic Behaviour', *Journal of Economic Theory*, 16: 425–42.

Simon, L. K. (1984), 'Bertrand, the Cournot Paradigm and the Theory of Perfect Competition', *Review of Economic Studies*, 51: 209–30.

Stahn, H. (1996), 'Un modèle de concurrence monopolistique: une approche a équilibre général', *Annales d'Economie et de Statistiques*, 43: 29–56.

Tirole, J. (1988), *The Theory of Industrial Organization*. Cambridge, Mass.: MIT Press.

Triffin, R. (1940), *Monopolistic Competition and General Equilibrium*. Cambridge, Mass.: Harvard University Press.

Ventura, L. (1994), 'On a Shareholder-Constrained Efficient Criterion for Strategic Firms', CORE Discussion Paper no. 9466, December.

Walras, L. (1874), *Elements d'economie politique pure*. Geneva: L. Corbaz.

Willig, R. D. (1991), 'Merger Analysis, Industrial Organization Theory and Merger Guidelines', *Brookings Papers: Microeconomics*. Washington DC: Brookings Institution.

8

Space and Value: an Outlook and New Perspectives

Suzanne Scotchmer and Jacques-François Thisse

8.1. Introduction

It is rare to find an economics text in which the problem of space is studied as an important subject, or even mentioned. This is despite its obvious importance in how markets function. For example, consider the debate raging within the European Union about the regional consequences of the Single Market.

The reason why space has been marginalized in economic theory is not clear. Certainly, a long list of eminent economists have turned their attention to the subject at least in passing, and Samuelson (1983) places the subject's founder, von Thünen (1826), in the pantheon of great economists.[1] (See Ekelund and Shieh (1986) for a historical perspective on other contributors.) Blaug (1985: ch. 14) attributes the subject's neglect to von Thünen's lack of clarity and to a formalism of other early contributors (such as Laundhart) that was inaccessible at the time. However, these explanations should not extend into the present.

Most economic activities are distributed over space, and for such activities *space moulds the very nature of competition between firms*. In this chapter we review the effect of space on competition and efficiency. We point out that spatial models of private goods and local public goods have treated space in fundamentally different ways, and suggest that each of these branches of the literature could be improved by adopting ideas from the other.

Space matters only if production involves scale economies. Otherwise each location would have an autarkic economy and there would be no transport of goods or consumers. But if production involves increasing returns, a finite economy accommodates only a finite number of firms, and these are imperfect competitors.

We thank Marcus Berliant, Jacques Drèze, Masa Fujita, André Grimaud, Vernon Henderson, Yorgos Papageorgiou, David Pines, Ken Small, and one referee for useful comments. We also thank the Institute of Business and Economic Research, University of California, Berkeley, CORE–Louvain-la-Neuve, Belgium, the Institute of Advanced Study at Indiana University, the Berkley–France Fund, and the Ministère de la Recherche (France) for financial support.

[1] The contribution of von Thünen to economic thought is so impressive that Nerlove and Sadka (1991) do not hesitate to consider him as the originator of marginalism.

Hotelling (1929), Kaldor (1935), and Lösch (1940) argued that space gives this competition a particular form. Since consumers buy from the firm with the lowest 'full price', defined as the posted price plus the transportation cost, each firm competes directly with only a few neighbouring firms, thus making the process of competition inherently strategic. Localized competition also arises in Lancasterian models of product differentiation, but the problem of firm location is more complex in geographical space than in characteristics space because consumers as well as firms are mobile, and their residential choices will typically interact with firms' choices of location.

In addition to localized competition, a second consequence of space is that it *blurs the line between private and public goods*. The model of pure public goods holds that, unlike private goods, pure public goods can serve unlimited numbers of consumers without (1) having quality degraded through congestion or (2) becoming more costly. In contrast to this model, most publicly provided goods suffer from congestion either directly, as when too many people attend an art exhibit, or indirectly, as when the public good is located in space. If a public good is located in space, congestion appears as competition for the limited land close to the public good. In addition, transportation costs are required to use the public good, which means that the social cost increases with the number of users. The literature following Tiebout (1956) and Buchanan (1965) has argued that both these effects compromise the 'purity' of public goods, and make them more similar to private goods.

Despite the conceptual similarity between private and public goods in the spatial context, economists studying these subjects have made fundamentally different modelling assumptions, which have different intellectual origins, and have led to different conclusions, particularly concerning efficiency. Hotelling (1929) wanted to introduce heterogeneity among consumers in the demand for private goods in order to smooth firms' demand functions and subvert the extreme conclusions that follow from Bertrand-style price competition. He did this by distributing consumers in space so they have different transportation costs to firms. For this purpose a land market was unnecessary. On the other hand, Tiebout wanted to solve the problem of preference revelation in the theory of public goods by allowing consumers to choose among jurisdictions with different public goods. By migrating to the jurisdictions that respect their tastes, consumers reveal their preferences. Jurisdictions (identified with land owners) can profit by respecting their residents' tastes, provided efficient provision of public goods is capitalized into land prices. For this a land market and consumer mobility are necessary, but transport costs are not. In fact, if non-residents could transport themselves to a jurisdiction to consume its public goods without paying for the land, the efficiency arguments of this literature could vanish.

In Section 8.2 we argue that attempts to integrate space into the general equilibrium model of private goods have been unsatisfactory. In Section 8.3 we summarize and evaluate the alternative framework of *location without land* proposed by Hotelling and successors, while Section 8.4 discusses the framework of the local public goods literature, which has *land without location*. In both of these latter sections we try to show how the conclusions of each branch of this literature depend on its modelling assumptions. Section 8.5 discusses gaps in our understanding of firm location, and tries to illuminate how capitalization arguments from the local public goods literature might lead to richer allocation mechanisms for governing firm location. Section 8.6 concludes.[2]

8.2. Space in the Competitive Model with Private Goods

The most elegant and advanced competitive model of a private goods economy is undoubtedly that developed by Arrow and Debreu (1954). These authors define a commodity not only by its physical characteristics, but also by the time and place in which it is made available. The same good traded at different places becomes different economic commodities. (The same idea was developed earlier by Allais 1943: 809.) Choosing a location is part of choosing a commodity, so location is treated in the same way as other decisions taken by economic agents. This definition integrates spatial interdependence of markets into general equilibrium in the same way as other forms of interdependence, and apparently obviates the need for a theory specific to the spatial context. But unfortunately, complications are buried in the details of the model.

First, in order to demonstrate existence of prices that simultaneously equilibrate all the markets, Arrow and Debreu suppose convexity of preferences and of firms' production sets. In addition, constant unit prices imply that consumers' budget constraints are linear. These hypotheses are restrictive in themselves, but we point out that in the context of space they become untenable. Second, with scale economies, space makes it impossible to define markets in such a way that the price-taking hypothesis is reasonable.

Convexity of preferences is not really necessary for the existence of a price-taking equilibrium if there is a large number (a continuum) of consumers. Nevertheless, it is worth pointing out that convexity of preferences is contradicted by the evidence regarding consumers' choice of housing. With convex preferences, a consumer would purchase a small quantity of a large number of goods—in particular, a small quantity of housing in many different locations. This is not what consumers typically do. Grimaud and Laffont (1989) relax the hypothesis of convex preferences by assuming a continuum of consumers and a finite set of locations, and establish existence of a competitive equilibrium in an exchange economy where consumers choose to reside in only one place.[3] The economy they consider is very simple in that there are no transport costs of the composite

---

[2] Strong 'potential' convergences between international trade and location theories similarly exist and are discussed by Krugman (1993a).

[3] A different proof that also deals with the non-convexity of preferences can be found in Schweizer et al. (1976) and Scotchmer (1985a).

good between locations (though the consumers may exhibit a utility loss associated with moving); the only price connected with space is land rent. A more general model with a continuum of consumers and a continuum of locations is considered by Fujita and Smith (1987). They show the existence of a competitive residential equilibrium in an economy where each consumer resides at one location only, while transportation costs to a given, finite set of points (business districts, public facilities, etc.) are positive.

If production involves scale economies, there will be only a finite number of firms (see below), and then shopping requires transport costs. A consumer will organize her shopping itinerary so as to minimize the total cost of purchases including transport costs. 'Trip-chaining' implies a particular structure of substitution between retail outlets which introduces non-convexities into the budget constraint. The consumer's problem is extremely complex: to determine the optimal geographic structure of purchases requires solving a particularly difficult combinatorial problem (Bacon 1971) for which there is no known algorithm that permits finding an optimal solution in a reasonable time. (In complexity theory, this means that this problem is NP-complete.) Furthermore, there are often considerable scale economies in carrying the goods bought by a consumer when shopping (Stahl 1987). In the extreme, consumers' outlays on transportation can be considered as independent of the purchased quantity. These non-convexities affect demand functions in complex ways which have not been investigated, and the implications for the existence of an equilibrium are not clear.

Non-convexities in production are troubling to competition in an even more fundamental way than convex preferences or nonlinear budget constraints. The hypothesis that production sets are convex implies that production exhibits no increasing returns to scale whatever its scale. Subdividing a firm into smaller units therefore can increase the output available from given inputs. In the limit, if the distribution of endowments is uniform the economy reduces to a Robinson Crusoe-type economy where each person produces for his own consumption (backyard capitalism). General equilibrium theorists skirt this problem either by supposing that the number of firms is fixed or by considering exchange economies without firms. But even with a fixed number of firms, convexity has an unsatisfying implication. Although the number of firms is given, each firm prefers a small plant at each of many locations. Each location could thus be a base for an autarkic economy where goods are produced on an arbitrarily small scale, except that, as in the neoclassical theory of international trade, trade might possibly occur if the geographic distribution of resources was non-uniform. While pertinent (see e.g. Courant and Deardoff 1992), unequal distribution of resources seems weak as the only explanation for local specialization and trade.[4] Hence, *increasing returns to scale are essential for explaining the geographical*

---

[4] See, however, Beckmann and Puu (1985) for an original approach to the location of production activities operating under constant returns to scale when space is heterogeneous.

distribution of economic activities. This observation might be called the 'Folk Theorem' of spatial economics.[5]

The introduction of increasing returns to scale into the general equilibrium model has generated much interest in recent years. (See Cornet (1988) for a survey of the main contributions.) Without denying that these attempts are interesting, they remain largely unsatisfactory, largely because they do not answer the question posed by Sraffa (1926: 545): to what extent is price-taking compatible with increasing returns to scale? Suppose the firm size that minimizes average production cost is 'large' relative to the size of the market. A price-taking equilibrium could not have 'many' firms, each operating at inefficiently small scale, because each such firm would have a profit incentive to increase its output. Hence the market can accommodate only a 'few' firms of efficient size. But with only a few firms, how does one justify the hypothesis that firms treat prices as given, since firms must realize that their size permits them to influence prices to their own advantage?[6]

This takes us to the problem of markets. Although the existence of a price-taking equilibrium does not in itself require a large number of agents, a large number of agents seem necessary to *justify* the hypothesis that agents are price-takers (see e.g. Aumann 1964). Even if the economy is large, so that the number of firms can be large, the geographic dispersion of consumption causes production to be dispersed and local markets to be 'small'. Thus, the combination of increasing returns and geographically dispersed consumption renders untenable the hypothesis that many firms compete in each market. If one returns to the suggestion of Arrow and Debreu of distinguishing goods by their location, *most markets are probably characterized by a small number of firms* (if any) which, as a consequence, do not behave competitively (see also Samuelson 1967).

It is therefore tempting to interpret the spatial market as geographically large in order to ensure a large number of firms. Firms are artificially grouped in the same 'market' even though they are very separated in space. It is in giving a sufficient expanse to regional markets that one saves the competitive hypothesis. This approach is hardly satisfactory, since the geographically separated firms have some monopoly power and will not voluntarily renounce it. The grouping of firms has another surprising implication for the structure of competition. The enterprises that are separated in space but situated in the same market are viewed as competitors selling their products at the same price; on the other hand, the nearby firms situated on either side of the boundary between markets are supposed to sell their products at different prices.[7]

---

[5] It is not easy to trace the origin of this claim, but it was made by Lösch (1940) and Koopmans (1957). (See Starrett (1978) for a modern presentation.) The same idea reappears in the new theories of international trade as developed by Helpman and Krugman (1985).

[6] The same problem appears in the theory of 'clubs' providing public goods, where the size of optimal groups is positive (but typically smaller than the population), thus leading to a small number of clubs in equilibrium that behave strategically (Scotchmer 1985*b, c*).

[7] A similar criticism was made by Lösch (1940) of neoclassical international trade theory.

Hence, in space, it is difficult to admit the hypothesis that firms face perfectly elastic demands except to suppose that exchange is organized by Walrasian auctioneers operating in a few market-places.

8.3. Spatial Competition: Location without Land

Thus, the model of perfect competition does not seem to integrate space satisfactorily. If firms and consumers are not geographically grouped, and if the number of firms is small relative to the number of consumers owing to indivisibilities in production, each firm has some monopoly power over the consumers in its immediate vicinity. Differences in consumer locations, and hence transport costs, are a source of market power. Thus, *spatial competition is by nature oligopolistic*, and should be studied according to the relevant theories of imperfect competition. In fact, the discussion below reminds us that some of the major insights of game theory were motivated by spatial economic problems.

The prototype of spatial competition is due to Hotelling, who studied firms' location and price decisions assuming that consumers' locations are fixed. Heterogeneity among consumers, introduced through transportation costs, ensures that each firm's demand is continuous, while permitting consumers to react discontinuously at the individual level (non-convex preferences). Hotelling's idea was to make sure that individual discontinuities are distributed such that they are not noticeable to the firm. (Formally, one supposes that the distribution is absolutely continuous.) To this end, he imagined a market where the consumers live at locations continuously and uniformly distributed along a line segment—Main Street—and where duopolists sell an identical good at different locations. For each pair of prices, each consumer purchases one unit from the firm which, for him, has the lower full price. The consumers are thus divided into two segments, with each firm's aggregate demand represented by the consumers in one segment. The boundary between the two firms' markets is given by the location of the consumer who is indifferent between the two firms. This boundary is endogenous, since it depends on the prices set by the firms. Because of the continuous dispersion of consumers, a marginal variation in price changes the boundary, and changes each firm's demand by the same order.[8]

Hotelling considers a two-stage decision process where the firms choose first (simultaneously) their locations and afterwards their prices. This decoupling of decisions captures the idea that firms select their locations in anticipation of later competing on price. For each location pair, Hotelling determines what he thinks will be the prices in a non-cooperative equilibrium of the corresponding price subgame. He includes these prices, which are functions of the locations, in the

---

[8] d'Aspremont *et al.* (1979) have demonstrated that the hypotheses of Hotelling do not guarantee continuity at the global level. For that, it is necessary to replace the assumption of linear transport costs by one in which transport costs are increasing and strictly convex in distance.

profit functions of the firms, which then depend only upon locations. These new profit functions are used to study the game of choosing locations. Hotelling finds an equilibrium where the two firms locate at the centre of the market, a tendency that has been named the Principle of Minimum Differentiation.

The idea of formulating a game on price and locations according to a two-stage procedure was extremely ingenious and original. (It preceeds by many years the work of Selten on perfect equilibrium.) Unfortunately, Hotelling's analysis was incorrect. When the two firms are sufficiently close, there does not exist an equilibrium in pure strategies for the corresponding price subgame. The study of the location game is accordingly incomplete. However, as established by d'Aspremont *et al.* (1979), if the transport costs are quadratic rather than linear, a price equilibrium will exist for any pair of locations. Reconstructing Hotelling's analysis, these authors then show that the two firms wish to place themselves at the two ends of the market segment. This tendency to spatial differentiation or dispersion always dominates when the firms sell an identical good. The Principle of Minimum Differentiation must thus be replaced by the Principle of Differentiation: *firms selling a homogeneous good wish to separate themselves geographically in a way that relaxes price competition.*

Space changes the nature of competition fundamentally in that, however many firms participate in aggregate, competition is *localized*: each firm competes more vigorously with its immediate neighbours than with more distant neighbours. To see this, suppose that n firms are distributed equidistantly along a circle. Firm i has two direct competitors, firms $i-1$ and $i+1$. The market situated between firms $i-1$ and $i+1$ is segmented according to the same principle as in the duopoly case: each consumer patronizes the firm with the lowest full price. Hence there are three groups of consumers in this market: those who buy from firm $i-1$, those who buy from firm $i+1$, and those who buy from firm i. Firm i has two market boundaries. A unilateral price cut by firm i will extend its own market only at the expense of firms $i-1$ and $i+1$, and the other firms will be unaffected. This competitive structure, first uncovered by Kaldor and rediscovered by Eaton and Lipsey (1977), is by nature oligopolistic in that each firm is concerned directly only with a small number of competitors, whatever the total number of firms in the industry. In this sense it differs fundamentally from the symmetric model of Chamberlin (1933), in which a firm that cuts its price will attract customers from *all* the other firms.

Consider now the efficient configuration: how many firms should be in the market and where should they be located? In the setting considered by Hotelling, the optimal number and locations of firms minimize the firms' fixed production costs plus consumers' total transport costs. (If individual demands were price-sensitive, efficiency should also consider the deadweight loss arising from oligopolistic prices.) There is a fundamental social trade-off in that *increasing the number of firms, hence fixed costs, reduces the aggregate tranport costs and vice versa* (see also Lösch 1940). Firms consider a similar trade-off when deciding whether to enter in equilibrium. A firm will enter only if it can locate sufficiently far from other firms so that it can serve enough consumers, and charge a high enough price, to cover its fixed costs. In general, the equilibrium number of firms is larger than the optimal number (see e.g. Anderson *et al.* (1992: ch. 6). Even if the equilibrium and optimum numbers of firms were the same, the firms in equilibrium might not locate efficiently. For example, if the optimal and equilibrium number of firms is two, the optimal locations on the interval from zero to one are at the first and third quartiles, whereas the equilibrium locations will be at the end-points.

With a homogeneous good, the Hotelling model leads to a geographical isolation of firms, each with localized monopoly power. However, this conclusion is based on the extreme price sensitivity of consumers. In the model, each consumer has a threshold price difference below which he will not switch firms, and above which he switches with probability one. Such extreme behaviour seems unwarranted, and psychologists have suggested an alternative model of consumer choice which softens it. This model imputes a random term to utility and makes the consumer's decision whether to switch firms probabilistic (see Anderson *et al.* 1992: ch. 2 for a survey). McFadden (1981) has pioneered the use of such models in economics. It changes the outcome of competition in the Hotelling model as follows.

We want to assume that the observer, e.g. the firm, assigns a probability between zero and one to whether a particular consumer on a particular date will respond to a price difference by switching firms. Probabilistic behaviour can be modelled by assuming that consumers maximize a stochastic utility rather than a deterministic utility. Firms implicitly sell heterogeneous products, and there is a random term in the consumer's utility which establishes her ranking of firms at the time of purchase. An interpretation is that consumers like product variety, and that, even if prices do not vary, they do not always purchase from the same firm.

In the Hotelling model, if two firms are located side by side with identical prices, a small price reduction of one firm will attract all the customers. If consumers' switching behaviour is probabilistic, the aggregate response to a price cut will not be so abrupt. This modification to the Hotelling model, which has been developed by Anderson *et al.* (1992: ch. 9), has two major implications. First, if consumers' purchasing behaviour becomes sufficiently dispersed, firms' demand functions are smoothed sufficiently when they are located close together so that a price equilibrium in pure strategies exists. Second, under the same condition, *firms tend to agglomerate at the market centre instead of dispersing geographically.*[9] Price competition at the centre is relaxed because of the (implicit) differentiation among vendors, which gives them market power even when they are agglomerated (Thisse 1993). Agglomeration can thus be a noncooperative equilibrium when transportation costs are low with respect to product heterogeneity.[10] In addition, the smoothing of firms' demand functions when

[9] If the dispersion were too small, aggregate demand would respond almost as abruptly to changes in firms' behaviour as in the Hotelling model, and the same conclusions would arise.

[10] A similar result is obtained by Fujita and Krugman (1995), who use a non-strategic model of monopolistic competition *à la* Dixit and Stiglitz (1977).

they are located close together can restore the existence of equilibrium in pure price strategies.

Thus, with homogeneous goods vendors disperse in order to avoid competitors. But if firms sell heterogeneous goods and consumers with different preferences among firms are themselves geographically dispersed, the tendency for firms to disperse may be overcome, and firms may agglomerate. The random utility model implies that on any marketing date consumers with different preferences among firms are geographically dispersed. The geographic dispersion of consumers with different tastes has the additional affect of overcoming the non-existence of equilibrium in prices when firms are agglomerated.

Models of spatial competition assume that consumers' locations are fixed. Consumer mobility requires a land market because otherwise all the consumers would locate right next to the firms. This brings us to the literature on local public goods in which consumers are assumed to be mobile.

8.4. Local Public Goods: Land without Location

Hotelling goods are similar to public goods: The firm has a high fixed cost and zero marginal cost of selling to additional customers. Thus, the Hotelling model is probably the simplest way to put public goods into the spatial setting, and there is no distinction between public and private goods. The public good is not 'pure' because using it requires transport costs.

Space has an important consequence that is ignored in spatial competition models but is central to local public goods models: namely, *capitalization*. Capitalization means that the price of land reflects the public services, local taxes, and transport costs incurred by the occupant. There is no capitalization in the Hotelling model because there is no land.

Capitalization and consumer mobility (mobility of residence, as opposed to choice of shopping centre) are inextricably linked; since consumers can move from unattractive locations to attractive locations, land prices and population densities will adjust to compensate for the differences in attractiveness. When an increase in local public goods or the building of a shopping centre is capitalized into an increased land price, each resident will typically consume less land, and the density of the population will increase. Through capitalization and consumer mobility, populations are endogenous to local policies.

In Hotelling-type models, consumers have fixed locations and do not pay for the land they occupy, and thus there is no market force driving capitalization. Hence firms locating in space cannot be viewed as landowners who can profit from the capitalized value of efficient location decisions. Nevertheless, such an idea is provocative, and in Section 8.5 we will ask whether similar mechanisms can be applied to firms providing private goods.

While the Hotelling model has location without land, the local public goods model has land without location. In the Hotelling model location means 'location relative to firms'; a consumer can purchase from any firm, provided he is willing to pay the transport cost to this firm, and thus the boundaries between firms are endogenous to firms' prices and locations. In the local public goods model described below, consumers are mobile in the sense that they choose what jurisdiction or location to occupy, but once there 'location relative to public goods facilities' is irrelevant. Consumers cannot use the public facilities of a neighbouring jurisdiction even if those facilities are closer. The tying of consumer benefits to residency in the jurisdiction is essential to the success of the model; without it, the land value that the jurisdiction maximizes would not capture all the benefits of its policies. This assumption is most vividly met in the islands model of Stiglitz (1977), where it is infeasible for a consumer on one island to consume the public goods of another.

The basic capitalization argument is that capitalization provides a natural measure of social surplus, or willingness to pay for an increase in public goods. If this is so, and if a jurisdiction views land value as 'profit', which it tries to maximize, public goods should be provided efficiently. In fact, something stronger is true: in addition to efficient provision of public goods, the population will be partitioned efficiently among the existing jurisdictions. Thus, if capitalized land values are included in profit, jurisdictions have an incentive to organize their affairs efficiently.

Appealing as the capitalization argument seems, it needs qualification. First, there may be issues of existence (Wildasin 1987). Second, the argument typically rests on the hypothesis that the attractiveness of other jurisdictions does not change when one jurisdiction changes its fiscal policy. Under this hypothesis, the increase in land value following the change of fiscal policy will reflect willingness to pay for the increased public goods, holding utilities fixed.

In order that utility opportunities elsewhere remain fixed, the price of land elsewhere, and the fiscal policies, must remain fixed. But, as pointed out above, capitalization and consumer mobility go hand in hand. Land prices rise in the improved jurisdiction because the improvement attracts residents from elsewhere, which pushes up demand for land, reduces per capita land consumption, and increases the population of the jurisdiction. Meanwhile, as residents leave the other jurisdictions, the land prices there fall, providing the remaining residents with more utility than they had before. In this way, utility is 'exported' from the jurisdiction that increased its public goods to the other jurisdictions. Because of the utility effect, the increase in land value in the jurisdiction that increased public goods will underestimate willingness to pay for the public goods, and in equilibrium public goods may be underprovided (Scotchmer 1986).[11]

The assumption that utility elsewhere is fixed is a 'competitive hypothesis' which may not be justified. If each jurisdiction were very small, then the prices of land in other jurisdictions, hence utility, would be almost unresponsive to one jurisdiction's change in fiscal policy. So we come naturally to the question of how large a jurisdiction should be.

---

[11] This problem has also been observed in the literature on cost–benefit analysis; for an early discussion see Polinsky and Shavell (1975) and Pines and Weiss (1976).

In the capitalization model, the boundaries of jurisdictions are *fixed* in geographic space,[12] in contrast to the spatial competition model, where the boundary between two firms is established by consumers' endogenous decisions concerning where to shop.[13] For land value maximization to yield efficiency, the jurisdiction must include all the beneficiaries of its fiscal policy. Consider, for example, a diffused public good like air quality. If the pollution produced by one jurisdiction is exported to another jurisdiction where it erodes property values, the polluting jurisdiction will have too little incentive to reduce pollution, since some benefits are not reflected in its own land value. Or consider a public good supplied at a specific site, such as a park, which residents of neighbouring jurisdictions can also visit. The neighbours' benefits will be capitalized into their own property values, which are outside the jurisdiction that provided the park. To avoid such uncounted spillovers, jurisdictions should be large. In addition, public goods by their very nature have indivisibilities in the sense that efficiency requires that many consumers share the costs and benefits of the public good, and this is another reason why jurisdictions should be large.

But if the jurisdiction is large relative to the economy, the competitive hypothesis may well fail.

This failure leads to underprovision if the jurisdictions compete only in public goods, essentially because increasing the public goods has conflicting impacts on property values. On the one hand, an efficient increase in public goods should increase property values; but on the other hand, increasing public goods induces immigration from elsewhere and reduces property values through the utility effect described above. A jurisdiction can do better if it has two instruments to govern these two effects. If the jurisdiction can charge an admission fee to control migration, public goods will be provided efficiently because their only purpose is to increase social surplus conditional on the population, which the jurisdiction now controls through the admission price. Thus, public goods can be provided efficiently within jurisdictions even without perfect competition (Scotchmer 1986).[14]

8.5. Towards a Synthesis

Introducing a land market and consumer mobility into Hotelling-type models has at least two important consequences: it permits the location decisions of

---

[12] Though generally accepted, this assumption is perhaps less obvious than it might seem at first sight, as shown by the debate between Henderson (1985) and Epple and Romer (1989)

[13] In models of local public goods with land, it is difficult to conceive a decentralized mechanism to partition space into jurisdictions. A parallel literature called 'club theory' (initiated by Buchanan 1965) has studied models without space. Ignoring space makes it easier to conceive entry; there is no problem of acquiring land or of dividing space into jurisdictions. Such models have been studied under the competitive hypothesis (for a summary see Scotchmer 1994), but the competitive hypothesis fails for the same reason as for indivisibilities in private goods production: the efficient size of the firm (club) is positive. Firms make positive profit in a non-cooperative equilibrium even with the efficient number of clubs, and therefore the incentive to enter can be too great (Scotchmer 1985*b*, *c*).

[14] See Myers (1990) for a similar result in a related but somewhat different context.

firms and consumers to be jointly endogenous, and it permits allocation mech-anisms based on land capitalization, as in the literature on local public goods. Very little work has been done along either dimension. In this section we record some speculations based on the little work that has been done, and try to indicate the form that further research might take.

If we introduce a land market and consumer mobility into the Hotelling model, the locations of firms and consumers become interdependent in that *the optimal location of a consumer depends on the locations chosen by the firms and vice versa* (Koopmans 1957: ch. II.9). Roughly speaking, two lines of research have been followed so far. In the former, all agents are assumed to be atomistic and, accordingly, there is no strategic interaction between firms. Both firms and consumers move simultaneously. In the latter, firms make strategic decisions while consumers behave competitively. In these models, firms move first and consumers second.

Assume first a 'large' number of firms and consumers. Firms sell differenti-ated products and each firm has a negligible impact on its competitors. Con-sumers like different goods on different days (e.g. a preference for variety by the Jensen inequality). Consequently, they have no incentive to locate close to any particular firm. However, if transportation costs are low and/or products differ-entiated enough, firms have an incentive to cluster at points where they are, on average, close to all their potential customers, while consumers distribute them-selves around firms according to the Thünian highest bid rent principle. In other words, firms agglomerate because the benefit for a firm to locate away from competitors (its price can be higher) is overcome by the fact that its demand is much lower than within the agglomeration. Hence, under the conditions stated above, the spatial equilibrium involves the formation of an agglomeration (see e.g. Papageorgiou and Thisse 1985; Abdel-Rahman 1988; Fujita 1988; and Fujita and Krugman 1995).[15]

Suppose now that firms are no longer atomistic but behave strategically, while consumers still behave competitively. (According to Henderson and Mitra (1994), modern cities would be replete by 'big' private firms and developers that are not atomistic agents.) Since firms have more market power than consumers, it seems reasonable to assume that firms locate first, anticipating the subsequent locations of consumers and the effect of firms' locations on their demand func-tions.[16] When products are homogeneous, such a process may reinforce the

---

[15] A similar approach is taken by Krugman (1991, 1993*b*), who emphasizes more the interaction between the product and labour markets but does not integrate land.

[16] This approach to firms' and consumers' locational choice is analogous to the Cournot–Walras model used in general equilibrium with imperfect competition (see Bonanno 1990 for a recent survey). In this model, firms select quantities, and prices are then established at the Walrasian equilibrium of the corresponding exchange economy. Hence firms are able to determine the demand functions relating the quantities they supply to the equilibrium market prices. Using these inverse demands, firms choose their outputs at the Cournot equilibrium. In the spatial setting, the locations of firms correspond to outputs, while the residential equilibrium, which is influenced by the loca-tions chosen by firms, corresponds to the competitive equilibrium in the Cournot–Walras model.

tendency towards dispersion that was discovered in Section 8.3. If the firms disperse, consumers pay smaller transport costs on average, and may also pay lower average land prices, since with dispersed firms the supply of attractive lots (those close to firms) is greater. The resulting income effect would increase consumers' demand for private goods, and make localized market power even more profitable than in the Hotelling model (Fujita and Thisse 1986). However, the mere existence of a public facility or of a major transportation node might be enough to attract firms within the same urban area, other things the same, because transportation costs are reduced for consumers, which leaves them with higher incomes with which to buy the good sold by firms (Thisse and Wildasin 1992). In other words, the existence of a pre-existing public facility yields an incentive for agglomeration of firms and consumers in an urban area. Clearly, more work is called for here. In particular, the role of product differentiation should be analysed when consumers are mobile. As in Section 8.3, it seems reasonable to expect product differentiation to lead to the formation of agglomerations when consumers at any given location have heterogeneous tastes (or a preference for variety). If this conjecture is correct, an important question is the number of cities that emerge in equilibrium as well as their relative sizes (Krugman 1993c).

Introducing a land market in Hotelling-type models also permits allocation mechanisms based on land capitalization. A model of private goods production in the spirit of Section 8.4 would interpret the jurisdiction as a 'company town'. The firm would own all the land occupied by its customers. Efficiency within the jurisdiction would mean marginal cost pricing and a socially optimal location for the firm within the jurisdiction. To purchase from a particular firm, a consumer must live in that firm's jurisdiction. The firm's payoff would be the profit earned by selling the good plus the capitalized value of its land. If the firms (jurisdictions) compete for customers only by setting unit prices for the goods, the unit prices would serve two purposes: to attract consumers to the jurisdiction, but also to determine how much of the good is consumed. In non-cooperative equilibrium (if any) these two purposes would conflict, and, based on the reasoning in Section 8.4, we find it reasonable to conjecture that the firms might not set efficient marginal cost prices, even if they locate efficiently within their jurisdictions. However, if a firm could affect migration by setting an admission fee as well as a unit price (nonlinear pricing), we conjecture that it would conduct its internal affairs efficiently; i.e., it would set price equal to marginal cost and locate optimally, controlling immigration through the admission fee.

Of course, it is unreasonable to take the geographic boundaries between firms' market areas as fixed, as the model does. In real markets, boundaries between firms are endogenous as in the Hotelling model. Recently Asami *et al.* (1993) have proposed an efficient allocation mechanism based on land capitalization in which consumer locations and market boundaries are both endogenous. Each firm's payoff is determined by its profit from selling the private good plus the capitalized value of the land in the whole area under consideration. Roughly speaking, in this mechanism each firm is made to treat the whole market served by all firms as its own jurisdiction. It is necessary to take such a broad definition of the jurisdiction because otherwise there would be uncounted spillovers: each firm's location and price decision affects consumers in the whole market. The capitalization mechanism works as follows. When a new firm enters, it changes the aggregate land rent. If each firm is given the aggregate land rent as revenue, minus some lump-sum tariff, firms in aggregate will choose optimal locations and prices equal to marginal cost, provided the utility achieved by consumers is fixed by an outside option. The land rent capitalizes the social value of the firms' activities, and by maximizing its contribution to capitalized value the firm maximizes social welfare. For the case of Hotelling-type homogeneous goods, Asami *et al.* identify tariffs that guarantee non-negative income to both the mechanism designer and the firms;[17] however, in general, finding such tariffs may be problematic. Furthermore, the existence of different firms supplying a consumer with different products makes it difficult to evaluate the contribution of each firm to the land rent prevailing where the consumer resides, and may call for new institutional arrangements in order to achieve efficiency (Hochman *et al.* 1994).

8.6. Conclusion

In location models with fixed costs, competition between firms is inevitably localized. With homogeneous goods, firms have a tendency to disperse, and, because of the monopoly profits that arise from geographical isolation, too many firms may enter. When consumers have a taste for product variety (or consumers with heterogeneous tastes are geographically dispersed), firms may agglomerate. In the random utility model with the logit distribution, the number of firms will be close to optimal. On the other hand, there has been little investigation into the joint location problem of firms and consumers.

A land market opens the possibility of allocation mechanisms based on capitalization. These are focal in the literature on local public goods, but, because of the absence of transport costs, that literature cannot be adopted without modification to the problem of firm location, even if we assume that firms can be landowners and therefore can profit from capitalization. In order for capitalization incentives to achieve efficiency, firms must own all the land occupied by their customers; thus, the boundaries between firms' markets must be fixed before they set prices. This conflicts with the idea behind the model of transport costs in which the boundary is endogenous to the prices.

We have discussed another type of allocation mechanism based on capitalization in which each firm collects the entire rent from all the land, so that endogenous

---

[17] Another example is provided by Fujita and Thisse (1993), who apply the same principle to decentralize the optimum in the quadratic assignment problem developed by Koopmans and Beckmann (1957).

boundaries are no longer a problem. However, such mechanisms must be implemented by a central authority, and cannot be implemented simply by distributing the land (whether by fiat or market) and then permitting firms to compete on price.

To study the simultaneous location decisions of firms and consumers, it seems that transportation costs and capitalization effects must be joined in the same model. This is partially done in the urban economics model of the central city (Fujita 1989), where consumers bear transport costs to the centre and their land rent capitalizes that cost. To our knowledge, such models have not been fully extended to allocation mechanisms that also govern the location decisions of firms. However, we have suggested that there may be mechanisms based on capitalization and/or nonlinear pricing rules that achieve efficiecy, but such mechanisms are not decentralized competitive models.

We conclude from our consideration of the literature on location and space that space introduces to economics a rich set of problems and possibilities that have not been fully explored. We are unsure why the subject has fallen out of fashion, but since space is basic to the conduct of economic activity, both domestically and internationally, the subject should certainly be revived.

REFERENCES

Abdel-Rahman, H. M. (1988), 'Product Differentiation, Monopolistic Competition and City Size', *Regional Science and Urban Economics*, 18: 69–86.

Allais, M. (1943), *A la recherche d'une discipline économique*. Paris; reprinted as *Traité d'économie pure*. Paris: Imprimerie nationale, 1952.

Anderson, S., de Palma, A., and Thisse, J.-F. (1992), *Discrete Choice Theory of Product Differentiation*. Cambridge, Mass.: MIT Press.

Arrow, K., and Debreu, G. (1954), 'Existence of an Equilibrium for a Competitive Economy', *Econometrica*, 22: 265–90.

Asami, Y., Fujita, M., and Thisse, J.-F. (1993), 'A Land Capitalization Approach to the Efficient Provision of Urban Facilities', *Regional Science and Urban Economics*, 23: 487–522.

Aumann, R. (1964), 'Markets with a Continuum of Traders', *Econometrica*, 32: 39–50.

Bacon, R. (1971), 'An Approach to the Theory of Consumer Shopping Behavior', *Urban Studies*, 8: 55–64.

Beckmann, M., and Puu, T. (1985), *Spatial Economics: Density, Potential and Flow*. Amsterdam: North-Holland.

Blaug, M. (1985), *Economic Theory in Retrospect*. Cambridge: Cambridge University Press.

Bonanno, G. (1990), 'General Equilibrium Theory with Imperfect Competition', *Journal of Economic Surveys*, 4: 297–328.

Buchanan, J. M. (1965), 'An Economic Theory of Clubs', *Economica*, 33: 1–14.

Chamberlin, E. (1933), *The Theory of Monopolistic Competition*. Cambridge, Mass.: Harvard University Press.

Cornet, B. (1988), 'General Equilibrium Theory and Increasing Returns: Presentation', *Journal of Mathematical Economics*, 17: 103–18.

Courant, P. N., and Deardoff, A. V. (1992), 'International Trade with Lumpy Countries', *Journal of Political Economy*, 100: 198–210.

d'Aspremont, C., Gabszewicz, J., and Thisse, J.-F. (1979), 'On Hotelling's Stability of Competition', *Econometrica*, 47: 1045–50.

Dixit, A., and Stiglitz, J. E. (1977), 'Monopolistic Competition and Optimum product Diversity', *American Economic Review*, 67: 297–308.

Eaton, B. C., and Lipsey, R. G. (1977), 'The Introduction of Space into the Neoclassical Model of Value Theory', in M. Artis, and A. Nobay (eds.), *Studies in Modern Economics*. Oxford: Basil Blackwell, 59–96.

Ekelund, R. B., and Shieh, Y. N. (1986), 'Dupuit, Spatial Economics and Optimal Resource Allocation: a French Tradition', *Economica*, 53: 483–96.

Epple, D., and Romer, T. (1989), 'On the Flexibility of Municipal Boundaries', *Journal of Urban Economics*, 26: 307–19.

Fujita, M. (1988), 'A Monopolistic Competition Model of Spatial Agglomeration', *Regional Science and Urban Economics*, 18: 87–124.

—— (1989), *Urban Economic Theory: Land Use and City Size*. Cambridge: Cambridge University Press.

—— and Krugman, P. (1995), 'When Is the Economy Monocentic? von Thünen and Chamberlin Unified', *Regional Science and Urban Economics*, 25: 505–28.

—— and Smith, T. E. (1987), 'Existence of Continuous Residential land-Use Equilibria', *Regional Science and Urban Economics*, 17: 549–94.

—— and Thisse, J.-F. (1986), 'Spatial Competition with a Land Market: Hotelling and von Thünen Unified', *Review of Economic Studies*, 53: 819–41.

—— —— (1993), 'Technological Linkages and Efficient Locations of Indivisible Activities', *Journal of Urban Economics*, 34: 118–41.

Grimaud, A., and Laffont, J.-J. (1989), 'Existence of a Spatial Equilibrium', *Journal of Urban Economics*, 25: 213–18.

Helpman, E., and Krugman, P. R. (1985), *Market Structure and Foreign Trade*. Cambridge, Mass.: MIT Press.

Henderson, J. V. (1985), 'The Tiebout Model: Bring Back the Entrepreneurs', *Journal of Political Economy*, 93, 248–64.

—— and Mitra, A. (1994), 'The New Urban Landscape: Developers and Edge Cities', mimeo, Brown University, Department of Economics.

Hochman, O., Pines, D., and Thisse, J.-F. (1994), 'On the Optimal Structure of Local Governments', *American Economic Review*, 85: 1224–40.

Hotelling, H. (1929), 'Stability in Competition', *Economic Journal*, 39: 41–57.

Kaldor, N. (1935), 'Market Imperfection and Excess Capacity', *Economica*, 2: 35–50.

Koopmans, T. C. (1957), *Three Essays on the State of Economic Science*. New York: McGraw-Hill.

—— and Beckmann, M. J. (1957), 'Assignment Problems and the Location of Economic Activities', *Econometrica*, 25: 53–76.

Krugman, P. R. (1993a), 'On the Relationship Between Trade Theory and Location Theory', *Review of International Economics*, 1: 110–22.

—— (1993b), 'First Nature, Second Nature, and Metropolitan Location', *Journal of Regional Science*, 33: 129–44.

Lösch, A. (1940), *Die Räumliche Ordnung der Wirtschaft*. Iena: Gustav Fisher. English translation: *The Economics of Location*, Yale University Press, New Haven, 1954.

McFadden, D. (1981), 'Econometric Models of Probabilistic Choice' in C. F. Manski and D. McFadden (eds), *Structural Analysis of Discrete Data with Econometric Applications*, MIT Press, Cambridge, Mass.: 198–272.

Nerlove, M. L. and Sadka, E. (1991), 'Von Thünen's Model of the Dual Economy', *Journal of Economics*, 54: 97–123.

Papageorgiou, Y. Y. and Thisse, J.-F. (1985), 'Agglomeration as Spatial Interdependence Between Firms and Households', *Journal of Economic Theory*, 37: 19–31.

Pines, D. and Weiss, Y. (1976), 'Land Improvement Projects and Land Values', *Journal of Public Economics*, 3: 1–13.

Polinsky, A. M. and Shavell, S. (1975), 'The Air Pollution and Property Value Debates', *Review of Economics and Statistics*, 57: 100–4.

Samuelson, P. A. (1967), 'The Monopolistic Competition Revolution' in R. Kuenne (ed.), *Monopolistic Competition Theory*, Wiley, New York: 105–38.

—— (1983), 'Thünen at Two Hundred', *Journal of Economic Literature*, 21: 1468–88.

Scotchmer, S. (1985a), 'Hedonic Prices, Crowding, and Optimal Dispersion of Population', *Journal of Economic Theory*, 37: 285–303.

—— (1985b), 'Profit Maximizing Clubs', *Journal of Public Economics*, 27: 25–45.

—— (1985c), 'Two-Tier Pricing of Shared Facilities in a Free-Entry Equilibrium', *Rand Journal of Economics*, 16: 456–72.

—— (1986), 'Local Public Goods in an Equilibrium: How Pecuniary Externalities Matter', *Regional Science and Urban Economics*, 16: 463–81.

—— (1994), 'Public Goods and the Invisible Hand' in J. Quigley and E. Smolensky (eds), *Modern Public Finance*, Harvard University Press, Cambridge, Mass., 93–125.

Schweizer, U., Varaiya, P. V., and Hartwick, J. (1976), 'General Equilibrium and Location Theory', *Journal of Urban Economics*, 3: 285–303.

Sraffa, P. (1926), 'The Laws of Return under Competitive Conditions', *Economic Journal*, 36: 535–50.

Stahl, K. (1987), 'Theories of Urban Business Location' in E. S. Mills (ed.), *Handbook of Urban Economics*, North-Holland, Amsterdam, 759–820.

Starrett, D. (1978), 'Market Allocations of Location Choice in a Model with Free Mobility', *Journal of Economic Theory*, 17: 21–37.

Stiglitz, J. (1977), 'The Theory of Local Public Goods' in M. S. Feldstein and R. P. Inman (eds), *The Economics of Public Services*, Macmillan, London, 273–334.

Thisse, J.-F. (1993), 'Oligopoly and the Polarization of Space', *Papers and Proceedings of the European Economic Association*, 37: 199–307.

—— and Wildasin, D. (1992), 'Public Facility Location and Urban Spatial Structure', *Journal of Public Economics*, 48: 83–118.

Tiebout, M. (1956), 'A Pure Theory of Local Expenditures', *Journal of Political Economy*, 64: 416–24.

von Thünen, J. H. (1826), *Der Isolierte Staat in Beziehung auf Landwirtschaft und Nationalökonomie*. Hamburg: Perthes. English translation: *The Isolated State*, Pergamon Press, Oxford, 1996.

Wildasin, D. E. (1987) 'Theoretical Analysis of Local Public Economics', *Handbook of Urban Economics*, in E. S. Mills (ed.), North-Holland, Amsterdam, 429–76.

9

The Future of Managerial Economics

Jean-Pierre Ponssard and Hervé Tanguy

The discipline of economics is generally associated with major issues facing nations: unemployment, trade, growth and fiscal problems for example. Thus, the economist becomes a sort of overall policy advisor. In these global analysis, firms may be conveniently considered as a black box, which mechanically optimize profits on the basis of input and output prices.

Obviously, the reality of management is much more complicated. Many applied economists study this black box for its own interest, generating relevant ideas for the analysis of (imperfect) competition and for the (more) efficient allocation of resources. These ideas have connections with the two traditional subjects discussed in formal research and categorized as exchange and production. What is the nature of these connections, how is theory influenced by applications and vice versa? Can we draw some conclusions on future research based on these interactions?

This paper starts from the tangible role of the applied economist within a company, and then goes on to describe the tools and techniques used, which have greatly developed and continue to develop according to the various issues encountered. It describes what managerial economics is supposed to do, what it was and where it could go. Then it suggests some ideas for future theoretical research.

This field approach is prefered from one in which one would start from the theoretical achievements and the open theoretical questions. This preference arises from a number of reasons, the main of which simply is the research experience of the authors devoted to analysing and describing how things are done in practice. Still this approach can be directly related to the theoretical views expressed in the present volume by two other authors.

Malinvaud, in Chapter 2 above, emphasizes the recurring cycle in the development of economic research, making a clear difference between operational versus analytical research, as well as between the search for positive explanation or the proposal of normative rules. Managerial economics typically deals with operational tools and normative rules. Malinvaud identifies the beginning of an 'applied' cycle with the 1960s. This is the point at which we shall also originate our discussion of managerial economic tools, mostly based at the time on optimization techniques and discounted cash flow analysis.

Malinvaud also points out that the current trend in theoretic research is mainly positive oriented and analytical in its purpose, reflecting the need to understand complex issues. Indeed, we shall illustrate the decline of traditional operational managerial economic tools because of the more 'complex' environment which firms had to face in the late 1970s. At the academic level a lot of the current formal research indirectly results from this decline. Models were developed to introduce the complexities that were recognized from the real world. Then an interesting question arises: does this understanding provides any new meaningful operational tools, or is this understanding still very remote to be 'applicable'?

Our opinion is that it is not as remote as it is often argued. Yet a major qualification should be made, a qualification which is rarely understood by pure theoreticians. It is worthwhile spending some time on this matter from the very beginning to properly focus the scope of this paper. Let us take two very 'applied' subjects such as poker and chess to illustrate our point. Poker appeared as an illustrating example in many early game-theoretic work with authors such as von Neumann, Nash, and Shapley. From this starting point, much more is now conceptually known about the strategic usage of information (adverse selection, moral hazard, signalling, etc.). Do these analytical achievements provide any operational guidance to playing poker? The answer is certainly no. On the other hand, very much is now known about designing computer programs to play chess efficiently. The corresponding conceptual work (in artificial intelligence, cognitive science and optimization theory) is almost ignored by economists.[1] Since the current analytical work is much closer to the former type of research than to the latter, this clearly suggests that no operational tools should be expected from the recent analytical achievements. What should be expected then?

Our view is that these analytical achievements can be used as 'models of knowledge' to develop new managerial economic tools to be progressively substituted to optimizing techniques of the 1960s. But significant contextualization is required to go from a model of knowledge to an operational tool. At this point a major difference appears with the approach of the 1960s. Instead of complexifying the tool, it now seems much more adequate to limit its complexity and to increase the cognitive capabilities of the agents that will use it. This view has important ramifications in terms of research orientations. First, it makes it much more essential to clarify what are the general and what are the more or less *ad hoc* assumptions, given that the capacity for economic theory to provide results that would have wide applications now seems much more doubtful than it ever was. Second, models of knowledge are normative in essence; that is to say, that they are meant to be tested not against data, but in relationship with their capacity to create organizational learning from current practices (i.e. to create a more efficient future rather than explain the past as they would as positive explanations of the world). It is unclear how this second idea should be put into evaluating techniques to generate valuable incentives for research.

---

[1] See Simon and Schaefer (1992) for an illuminating discussion of how chess is played by human and computers, and related developments.

These introductory comments should be put into perspective with more specific ones about the future of game theory. Game theory has now become one of the basic conceptual tools of the modern microeconomist. In this respect, it is interesting to observe that van Damme, in Chapter 10 below, suggests that research in that field should give more attention to the context. Pure hypothetico-deductive analysis of rationality in formal games provided a very profound understanding of the concept of common knowledge. This concept is a key issue in applications (e.g., how credible is rational behaviour? what kind of bounded rationality should be introduced and in what form?). To focus on the theoretical analysis, it seems almost inevitable to introduce some specificities about the situation under study. This had been pointed out a long time ago by Schelling. It may now be the appropriate time to embark on such an approach, given the state of the analytical tools that have been developed and the operational needs in many management areas.

9.1. The Economist Job in a Company: a Starting Point

The position of the applied economist in a company is usually part of financial services. His main activity is devoted to producing indicators and quantitative assessments. But the applied economist is not an accountant. Historically, these two functions have been separated, which is unfortunate.[2] The economist does accounts for the future, whereas the accountant keeps track of past income and expenditure. The economist contributes to decision-making, whereas the accountant is a bookkeeper ensuring the legal soundness of the accounts.

This dichotomy is unfortunate, because the first of these functions is not mandatory, whereas the second is. Companies are subject to numerous onlookers: the shareholders, the tax man, the employees representatives, the competitors and other stake-holders. The result is that the economist may distrust the legal accounts which are subject to conventions and may be arbitrary or even vague (with various degrees of intention) and thus difficult to interpret. Therefore the economist uses his own data,[3] and constructs his own accounts, an approach that lays him open to being cut off from reality, the reality that has the force of the law and the force of a reference which is automatically communicated to the stake holders. Furthermore, the updating of his own data base may be problematic.

---

[2] Johnson and Kaplan (1987) suggest that this historical separation is partly due to the cost of maintaining several management information systems in a coherent way (that is with possibilities to go from one to the other). That it should now be possible to handle all relevant business information in one unique data base remains an implicit view of many consultancy companies.

[3] A key reason for developing his own data comes from the idea that there should be a difference between economic cost, i.e. opportunity cost, and accounting cost (see e.g. Alchian 1977 for an early approach to economic cost relevant for managerial economics). Still, it is rarely recognized that the very notion of opportunity cost requires a theory of price formation. This requires the introduction of an undisputable solution concept (and there is none) in a world of imperfect competition since in such a world market prices and individual firm decisions clearly interact. The discrepancy between standard accounting cost allocation procedures and more economic cost allocation procedures may then be more arbitrary than it is usually argued, both relying on conventional assumptions.

Beyond participating in the forecasting of accounts and their interpretation, the company economist is often involved into analysing the expected profitability of various assets.

Analysis of asset profitability is only one step away from modelling the major functions associated with the overall management of industrial activity. This step is all the more easily made when the investment concerned is the acquisition of other companies, a situation quite common nowadays.[4] The economist is supposed to validate a qualitative assessment and to provide some indicators that illustrate the value creation process associated with the investment. Such an analysis involves considerations about the competitive strengths and weaknesses of the proposed strategy in terms of price policy, product range, production management, further capital expenses, choice of a financial structure, and many other issues. This analysis thus risks becoming excessively complex, and consequently difficult to believe: how can the economist pretend to be competent in all these different areas? Rather than being an outside analyst, this suggests that the managerial economist should redefined as a middle man between experts, his own expertise coming from his ability to organize an efficient coordination procedure among company experts (Ponssard and Tanguy 1993). This point will be further discussed in later sections. Most of the time, the economist job only consists in providing a general methodology and company experts translate their subjective beliefs into the standard quantified framework.

The methodology may address such questions as which time span to consider for the analysis, what to do with the goodwill in case of an acquisition, how to compute cash flows, which terminal value to attribute at the end of the period, particularly if growth is expected to exceed that horizon, and so on. This methodology is in fact a way to model the company and to evaluate the resulting financial flows.

Once the decision to invest is taken, another task devolves to the economist: management control. Usually, this consists of checking that the reality of what is happening does not stray too far from forecasts. In some companies, the management controller is a sort of financial inspector, who on the fourth or fifth of every month records the results of the previous month's activity. The directors can then discuss the findings, and if they are too far below the forecasts the executive responsible may simply be sacked. Thus, as a support to decision-making, this function is concrete.

Ordinarily, an executive knows how to handle a difference between the economist's accounts and the accountant's results sheet to his own advantage. He can plead the changing circumstances between the time at which the forecasts were made and the period of activity, reorganizations made essential by these changes, the impossibility of identifying what is caused by the environment (which is uncontrollable) and what results from his own sound decisions (the benefits of which will soon be evident). If applied too soon, management control

---

[4] A typical managerial economics approach to this issue is detailed in Copeland *et al.* (1990).

does not function, if too late, it has to reassess completely the overall state of affairs, which is technically difficult and politically sensitive. Thus, the use of *ex ante* economic analysis for *ex post* control is an important and delicate matter.

As a starting point for discussion, the job description of a managerial economist requires the ability to handle the following three tasks through a set of well identified operational tools:

1. defining a framework to evaluate a decision through collecting appropriate data;
2. in particular, modelling the future consequences of a decision in a credible way;
3. controlling the *ex post* performance of past decisions.

9.2. What Managerial Economics Was About

The 1960s was the golden age of managerial economics. It was the time when the basic tools of 'economic calculus'[5] were developed: techniques for forecasting, pricing, capital investment planning. The general environment was considered to be fairly stable, and if models of the future did not always perform as expected it was felt that this was just a question of further work: with more time and more extensive calculation techniques, the models could be perfected.

With the crises of the 1970s and the subsequent major changes, the context did not, perhaps, fundamentally evolve, but businessmen became much more circumspect when dealing with economists and their models for predicting the future. Decisions had to be made in a context of doubt, knowing that the doubt was intrinsic and that it could not be eliminated by economists, or anyone else.

All this is now well known, and can be summarized by a classic illustration, termed the so-called golf club. The accuracy of (usually very optimistic) forecasts in face of a changing reality has been deceiving (see Fig. 9.1). As a consequence, internal economic services in charge of producing forecasts have been dismantled. Where they did not disappear, they had to adapt by using more flexible and more qualitative tools, such as strategic analysis. They changed their name and relabelled themselves as strategic departments.

Strategic analysis aims to position an activity or a project relative to what is known about the competition. Then, the objective is to maintain a so-called durable competitive advantage[6] as a proxy to secure future profits.[7]

---

[5] In France, there has been a long tradition of managerial economics combining economic theory with operational research. It culminated under the impulsion of Lesourne, with the creation of SEMA, a consultancy company. The existence of large French state entreprises such as Electricité de France is a key historical factor of this development.

[6] Porter (1980) is the basic reference that illustrates this change.

[7] A tangible contribution to strategic analysis refers to typologies of businesses such as 'dogs, cash cows, stars and dilemma' with respective generic strategies. (See the well known Boston Consulting Group booklets, a presentation of which is given in Ponssard (1988: ch. 2.)

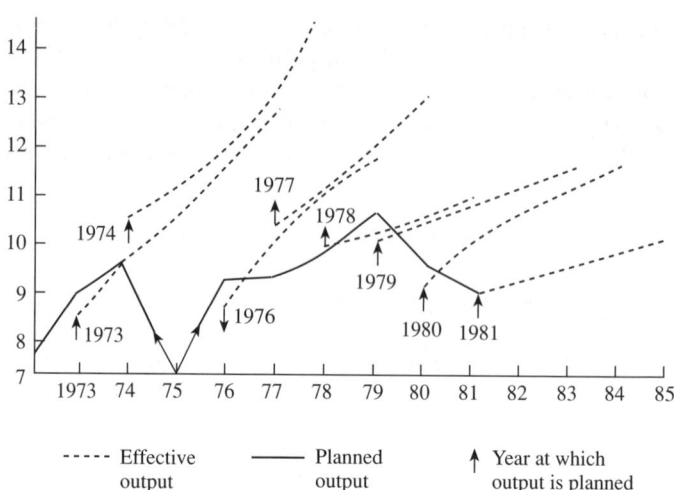

Fig. 9.1. Effective versus planned output for ethylene in the EEC, 1973–1985
Source: Chemistry and Industry: CEFI

However, subjectivity plays a large role in identifying a business segment and the key factors that structure competition, and in selecting a reasonable strategy. The data collection process to validate that strategy can be an elusive task. The issue of controlling the *ex post* validity of a strategic choice may become very political. Quite rapidly it may become apparent that strategic analysis does not yield quantitative models in any way comparable to the operationality of previous approaches, and this explains why the staff size of many internal strategic departments, after a flourishing period, is later been considerably reduced.

This evolution towards more qualitative strategic analysis had major impacts: first, the externalizing of strategic departments to consulting firms; second, the increased discrepancy between the control process, which remained internal to the company, focusing more and more on financial data instead of on key strategic factors; third, the relevance of the strategic analysis methodology provided by consulting firms, which became progressively cut off from the direct empirically rooted experience of operational managers, reinforcing the divorce between the recent theoretical developments and the empirical challenges managers face. This evolution left little room for genuine managerial economics.

From an empirical standpoint, the challenges did not concern the need for more sophisiticated market analysis but rather the need to adapt production techniques to an ever changing environment. Since, after all, production is at the core of the firm activity, there may be something to learn from the way this challenge has been addressed and from the tools that have developed.

9.3. What Happened in Production Management

Production management is one of the areas of business activity where there has been a revolution. The approach to production management has drastically changed away from the Taylorism approach. With a large variety of final products and multiple intermediate parts or components (cars, computers, airplanes, military equipment transmission systems, and radars all illustrate the trend towards customized production in many different areas[8]), the recourse to a well designed *ex ante* optimal resource allocation plan would be excessively complex without providing much *ex post* efficiency.

The selected practical approaches allow much more reactivity to on-line information flows. In this context, our starting point to formalize an economic methodology could be redefined as follows:

1. The question refers not to assessing a decision but to assessing a coordination procedure.
2. The problem of forecasting data for a central planner is replaced by the problem of designing an information system that aims to transfer the relevant information to where it needs to be as quickly as possible.
3. Management control is not on *ex post* evaluation but involves continuous adjustments so as to remain on some 'ideal overall trajectory', independently of any temporary observed deviation.

As for how this 'ideal overall trajectory' is economically evaluated, it relies on intuitive principles about so-called key cost and value drivers: date, quantity, quality commitments, etc. The economic performance of such intuitive rules involves a large part of wishful thinking with the expectation of self-fulfilling prophecies. And it seems to work most of the time.

Indeed, the originality of this new production system[9] is the true symbiosis between 'hard' (technology and machines to be as flexible as possible) and 'soft' elements (continuous information exchanges and readjustments of flows among services on one hand, labour management across services so as promote better understanding about a common task to be performed on another). This approach is far from the traditional allocation of resources to well identified services.[10]

That these pragmatic approaches could cope successfully with the increased complexity of production without major psychological stress is far from obvious.

In this respect, it is interesting to point out that the main empirical difficulties come from the design of the relevant information flows, the motivation to

---

[8] Continuous production processes such as aluminium, steel, cement, etc., have been less affected by this revolution. Still, this revolution in production is now extended to production of services and as such is of relevance to any organization.

[9] A stimulating introduction to the new versus the traditional approaches to production management can be found in Goldratt and Cox (1993).

[10] See Aoki (1990) for a discussion emphasizing these differences.

have the information circulated, and the early recognition that on-line operation should not be complete, rather than from pure opportunistic behaviour from the agents.[11] It is also interesting to note that the operational tools that have been developed are usually quite simple and do not rely on sophisticated optimizing techniques. They are often constructed along the underlying physical flows that arise from the selected production process.

How does these well documented empirical observations eventually relate with the actual trend of economic research in organization theory?

9.4. Production Management and Organization Theory

The preceding observations can be summarized as follows.

In modern production management, each agent is in interaction with a limited number of other agents. A general task is identified. Two assumptions are crucial to the analysis. First, these agents have distinct knowledge in the sense that they cannot *ex ante* communicate their full capabilities to one another in a limited time period. Second, the decision process is to be conducted on line with only a few possibilities to formally exchange information between agents. Efficient *ex post* efficiency of decentralized decision making is incompatible with the urgency of the actual functioning of the modern firm.[12]

Consider now two ways of formalizing this problem. In a standard approach, this production problem would be investigated in terms of the feasibility of a Paretian outcome under incentive compatibility constraints, given the agents' individual action spaces and utility functions.[13]

Milgrom and Roberts (1992) have suggested another approach which seems more in line with the ideas currently developed in production management. They suggest a two-step approach, first to identify an overall feasible and satisfactory strategy for the firm, and then to design appropriate incentives to ensure that this strategy is followed.

This two-step approach to formalizing the problem has two advantages: it does not start with utility functions but with proxies of firm profits; and it does not need to model the way agents optimize their actions using such unpalatable notions as risk aversion, Bayesian beliefs, and reservation wages, but rather with the mutual observability of objective facts such as physical and information flows arising from a given production strategy. More importantly, it recognizes the intrinsic difficulty in finding a feasible production strategy simply because of the multitude of technical and financial constraints and capabilities which have to be combined. Combinatorial (and non-convexity) aspects arising from

---

[11] See Asanuma (1991) for a suggestive case study in the automobile industry.

[12] It is quite easy to simulate such a process in a laboratory, the results are amazingly poor in terms of ex-post efficiency. A well known example in the USA is the 'beer game' (Sterman 1989; see also Schon (1997) for a game illustrating difficulties of communication without a common langage.

[13] Holmström (1982) is representative of this line of approach.

space and time complementarities[14] are more crucial than pure incentive compatibility constraints.[15]

This second avenue is certainly worth more attention than it currently obtains from theoreticians. Significant contributions should address questions such as the best coordination rules to be used and the design of the appropriate information systems which should be put into place to support these rules.[16]

Still, an interesting question comes to mind. What would be the operationality of the corresponding theoretical achievements? From a positive standpoint (as it would be in the traditional view of economic theory), predictions on the outside world based on such models are of very limited value. Still these models can be useful in a learning process for those who will be operationally involved in handling the production task.[17]

The status of economic models can be illustrated through a critical discussion of some recent game theoretical advances.

9.5. Models of Knowledge versus Operational Models: Some Ideas Originating from Game Theory

Game theory is now used as a pedagogical tool in most microecomics textbooks.[18] At the same time, its foundation has never been as shaky as it now appears because of the profusion of Nash refinements.[19] That most applications of game theory to economic problems require implicit rationality conditions is admitted, but the consequences of this fact has not been fully recognized.[20]

Consider Fig. 9.2. In this diagram several distinctions are made. What concerns the 'real' world is depicted on the left. Managers more or less address this

[14] This question of solvability is almost never addressed in economics in spite of the fact that many economic models are extremely difficult to solve numerically (see Paradimitriou and Tsitsiklis 1986). To design an economic model which is solvable and acceptable to the various parties involved is a major practical task.

[15] This is not to say that incentive constraints are not important but that if these are operationalized on proxies which are not properly related to the on going process, many perverse outcomes arise. See Ponssard (1983) for the unexpected results obtained from incentive constraints in military procurement in France: such contracts are most useful when minor productivity gains remain at the end of a program rather than at the early stage when major uncertainties coexist. In a similar vein, see Midler (1994) for a discussion of how the incentive issue varies from a creativity one to a commitment one along the evolution of a project.

[16] See Aoki (1986) for a tentative formalization along these lines. See also Cremer (1980) for an interesting formalization of Chandler's analysis of Sears and Roebuck reorganizations (Chandler 1962). These contributions give only limited attention to the static and dynamic complementarities resulting from the underlying production functions.

[17] This view relates to the one originally developed in the organizational learning litterature Argyris and Schon (1978), Moisdon and Weil (1992), illustrate the role of full size models to work on the technical interfaces in the automobile industry.

[18] See Kreps (1990) as well as Milgrom and Roberts (1992); see also Kreps (1984) for an advocacy paper on the subject.

[19] See van Damme (1992) for a survey of this litterature trigered by the work of Kohlberg and Mertens (1986) on forward induction criteria.

[20] See Ponssard (1990) for a discussion of that point.

Phase 1: Planning

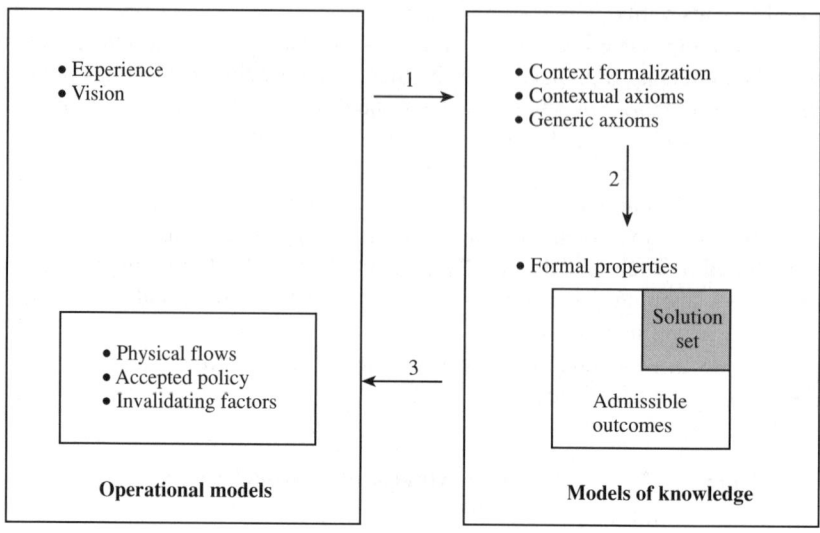

Phase 2: Decentralized actions
- Agents with idiosyncratic knowledge
- Radical uncertainty about the future
- Mutual adjustments
- Crises (generating experience and knowledge)

Fig. 9.2. The role of economic models in management

real world in two steps: they design planning and control devices (referred as operational models) to assess the *ex ante* validity of some feasible strategy; then they react in a decentralized fashion to local uncertainties with a very limited possibility of redesigning an overall strategy.

What concerns game theory, and economic theory in general, is depicted on the right of the diagram, under the heading of what is referred to as models of knowledge. Theoreticians care about conceptualization of some context and the solutions that could logically be inferred from various rationality assumptions. This corresponds to arrow 2.

From a theoretical perspective, a difference is usually made between the context and the model used to talk about it. But, surprisingly, many game theorists have lost this distinction and consider that a game tree or a normal form game is meant to be played as it is. They forget about arrows 1 and 3. A lot of confusion comes from this: what is the more 'real' representation? are the two equivalent? when is the 'actual' reasoning taking place—at the beginning of the game or after an actual move, the validity of which is still under consideration? And so on.

Given this confusing state of affairs, many paradoxes have been discussed (such as outcomes resulting from backward induction). In many extensive-form solutions it is not unusual to show that a proposed result arises from implicit assumptions that would be unintuitive if applied in another extensive game. This is very embarassing from a normative standpoint.

However, if one starts from the idea that generic rationality principles will produce interesting results only if they are combined with some contextual assumptions, then this completely changes the current perspective. The major task consists in identifying the relevant details of the context and in properly formalizing them (this refers to arrow 1). In our terminology, the elaboration of a model of knowledge implies a model-building activity. This is a major task which refers to finding the most adequate combination of some generic and contextual rationality principles to address a well identified practical problem. When it comes to interpreting the solution of a model of knowledge, a major difference arises from the standard discussions found in most game-theoretical papers: the formal solution of a model of knowledge can be relevant only as long as the actual players in the real world know that they share the same contextual axioms.

Why and how this can be the case should not be taken for granted. Only if this is the case is the understanding of the reasoning that underlies a model of knowledge of some interest. And this reasoning is more important than the identification of a detailed solution. All the solutions that are compatible with the assumptions should be identified to clarify what, in a model, connects the premises with the consequences. (Arrow 2 requires much more work than providing one solution to a given set of assumptions; the main task very often amounts to working backwards on the assumptions to obtain a desirable solution set and *only* that set.)

Crawford and Haller's analysis of pure coordination games (1990) provides a good pedagogical example illustrating this point. Their solution requires both some general rules and some conventions. In their game, since the labelling of the moves is private, the players cannot rely on such things as alphabetic order to coordinate. Their players have to make some joint inference based on *ad hoc* rules for constructing dynamic focal points using past observations. This cannot arise simply from generic Nash equilibrium considerations.[21] That conventions are needed is an interesting contribution to the formalization of corporate culture, so far discussed mainly through general reputation principles.

It is the entire line of reasoning corresponding to arrow 2, if any, that can be injected into an operational model. As such, it should be considered only as a reference to the implementation phase (arrow 3). And, as a reference, the model of knowledge need not be known in details to actual players. From an applied

---

[21] See Ponssard (1994) for a detailed discussion of this point and in particular for the notion of 'interactive rationality' which embeds conventions into the design of game-theoretical concepts through adopting a position '*à la* Rawls'.

perspective, the role of learning in model-building, the empirical difficulties to communicate knowledge across experts, and the reinforcing role of simple devices to sustain efficient coordination are the important things to be emphasized. Sophistication in modelling and robustness as a predictive device is replaced by transparency in assumptions and the limited efficiency to cope with varying circumstances.[22]

9.6. Is There a Future for Managerial Economics?

At this point we have characterized the current empirical trend in production management, a key area to understand what happened to the internal resource allocation process. Some possible connections with organization theory have been pointed out. What should be expected from theoretical research has been discussed. Can one reformulate the economist job in a company along the three dimensions identified Section 9.1?

1. *Defining a framework to assess a decision or designing an organization to implement a strategy*
Designing procedures of interaction between organizational agents is not identical to evaluating a one-spot decision for a well identified decision-maker. The explicit introduction of both the time dimension and the asymmetry of information (and knowledge) becomes necessary, and this is not correctly addressed by the standard modelling strategy. These organizational agents have cognitive capabilities that allow them to integrate new and relevant information as uncertainties unfold and time elapses as long as they have agreed on a set of more or less conventional rules. These rules allow them efficiently to coordinate decentralized actions without endangering the ongoing decision process. Thus, the major task refers to identifying such rules, making them common knowledge, and designing an appropriate information system that reinforces the time consistency of the decision process along the way. From the simple task of collecting opportunity costs to evaluate a decision, one goes to the more difficult issue of assessing the reactivity of an organizational structure to successfully implement a somewhat idealized generic strategy.

2. *Modelling the future in a credible way versus learning how to cooperate*
Standard approaches to decision-making under uncertainty typically amount to identifying a set of alternatives, a set of possible states of the world, and then optimizing a relevant criterion such as profit maximization. The relevance of the approach comes from the ability to model the future in a credible way. When the future is seen as a construction of a decentralized project, the economic

---

[22] For examples of operational models explicitly designed from models of knowledge, see Hatchuel and Molet (1986); Soler and Tanguy (1997). De Jaegere and Ponssard (1990) developed an experimental game illustrating economic modelling as an *ex ante* efficient communication device.

value of which will depend largely on the efficient ability to incorporate in due time information not known at the beginning, the issue focuses on evaluating coordination rules rather than on evaluating outcomes. The *ex ante* exploration of the production set is an enormously complex task which cannot be combined with a formal criterion. The future outcome of a strategy cannot be convincingly modelled, but the adequacy of generic strategy with some environmental assumptions can still be argued and theory can help in structuring this discussion. When the time comes to implement this strategy, many unnecessary details can remain unspecified, as long as agents are fully aware of the interdependence that results from technical and financial mutual constraints. The *ex ante* identification of the relevant mutual set of constraints and the robustness of proxies to keep on track can be logically explored and simulated on a simple model. This refers to the learning aspect of model-building.

3. *Controlling the ex post performance of a decision or contributing with efficiency to readjusting ongoing projects.*

Management control as traditionally depicted in terms of *ex post* assessments now becomes a centralized task, the goal of which is to challenge the relevance of the selected strategy given the progressive accumulation of data. Since the decentralized actions have not been precisely detailed and adaptability to local uncertainty is a key success factor of the firm, the notion of control has to be reformulated. It should take the role of auditing the relevance of the selected generic strategy and should eventually be prepared to invalidate it totally. This may be calling for crisis meetings in case of emergencies. Formally, this form of control is closer to classical test hypothesis than to Bayesian updating in which the very idea of control is simply ignored.

Is there a room along these lines for a set of core concepts similar to the ones that existed in the 1960s? Or is it the case that the concepts have to be so much adapted to the different contexts that this idea has become obsolete? The recent evolution of economics departments in business schools provides an empirical answer. In many of them, the staff of managerial economics (or decision sciences) departments has been reduced or dispersed to production, as well as finance, marketing, accounting, etc. In a way this is a pity, since quantitative managerial economics was a way of providing a global conceptual representation of management decision-making.

This creates a feeling of discomfort, since formal research in microeconomics may appear more and more remote from applied work. The optimistic view of this paper is that the gap may not be as large as it is sometimes advocated as long as one is willing to move out from a naïve relationship in which sound theory would give rise to simple and undisputable operational tools. Moreover, our discussion suggests that the question of rationality, a major issue in economic theory, will remain central on the research agenda for many years to come. This is good news for theory, be it analytical or normative.

REFERENCES

Alchian, A. (1977), 'Costs and Outputs', in *Economic Forces at Work*. Indianapolis: Liberty Press.

Aoki, M. (1986), 'Horizontal versus Vertical Information Structure of the Firm', *American Economic Review*, 76: 971–83.

—— (1990), 'Towards an Economic Model of the Japanese Firm', *Journal of Economic Literature*, 28: 1–27.

Argyris, C., and Schon, D. A. (1978), *Organisational Learning*. Reading, Mass.: Addison-Wesley.

Asanuma, B. (1991), 'Coordination between Production and Distribution in a Globalized Network of Firms: Assessing Flexibility Achieved in the Japanese Automobile Industry', Unpublished paper, Kyoto University Department of Economics.

Chandler, A. D. (1962), *Strategy and Structure*, Cambridge, Mass.: MIT Press.

Copeland, T., Koller, T., and Murrin, J. (1990), *Valuation: Measuring and Managing the Values of Companies*. New York: John Wiley.

Crawford, V. P., and Haller, H. (1990), 'Learning How to Cooperate: Optimal Play in Repeated Coordination Games', *Econometrica*, 58: 571–96.

Cremer, J. (1980), 'A Partial Theory of the Optimal Organization of a Bureaucracy', *Bell Journal of Economics*, 11: 000–00.

de Jaegere, A., and Ponssard, J. P. (1990), 'La Comptabilité: Genèse de la modélisation en économie d'entreprise', *Annales des Mines: Gérer et Comprendre*, March: 90–98.

Goldratt, E. M., and Cox, J. (1993), *The Goal*, UK: Gower (2nd edition).

Hatchuel, A., and Molet, H. (1986), 'Rational Modelling in Understanding and Aiding Human Decision Making', *European Journal of Operation Research*, 24: 178–86.

—— and Sardas, J.-Cl. (1990), 'Métiers et réseaux: les paradigmes industriels de la GPAO', *Revue Réseaux*, 4 (April–May): 27–35.

Holmström, B. (1982), 'Moral Hazard in Teams', *Bell Journal of Economics*, 13: 324–40.

Johnson, H. T., and Kaplan, R. S. (1987), *Relance Lost: the Rise and Fall of Management Accounting*. Boston: Harvard Business School Press.

Kohlberg, E., and Mertens, J.-F. (1986), 'On the Strategic Stability of Equilibria', *Econometrica*, 54: 1003–38.

Kreps, D. M. (1984), 'Corporate Culture and Economic Theory', in J. Alt and K. Shepsle (eds.), *Perspective on Positive Political Economy*. New York: Cambridge University Press, 90–143.

—— (1990), *A Course in Microeconomic Theory*. New York: Harvester Wheatsheaf.

Midler, C. (1994), 'Evolution des règles de gestion et processus d'apprentissage', in A. Orléan (ed.), *Analyse économique des conventions*. Paris: PUF, 335–69.

Milgrom, P., and Roberts, J. (1992), *Economics, Organization and Management*. Englewood Cliffs, NJ: Prentice-Hall.

Moisdon, J-C. and Weil, B. (1992), 'L'Invention d'une voiture: un exercice de relation sociales?' *Annales des Mines: Gérer et Comprendre*, September: 30–41; Décembre: 50–8.

Paradimitriou, C., and Tsitsiklis (1986), 'Intractable Problems in Control Theory', SIAM *Journal of Control and Optimization*, 24: 639–54.

Ponssard, J.-P. (1983), 'Military Procurement in France: Towards a Long Term Institutional Perspective', in M. Shubik (ed.), *Auctions, Bidding and Contracting: Uses and Theory*. New York: New York University Press.

—— (1988), *Stratégie d'entreprise et économie industrielle*. Paris: McGraw-Hill.

—— (1990), 'Self-Enforceable Paths in Games in Extensive Form: a Behavior Approach Based on Interactivity', *Theory and Decision*, 29: 69–83.

—— (1994), 'Formalisation des connaissances, apprentissage organisationnel et rationalité interactive', in A. Orléan (ed.), *Analyse économique des conventions*, Paris: PUF.

—— and Tanguy, H. (1993), 'Planning in firms as an interactive process', *Theory and Decision*, 34: 139–159.

Porter, M. E. (1980), *Competitive Strategy: Techniques for Analysing Industries and Competitors*. New York: Free Press.

Schon, D. (1997), 'Organization learning and the epistemology of practice', in B. Reynaut (ed.), *Les limites de la rationalité*, Paris, La Déconcerte.

Simon, H., and Schaeffer, J. (1992), 'The Game of Chess', in S. Hart and R. Aumann (eds.), *Handbook of Game Theory*, 1, Amsterdam, Elseiner: 1–18.

Sterman, J. D. (1989), 'Modeling Managerial Behavior: Misperceptions of Feedback in a Dynamic Decision Making Experiment', *Management Science*, 35: 321–39.

Soler, L.-G., and Tanguy, H. (1997), 'Coordination Between Production and Commercial Planning: Informational and Modelling Issues', forthcoming in *International Transactions in Operations Research*.

van Damme, E. (1992), 'Refinements of Nash Equilibrium', in J-J. Laffont (ed.), *Advances in Economic Theory*, sixth world congress, vol. 1, Econometric Society Monographs, 20, Cambridge University Press, 32–75.

10

Game Theory: the Next Stage

Eric van Damme

> The next stage develops when the theory is applied to somewhat more com-
> plicated situations in which it may already lead to a certain extent beyond
> the obvious and the familiar. Here theory and application corroborate each
> other mutually. Beyond this lies the field of real success: genuine prediction
> by theory.
>
> von Neumann and Morgenstern (1947: 7–8)

10.1. Introduction

Game theory provides a framework, a language, for modelling and analysing interactive decision situations, that is, situations in which multiple decision-makers
with (partially) conflicting objectives interact. It aims at understanding human
behaviour in such conflict situations and at grasping how the resulting outcome
depends on the 'rules of the game'. Such understanding then enables advice to
be given on which changes in the rules might allow more desirable outcomes to
be reached. Three different types of game theory might be distinguished:

1. *normative game theory*, in which one analyses the consequences of strategic behaviour by super-rational players;
2. *descriptive game theory*, which is concerned with documenting how people
   actually make decisions in game situations; and
3. *prescriptive game theory*, which aims at giving relevant and constructive
   advice that enables players to reach better decisions in game situations.

Of course, it is not always straightforward to categorize a game-theoretic contribution as descriptive, normative, or prescriptive. To enhance understanding of
an actual conflict situation, elements from all branches may be needed.

In the past, mainly the normative branch of game theory has been developed.
This theory is based on strong rationality principles. The players are assumed to
know what they want, to be exclusively motivated to obtain what they want, and
to have an unbounded, costless, calculating ability to analyse any situation. In addition, the theory assumes that these players analyse the situation by means of a
common model. The rules of the game are assumed common knowledge, i.e.

The author thanks Hans Carlsson, Stef Tijs, Oscar Volij and an anonymous reviewer for comments
on an earlier version. The usual disclaimer applies.

everybody knows that everybody knows that [such and such] are the rules. As Aumann puts it, 'The common knowledge assumption underlies all of game theory and much of economic theory. Whatever the model under discussion . . . the model itself must be assumed common knowledge; otherwise the model is insufficiently specified, and the analysis incoherent' (Aumann 1987: 473).

Normative game-theoretic analysis is deductive; the theory analyses which outcomes will result when (it is common knowledge that) the game is played by rational individuals. The main aim is 'to find the mathematically complete principles which define "rational behavior" for the participants in a social economy, and to derive from them the general characteristics of that behavior' (von Neumann and Morgenstern 1947: 31). In other words, 'the basic task of game theory is to tell us what strategies rational players will follow and what expectations they can rationally entertain about other rational players' strategies' (Harsanyi and Selten 1988: 342). Of course, the theory of rationality should not be self-destroying; hence, in a society of people behaving according to the theory, there should be no incentive to deviate from it. In consequence, normative theory has to prescribe the play of a Nash equilibrium.

In the last two decades, game-theoretic methods have become more and more important in economics and the other social sciences. Many scientific papers in these areas have the following basic structure. A problem is modelled as a game, the game is analysed by computing its equilibria, and the properties of the latter are translated back into insights relevant to the original problem. The close interaction between theory and applications has, inevitably, led to an increased awareness of the limitations of the theory. It has been found that the tools may not be powerful enough, or that they may yield results that do not provide a useful benchmark for the analysis of actual behaviour. For example, many models admit a vast multiplicity of equilibrium outcomes so that the predictive power of game-theoretic analysis is limited. To increase understanding, therefore, it may, be necessary to perfect the tools. In other models, such as in Selten's (1978) chain store paradox, the theory yields a unique recommendation, but it is one that sensible people refuse to take seriously as a guide for actual behaviour. Hence, new tools need to be developed as well.

Of course, one should not be surprised to find discrepancies between predictions based on normative game theory and outcomes realized in practice. The rationality of human beings is limited. Human players are not mental giants with nerves of steel; they do not always know what they want, they may not be motivated to obtain what they want, and their cognitive abilities are severely bounded. Furthermore, in many real-life games it is not clear what the rules of the game are. Even if they are clear, it is not certain that people are aware of them, let alone that they are common knowledge. Consequently, one may raise the important question of the empirical relevance of normative game theory. How can it be that a theory based on such idealizing assumptions can say anything sensible about the real world? Can it actually say something sensible? In which contexts does a game-theoretic solution concept, or a prescription on the basis of it, make sense?

Harsanyi (1977) expresses an optimistic attitude. According to Harsanyi, a normative solution concept is useful not only to clarify the conceptual issues involved in the definition of rationality: it is also prescriptively relevant, since it can serve as a benchmark for actual behaviour, in the following ways.

1. It can help with explaining and predicting the behaviour of players in those cases where they can be expected to behave *as if* they are rational.
2. It can lead to a better understanding of actual behaviour in situations different from those covered by 1; i.e., the behaviour might be explained as an understandable deviation from rationality.

Of course, this leaves open the question of when people can be expected to behave as if they are rational, and hence in which contexts a solution concept is a useful benchmark.

Other game theorists are much more pessimistic than Harsanyi. For example, Raiffa expresses the frustration that he experienced after having accepted an appointment at the Harvard Business School, just after *Games and Decisions* was published in 1957:

I began by studying loads of case studies of real-world problems. Practically every case I looked at included an interactive, competitive decision component, but I was at a loss to know how to use my expertise as a game theorist. (Raiffa 1982: 2)

Raiffa continues by pointing out the limitations of the normative theory, the gap that exists with descriptive theory, and the difficulties of erecting a meaningful prescriptive theory on the basis of foundations provided by existing theory:

The theory of games focuses its attention on problems where the protagonists in a dispute are superrational, where the 'rules of the game' are so well understood by the 'players' that each can think about what the others are thinking about what he is thinking, ad infinitum. The real business cases I was introduced to were of another variety: Mr X, the vice-president for operations of Firm A, knows he has a problem, but he's not quite sure of the decision alternatives he has and he's not sure that his adversaries (Firms B and C) even recognize that a problem exists. If Firms A, B, and C behave in thus-and-such a way, he cannot predict what the payoffs will be to each and he doesn't know how he should evaluate his own payoffs, to say nothing about his adversaries' payoffs. There are uncertainties all around besides those that relate to the choices of Firms B and C; no objective probability distributions for those ancillary uncertainties are available. Mr X has a hard time sorting out what he thinks about the uncertainties and about the value trade-offs he confronts, and he is in no frame of mind to assess what Mr Y of Firm B and Mr Z of Firm C are thinking about what he's thinking. Indeed, Mr X is mainly thinking about idiosyncratic issues that would be viewed by Y and Z as completely extraneous to their problems. Game theory, however, deals only with the way in which ultrasmart, all-knowing people *should* behave in competitive situations, and has little to say to Mr X as he confronts the morass of his problem. (Raiffa 1982: 2)

The challenge of game theory is to bridge the gap from the ideal world of mathematics to the study of actual behaviour in the real, complex world. A main lesson from the past seems to be that exclusive development of a normative theory does not bring success: the hope of obtaining precise, reasonable predictions on the basis of general rationality principles was idle. A really useful theory with high predictive power that can be used for prescriptive purposes has to stand on two legs, a deductive one and descriptive one. At the present stage, the marginal return to developing the latter leg is higher.

To realize the potential of game theory, it is first of all necessary to improve its empirical base. In order to obtain a broad set of facts on which to theorize, we need to do fieldwork and careful laboratory experimentation. We have to study actual human behaviour in order to find regularities in that behaviour so as to be able to construct meaningful theories of procedural and bounded rationality. Indeed, we need to construct such theories. In order to develop applied game theory successfully, it is also useful to document what has been learned in the past, to make an overview of the cases in which existing game theory has been successfully applied, and to document why the theory does not work in the cases where it does not work. In which situations can we expect existing theory to improve our understanding of the real world? What is the range of successful applications of existing theory? Which models and which solution concepts are most appropriate in which contexts?

In this paper I comment on some recent developments in game theory that are building blocks towards a better theory. Since the bulk of the work is in normative (non-cooperative) game theory, I restrict myself mainly to this branch. To provide a perspective, I start in Section 10.2 by giving a broad overview of the developments in game theory in the last forty years. In Section 10.3 I discuss game-theoretic models and some applications of game theory: what can experiments and fieldwork tell us about the domain of applicability of the models and the solution concepts? In Section 10.4 I discuss three rationales underlying the notion of Nash equilibrium, one involving perfect rationality, another involving limited rationality, and the final one based on perfect absence of rationality. Section 10.5 is devoted to issues of bounded rationality. It describes some recent research into the consequences of the players having bounded information processing devices and discusses the difficulties associated with modelling human reasoning processes. Section 10.6 offers a brief conclusion.

10.2. History: Problems Solved and Unsolved

In the preface of the *Contributions to the Theory of Games* Vol. 1 the editors Harold Kuhn and Albert Tucker (1950) list fourteen outstanding problems in the theory of games. Half of these deal with two-person zero-sum games, and the most important problem listed is 'to find a computational technique of general applicability for finite zero-sum two-person games with a large number of pure strategies'. Other problems in this class concern determining the existence of a value for games with an infinite number of strategies, characterizing the structure of the set of solutions, and constructing efficient algorithms to find solutions. As evidenced by the dearth of activity in this area at present, these problems have been solved satisfactorily. In particular, optimal strategies can be found efficiently by linear programming techniques.

In cooperative game theory, the problems that Kuhn and Tucker list are (1) to ascribe a formal value to an arbitrary n-person game, (2) to establish significant asymptotic properties of n-person games for large n, (3) to establish existence of von Neumann–Morgenstern (vNM) stable sets for arbitrary n-person games and to derive structural characteristics of such stable sets, and (4) to extend the theory to the case where utility is not transferable. To some extent these problems have also been satisfactorily solved. Shapley (1953) defined and axiomatized a value for n-person games. Extensions to non-transferable utility (NTU) games were given in Harsanyi (1963) and Shapley (1968), with axiomatizations being provided in Aumann (1985) and Hart (1985). Asymptotic properties were studied in Aumann and Shapley (1974). Of particular importance were the equivalence theorems for large games and markets (see Aumann 1964; Debreu and Scarf 1963; and Mas-Colell 1989). As far as vNM stable sets are concerned, the picture is somewhat less satisfactory: stable sets do not always exist (Lucas 1968), and the concept is so difficult to work with that few general structural properties are known.

One problem on the Kuhn–Tucker list has cooperative as well as non-cooperative aspects. It is:

to study n-person games with restrictions imposed on the forming of coalitions (e.g. embargo on side payments or on communication, or on both), thus recognizing that the cost of communication among the players during the pregame coalition-forming period is not negligible but rather, in the typical economic model with large n, is likely to be the dominating consideration. One approach to this question might be to formalize the coalition-forming period as a noncooperative game in the sense of Nash. (Kuhn and Tucker 1950: xi)

In this area we have seen less progress than in the ones mentioned before. The process of coalition formation (and coalition dissolution) is still not well understood and it is only very recently that we have seen non-cooperative formalizations of the coalition formation process along the lines suggested by Kuhn and Tucker (see Harsanyi 1974; Selten 1981, 1991a; and, for an overview of the special case where only two-person buyer–seller coalitions are relevant, Osborne and Rubinstein 1990). Much of the recent work, however, is plagued by the fact that the extensive forms studied admit infinitely many equilibria. It seems safe to conjecture that we will see more work in this area in the near future.

Within non-cooperative game theory, Kuhn and Tucker mention two problems that 'need further classification and restatement above all'. Here 'we find the zone of twilight and problems which await clear delineation'. The problems are:

(a) To develop a comprehensive theory of games in extensive form with which to analyze the role of information, i.e. the effect of changes in the pattern of information.

(*b*) To develop a dynamic theory of games:
  (i) In a single play of a multimove game, predict the continuation of the opponent's strategy from his early moves.
  (ii) In sequence of plays of the same game, predict the opponent's mixed strategy from his early choices of pure strategies. (Kuhn and Tucker 1950: xii)

The seminal work of Kuhn (1953) and Selten (1965, 1975) on extensive form games, and of Harsanyi (1968) and Aumann (1976) on information and knowledge, has enabled more formal restatements of these problems as well as theory development. In the past two decades much effort has been devoted to try to solve problem (a), i.e. to define solution concepts that capture rational behaviour in extensive form games. Various concepts have been proposed and their properties have been vigorously investigated. In the process, severe difficulties in the foundations of game theory have been uncovered. Some authors (e.g. Basu 1990, Reny 1986) have even argued that game theory is inconsistent since the theory's basic assumption, the common knowledge of players' rationality, cannot hold in non-trivial extensive-form games.

By using the newly developed solution concepts, a start has been made to study the influence of the distribution of information on the outcome of play. It was found that there is a disturbing lack of robustness of the rational outcome: small changes in the information structure may have drastic consequences. In particular, inserting a tiny bit of irrational behaviour may have a large impact on the rational solution of a game. Furthermore, when rationality is not common knowledge, a rational player may benefit by pretending to be somewhat irrational, so that the superiority of 'rational behaviour' over other behaviour is not clear. The latter poses a challenging problem for game theory since it goes to the heart of it: namely, as the founding fathers already wrote, 'The question remains as to what will happen if some of the participants do not conform. If that should turn out to be advantageous to them . . . then the above "solution" would seem very questionable' (von Neumann and Morgenstern 1947: 32). We will return to this problem area in Section 10.4.

Within normative theory, the Kuhn–Tucker problem (b)(i) about learning and prediction reduces to a routine computation using Bayes's rule, since this theory imposes the assumptions of perfect rationality and equilibrium. Important results were obtained, for example, concerning information revelation in repeated games of incomplete information. As a consequence of the growing awareness of the limitations of the rationality and equilibrium assumptions, however, there has recently been a renewed interest in the actual learning of boundedly rational players in dynamic games, as well as in processes of evolutionary selection in such situations. We return to this topic in Sections 10.4.2 and 10.4.3.

With respect to the Kuhn–Tucker problem (b)(ii) about repeated games, we note that the most important result obtained is the folk theorem. This result establishes a link between cooperative and non-cooperative game theory: repetition (with 'enough' information being transmitted to players during the game) may allow players to reach more efficient outcomes in equilibrium (Aumann and

Shapley 1976; Rubinstein 1978; Fudenberg and Maskin 1986). Since the result shows that under weak assumptions almost anything can happen, it can also be interpreted as a negative result. Cooperation might result, but it need not; also, less efficient outcomes may be sustained by equilibria of repeated games. There is an embarrassing multiplicity of equilibria, and this raises the important question of why one should expect any equilibrium at all. We return to this question in the Section 10.4.1.

To summarize, although the theory has been developed substantially, progress has uncovered many new conceptual and technical problems. These include problems with the foundations of the theory and with the justification of the solution concepts, problems of multiplicity (making the analysis inconclusive), and problems of lack of robustness of the outcomes with respect to the assumptions underlying the model. At the same time, the better developed theory has enabled more extensive application. Inevitably, the increased number of applications has led to an increased awareness of the limitations and weaknesses in the theory. In particular, the applications have thrown doubt on the relevance of strong rationality assumptions, in that it has been found that game-theoretic solutions may be hard to accept as a guide to successful practical behaviour. In the following sections we describe these drawbacks in more detail and discuss how game theorists try to overcome them.

10.3. The Rules of the Game

Two types of game model can be distinguished: cooperative and non-cooperative. Cooperative models assume that binding contracts can be concluded outside the formal rules of the game. In a non-cooperative game, no external enforcement mechanism is available. To put it differently, these models differ in the amount of detail they require to be specified. At the macro level, we have the cooperative model in which the actual process of play is abstracted away from. In this model attention is focused on the options and alternatives that the various coalitions have. At the other extreme, we have the non-cooperative, extensive-form model, which allows faithful modelling of actual real-life institutions. In this model emphasis is on the process of play, and the analyst is forced to specify the fine structure of the game, i.e. the strategic variables that are relevant, the timing of the moves and the distribution of information among the players at the relevant points in time. At the intermediate level, we find the (non-cooperative) strategic form which focuses on the strategies that individual players have available and the resulting outcomes. Each of these models has its attractive features as well as its drawbacks. Broadly speaking, incorporating more detail allows a more refined prediction, but that prediction might depend very strongly on those details; hence the prediction might not be robust.

Already in the modelling stage game theory can provide important insights as it forces the analyst to go through a checklist of questions that afford a classification of the situation at hand. (How many players are there? Who are they? What do they want? What can they do? When can they do it? What do they know? Can they sign binding contracts? etc.) This classification in turn allows one to see similarities in different situations and allows the transfer of insights from one context to another.

The theoretical development of the extensive-form model, and of games with incomplete information that followed the seminal work of Aumann, Harsanyi, Kuhn, and Selten, made non-cooperative game theory more suitable for application, and in the past two decades game-theoretic methods have pervaded economics as well as the other social sciences. Game-theoretic methods have come to dominate the area of industrial organization, and game-theoretic tools have been essential for the understanding of economies in which information is asymmetrically distributed. The rapid growth of the use of game theory in economics in the last two decades can be attributed in part to the fact that the extensive-form model allows a tremendous degree of flexibility in modelling. Any real-life institution can be faithfully modelled, and the explicitness allows scrutinizing the model's realism and limitations. The richness of the model also has its drawbacks, however. First of all, richer models allow more flexibility in classifying conflict situations; hence it is more difficult to obtain general insights. Second, it is more difficult to do sensitivity analysis. Third, and most importantly, it will only rarely be the case that the situation at hand dictates what the model should be. Frequently, there is considerable scope for designing the model in various ways, each of them having something going for it. Judgement on the appropriateness of the model is essential.

If there is freedom in filling in the details of the game, one would ideally want the outcome to be robust with respect to inessential changes. Unfortunately, this happy state of affairs seems to materialize only for solution concepts that are based on weak rationality assumptions, i.e. concepts that do not make sharp predictions. Outcomes generated by stronger solution concepts, such as subgame-perfect equilibrium or stable equilibrium (Kohlberg and Mertens 1986), frequently depend critically on these details. The application of these concepts then requires the modelling of all details. Indeed, Kohlberg and Mertens do make the assumption that the model is isomorphic to reality rather than to an abstraction of it: 'we assume that the game under consideration fully describes the real situation—that any (pre-)commitment possibilities, any repetitive aspect, any probabilities of error, or any possibility of jointly observing some random event, have already been modelled in the game tree' (Kohlberg and Mertens 1986: fn. 3). The appropriateness of such an assumption for applied work may be questioned, especially since human beings are known not to perceive all details of a situation.

In the recent past we have seen a tendency for models to get more detailed and more complex. For example, models with incomplete information rely on Harsanyi's (1968) trick of adding a fictitious chance move to ensure the common knowledge of the model. This construction quickly yields a complicated game so that, even in the case where the analyst can solve the game, the question remains as to how relevant that solution is for real-life players with bounded computational complexities. Furthermore, at the intuitive level one might argue that, the more detail one adds to the model, the less likely it is that this detail is commonly perceived by all parties involved in the actual conflict, hence the less credible the common knowledge assumption. The extensive quotation from Raiffa in Section 10.1 suggests that, by making the assumption that the model is common knowledge, game theory abstracts away from the most basic problem of all: 'What is the problem to be solved?' We return to this issue in Section 10.5.

10.3.1. LABORATORY EXPERIMENTS

The structural characteristics of the game can be controlled in laboratory experiments, but even in experiments it is hard to control the preferences and beliefs of the players and the manner in which they perceive the situation. Experiments with ultimatum bargaining games have shown that proposers do not ask for (almost) the entire cake, but we do not know why they do not do so. We do not know what motivates people and what they believe about the motivations of others. Do people make 'fair' proposals because they are intrinsically motivated by 'fairness', or because they believe the opponent cares about the distribution of payoffs and not just about his own share? The experimental data contradict the joint hypotheses that is common knowledge that players (*a*) are only interested in their own monetary payoffs and (*b*) want to maximize these payoffs, but this conclusion is not very informative. We want to dig deeper and get to know why the results are as they are and why the results depend on the context in the way they do. (See Güth and van Damme (1994) for a systematic investigation of how the results depend on the amount of information that is transmitted from the proposer to the responder.)

Experiments may give us a better idea of the settings in which the use of a game-theoretic solution concept such as Nash equilibrium is justified. An important and intriguing puzzle is offered by the experimental research on double auctions (Plott 1987; Smith 1990). The experiments show that Nash equilibria may be reached without players consciously aiming to reach it. However, the Nash equilibrium that is obtained is not an equilibrium of the complex, incomplete information game that the players are playing: rather, it is the (Walrasian) equilibrium of the associated complete information game. In addition, giving players information that allows them to compute the equilibrium may make it less likely that this equilibrium is reached. In these experiments there is a number of traders, each trader i assigning a value $v_i(n)$ to n units of the good that is traded. All the information is private. Agents act both as price-makers (by announcing bids and asks) and as price-takers (by accepting bids or asks from other traders). The prices and allocations converge quickly to the Walrasian equilibria of the complete information economy, even though none of the traders has the information to compute this outcome and none is aware of the fact that traders are maximizing profits in this way. Subjects participating in these experiments describe them as 'non-transparent'; hence the question to be answered is 'Which institutional aspects help players in reaching the equilibrium?' In other words, which mechanisms provide sufficient feedback for players to learn the equilibrium? We will return to this question at a more abstract level in the next section.

The interaction between individual behaviour and the institutional setting is not very well understood yet, and no doubt much research will be done in this area in the next decade. It is interesting to compare the 'good news' from the previous paragraph with the 'bad news' obtained by Kagel and Levin (1986). These authors study common value auctions in which participants can fall prey to the winners' curse. It turns out that, given enough experience, players learn to avoid making losses. However, they certainly do not learn to understand the situation and play the equilibrium. In fact, their learning does not allow them to cope with a change in the circumstances: if the number of bidders is increased, the players increase their bids, while equilibrium behaviour would force them to shade their bids even more. As a consequence, players make losses for some time until they have learned to cope with the new situation. It would be interesting to know what would happen if players gained experience in many circumstances. An example, from a completely different context, suggests that learning from different environments may allow people to learn more: Selten and Kuon (1992) study three-person bargaining games in which only two-person coalitions can form. They find that players who gain experience with many diverse situations learn to understand the logic of the quota solution and come to behave in accordance with it. In contrast, the behaviour of bargainers who draw from a more limited set of experiences does not seem to settle down.

10.3.2. APPLIED GAME THEORY

One of the areas in which game-theoretic tools have been extensively applied in the last two decades is industrial organization. Several commentators (Fisher 1989; Pelzman 1991) have argued that these applications have not been successful as the theory has been unable to reach general insights. Part of the reason, no doubt, lies in the three drawbacks of the extensive-form model that were mentioned above. The flexibility of that model has enabled the theoretical explanation of any type of behaviour. In addition, it seems that, when writing the details in the extensive form, theorists have not been guided by detailed empirical work. Of course, the problem might lie not in the tool but in the subject of study: it might be that no general insights are possible. Furthermore, the rapid spread of game-theoretic ideas through this literature can probably be attributed more to the absence of good competitors to game theory than to the fact that the field is ideally suited to the application of game-theoretic techniques: The basic assumptions underlying game theory (common knowledge of rationality and of the rules of the game) are not particularly realistic in this area. Since the formal rules governing competition are not very detailed, industrial organization is not the first area one thinks of for successful application of game theory based on the extensive form.

Game theory may be more successful in situations that are closer to its base, situations in which the rules are clear and where one can have more faith in the players' rationality. Financial markets immediately come to mind: the rules are clear, the game offers opportunities for learning, and the stakes are high, so that one could at least hope that irrational behaviour is driven out. However, as evidenced by the large number of anomalies in this area, one should not expect too much here, either (De Bondt and Thaler 1992). Nevertheless, it seems that game theory could contribute something to the analysis of financial markets. For example, following the Big Bang in London, European stock exchanges have gone through a series of restructurings in order to try to increase their competitiveness. Such restructurings involve changes in the rules of the trading game, and hence problems of mechanism design (Pagano and Roell 1990).

Auctions are another case in which the context pins down the structural characteristics of the game, i.e. the actions and their timing, although not the distribution of information. Standard auction models can make definite predictions about outcomes, and indeed in some cases the predictions match the data reasonably well (Hendriks and Porter 1988).

Another case in which the institutional structure of interaction is well-defined is that of centralized matching markets studied by Al Roth (Roth 1984; Roth and Sotomayor 1990; Roth and Xing 1994). Although the rules of the non-cooperative game are well-defined, Roth's point of departure for the analysis lies in co-operative game theory, viz. in the Gale and Shapley (1962) investigation of whether the core of such a game, the set of stable matchings, is nonempty. Roth investigates whether rules that produce stable outcomes will remain in place, and whether rules that produce unstable outcomes will induce market failure and hence be abolished after some time. The hypothesis, indeed, is powerful enough to explain the success of various market rules; hence we have a clear example not only of the rules determining the play but, vice versa, of the play influencing the rules. It would be nice to see more examples of this phenomenon and to know whether there is a tendency for 'efficient' rules to evolve. What is particularly interesting here is the combination of 'cooperative' and 'non-cooperative' elements in the analysis, providing an example that might be successful also in other contexts.

I expect that in the next decade the pendulum will swing back again from non-cooperative theory towards cooperative game theory. In some cases it will not pay the analyst to model the game to the greatest possible detail: rather, it might be more attractive to consider the situation at a more aggregate level and to make broad qualitative predictions that hold true for a large range of detailed specifications of the actual process. To some extent, this redirection is already occurring in two-person bargaining theory. The non-cooperative underpinnings of Nash's solution (which were enabled by the seminal paper by Rubinstein

1982) are useful in that they increase our confidence in that solution and show us how to include 'outside options' in Nash's original cooperative model. (See Binmore *et al.* (1992) for an overview.) Once this has been established, rational advice to bargainers concerning what policies to pursue, as well as comparative statics properties (for example concerning risk aversion), can be derived from (an appropriate modification) of Nash's original cooperative model.

Of course, cooperative game theory is still underdeveloped according to several dimensions. We know little about the dynamic processes of coalition formation and coalition dissolution and very little about cooperation under incomplete information. I expect to see some work on these problems in the near future.

10.4. Equilibrium and Rationality

Non-cooperative game-theoretic analysis centres around the notion of Nash equilibrium; hence it is essential to address the relevance of this solution concept. Why do we focus on Nash equilibria? When, or in which contexts, is Nash equilibrium analysis appropriate? Where do equilibria come from? How can one choose among the equilibria?

There are at least three interpretations (justifications) of the notion of Nash equilibrium:

1. It is a necessary requirement for a self-enforcing theory of rational behaviour.
2. It results as the outcome of a learning process.
3. It results as the outcome of an evolutionary process.

In the three sub-sections that follow, we shall consider these justifications in turn along with some recent literature dealing with each topic.

10.4.1. PERFECT RATIONALITY

The first justification of Nash equilibrium is a normative one. Nash equilibrium arises in addressing the question, 'What constitutes rational behaviour in a game?' A theory of rationality that prescribes a definite (probabilistic) choice (or belief) for each player has to prescribe a Nash equilibrium, since otherwise it is self-contradictory. In Nash's own words, 'By using the principles that a rational prediction should be unique, that the players should be able to deduce and make use of it, and that such knowledge on the part of each player of what to expect the others to do should not lead him to act out of conformity with the prediction, one is led to the concept' (Nash 1950: 23). Nash also comments on the limited scope of this justification: 'In this interpretation we need to assume the players to know the full structure of the game in order to be able to deduce the prediction for themselves. It is quite strongly a rationalistic and idealizing interpretation' (Nash 1950: 23).

This rationalistic interpretation relies essentially on the assumptions that each game has a unique rational solution and that each player knows this solution. To address the question of how players get to know the solution, one needs a formal model that incorporates players' knowledge. Such a model has been developed by Aumann, and readers are referred to Aumann and Brandenburger (1991) for a discussion of the epistemic conditions underlying Nash's concept. Here I shall just remark that in the two-player case less stringent conditions suffice than in general n-player games. (Roughly speaking, in the two-player case, mutual knowledge of beliefs, rationality, and payoffs suffices, while in the n-player case, one needs common knowledge assumptions, as well as a common prior on the beliefs.)

While the rationalistic interpretation of the Nash equilibrium concept relies on the assumption that each game has a unique strategy vector as its rational solution, it is the case that many games admit multiple Nash equilibria. Hence the rationalistic interpretation requires us to address two questions: (1) Can a theory of rational behaviour prescribe any Nash equilibrium? (2) What constitutes rational behaviour in cases where there are multiple equilibria? These questions are addressed, respectively, in the literatures on equilibrium refinement and equilibrium selection.

The research that has been performed on extensive-form games has made it clear that the answer to the first question must be in the negative: certain Nash equilibria are not compatible with perfect rationality as they rely on incredible threats. To rule out these equilibria, Selten (1965) started a programme of refining the equilibrium concept. Many different variations were proposed, each imposing somewhat stronger rationality requirements than the Nash equilibrium does (see van Damme 1987 for an overview). Game theorists have not yet agreed upon the ultimate refinement: we certainly do not yet have a convincing answer to the question, 'What constitutes rational behaviour in an extensive-form game?'

Recently the relevance of the refinements programme has been questioned. Namely, most refinements (in particular, subgame-perfect and sequential equilibrium) insist on 'persistent rationality'; i.e., it is assumed that, no matter what has happened in the past, a rational player will play rationally in the future. This assumption might well be a sensible one to make for perfectly rational players, but it is a problematic one in the applications of theory, especially, if the application involves a simplified model. Human players are not perfectly rational; they make mistakes, and they might deviate from perfect rationality in a systematic way. Once, in a real game, one sees that a player deviates from the rational solution of the game, one should not exclude the possibility that one's model of the situation or one's model of that player is wrong. Of course, what one should then believe cannot be determined by that original model: the model has to be revised. If the model of the exogenous environment is appropriate, one is forced to enrich the model by incorporating actual human behaviour. Hence in extensive-form games the perfectly rational solution might not be a good benchmark against which to compare actual behaviour.

	c	*d*
c	2,2	0,*x*
d	*x*,0	*x*,*x*

Fig. 10.1. Stag Hunt Game $g(x)$ ($0 < x < 2$)

With regard to changes in the model, it is worrisome that the perfectly rational solution might change drastically with minor changes in the data of the game. For example, if there is a small probability of there being irrational players around, rational players might play very differently than in the case where this possibility does not exist (Kreps *et al.* 1982). Human players have free will; if a player can profit from behaving differently than the theory of perfect rationality prescribes, there is nothing that can prevent him from doing so.

Nash had already stressed that the normative interpretation of equilibrium requires one to solve the problem of equilibrium selection. A solution to this problem has been provided in Harsanyi and Selten (1988), in which a coherent single-valued theory of rationality for interactive decision situations has been constructed. However, the Harsanyi–Selten book also shows that such a theory necessarily has to violate certain intuitively desirable properties. For example, a theory of rationality that depends only on the best reply structure of the game necessarily has to pick a Pareto-inferior Nash equilibrium in some games. In the stag hunt game $g(x)$ of Fig. 10.1, (c, c) is the Pareto-dominant equilibrium if $x < 2$. This game, however, is best-reply-equivalent to a common payoff coordination game with diagonal payoffs equal to $2 - x$ and x and off-diagonal payoffs equal to zero. In the latter game, the Pareto-dominant equilibrium is (d, d) if $x > 1$.

Since there is room for alternative theories of equilibrium selection—the Harsanyi–Selten theory violates certain desirable properties—as well as improvements, some work on rational equilibrium selection will continue. Carlsson and van Damme (1993*b*) compare several (partial) theories which all derive their inspiration from Nash's (1953) bargaining paper. Nash (1953) suggested selecting equilibria on the basis of their relative stability properties. Specifically, he suggested investigating robustness with respect to perturbations in the knowledge structure of the game. Hence an equilibrium should survive in a 'more realistic' version of the model. In a specific implementation of this idea, Carlsson and van Damme (1993*a*) show that 'absence of common knowledge' may serve as an equilibrium selection device. Only some equilibria may be viable when there is just 'almost common knowledge' (see also Rubinstein 1989). Interestingly, in the Carlsson–van Damme model there is a form of 'spontaneous coordination': one does not need to assume equilibrium behaviour in the perturbed game to obtain equilibrium selection in the original game—iterated dominance arguments suffice. Hence the model illustrates a possibility of how rational players might derive the solution.

In the Carlsson—van Damme model it is common knowledge that a game from a certain class has to be played; players make observations on which game is played, but observations are noisy, with the errors of different players being independent. As a concrete example, suppose the game is as in Fig. 10.1 but each player i makes a noisy observation $x_i = x + \varepsilon_i$ on the parameter characterizing the game. As a result of the noise, rational players have to analyse all games $g(x)$ at the same time. What is optimal for a player i at x_i depends on what his opponent does at points in the interval $[x_i - 2\varepsilon, x_i + 2\varepsilon]$, which in turn depends on what the opponent believes i will do on $[x_i - 4\varepsilon, x_i + 4\varepsilon]$. Clearly, player i will choose $c(d)$ if x_i is close to zero (two), since then chances are good that this action is dominant for the actual value of x. Having determined the behaviour at the 'end points', a recursive argument allows determination of the optimal behaviour at the other observations. Carlsson and van Damme show that with vanishing noise players will coordinate on the risk-dominant equilibrium; i.e., they will play c if and only if $x < 1$.

Formally, in a 2×2 game, one equilibrium is said to risk-dominate another if its associated (Nash) product of deviation losses is larger. In Fig. 10.1, a player's deviation loss from (c, c) is $2 - x$, while that from (d, d) is x, hence (c, c) is risk-dominant if and only if $(2 - x)^2 > x^2$. This concept of risk dominance was introduced in Harsanyi and Selten (1988), and it has proved important in other contexts, also. We will return to it below. It should be noted, however, that for games larger than 2×2, the definition of risk dominance is by means of the tracing procedure, and that in these cases the equilibrium selected by the Carlsson–van Damme technique may be different from the risk-dominant one (see Carlsson and van Damme 1993*b* for further details). In particular, that paper derives the intuitive result that cooperation is more difficult when there are more players: in an *n*-player version of Fig. 10.1, the observation where players switch from c to d is strictly decreasing in *n*.)

One interpretation of the Carlsson–van Damme model is that the observations correspond to the players' models of the actual situation. Models of different players are highly similar, but they are not identical. The conclusion, then, is that this more realistic modelling implies that certain Nash equilibria are not viable. (Note the link with the discussion on perception in Section 10.5.)

Incorporating more realistic knowledge assumptions need not always reduce the number of equilibria. For example, Neyman (1989) shows that small changes in the knowledge structure may allow new equilibria to arise. He demonstrates that, in the finitely repeated prisoner's dilemma, if players do not have a common knowledge upper bound on the length of the game, cooperation until near the end of the game is an equilibrium outcome. In the simplest of Neyman's models, the actual length *n* of the game is a draw from a geometric distribution, and each player i gets a signal n_i on the length of the game with $|n_i - n| = 1$ and $|n_1 - n_2| = 2$. Hence player i knows that the actual length is either $n_i - 1$ (and his opponent has signal $n_i - 2$) or $n_i + 1$ (with the opponent having the signal $n_i + 2$). It is now easily seen that, if each player follows the strategy of defecting only after a previous defection, or when he is sure that the current round is the last one, an equilibrium results. In this equilibrium players cooperate until the next-to-last round.

From the above two examples, it is clear that much work remains to be done before we have a clear picture of how the equilibrium outcomes depend on the distribution of knowledge in the game. Hence there is a need for further development of rationalistic theories, even though it may be questioned whether such theories will provide a useful benchmark for actual decision-making.

10.4.2. LIMITED RATIONALITY: LEARNING

The second interpretation of equilibrium Nash calls the 'mass-action' interpretation. 'It is unnecessary to assume that the participants have full knowledge of the total structure of the game, or the ability or inclination to go through any complex reasoning processes. But the participants are supposed to accumulate empirical information on the relative advantages of the various pure strategies at their disposal' (Nash 1950). If we assume that there is a stable frequency with which each pure strategy is used, players will learn these frequencies and they will play best responses against them. Consequently, a necessary condition for stability is that the frequencies constitute a Nash equilibrium. Nash remarks that 'Actually, of course, we can only expect some sort of approximate equilibrium, since the information, its utilization, and the stability of the average frequencies will be imperfect.'

It is clear that Nash's remarks raise many intriguing questions which cry for an answer. Under which conditions will there exist stable population frequencies? What will happen if the frequencies do not settle down? When will there be a limit cycle? Is it possible to have strange attractors or chaos? How does an approximate equilibrium look like? How long does it take before the process settles down? In what contexts is the long run relevant? How does the outcome depend on the information that players utilize? Does limited information speed up the process? Or might more limited information lead to completely different outcomes? What if the game is one in the extensive form and players get to see only the actual path of play and not the full strategies leading to the path? Do we get to more refined equilibrium notions? Can the concept of subgame-perfect equilibrium be justified by some learning concept? Might non-Nash equilibria be asymptotically stable fixed points of learning processes? How does the outcome depend on the complexity of the reasoning processes that players utilize?

Although some of these questions were already addressed in the 1950s and 1960s, particularly in relation to the Brown–Robinson process of fictitious play, interest dwindled after Shapley (1964) had given an example of a non-zero sum game for which this process does not converge, but rather approaches a limit cycle. Recently, interest has shifted again in this direction. At present, the above questions are being vigorously researched, and such research will continue in the near future.

The interest in these questions, of course, arises from the observation that 'There are situations in economics or international politics in which, effectively, a group of interests are involved in a noncooperative game without being aware of it, the non-awareness helping to make the situation truly noncooperative' (Nash 1950: 23). Hence players have only local information; they do not see through the system, but nevertheless they get such feedback from the system so as to be able to reach an equilibrium (cf. the discussion on the double auction in Section 10.3). Consequently, this second interpretation suggests a domain of relevance for Nash equilibrium that is completely different from the one suggested by the first interpretation. Whereas the first make sense in simple situations ('with an obvious way to play'—Kreps 1990), the second relies on the situation not being obvious at all.

Formal models that address the questions raised above postulate that players behave according to certain rules, and are seen as information-processing machines. The machine has a certain memory and an output rule that associates a decision with each possible state of memory. After each stage of play, the machine processes the information about this period's play and incorporates it into its memory, thereby possibly changing its state. A collection of rules, one for each player, then determines the evolution of play, hence the payoffs for each player (cf. the discussion in Section 10.5). The questions mentioned above then correspond to asking what consequences various rules will have. In the future we should expect to see purely theoretical research (analysing the properties of mathematically tractable processes), simulation studies of more complicated processes, and empirical research: what kinds of learning processes do people adopt, and what types of outcomes do these processes imply?

Most of the research conducted up to now has been theoretical, but there have also been some simulation studies (see e.g. Marimon *et al.* 1990). The work is so diverse and vast that it is impossible to summarize it here. I will confine myself to a simple illustration which is based on Young (1993). (See also Kandori *et al.* 1993; Ellison 1993.)

Assume that the game $g(x)$ from Fig. 10.1 is played by members of two finite populations of size N. Each time period, one member of each population is picked at random to play the game. In deciding what to do, a player (randomly) asks $k(k \ll N)$ members of his population what their most recent experience was in playing this game (i.e. what their opponents did), and he then plays a best response against this frequency distribution. Obviously, the system has two stationary states: all play c or all play d. Hence, in the long run, an outside observer will only see a Nash equilibrium being played.

Now let us add some small amount of noise. Assume that each player's memory may be imperfect: with small probability ε, a player remembers $c(d)$ when the actual experience was $d(c)$. The imperfection implies that the system may move from one equilibrium to the other. However, such movements are unlikely. To move away from 'all c', one needs simultaneous mutation (i.e. imperfect recall) of a fraction $1 - x/2$ of the sample. To move away from 'all d', a fraction $x/2$ needs to mutate simultaneously. If ε is very small, then the first possibility is much more likely if $x > 1$, while the second is much more likely if $x < 1$. Hence if $x < 1$ ($x > 1$) the system will remain much longer in 'all c' ('all d') than in 'all d' ('all c'). In the ultra long run, we get equilibrium selection according to the risk dominance criterion. Again, the introduction of random variation leads to equilibrium selection.

10.4.3. ZERO RATIONALITY: EVOLUTION

The third justification of Nash equilibrium has its origins in biology and was proposed first in Maynard Smith and Price (1973). In this interpretation there is no conscious choice at all: individuals are programmed to play certain strategies, and more successful strategies reproduce faster than others, so that eventually only the most successful strategies survive. If the population reaches a stable state, all existing strategies must be equally successful, and strategies that are not present cannot be more successful. Hence a stable state must be a Nash equilibrium. This interpretation, then, involves perfect absence of rationality.

In the most basic model of this type, there is an infinite population of individuals who are randomly matched in pairs. Individuals are programmed to play strategies from a certain set S, and if an s-individual meets a t-individual then the expected number of offspring to s is $u(s, t)$ where u is some symmetric bimatrix game. A monomorphic population in which only s^*-individuals are present is stable if any mutant $s \neq s^*$ who enters in the population with a small frequency is selected *against*. The formal condition for such stability is that (s^*, s^*) is a symmetric Nash equilibrium of u with $u(s^*, s) > u(s, s)$ for all alternative best replies s against s^*. A strategy s^* satisfying these conditions is said to be an evolutionarily stable strategy (ESS). Hence, ESS is a refinement of Nash equilibrium. In the game of Fig. 10.1, for example, both c and d are ESS, but the mixed-strategy equilibrium does not correspond to an ESS. Within this framework, one can also investigate the evolution of a polymorphic population. If the set of all possible strategies is finite, then, if the time between successive generations is small, the population proportions evolve according to the replicator dynamics $\dot{x}_s = x_s(u(s, x) - u(x, x))$. (In this expression, x_s denotes the fraction of s-individuals in the population, $u(s, x)$ is the expected number of offspring of an s-individual, and $u(x, x)$ is the average fitness of the population). Broadly speaking, s^* is an ESS if and only if it is an asymptotically stable fixed point of the replicator dynamics.

Within this area several questions are presently being investigated. The answers at present are far from complete, so that the research will continue. A typical question is whether evolutionary forces will wipe out irrational behaviour; i.e., if $x(t)$ is a trajectory of the replicator equation and s is an (iteratively) dominated strategy, will $x_s(t)$ tend to zero as t gets large? Another question is whether evolutionary forces will produce equilibria; i.e., in which contexts does $\lim_{t\to\infty} x(t)$ exist, and is such a limit an equilibrium of the game? Also, we want to know the properties of ESS in specific classes of games. For example, do evolutionary pressures lead to efficient equilibria? In repeated games, does evolution force cooperation (Axelrod 1984)? Furthermore, the basic model of a symmetric strategic form game is very limited; hence how should evolutionary stability be defined in extensive-form games or in asymmetric games? What are the properties of ESSs in these games? Furthermore, how should the definition be modified if mutants appear more frequently, or if there is local interaction, i.e. viscosity? What happens if there can be drastic innovations that can change the character of the game (Holland 1992)?

Preliminary research on the above questions has shown that many games fail to have ESS. Theorists have been reluctant to give up the idea of equilibrium and have proposed weaker concepts with better existence properties. Also, set-valued concepts have been proposed. These are attractive for extensive-form games, especially if the strategies in the set differ only off the equilibrium path. Finally, it has been argued that in economic contexts it might be more appropriate to assume a bit more rationality on the part of mutants: new strategies will be introduced only if they have some chance of survival. Corresponding solution concepts have been defined, and the properties of these are currently being investigated. As the literature dealing with this topic is vast, I give only one example, and refrain from further comments. I refer to van Damme (1994) for further details and references.

The example concerns the evolution of language. There is the common wisdom that, if players could communicate before playing the game $g(x)$ of Fig. 10.1, they would talk themselves into the efficient equilibrium (c, c). However, Aumann (1990) has argued that the conventional story may not be fully convincing. Furthermore, the intuition has been hard to formalize using equilibrium concepts that are based on perfect rationality. Recently, some progress has been made by using evolutionary concepts. The basic idea is very simple: in a population playing the inefficient equilibrium (d, d), a mutant who sends a special signal and who reacts to the signal by playing c could possibly invade. Things are not that simple, however; success is not guaranteed. If the existing population punishes the use of the new signal (for example by playing the mixed strategy in response to it), then the mutant does worse than the existing population. Hence if the mutant enters at the wrong point in time, it will die out. However, the existing population cannot guarantee such punishment. Strategies that do not punish and behave on the equilibrium path just as other members of the population do equally well as the population and can spread through it. If the mutant arises at a point in time when there are only few punishers around, it will thrive and eventually take over the entire population. Hence, with communication, the outcome (d, d) is not evolutionarily stable; the population will drift to (c, c) (see Kim and Sobel 1991).

10.5. Bounded Rationality

Standard game-theoretic analysis assumes that it is common knowledge that players are rational in the Bayesian sense; hence it is assumed to be common knowledge that each player (1) knows the set of all feasible alternatives, (2) knows the exact consequences of each action combination, and (3) has a globally consistent preference relation on the set of all possible consequences. The behaviour of each player is assumed to be substantively rational; i.e., 'it is appropriate to the achievement of given goals within the limits imposed by given conditions and constraints' (Simon 1976: 130). Hence each player has a skill in computation that enables him to calculate infinitely rapidly, and without incurring any costs, the action that is optimal for him in the situation at hand.

Experiments and fieldwork have shown that already, in relatively simple situations, human subjects may not behave *as if* they are substantively rational; at least, it may take a very long time before they behave this way. Hence the empirical relevance of the Bayesian theory is limited. One of the virtues of game theory is that, by taking the Bayesian model to its logical extremes, it has clearly revealed the limitations of that model. As Simon wrote as early as 1955, 'Recent developments . . . have raised great doubts as to whether this schematized model of economic man provides a suitable foundation on which to erect a theory— whether it be a theory of how firms *do* behave or how they rationally "should" behave' (Simon 1955: 99). He also wrote that the task we face is 'to replace the global rationality of economic man with a kind of rational behaviour that is compatible with the access to information and the computational capacities that are actually possessed by organisms, including man, in the kinds of environments in which such organisms exist' (Simon 1955: 99).

Recent game theory papers have taken up this task. They deal with all kinds of cognitive limits—with respect to perception, memory, information-processing capacity, knowledge, computational abilities, etc.—by including them explicitly in the model, and they deduce the consequences of the presence of these limits on outcomes. In these models agents are information-processing devices, and the bounded rationality arises from the bounded capacity of the system. The models retain the optimization assumption: how should the machine be optimally designed within the constraints that are specified? Hence it is assumed that the 'system designer' is substantively rational. One interpretation of this meta-player is as an unconscious evolutionary process. Alternatively, it is a super-rational player who correctly foresees the constraints that he will face and who takes these optimally into account.

As there are infinitely many possibilities for adding constraints, work of this type will certainly continue for quite a while. We will describe some of it in the following sub-section. It is noteworthy that these models are not based on the empirical knowledge of actual thinking processes. In Section 10.5.2 we consider why more input from psychology is not used.

10.5.1. AN OPTIMIZATION APPROACH

The first models of bounded rationality in the game theory literature deal with repeated games, and they depart from perfect rationality by taking complexity costs of implementing strategies into account. It is assumed either that strategies that are too complicated cannot be used (Neyman 1985), or that more complex strategies have higher costs (Rubinstein 1986; Abreu and Rubinstein 1988). Hence Neyman's approach amounts to eliminating strategies from the original game, while Rubinstein's approach changes the payoffs. Both models view a strategy as an information-processing rule, a machine. The machine has a number of states and each state induces an action. In addition, there is a transition function. Depending on the information that the machine receives (i.e. on which action combination is played by the opponents), the machine moves to another state. The complexity of a strategy is measured by the number of states in the machine. Neyman assumes that players have only a certain number of states available; Rubinstein assumes that states are costly and that players care, lexicographically, about repeated game payoffs and complexity costs. Each player has to choose a machine at the beginning of the game, the chosen machines then play the repeated game against each other, and each player receives the resulting payoff. Hence we have a game in strategic form where the strategy set of each player is the set of all possible machines and we can investigate the Nash equilibria of this 'machine game'.

One can easily see what causes the action in Neyman's setup: by eliminating strategies, one might create new, possibly more attractive, equilibria. Indeed, Neyman shows that, if players cannot use too complicated machines, cooperation might be an equilibrium outcome in the finitely repeated prisoner's dilemma. In Rubinstein's setup the results are driven by the observation that there are many ties in the payoff matrix of a repeated game (many strategy profiles induce the same path), hence small changes in these payoffs may have large effects. Introducing explicit costs for implementing a strategy has drastic consequences indeed: In the repeated prisoner's dilemma, for example, only the 'diagonals' of the set of feasible payoffs can be obtained as Nash equilibrium payoffs of the machine game (Abreu and Rubinstein 1988). By introducing costs also for the number of transitions, the set of equilibrium payoffs shrinks even further: only the repetition of the one-shot equilibrium survives (Banks and Sundaram 1990). The contrast with the folk theorem is remarkable.

Note that in these models the cost of calculating an equilibrium strategy are not taken into account, and that this calculation might be more complicated than calculating an equilibrium in the unrestricted game. In addition, there is the question of why Nash equilibria of the machine game are relevant. Binmore and Samuelson (1992) argue in favour of an evolutionary interpretation of the machine game in which equilibrium results from an evolutionary adaption process. Hence nature might endow the players with the equilibrium and there is no issue of finding or computing it.

A next generation of models builds on the above ideas by incorporating limits on the information-processing abilities of players. A player is viewed as an information-processor: information flows in, is processed in some way, and a decision results as an output. The processor has limited capacity; he can carry out only a certain number of operations per time period. Perhaps the capacity can be extended, but extensions are costly. A seminal paper is Rubinstein (1993), in which the consequences of heterogeneity in information-processing ability are investigated. Some players can only distinguish high prices from low ones: they cannot make fine distinctions. The *ex ante* decision that such a player has to make is which prices to classify as low and which as high, knowing that his final decision (whether to buy or not) can depend only on the classification of the price and not on the price itself. The question addressed is how one can optimally exploit such 'naive' players. Formally, the model is a two-stage game in which a kind of sequential equilibrium is computed: players optimize taking their own constraints and those of other players into account.

In Rubinstein's model, there is a monopolistic shop owner and two types of customer, *A* and *B*. The shop owner is privately informed about which state of nature prevails, and to maximize his profit he would like to reveal this information to the type *B* individuals, but not to those of type *A*. Specifically, in a certain state of nature the monopolist would prefer to sell only to type *B*. It is assumed that the only signal the monopolist has available is the price that he sets. Since the optimal price reveals the state, the monopolist's most desired outcome cannot be realized if all consumers can perfectly perceive the price: the type *A* consumers would correctly infer the state from the price. However, if perceptions of the type *A* consumers are imperfect, then the monopolist can do better. He can add some noise to his price signal and force consumers to pay attention to this noise by, possibly, hiding some relevant information behind it. By distracting their attention, the consumers might not notice information that is really essential and the monopolist might be better off.

Fershtman and Kalai (1993) consider a similar model of a multi-market oligopolist with a limited capacity to handle information. The oligopolist can pay attention to only a limited number of markets, and he has to decide how to allocate his attention: should he stay out of markets where there is competition and where, in order to play well, he is forced to monitor the competitors' behaviour closely, or should he rather devote much effort to those markets and go on 'automatic pilot' in the monopolistic markets?

Models of limited attention like the above (but see also Radner and Rothschild 1975, and Winter 1981) seem to me to be extremely relevant for actual decision-making and to evaluate the role that game theory can play in such situations. For example, should a business manager with limited time and attention best focus his attention on the strategic interaction with the competitors, or is he better off trying to improve the organization of production within the firm? It is obvious that in real life we are involved in many games at the same time, and that we do not devote equal time to analysing each of them. *Ceteris paribus*, more important games deserve more attention, but certainly, the complexity of a game also plays a role. I think it is important to find out how much time to devote to each game that one plays and I expect to see some research in this area in the future.

Summarizing the above, we might say that, although the initial papers in this area dealing with the complexity of executing strategies were perhaps not directly practically relevant, they were tremendously important and improved our tools for the analysis of other aspects of bounded rationality. Nevertheless, a drawback is that this work does not take into account the cost of computing an optimal strategy. Probably, most actual situations are so complex that it is simply impossible to find an optimal strategy within the time span that is allowed. In such cases, one has to settle for a 'good' solution. Such a solution may be obtained either from solving a drastically simplified problem exactly or from a heuristic procedure applied directly to the complex situation. Game theory at present does not offer much advice on what to do when one has to rely on heuristics. The literature focuses exclusively on the question, 'What is optimal given the constraints?' It does not address the question, 'What is an efficient procedure for coming up with a reasonable solution?' The theory does not deal with 'satisficing behaviour'; it has not yet made the transition from studying behaviour that is substantively rational to studying behaviour that is procedurally rational, i.e. 'behaviour that is the outcome of appropriate deliberation' (Simon 1976: 131).

It seems reasonable to expect that, if computations are complicated and costly, and if the computation process is not deterministic, one will not be able to determine exactly the point at which the other players stop computing; hence one will not be able to figure out what the others will do. Each player will face uncertainty, and there will be private information. Each player will stop computing only if he has a strategy that is a reasonably good response against the average expected strategy of the others. We do not necessarily end up at an equilibrium. It will be extremely interesting to see what such 'robust choices' look like, and whether or not they bear any relationship to existing game-theoretic solution concepts.

10.5.2. A BEHAVIOURAL APPROACH

The research discussed in the previous sub-section is firmly entrenched in the deductive branch of game theory: a well-specified game is set up and the equilibria of the game are analysed. Elements of bounded rationality are introduced within a given well-specified model: the problem to be solved is assumed given. Most actual decision problems, however, are unstructured and complex. In reaching a decision, one first has to construct a model and then to evaluate the decisions within that model. The papers discussed above do not deal with the question of how to generate an appropriate model. In most actual decision-taking situations, however, most time is spent on trying to visualize and understand the situation, and hence on the formulation of a model that is appropriate for the situation. So it is probably at the modelling stage that aspects of bounded rationality are most important. It is remarkable that none of the papers discussed above contains an explicit model of the reasoning process of a player, let alone takes detailed empirical knowledge of the actual human thinking processes into account. In this sub-section I discuss some of these behavioural aspects of bounded rationality.

Most actual decision-taking situations are complex. It is better to speak of the *emergence* of decisions than of *decision-taking*. Broadly speaking, in reaching a decision, the actor has to perform the following steps of perceiving, thinking and acting:

1. *perception* of the situation and *generation* of a model for analysing it;
2. *problem solving*: searching for patterns, for similarities with other models and situations, and for alternative plans of action;
3. *investigating* the consequences of (a subset of the) actions and *evaluating* them;
4. *implementing* an action;
5. *learning*: storing relevant information in memory so as to facilitate solving a similar problem later.

Selten (1978) develops an informal model of the human reasoning process that takes these steps into account. He emphasizes the importance of perception: how does a player view the problem? what elements does he consider to be relevant? what patterns does a player see? what types of similarity with other decision situations does a player notice? Selten suggests a model of the human reasoning process that is based on the idea that a decision may be reached on three levels: those of routine, imagination, and reasoning. It is assumed that each higher level uses more information and needs more effort than the lower one. Hence, because of the costs involved, the player may decide not to activate all levels. Furthermore, it is not necessarily true that the decision reached by the highest activated level will be taken. As Selten writes, 'The reason is quite simple. It is not true that the higher level always yields a better decision. The reasoning process is not infallible. It is subject to logical and computational mistakes' (Selten 1978: 150).

Actually, Selten makes an argument for decisions arising from the level of imagination. In game situations it is important to put oneself in the shoes of the other players in order to form expectations about their behaviour. Since a player who makes decisions at the routine level 'is likely to make some mistakes which can be easily avoided by imagining oneself to be in the other player's position', this level is unattractive in game situations. On the other hand, 'If a player tries to analyze the game situation in a rigorous way, then he will often find that the process of reasoning does not lead to any clear conclusion. This will weaken his tendency to activate the level of reasoning in later occasions of the same kind'

(Selten 1978: 152). Furthermore, rigorous reasoning has to be applied to a model of the situation, and to construct such a model one has to rely on the level of imagination. Since 'the imagination process is not unlikely to be more reliable as a generator of scenarios than as a generator of assumptions for a model of the situation', this level will yield good solutions in many cases, so that Selten concludes that 'one must expect that the final decision shows a strong tendency in favor of the level of imagination even in such cases where the situation is well structured and the application of rigorous thinking is not too difficult' (Selten 1978: 153).

The concrete problem that Selten addresses is why a game theorist familiar with the backward induction argument in the finite-horizon chain-store game, and who accepts the logical validity of that argument, nevertheless decides to fight entry if entry would occur in the first period. Hence Selten discusses why a human player might deliberately neglect the advice offered by a rationality based theory. So he deals with 'motivational bounds' of human rationality, rather than with 'cognitive bounds'. The solution that Selten offers is that, at the level of imagination, a player might not perceive the situation in the same way as the game theorist views the extensive game. A player's model of the situation need not contain all detail that the extensive form provides. Psychologists tell us that an observer exercises control over the amount of detail he wishes to take in, and that people sometimes see things that are not there (also see Schelling 1960: 108, fn. 18). It matters: if the entrants believe that the monopolist classifies the situation simply according to whether the horizon is far away or near, and that he views a game with a horizon that is far away as one with an infinite horizon, then the deterrence equilibrium becomes possible.

The classical interpretation of a game is as a full description of the physical rules of play. Following Selten's lead implies taking seriously the idea that a player's model of a situation depends on how the player perceives the situation. In a game context, the fact that a player's perception of the situation need not coincide with the actual situation forces us to discuss a player's perception of the other players' perceptions. Rubinstein (1991) advocates viewing the extensive form as the players' common perception of the situation rather than as an exhaustive description of the situation. Hence the model should include only those elements that are perceived by the players to be relevant. It is unknown what the consequences are of this reinterpretation of the game model. However, it should be noted that Schelling already stressed that the locus where strategic skill is important is in the modelling stage: the trick is to represent the situation in such a way that the outcome of the resulting model is most favourable to one's side (Schelling 1960: 69).

It is a challenging task to formalize the above ideas, i.e. to develop models of procedural rationality. However, procedural rationality cannot be fruitfully studied without taking empirical knowledge of the actual thinking processes into account. Without having a broad set of facts on which to theorize, there is a certain danger of spending too much time on models that are mathematically elegant, yet have little connection with actual behaviour. At present our empirical knowledge is inadequate, and it is an interesting question why game theorists have not turned more frequently to psychologists for information about the learning and information-processing processes used by humans. One reason might be that this knowledge is not available in a sufficiently precise form to be meaningfully incorporated into a formal mathematical model. Another might be that other social sciences might not have much knowledge available. Wärneryd (1993) explains that economists might have little to learn from psychologists since psychologists have shown remarkable little interest in economic issues. Also, Selten is of the opinion that little of value can be imported. His 1989 Nancy L. Schwarz memorial lecture is entirely devoted to the question, 'What do we know about the structure of human economic behavior?' After having discussed this question for eighteen pages, he concludes:

I must admit that the answer is disappointing. We know very little. . . . We know that Bayesian decision theory is not a realistic description of human economic behavior . . . but we cannot be satisfied with negative knowledge—knowledge about what human behavior fails to be. . . . We must do empirical research if we want to gain knowledge on the structure of human economic behavior. (Selten 1989: 25)

To improve our understanding of human behaviour, laboratory experimentation is essential. Unlike many current experiments, which just inform us that the rationalistic benchmark is not very relevant, we need experiments that inform us *why* the deviations occur and *how* players reason in these situations.

10.6. Conclusion

The starting point of this paper was the observation that, while standard game theory is based on the assumption of perfectly rational behaviour in a well-defined model that is common knowledge, real-world problems, in contrast, are often unstructured and human players are far from rational. As a consequence, it follows that much of standard game theory is largely irrelevant for prescriptive (or explanatory) purposes. In order to increase the applicability of the theory, it is necessary to develop models that incorporate aspects of bounded rationality. At present such models are indeed developed, yet they retain the assumption of optimizing behaviour. Hence they limit themselves to situations that are simple enough to enable the optimization to be carried out. Complex situations offer less scope for optimizing behaviour and force us to address the problem-solving aspects associated with procedural rationality: how is the situation perceived, how is it modelled, and how do humans go about solving them?

That aspects of mutual perception and joint problem-solving might be more important than individual optimization was already stressed by Schelling, who formulated the essential game problem as 'Players must together find "rules of the game" or together suffer the consequences' (Schelling 1960: 107). Up to now, the road that Schelling pointed to has not been frequently travelled. Game theorists have instead followed the road paved by Nash. I conjecture that there will be a reorientation in the near future, i.e. that game theory will focus more on the aspects of imagination stressed by Schelling and less on those of logic stressed by Nash. Of course, I might be wrong. The game of which route to take is one of coordination with multiple equilibria: being on one road is attractive only if sufficiently many (but not too many) others travel that road as well. As the discussion of Fig. 10.1 has shown, there is no reason to expect the Pareto-efficient equilibrium to result.

Schelling also already stressed that, in order to increase the relevancy of game theory, it is necessary to develop its descriptive branch. Prescriptive theory has to stand on two strong legs:

A third conclusion . . . is that some *essential* part of the study of mixed-motive games is necessarily empirical. This is not to say just that it is an empirical question how people do actually perform in mixed-motive games, especially games too complicated for intellectual mastery. It is a stronger statement: that the principles relevant to *successful* play, the *strategic* principles, the propositions of a *normative* theory, cannot be derived by purely analytical means from a priori considerations. (Schelling 1960: 162–3)

Hence we may conclude with a message that is somewhat depressing for theorists. Just as at the inception of the theory, it might still be true that

the most fruitful work may be that of careful patient description; indeed this may be by far the largest domain for the present and for some time to come. (von Neumann and Morgenstern 1947: 2)

REFERENCES

Abreu, D., and Rubinstein, A. (1988), 'The Structure of Nash Equilibrium in Repeated Games with Finite Automata', *Econometrica*, 56: 1259–82.

Aumann, R. J. (1964), 'Markets with a Continuum of Traders', *Econometrica*, 32: 39–50.

—— (1976), 'Agreeing to Disagree', *Annals of Statistics*, 4: 1236–9.

—— (1985), 'An Axiomatization of the Non-Transferable Utility Value', *Econometrica*, 53: 599–612.

—— (1987), 'Game Theory', in J. Eatwell, M. Milgate, and P. Newman (eds.), *The New Palgrave Dictionary of Economics*. London: Macmillan, 460–82.

—— (1990), 'Nash Equilibria Are Not Self-Enforcing', in J. J. Gabszewicz, J.-F. Richard, and L. A. Wolsey (eds.), *Economic Decision-Making: Games, Econometrics and Optimisation*. Amsterdam: North Holland, 201–6.

—— and Brandenburger, A. (1991), 'Epistemic Conditions for Nash Equilibrium', Working Paper no. 91–042, Harvard Business School.

—— and Shapley, L. S. (1974), *Values of Non-Atomic Games*. Princeton: Princeton University Press.

—— —— (1976), 'Long-Term Competition: a Game-Theoretic Analysis', mimeo, Hebrew University; also published as Working Paper 676, Department of Economics, University of California, Los Angeles, 1992.

Axelrod, R. (1984), *The Evolution of Cooperation*. New York: Basic Books.

Banks, J., and Sundaram, R. (1990), 'Repeated Games, Finite Automata and Complexity', *Games and Economic Behavior*, 2: 97–117.

Basu, K. (1990), 'On the Non-Existence of a Rationality Definition for Extensive Games', *International Journal of Game Theory*, 19: 33–44.

Binmore, K., and Samuelson, L. (1992), 'Evolutionary Stability in Repeated Games Played by Finite Automata', *Journal of Economic Theory*, 57: 278–305.

—— Osborne, M. J., and Rubinstein, A. (1992), 'Noncooperative models of bargaining', in R. J. Aumann and S. Hart (eds.), *Handbook of Game Theory*, i. Amsterdam: North-Holland, 179–225.

Carlsson, H., and van Damme, E. (1993*a*), 'Global Games and Equilibrium Selection', *Econometrica*, 61: 989–1018.

—— —— (1993*b*), 'Equilibrium Selection in Stag Hunt Games', in K. G. Binmore and A. Kirman (eds.), *Frontiers of Game Theory*. Cambridge, Mass.: MIT Press, 237–54.

De Bondt, W. F. M., and Thaler, R. (1992), 'Financial Decision Making in Markets and Firms: a Behavioral Perspective', mimeo, School of Business, University of Wisconsin.

Debreu, G., and Scarf, H. (1963), 'A Limit Theorem on the Core of an Economy', *International Economic Review*, 4: 236–46.

Ellison, G. (1993), 'Learning, Local Interaction, and Coordination', *Econometrica*, 61: 1047–72.

Fershtman, C., and Kalai, E. (1993), 'Complexity Considerations and Market Behavior', *Rand Journal of Economics*, 24: 224–35.

Fisher, F. M. (1989), 'Games Economists Play: a Noncooperative View', *Rand Journal of Economics*, 20: 113–24.

Fudenberg, D., and Maskin, E. (1986), 'The Folk Theorem in Repeated Games with Discounting and with Incomplete Information', *Econometrica*, 54: 533–54.

Gale, D., and Shapley, L. S. (1962), 'College Admission and the Stability of Marriage', *American Mathematics Monthly*, 69: 9–15.

Güth, W., and van Damme, E. (1994), 'Information, Strategic Behavior and Fairness in Ultimatum Bargaining', Discussion Paper no. 9465, CentER for Economic Research, Tilburg University.

Harsanyi, J. C. (1963), 'A Simplified Bargaining Model for the *n*-person Cooperative Game', *International Economic Review*, 4: 194–220.

—— (1968), 'Games with Incomplete Information Played by "Bayesian" Players, parts I, II, and III', *Management Science*, 14: 159–82, 320–32, 468–502.

—— (1974), 'An Equilibrium Point Interpretation of Stable Sets and a Proposed Alternative Definition', *Management Science*, 20: 1472–95.

—— (1977), *Rational Behaviour and Bargaining Equilibrium in Games and Social Situations*. Cambridge: Cambridge University Press.

—— and Selten, R. (1988), *A General Theory of Equilibrium Selection in Games*. Cambridge, Mass.: MIT Press.

Hart, S. (1985), 'An Axiomatization of Harsanyi's Nontransferable Utility Solution', *Econometrica*, 53: 1295–1314.

Hendriks, K., and Porter, R. H. (1988), 'An Empirical Study of an Auction with Asymmetric Information', *American Economic Review*, 78: 301–14.

Holland, J. H. (1992), *Adaptation in Natural and Artificial Systems*. Cambridge, Mass.: MIT Press.

Kagel, J. H., and Levin, D. (1986), 'The Winner's Curse and Public Information in Common Value Auctions', *American Economic Review*, 76: 894–920.

Kandori, M., Mailath, G. J., and Rob, R. (1993), 'Learning, Mutation and Long Run Equilibria in Games', *Econometrica*, 61: 29–56.

Kim, Y.-G., and Sobel, J. (1991), 'An Evolutionary Approach to Pre-Play Communication', mimeo, University of California, San Diego.

Kohlberg, E., and Mertens, J.-F. (1986), 'On the Strategic Stability of Equilibria', *Econometrica*, 54: 1003–39.

Kreps, D. M. (1990), *Game Theory and Economic Modelling*. Oxford: Oxford University Press.

—— Milgrom, P., Roberts, J., and Wilson, R. (1982), 'Rational Cooperation in the Finitely-Repeated Prisoner's Dilemma', *Journal of Economic Theory*, 27: 245–52.

Kuhn, H. W. (1953), 'Extensive Games and the Problem of Information', in H. W. Kuhn, and A. W. Tucker (eds.), *Contributions to the Theory of Games*, vol. 2. *Annals of Mathematics Studies*, xxviii. Princeton: Princeton University Press, 193–216.

—— and Tucker, A. W. (1950), *Contributions to the Theory of Games*, vol. 1. *Annals of Mathematics Studies*, xxiv. Princeton: Princeton University Press.

Lucas, W. F. (1968), 'A Game with no Solution', *Bulletin of the American Mathematics Society*, 74: 237–9.

Luce, R. D., and Raiffa, H. (1957), *Games and Decisions: Introduction and Critical Survey*. New York: John Wiley.

Marimon, R., McGrattan, E., and Sargent, T. (1990), 'Money as a Medium of Exchange in an Economy with Artificial Intelligent Agents', *Journal for Economic Dynamics and Control*, 14: 329–73.

Mas-Colell, A. (1989), 'An Equivalence Theorem for a Bargaining Set', *Journal of Mathematical Economics*, 18: 129–39.

Maynard Smith, J. (1982), *Evolution and the Theory of Games*. Cambridge: Cambridge University Press.

—— and Price, G. R. (1973), 'The Logic of Animal Conflict', *Nature* (London), no. 246: 15–18.

Nash, J. F. (1950), 'Non-Cooperative Games', Ph.D. dissertation, Princeton University.

—— (1953), 'Two-Person Cooperative Games', *Econometrica*, 21: 128–40.

Neyman, A. (1985), 'Bounded Complexity Justifies Cooperation in the Finitely Repeated Prisoner's Dilemma', *Economics Letters*, 19: 227–9.

—— (1989), 'Games without Common Knowledge', notes, Hebrew University.

Osborne, M. J., and Rubinstein, A. (1990), *Bargaining and Markets*. San Diego: Academic Press.

Pagano, M., and Roëll, A. (1990), 'Trading Systems in European Stock Exchanges: Current Performance and Policy Options', *Economic Policy*, 10: 63–115.

Pelzman, S. (1991), 'The Handbook of Industrial Organization: a Review Article', *Journal of Political Economy*, 99: 201–17.

Plott, C. R. (1987), 'Dimensions of Parallelism: Some Policy Applications of Experimental Methods', in A. E. Roth (ed.), *Laboratory Experimentation in Economics: Six Points of View*. Cambridge: Cambridge University Press.

Radner, R., and Rothschild, M. (1975), 'On the Allocation of Effort', *Journal of Economic Theory*, 10: 358–76.

Raiffa, H. (1982), *The Art and Science of Negotiation*. Cambridge, Mass.: Harvard University Press.

Reny, P. (1986), 'Rationality, Common Knowledge and the Theory of Games', Ph.D. dissertation, Princeton University.

Roth, A. E. (1984), 'The Evolution of the Labor Market for Medical Interns and Residents: a Case Study in Game Theory', *Journal of Political Economy*, 92: 991–1016.

—— and Sotomayor, M. (1990), *Two-Sided Matching: a Study in Game-Theoretic Modelling and Analysis*. Cambridge: Cambridge University Press.

—— and Xing, X. (1994), 'Jumping the Gun: Patterns and Pathologies in the Timing of Market Transactions', *American Economic Review*, 84: 992–1044.

Rubinstein, A. (1978), 'Equilibrium in Supergames with the Overtaking Criterion', *Journal of Economic Theory*, 21: 1–9.

—— (1982), 'Perfect Equilibrium in a Bargaining Model', *Econometrica*, 50: 97–109.

—— (1986), 'Finite Autonoma Play the Repeated Prisoner's Dilemma', *Journal of Economic Theory*, 39: 83–96.

—— (1989), 'The Electronic Mail Game: Strategic Behavior under Almost Common Knowledge', *American Economic Review*, 79: 385–91.

—— (1991), 'Comments on the Interpretation of Game Theory', *Econometrica*, 59: 909–24.

—— (1993), 'On Price Recognition and Computational Complexity in a Monopolistic Model', *Journal of Political Economy*, 101: 473–84.

Schelling, T. C. (1960), *The Strategy of Conflict*. Cambridge, Mass.: Harvard University Press.

Selten, R. (1965), 'Spieltheoretische Behandlung eines Oligopolmodells mit Nachfrageträgheit', *Zeitschrift für die gesamte Staatswissenschaft*, 12: 301–24.

—— (1975), 'Re-examination of the Perfectness Concept for Equilibrium Points in Extensive Games', *International Journal of Game Theory*, 4: 25–55.

—— (1978), 'The Chain Store Paradox', *Theory and Decision*, 9: 127–59.

—— (1981), 'A Noncooperative Model of Characteristic Function Bargaining', in V. Böhm and H. H. Nachtkamp (eds.), *Essays in Game Theory and Mathematical Economics in Honor of Oskar Morgenstern*. Mannheim: Bibliographisches Institut, 131–51.

—— (1989), Evolution, Learning and Economic Behavior. Nancy Schwartz Memorial Lecture. J. L. Kellogg Graduate School of Management, Northwestern University, Evanston, Ill.

—— (ed.) (1991*a*), *Game Equilibrium Models*, iii, *Strategic Bargaining*. Berlin: Springer Verlag.

—— (1991*b*), 'Evolution, Learning and Economic Behavior', *Games and Economic Behavior*, 3: 3–24.

—— and Kuon, B. (1992), 'Demand Commitment Bargaining in Three-Person Quota Game Experiments', Discussion Paper no. B219, Bonn University.

—— Mitzkewitz, M., and Uhlich, H. R. (1988), 'Duopoly Strategies Programmed by Experienced Players', Discussion Paper no. B106, Bonn University.

Shapley, L. S. (1953), 'A Value for *n*-person Games', in H. W. Kuhn and A. W. Tucker (eds.), *Contributions to the Theory of Games*, vol. 2. *Annals of Mathematics Studies*, xxviii. Princeton University Press, Princeton, 305–17.

—— (1964), 'Some Topics in Two-Person Games', in M. A. Dresher, L. S. Shapley and A. W. Tucker (eds.), Advances in Game Theory. *Annals of Mathematics Studies*, 52. Princeton University Press, Princeton, 1–28.

—— (1968), 'Utility Comparison and the Theory of Games', in G. T. Guilbaud, *La Décision: aggregation et dynamique des ordres de preference*. Paris: Editions du CNRS.

Simon, H. (1955), 'A Behavioral Model of Rational Choice', *Quarterly Journal of Economics*, 69: 99–118.

Simon, H. (1976), 'From Substantive to Procedural Rationality', in S. J. Latsis (ed.), *Methods and Appraisal in Economics*. Cambridge: Cambridge University Press, 129–48.

Smith, V. L. (1990), 'Experimental Economics: Behavioral Lessons for Microeconomic Theory and Policy', Nancy L. Schwarz Memorial Lecture, J. L. Kellogg Graduate School of Management.

van Damme, E. (1987), *Stability and Perfection of Nash Equilibria*. Berlin: Springer Verlag; 2nd edn. 1991.

—— (1994), 'Evolutionary Game Theory', *European Economic Review*, 38: 847–58.

von Neumann, J., and Morgenstern, O. (1947), *Theory of Games and Economic Behavior*. Princeton: Princeton University Press.

Wärneryd, K. E. (1993), 'A Closer Look at Economic Psychology', Discussion Paper no. 9362 CentER for Economic Research, Tilburg University.

Winter, S. (1981), 'Attention Allocation and Input Proportions', *Journal of Economic Behavior and Organization*, 2: 31–46.

Young, P. (1993), 'The Evolution of Conventions', *Econometrica*, 61: 57–84.

III

Issues in Econometrics

Introduction to Part III

Russell Davidson

A decade is a long time in econometrics. Enough time for passing fads to be revealed as just that, and enough time too for valuable new methods to be recognized for their worth, and employed in serious empirical applications. And ten years more data for numerous time series, allowing us to try to answer questions that we simply didn't have enough information to tackle before.

It seems to be the case these days that, for the people who decide on the basis of research proposals just who is worthy to receive research funding, it is essential to know in advance what results we are going to come up with over the next three years or whatever the period may be for which funding is requested. As we all know (although these administrators don't seem to), the whole point about research is that, if you knew in advance what your results were going to be, you wouldn't need to do the research. Since I fully expect that econometricians will be just as busy doing research beyond the millenium as they have been up to now, it seems safe to assume that the only results to be obtained in the future that I can reasonably foresee at this point are the uninteresting ones!

Even so, it may still be possible to discern the general directions that will be occupying our interests for a few years to come. Indeed, the four papers in this part of the book were solicited in the hope that they would be in some sense prophetic, as well as informative about the current state of econometrics. It would be impertinent of me to try here to explain to readers what these papers contain—by similar reasoning to that used above, if I could, the papers would hardly be worth reading!—but what I can perhaps do usefully is to say how I, at least, situate the papers in the context of the diverse strands of research at present attracting econometricians' interest, and speculate as to how these strands will develop over the next few years.

In this part of the book, a surprisingly wide range of approaches can be seen in just four articles—Bayesian and frequentist, macro- or micro-oriented, empirical and methodological. For various reasons, good and bad, different people have different approaches to econometrics. The differences associated with whether one is addressing problems in micro- or macroeconometrics are obvious, and obviously necessary. Different sorts of questions and different types of data require different techniques. But in addition, there is the long-standing divide between the Bayesian and frequentist approaches, not in econometrics alone, but throughout all statistical disciplines. (Since both flavours of econometrician are to be found at GREQE, or GREQAM, as we have had to learn to call it now, I say 'frequentist' rather than 'classical', a term that does rather bias the argument

in one direction.) The divide is a deep one, and well known to provoke arguments of religious fervour. This being so, I doubt greatly that much will happen
in the near future to diminish the divide. I have (of course!) my own views as
to what approach is better in various sets of circumstances, but, for fear of
getting involved in religious controversy, I will not say a word about these views
here, except that the side I favour does indeed depend on circumstances, and is
not uniformly either frequentist or Bayesian.

Econometric modelling in the subject of Christian Gouriéroux's paper (Chapter
11). The last couple of decades have seen enormous advances in our techniques
of modelling, with the result that very little in the paper would have been at all
familiar to an econometrician in 1980. Perhaps a paper written in twenty years'
time will be just as remote from our present understanding, but I would be
surprised if that were to turn out to be the case. My reasoning is that many of
the techniques discussed in Gouriéroux's paper are fundamental. They will no
more go away in the next few years than will ordinary least squares. The point
I am trying to make is that over recent years we have developed methodologies
for dealing with most of the econometric issues we face, so that future advances
will be in the direction either of applying these methodologies or of refining
them. I don't foresee revolutionary change of the sort that attended the awaken-
ing of interest in unit roots and cointegration, for instance. But then, practically
all revolutionary scientific advances were not foreseen by anyone but their insti-
gators, and so my last sentence may well be simply worthless.

I will not try to describe, even in summary form, the methods discussed in so
masterly a fashion by Gouriéroux. Rather, let me focus on some aspects of those
methods that I find of particular interest, and that I think will reappear in the
work of the next few years.

First of all, there has been a tremendous burgeoning of techniques that use
computer simulation, in one way or another. I remember that, back in the 1960s,
computers were massive installations, not readily accessible to ordinary mortals;
only nuclear physicists and their like, backed by the power bestowed by substantial research grants, could make free of them. But for those few who could
use up a lot of computer time, my recollection is that they devoted much of it
to simulation. Then, as now, there was a trade-off between clever analytical
calculation and brute-force numerical methods. But since the 1960s, we humans
have not got any faster at analytical calculation, while computers have got
immeasurably faster and vastly more accessible. Economists as well as nuclear
physicists can now make extensive use of simulation methods.

Now that computers run so fast, there are all sorts of things they can do, by
simulation, that just wouldn't be feasible analytically. In fact, it is interesting
that a good deal of analytical cleverness has been devoted recently to developing
ever more sophisticated simulation techniques. One of the most spectacularly
successful of these is Efron's bootstrap. This very computationally intensive
technique was invented more than fifteen years ago, as computers were enter-
ing their phase of rapid evolution towards greater speed at lower cost. It is a
prime example of a wonderfully simple idea that turned out to be astonishingly
productive, but that just wouldn't have occurred to anyone if cheap computing

power had not been available. The basic idea was indeed simple enough—with hindsight, anyway—but it has since been made the subject of some profound theoretical analysis, of the sort we can do but computers cannot. The result of this analysis is that we can use the bootstrap for all sorts of things undreamt of when it was invented.

Widespread interest in bootstrap methods has sprung up only very recently among econometricians. Statisticians and econometricians do not always think the same way, and what excites one discipline can leave the other cold. For whatever reason, somewhere between five and ten years ago the bootstrap, till then exclusively a tool of statisticians, began to interest and excite econometricians. Today, it interests them more the more they learn about it. The phrase 'Bayesian bootstrap' has appeared in the title of a number of seminars I have attended recently, and it is clear that interest in the bootstrap, as indeed in all sorts of simulation methods, extends to all sorts of econometricians.

The bootstrap is almost always implemented by means of a Monte Carlo experiment—that is why it is computationally intensive. Monte Carlo experiments appeared on the scientific scene at almost the same time as computers: in the 1940s. They were already much in evidence among physicists in the 1960s. Even so, econometricians have contributed substantially to Monte Carlo methodology. However much computing time you have, you can always think up a problem that will use more, and econometricians are no exception to that rule. There are two possible solutions. The first is easy: you just wait, and, as computer hardware becomes faster and faster, what was impossible drifts into the realm of the possible. The second is harder. It involves the use of what are called variance-reduction techniques, and such techniques are discovered and implemented by use of analysis, not computing time. Some of the most successful of these variance-reduction methods have been thought up by econometricians, and continued improvements in Monte Carlo methodology can reasonably be forecast as one of the results of econometricians' activity over the next ten years.

As I mentioned earlier, and as Richard Blundell discusses at much greater length in his contribution (Chapter 14), available data sets have become much larger over the last decade. Not just the lapse of time is responsible for this. Econometricians, in company with statisticians and others, have set wheels in motion for data to be collected in new and interesting ways. National statistical agencies have been in this business for some time, but the scale of the endeavour has been growing. Panel data sets are a particularly important output of this enterprise. Quite recently, a number of new books have appeared devoted to the analysis of panel data. This, too, is a field in which econometricians have been active for at least two decades, but greater availability of data has caused panel data analysis to occupy a much more central position in econometric theory and practice.

Another field that has seen the appearance recently of large, sometimes very large, data sets is financial economics. Here time series are involved rather than panel data. Even if time rolls on at an unvarying rate, time series can get longer faster than that if the frequency of observations increases. This is just what has been happening with financial data. Conventional macroeconomic time series have yearly, or quarterly, or perhaps monthly frequencies, but it is not unusual for financial data to be generated every minute—at least every minute of the time stock markets are open.

Whether panel data or high-frequency time series are involved, the large number of observations makes it possible to use methods that are not practical with smaller data sets. I refer to the whole battery of non-parametric, semi-parametric, and semi-nonparametric methods. As with simulation methods, these too have come to us from the world of statisticians, and these too have been made over for the needs of econometrics. And, as one might expect, econometricians have made substantial contributions to the theory of these methods.

It is a commonplace in any realm of statistical inquiry that reliable inference can be obtained only if the models used for estimation and inference are correctly specified. Non-parametric methods can be of great help in the search for a correctly specified model provided enough data are available. Parametric models can, to a limited extent, handle nonlinearities, and they can do so very well if the exact nature of a nonlinearity is known. But if not, it is easy to end up with a misspecified model if one sticks exclusively to parametric models. Econometricians seem to be coming to the realization that non-parametric methods can be used on order to tease the nature of possible nonlinearities out of the data themselves, in such a way that a more efficient, but well specified, parametric model can be constructed based on the information given by a less efficient non-parametric procedure. It seems likely that the next decade will see growing use of non-parametric methods, as I describe here, and no doubt also in new and as yet unthought-of ways.

The commonplace of the preceding paragraph is no longer quite true, as Gouriéroux explains in Chapter 11. The new technique of indirect inference quite deliberately and explicitly uses misspecified models. The catch—for there has to be one, of course—is that one has to be aware of what the correctly specified model is. Not much further forward? Well, yes, in fact, because the correctly specified model may well be so complicated that ordinary procedures of estimation and inference cannot, even with present-day computer hardware, be used on it. If so, then it is often easy to come up with a slightly misspecified model that is greatly simpler. The results of estimating such a misspecified model can then be converted into results for the correctly specified model by means of—simulation, of course, what else? The technique of indirect inference, and some of the new methods of variance reduction, together promise to make it possible to work with models that, although highly satisfactory on theoretical grounds, have been too complex to deal with hitherto. It is hard for me to foresee just what benefits we will gain in the near future from these new possibilities, but that is just my own failure of imagination. There will certainly be significant gains.

One aspect of econometrics that is absolutely central in the work of those who work for governments is forecasting. Academic economists, on the other hand, often pay little attention to it. Augustín Maravall's paper (Chapter 12) shows that the latter statement has many exceptions! In some ways, this difference in the focus of interest is right and proper. Academics are, or should be, scientists, interested in analysing evidence and formulating hypotheses as to the workings of the world, the economic world in our case. For people with that point of view, forecasting can seem at best a distraction, and at worst necromancy and crystal-ball gazing—wholly unscientific in any case. But forecasting the economy is necessary if the economy is to be managed successfully, and obviously we can-not shirk responsibility in this matter. Something other than duty attracts other academic economists to the study of forecasting, namely the fact that the *theory* of forecasting is a fascinating field of study.

I have been impressed recently by just how different are the proper views to econometric modelling when forecasting rather than analysis of past events is the aim. The starting point for econometrics as historical analysis is cogently expressed at the beginning of Gouriéroux's paper:

The available data are a realization of a stochastic process . . . whose distribution is of course unknown, and the aim of econometrics is to use the data to derive relevant infor-mation on this underlying distribution. (see p. 222)

And, of course, econometrics for forecasting purposes will wish to make the fullest use of the relevant information provided by the other sort of economet-rics. But there's more to it. The main reason is that, in economics at least, there is simply no guarantee that the stochastic process that will operate in the future will be the same as the one that operated in the past, the one about which all that relevant information was derived.

The title of the paper by Bauwens and Lubrano is a bit of a play on words. Trends and breaking points, not in the Bayesian econometric literature, but rather in the operation of the economy, have been a central concern to time-series analysts recently. The point is simple: trends are forecastable; breaking points are not. Hence the forecaster's dilemma: will there be a breaking point in the period for which a forecast is being constructed, or will past trends continue? It is of course possible to talk about the probability of a breaking point, and of its amplitude, over some time horizon, and this is what the forecaster must do in order to have any realistic notion of the reliability of his or her forecasts. But this is not a concern for the econometrician who deals only with observed data without trying to extrapolate from them. One may discuss evidence for or against the hypothesis of a breaking point in the French economy in such-and-such a year, but this is a question of the interpretation of the factual record. It is my opinion here that it is in the realm of forecasting that the Bayesian approach can be most fruitful. That approach can deal naturally with things like the prob-ability of a future breaking point, and also with the costs of making mistakes about such things. Forecasting, after all, is almost always used as an aid to statistical decision making, and a Bayesian approach handles that nicely.

Whether or not econometricians will follow the division of labour I outline above, using primarily Bayesian methods in order to forecast, and primarily frequentist methods to analyse the economic record, is not something about which I feel competent to formulate any sort of forecast. Ask me about it again some time in the future, and I will try to answer on the basis of the data that will have been accumulated over that period!

11

Econometric Modelling: Methodologies and Interpretations

Christian Gourieroux

11.1. Introduction

As predicting the development of econometrics into the next millennium is a very hazardous task, I prefer to give some benchmarks for a better understanding of the recent evolution of econometric methodologies. To an outsider, this evolution certainly appears as a sequence of estimation and testing procedures, with the corresponding abbreviations and softwares. Some terms will be remembered —cointegration, GMM, encompassing, indirect inference. However, these technologies are byproducts of a deeper reflection on the models and on their use; this is the point I want to discuss.

The whole econometric approach, and statistical inference in general, is based on an axiom: that the available data are a realization of a stochastic process, often called the data generating process (DGP), whose distribution is unknown, and the aim of econometrics is to use the data to derive a relevant information on this underlying distribution.

To keep the presentation simple, I consider that the data are values taken by some variables (vectors) y_t indexed by time t, $t \in Z$, and I assume that the process is stationary. Thus, the DGP is characterized entirely by the conditional distribution of y_t given the past values $\underline{y}_{t-1} = \{y_{t-1}, y_{t-2}, \ldots\}$; I denote by

$$l_0 \left(y_t / \underline{y}_{t-1} \right) \tag{1}$$

the associated probability density function (p.d.f.).

The above assumptions—existence of an underlying distribution, the stationarity of the process, and the existence of a p.d.f.—are made in all that follows unless otherwise indicated. This will provide us with a minimal set of assumptions which will allow us to derive a complete statistical analysis. Such a set of assumptions is not very constraining, nor does it provide any information on the unknown p.d.f., l_0. This p.d.f. will be called the *true distribution*.

Other sets of assumptions could have been introduced, in particular for describing nonlinear dynamics, the existence of different underlying regimes, etc. However, I shall keep the above assumptions in the presentation that follows.

The results are presented in the time series framework. Indeed, it is often for macroeconomic or financial applications that these new approaches have been developed.

This may be a consequence of the relative weakness of structural theories in these domains, which in particular gives rather limited information on the dynamic aspects, but it is also due to the complexity of the real dynamics, which leads us to consider cautiously all the results deduced from linear formulations.

Section 11.2 recalls the traditional view of well specified models, and the approach 'from general to specific' used to determine such models. Section 11.3 covers the analysis of misspecified models, the understanding of the information that they may contain, and the interest of jointly studying several models of this kind (encompassing theory).

The next two sections concern the use of models as intermediate tools. In Section 11.4 I explain how to use a simple misspecified auxiliary model in analysing a complicated well specified model (theory of indirect inference), and in Section 11.5 I show how to use such misspecified models as a basis for deriving interesting classes of strategies (controls in macroeconomy, hedging or pricing strategies in finance), from which I shall choose the best.

The final section discusses the issue of model maintenance.

11.2. Well Specified Models

11.2.1. DEFINITION

Historically, the search for information on the true distribution has been based on the notion of well specified model. Let us consider a parametric framework, in which a model (M) is defined as a family of possible conditional p.d.f.s of y_t given $\underline{y_{t-1}}$, parameterized by θ whose dimension is p. Therefore we have

$$(M) = \{l(y_t/\underline{y_{t-1}}; \theta), \theta \in \Theta\}. \tag{2}$$

This model is well specified if the previous family contains the unknown true distribution, i.e. if there exists a true value θ_0 of the parameter such that:

$$l_0(y_t/\underline{y_{t-1}}) = l(y_t/\underline{y_{t-1}}; \theta_0). \tag{3}$$

Furthermore, if one value at most satisfies this condition (we say that θ_0 is identifiable), then we may assimilate the true unknown distribution and the *true* unknown *value of the parameter*. Searching for the true distribution l_0 is equivalent to searching for the true value θ_0. For this purpose different approaches are available; the best known one is the *maximum likelihood method* (Wald 1949). This consists in looking for the solution $\hat{\theta}_T$ of the maximization problem:

$$\hat{\theta}_T = \arg\max_{\theta} \sum_{t=1}^{T} \log l(y_t/\underline{y_{t-1}}; \theta). \tag{4}$$

Indeed, we may establish that if the model is well specified the estimator $\hat{\theta}_T$ tends to the true unknown value θ_0, when the number of observations T tends to infinity. Therefore $\hat{\theta}_T$ is a good approximation of θ_0 in large samples.

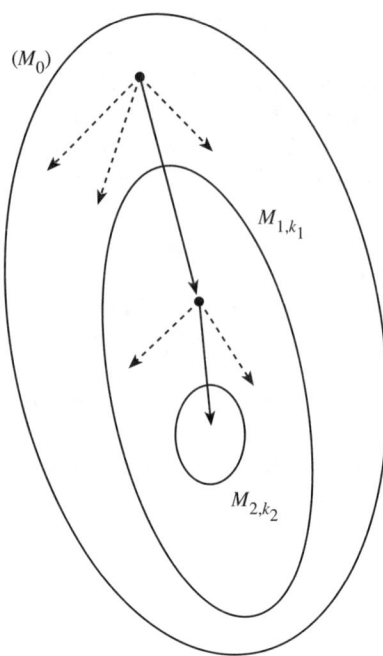

Fig. 11.1. From the General to the Specific

11.2.2. FROM GENERAL TO SPECIFIC

How can we exhibit a well specified (or approximately well specified) model in practice? The following approach, called 'from general to specific', offers one solution to this problem (Fig. 11.1). The idea is to start from a model (M_0) that is sufficiently unconstrained to allow us to consider the 'well specified' condition as plausible. In the case of macroeconomic aggregates, we generally consider that multivariate autoregressive (VAR) models may play such a role. The drawback of this initial model (M_0) is that it often depends on a large number of parameters, which are not accurately estimable and are difficult to interpret from an economic point of view. Therefore we will apply a sequence of tests in order to detect some constraints on these parameters, or equivalently to reduce the family of possible true distributions. For instance, for the case of macro-economic series, we may begin by separating the series (or combination of series) that are stationary from those that exhibit trend or seasonality (cointegration); then we may distinguish in the dynamics the long-run relationships and the adjustments around these relations (error correction model). If we now consider some processes summarizing the adjustment phenomena, we may study the causal links, the sensitivity with respect to exogenous or endogenous shocks (codependence). From an empirical point of view, such studies may be seen as a kind of factor analysis applied to a dynamic framework. This explains why the 'general to specific' approach appears in all factor models (see e.g. Anderson 1958; Gouriéroux *et al.* 1995*b*). From a theoretical point of view, this downward approach may be seen as a sequence of testing procedures. We first introduce different competing submodels $M_{1,1}, M_{1,2}, \ldots M_{1,K_1}$ corresponding to analogous kind of restrictions (approximately the same number of constraints, the same kind of complexity for these constraints, etc.), and we look for the model M_{1,k_1} that appears to be the best specified, generally using Wald test statistics. Then we introduce different submodels of M_{1,k_1} corresponding to some other similar restrictions—$M_{2,1}, \ldots, M_{2,K_2}$, say—and we look for the one that appears to be the best specified; M_{2,k_2} denotes this second-step model. And so on until the first time at which $M_{l+1,k_{l+1}}$ is clearly misspecified; and then we retain the previous model M_{l,k_l}.

The methodology just described is coherent, but it is also difficult to implement rigorously in practice. (See however Monfort and Rabemananjara (1990) for an application to the price–wage loop.) Indeed, it is not clear how, at each step, to select the best model among the competing ones, or how to perform the tests taking into account the errors arising from the tests performed in the previous steps. Moreover, the choice of the initial model (M_0) is not so easy. For instance, the choice of a VAR model assumes that the underlying dynamics is mainly a linear one, and this hypothesis itself should be tested.

11.2.3. PARAMETER OF INTEREST AND SEMI-PARAMETRIC APPROACHES

The difficulty of obtaining a well specified model has led many to circumvent the problem by considering that the different aspects of the true distibution do not have the same importance. Then we have to state precisely what the most important features of the distribution are, and to search for a well specified model bearing these features alone. This idea has been taken up since econometrics began, where for instance the conditional linear prediction of y_t, given the information $\underline{y_{t-1}}$ available at $t-1$, has been emphasized. So we introduce the notion of a first-order semi-parametric model by considering a parameterized set of conditional means,

$$(\overline{M}) = \{m(\underline{y_{t-1}}; \alpha), \alpha \in A\}, \tag{5}$$

assumed to be well specified:

$$\exists \alpha_0 : \underset{0}{E}(y_t / \underline{y_{t-1}}) = m(\underline{y_{t-1}}; \alpha_0). \tag{6}$$

Such a value gives all the information on the unknown form of the conditional mean. The model is semi-parametric since the knowledge of α_0 is not equivalent to the knowledge of the whole unknown conditional distribution l_0.

From such a well specified semi-parametric model, we can deduce an approximate value for α_0. For instance, we may apply a *nonlinear least squares (NLS) method*; i.e., we may look for the solution

$$\bar{\alpha}_T = \arg\min_{\alpha} \sum_{t=1}^{T} \left[y_t - m\left(\underline{y_{t-1}}; \alpha\right) \right]^2, \tag{7}$$

which is known to converge asymptotically to α_0 (Jennrich 1969; Malinvaud 1970), or we may apply some other techniques, such as the *pseudo-maximum likelihood approach*, introduced by Gouriéroux *et al.* (1984).

The search for a well specified semi-parametric model may be made through a 'general to specific' approach applied to the conditional mean. The testing procedures have to be performed without introducing too restrictive conditions on the conditional variance. This explains the importance of the methods correcting for conditional heteroscedasticity (White 1980; Newey and West 1987).

As mentioned at the beginning of this sub-section, a semi-parametric approach requires us to decide which parameters are the most important. This difficulty has a positive aspect, since it implies that the aim of any study must be made clear. It is the main contribution of the paper by Hansen (1982) that these most important parameters are shown not to be (in general) simple functions of the predictions of y_t. In fact, from some theory of optimal intertemporal behaviour in uncertain environment, we often deduce some first-order conditions (*Euler conditions*) of the kind

$$\underset{0}{E} \left\{ g(y_t, \underline{y_{t-1}}; \alpha_0) / \underline{y_{t-1}} \right\} = 0, \quad \forall \underline{y_{t-1}}, \tag{8}$$

where g is a given function and α_0 a true unknown value of some parameter. The functions g cannot in general be written as

$$g(y_t, \underline{y_{t-1}}; \alpha) = y_t - m(\underline{y_{t-1}}; \alpha), \tag{9}$$

which would bring us back to semi-parametric models based on prediction functions. Moreover, we have a joint definition of the value α_0, and of the *estimating constraint*, as soon as the following identification condition is satisfied:

$$\exists! \alpha_0 : \underset{0}{E} \left[g(y_t, \underline{y_{t-1}}; \alpha_0) / \underline{y_{t-1}} \right] = 0. \tag{10}$$

Such an unknown value α_0 may be approximated by solving a problem of the kind

$$\bar{\alpha}_T = \arg\min_{\alpha} \left[\sum_{t=1}^{T} z(\underline{y_{t-1}}) g(y_t, \underline{y_{t-1}}; \alpha) \right]'$$

$$\Omega \left[\sum_{t=1}^{T} z(\underline{y_{t-1}}) g(y_t, \underline{y_{t-1}}; \alpha) \right], \tag{11}$$

where Ω is a symmetric non-negative matrix with suitable size and $z(\underline{y_{t-1}})$ are matrices depending on past values: the *instrumental variables*. Such an estimation method is called a *generalized method of moments* (GMM) (Hansen 1982). GMMs generalize the instrumental variable estimation method and the two-stage least-squares introduced in the 1960s for the treatment of simultaneous equations models (Sargan 1958).

11.3. Misspecified Models

11.3.1. PSEUDO-TRUE VALUES

In order to simplify the presentation, we now consider parametric models. Such a model may be written as

$$(M) = \{l(y_t/\underline{y_{t-1}}; \theta), \theta \in \Theta\}.$$

It is *misspecified* if it does not contain the true unknown p.d.f.:

$$(M) \text{ is misspecified} \Leftrightarrow l_0(y_t/\underline{y_{t-1}}) \notin \{l(y_t/\underline{y_{t-1}}; \theta), \theta \in \Theta\}. \tag{12}$$

The study of such a model cannot be performed without being specific about what estimation method we will use to get a value of the parameter (see also Section 11.5). For illustration we will retain a *pseudo-likelihood method*. The estimator is defined by

$$\hat{\theta}_T = \arg\max_{\theta} \sum_{t=1}^{T} \log l(y_t/\underline{y_{t-1}}; \theta). \tag{13}$$

It may be shown (White 1982) that this estimator converges to a limit point given by

$$\lim \hat{\theta}_T = \theta^*(l_0) = \arg\max_{\theta} E_0 \log l(y_t/\underline{y_{t-1}}; \theta). \tag{14}$$

This limit depends on the true unknown distribution; it is called *pseudo-true value* (Fig. 11.2). It has to be noted that no notion of the true value of a parameter exists in this framework of misspecification.

How can we interpret this pseudo-true value? It is easily seen that

$$\theta^*(l_0) = \arg\max_{\theta} E_0 \log l(y_t/\underline{y_{t-1}}; \theta)$$

$$= \arg\min_{\theta} E_0 \log \frac{l_0(y_t/\underline{y_{t-1}})}{l(y_t/\underline{y_{t-1}}; \theta)}, \tag{15}$$

and that the quantity

$$KLIC(l_0, l_\theta) = E_0 \log \frac{l_0(y_t/\underline{y_{t-1}})}{l(y_t/\underline{y_{t-1}}; \theta)}, \tag{16}$$

called *Kullback–Leibler information criterion*, is a measure of the proximity between the two conditional distributions l_0 and l_θ. Therefore the pseudo-true value $\theta^*(l_0)$ provides the pseudo-true distribution $l(y_t/\underline{y_{t-1}}; \theta^*(l_0))$, which is the conditional distribution of (M) that is closest to the true unknown conditional distribution with respect to the previous criterion.

More generally, the pseudo-true value will depend on both the model (M) and the estimation method, or, equivalently, on both the model (M) and the measure of proximity (see also Section 11.5).

Under misspecification, the crucial question concerns the interpretation of the pseudo-true value. It is a difficult problem, well illustrated by the example of consumption functions. Let us consider data on aggregate consumption and income, C_t, R_t. We may introduce two simple regression models:

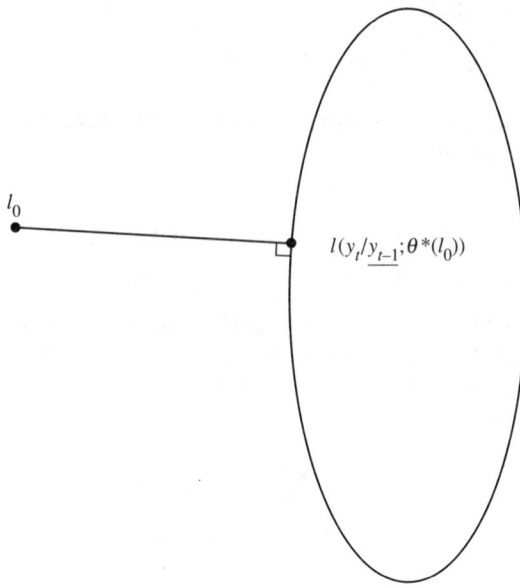

Fig. 11.2. Pseudo-true Value

$$\log C_t = a + b \log R_t + u_t, \quad u_t \sim IIN(0, \sigma^2), \tag{17}$$
$$u_t \text{ uncorrelated with } R_t;$$

$$\log C_t = \alpha + \beta \log R_t + \gamma C_{t-1} + v_t, \quad v_t \sim IIN(0, \sigma^2), \tag{18}$$
$$v_t \text{ uncorrelated with } R_t, R_{t-1}, \dots,$$

and we may estimate the various coefficients a, b, α, β, γ by ordinary least squares. What are the interpretations of the limits of the estimators $\hat{b}_T$, $\hat{\beta}_T$, and how can we use the these estimations? Is $\hat{b}_T$ an approximation of a long-run elasticity and $\hat{\beta}_T$ of a short-run elasticity? How can we take into account in the interpretation the omission of some variables which may also have an effect on the dynamics?

11.3.2. THE SEARCH FOR A WELL SPECIFIED MODEL FROM MISSPECIFIED ONES

For such a search, we may use an approach that is the converse of the 'general to specific' approach, i.e. the 'upward' approach (Fig. 11.3). The idea is to start from a structural model with a small number of parameters. Such a model (M_0) is usually deduced from economic theories. Since it may be very constrained, it usually does not fit the data well, and is clearly misspecified. An upward approach consists in introducing several models $M_{1,1}, \dots, M_{1,K_1}$, containing ($M_0$), by weakening the constraints in several directions, then selecting one of them, M_{1,k_1}, to correct partly for the specification error. In the second step we introduce several models, $M_{2,1}, \dots, M_{2,K_2}$, containing M_{1,k_1}, we select one of

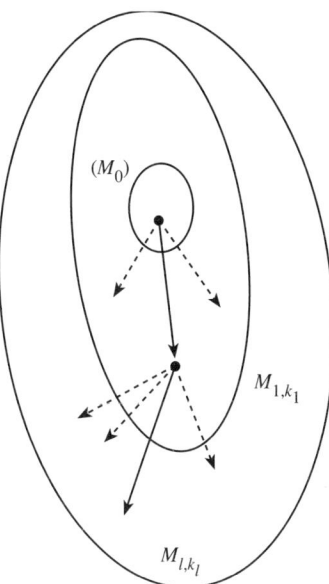

Fig. 11.3. The Upward Approach

them, M_{2,k_2}, and so on until we get the first model, M_{l,k_l}, that does not have a clear specification error.

This approach is symmetric of the downward approach described in Section 11.2.2, and uses different statistical techniques. Let us for instance consider the first step. The estimations are naturally performed under the more constrained model (M_0), and will serve as a basis for the selection of a larger model. The testing procedures are of the *Lagrange multiplier* type (Silvey 1959; Breusch and Pagan 1980; Engle 1982), and may be based on more empirical analyses using *generalized residual* plots for both linear and nonlinear models, possibly including unobservable latent variables (Gouriéroux *et al.* 1987; Chesher and Irish 1987).

11.3.3. STRUCTURED REDUCTION OF MISSPECIFIED MODELS

The 'general to specific' approach proposed for deriving a sufficiently constrained structure for a well specified model has its analogue in the framework of misspecified models. It is necessary to compare several misspecified models, each of them providing some information on the reductions that may be performed on the other ones. Since these competing models are generally non-nested, such an approach is naturally based on the theory of tests of non-nested hypotheses (Gouriéroux *et al.* 1983; Mizon and Richard 1986). Its extension to misspecified models gives the *encompassing theory* (Hendry and Richard 1990; Hendry 1993; Gouriéroux and Monfort 1993, 1995*a*).

We describe this approach for two a priori misspecified competing models. These models correspond to two parameterized families of conditional distributions:

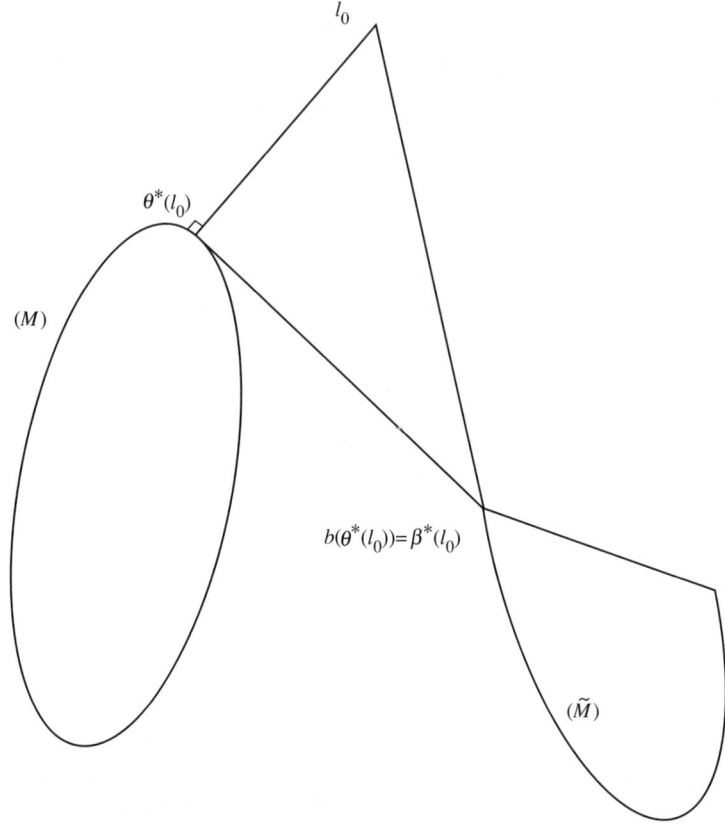

Fig. 11.4. The Encompassing Condition

$$(M) = \{l(y_t/\underline{y_{t-1}}; \theta), \theta \in \Theta\},$$
$$(\tilde{M}) = \{\tilde{l}(y_t/\underline{y_{t-1}}; \beta), \beta \in B\}. \tag{19}$$

With these models are associated pseudo-true values, denoted by $\theta^*(l_0)$ and $\beta^*(l_0)$ respectively.

It is said that model (M) encompasses model $(\tilde{M})$ if the results obtained with $(\tilde{M})$ can be understood by reasoning as if (M) were well specified. Thus, the idea is to be able to explain the results of the competitors (see Fig. 11.4). How can such an idea be formally translated? If model (M) were well specified, if the true distribution were reached by a true value θ of the parameter, a pseudo-maximum likelihood approach applied under $(\tilde{M})$ would lead asymptotically to a value $b(\theta)$ for the parameter β. The distribution $\tilde{l}(y_t/\underline{y_{t-1}}; b(\theta))$ is the distribution of $(\tilde{M})$, which is the closest to $l(y_t/\underline{y_{t-1}}; \theta)$. We call the application $b: \theta \mapsto b(\theta)$ a *binding function* (Gouriéroux and Monfort 1996).

The encompassing condition depends on the two competing models and on the true unknown distribution. It is as follows. The true distribution l_0 is such that (M) encompasses $(\tilde{M})$ if and only if:

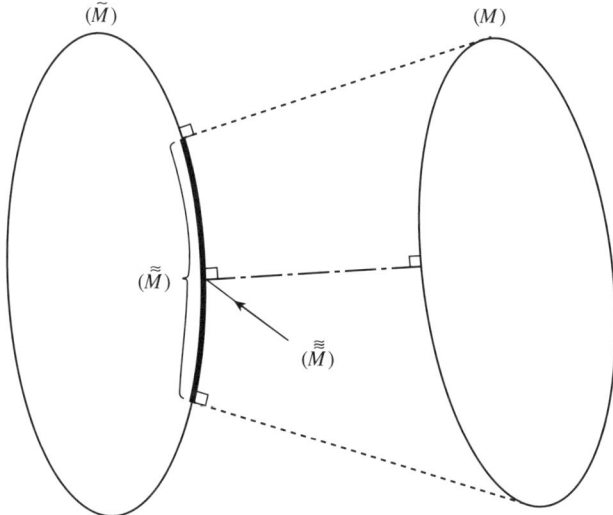

Fig. 11.5. Reductions on $\tilde{M}$

$$b(\theta^*(l_0)) = \beta^*(l_0). \tag{20}$$

This condition is denoted as

$$l_0 : (M)\,\varepsilon\,(\tilde{M}). \tag{21}$$

The knowledge that the true distribution is such that (M) encompasses $(\tilde{M})$ brings useful information about l_0, and allows us to simplify the encompassed model without loss of information. The idea is a simple one. If the encompassing condition is satisfied, only the distributions of $(\tilde{M})$, the 'mirror image' of distributions of (M), i.e. of the kind $\tilde{l}(y_t/\underline{y_{t-1}}; b(\theta))$, θ varying, are interesting. Therefore we may replace the misspecified model $(\tilde{M})$ with the misspecified submodel

$$(\tilde{\tilde{M}}) = \{\tilde{l}(y_t/\underline{y_{t-1}}; b(\theta)), \theta \in \Theta\},$$

which brings the same information about l_0 as $(\tilde{M})$.

In some case the true distribution may be such that mutual encompassing exists (Hendry and Richard 1990). Then the reduction will concern both models (M) and $(\tilde{M})$, and is often more important. Indeed, we may for instance replace model $(\tilde{M})$ with the submodel

$$(\tilde{\tilde{M}}) = \{\tilde{l}(y_t/\underline{y_{t-1}}; \beta), \text{ where } \beta \text{ such that } \beta = bo\,\tau(\beta)\},$$

where τ is the binding function from $(\tilde{M})$ to (M). These reductions are summarized in Fig. 11.5. In the figure the reduction of $(\tilde{M})$, the result of its encompassing by (M), corresponds to the mirror image of (M) in $(\tilde{M})$, represented by the projection of this set. The reduction of $(\tilde{M})$ in the case of mutual encompassing corresponds to the distribution of the $(\tilde{M})$ closest to (M).

It is worth noting that the encompassing hypothesis, which concerns the true unknown distribution, can be consistently tested without trying to estimate l_0

(Govaerts *et al.* 1994; Gouriéroux and Monfort 1995*a*). However, the encompassing approach has not been developed to its maximum. This point can be illustrated using a photographic comparison. To understand the shape of a three-dimensional object (the true unknown distribution l_0), we may take several photographs from different points. (Each point is one of the models.) The reduction procedure previously described is a way of using the different photographs (models) together to make the object (distribution) as clear as possible. It remains for us to explain how to use these two-dimensional photographs to reconstruct the object, which has a larger dimension. For us the last step is the most difficult, since the object (the true distribution) is in an infinite-dimensional space, whereas each parameter belongs to a finite-dimensional space. Therefore from a finite number of misspecified models we cannot hope to obtain a perfect reconstitution, even with a large number of observations.

Consequently such reconstitutions will require us to increase either the number of competing models or the dimension of the parameters with the number of observations. Some non-parametric approaches (kernel, orthogonal polynomials, etc.) are of this kind.

However, a partial reconstitution may be performed in some simple cases, especially for linear misspecified models. For instance, from the results of two simple linear regressions,

(M) $\qquad\qquad y_t = \theta\, y_{t-1} + u_t, \quad u_t \sim IIN(0, 1),$

$(\tilde{M})$ $\qquad\qquad y_t = \beta\, y_{t-2} + v_t, \quad v_t \sim IIN(0, 1),$

we can find (asymptotically) the estimation results corresponding to the model

(M^*) $\qquad\qquad y_t = \alpha_1\, y_{t-1} + \alpha_2\, y_{t-2} + w_t, \quad w_t \sim IIN(0, 1).$

Therefore we can pass from two pictures in dimension 1 (the size of the parameter in models (M) and $(\tilde{M})$) to one picture in dimension 2, and this even if the three models are misspecified.

11.4. Indirect Inference

In this section we will discuss another joint use of two models. The first one,

$$(M) = \{l(y_t/\underline{y_{t-1}}; \theta), \theta \in \Theta\},$$

is assumed to be well specified with a true value θ_0 of the parameter, but the analytical expression of l is too complicated to provide even numerically the maximum likelihood estimates. The second model,

$$(\tilde{M}) = \{\tilde{l}(y_t/\underline{y_{t-1}}; \beta), \beta \in B\},$$

is a misspecified model, which is simple to estimate. It will serve as an intermediate tool to bring information on the difficult 'right' model.

The approach by indirect inference (Smith 1993; Gouriéroux, Monfort and Renault 1993; Gallant and Tauchen 1996) uses the possibility of simulating artificial data under the initial model (M). Indeed, even if it is difficult to explicit the log-likelihood function for models containing nonlinearities, unobservable underlying factors, etc., it is often easy to simulate them.

In parallel to the set of available data, $y_1, \ldots, y_T$, we will introduce some sets of artificial data, $y_1^s(\theta), \ldots, y_T^s(\theta)$, $s = 1, \ldots, S$, simulated under model (M) with a value θ of the parameter. The auxiliary model $(\tilde{M})$ will be used to calibrate the observed and simulated paths. More precisely, we compute the pseudo-maximum likelihood estimator of β under $(\tilde{M})$:

$$\hat{\beta}_T = \arg\max_{\beta} \sum_{t=1}^{T} \log l(y_t/\underline{y_{t-1}}; \beta), \qquad (22)$$

which tends to the pseudo-true value, when T tends to infinity:

$$\lim \hat{\beta}_T = \beta^*(l_0) = b(\theta_0), \qquad (23)$$

where b is the binding function defined in the previous section. (We have automatic encompassing when the true distribution l_0 belongs to (M).)

Then we compute the pseudo-maximum likelihood estimator of β based on the simulations:

$$\hat{\beta}_{ST}(\theta) = \arg\max_{\beta} \sum_{s=1}^{S} \sum_{t=1}^{T} \log l(y_t^s(\theta)/\underline{y_{t-1}^s}(\theta); \beta), \qquad (24)$$

which tends to

$$\lim_{T} \hat{\beta}_{ST}(\theta) = b(\theta). \qquad (25)$$

Thus, from the artificial data, we exhibit an estimation method for the binding function: $\hat{\beta}_{ST}(\cdot) \simeq b(\cdot)$.

The rest of the approach consists in looking for a value of the initial parameter such that we get similar results for observed and simulated data. An *indirect inference estimator* is:

$$\hat{\theta}_{ST} = \arg\min_{\theta} \left\| \hat{\beta}_T - \hat{\beta}_{ST}(\theta) \right\|^2. \qquad (26)$$

This approach is summarized in Fig. 11.6. In practice, the second model is often deduced from the initial one by some simplifications, such as the linearization of nonlinearities, the discretization of a set of states or of dates (Gouriéroux and Monfort 1996). For illustration, let us consider a dynamic macromodel defined by the system

$$(M) \qquad\qquad y_t = g(y_t, y_{t-1}, u_t; \theta), \quad u_t \sim IIN(0, Id), \qquad (27)$$

where y_t is n-dimensional, u_t is an error term with dimension $m \geq n$, θ is an unknown parameter, and g is a given function. It is often difficult to get the analytical form of the conditional distribution of y_t given $\underline{y_{t-1}}$, even by assuming the existence of a well defined reduced form. Indeed, it is necessary to 'invert' the nonlinear function g, and partly to integrate out the errors whose dimension may be strictly larger than n. The initial model is often replaced by an approximated model obtained by linearizing the function g around some stationary deterministic sample paths for y_t and u_t. If they are denoted by α_0 and α_1, respectively, we get

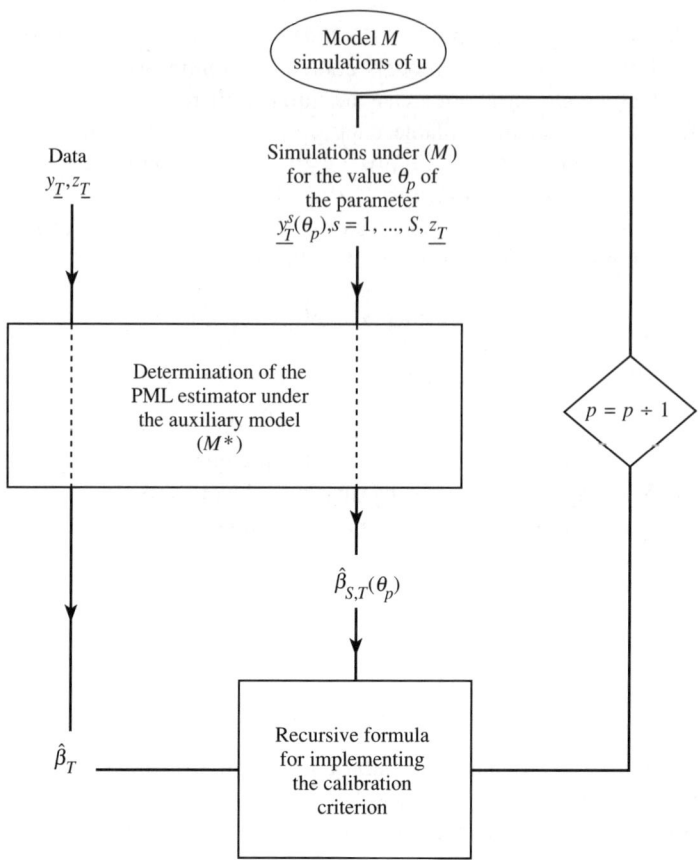

Fig. 11.6. Indirect Inference

$$g(y_t, y_{t-1}, u_t; \alpha) \simeq \frac{\partial g}{\partial y_t'}(\alpha_0, \alpha_0, \alpha_1; \alpha)(y_t - \alpha_0)$$

$$+ \frac{\partial g}{\partial y_{t-1}'}(\alpha_0, \alpha_0, \alpha_1; \alpha)(y_{t-1} - \alpha_0)$$

$$+ \frac{\partial g}{\partial u_t'}(\alpha_0, \alpha_0, \alpha_1; \alpha)(u_t - \alpha),$$

and the initial model is naturally replaced by the linearized model:

$$(\tilde{M}) \qquad y_t = \frac{\partial g}{\partial y_t'}(\alpha_0, \alpha_0, \alpha_1; \alpha)(y_t - \alpha_0)$$

$$+ \frac{\partial g}{\partial y_{t-1}'}(\alpha_0, \alpha_0, \alpha_1; \alpha)(y_{t-1} - \alpha_0)$$

$$+ \frac{\partial g}{\partial u_t'}(\alpha_0, \alpha_0, \alpha_1; \alpha)(u_t - \alpha_1), \quad u_t \sim IIN\,(0, Id). \tag{28}$$

It is an autoregressive model:

$$(\tilde{M}) \qquad y_t = a(\alpha_0, \alpha_1; \alpha) + \Phi(\alpha_0, \alpha_1; \alpha) y_{t-1}$$

$$+ \Theta(\alpha_0, \alpha_1; \alpha) u_t, \ u_t \ IIN(0, Id), \tag{29}$$

where:

$$a(\alpha_0, \alpha_1; \alpha) = -\left[Id - \frac{\partial g}{\partial y'_t}(\alpha_0, \alpha_0, \alpha_1; \alpha) \right]^{-1} \cdot \left\{ \frac{\partial g}{\partial y'_t}(\alpha_0, \alpha_0, \alpha_1; \alpha) \alpha_0 \right.$$

$$+ \frac{\partial g}{\partial y'_{t-1}}(\alpha_0, \alpha_0, \alpha_1; \alpha) \alpha_0 + \frac{\partial g}{\partial u'_t}(\alpha_0, \alpha_0, \alpha_1; \alpha) \alpha_1 \left. \right\},$$

$$\Phi(\alpha_0, \alpha_1; \alpha) = \left[Id - \frac{\partial g}{\partial y'_t}(\alpha_0, \alpha_0, \alpha_1; \alpha) \right]^{-1} \frac{\partial g}{\partial y'_{t-1}}(\alpha_0, \alpha_0, \alpha_1; \alpha),$$

$$\Theta(\alpha_0, \alpha_1; \alpha) = \left[Id - \frac{\partial g}{\partial y'_t}(\alpha_0, \alpha_0, \alpha_1; \alpha) \right]^{-1} \frac{\partial g}{\partial u'_t}(\alpha_0, \alpha_0, \alpha_1; \alpha).$$

In order to have a less constrained model, it is preferable to leave unconstrained the parameters α_0, α_1 around which are performed the expansions, and not, as is the usual practice, to fix α_0 equal to an empirical average of the y_t and α_1 equal to zero, i.e. to the theoretical mean of the error term. The parameter of the auxiliary model is $\beta = (\alpha'_0, \alpha'_1, \alpha')'$. Indirect inference is decomposed in two steps. First, there is a direct estimation of the auxiliary parameters α_0, α_1, α by maximum likelihood applied to model $(\tilde{M})$; in particular, we get values $\hat{\alpha}_0$, $\hat{\alpha}_1$ approximating the long-run pseudo-values corresponding to the observations and to the error terms. Despite the temptation to identify the parameters α of model $(\tilde{M})$ and θ of model (M), the estimator $\hat{\alpha}_T$ provides a biased approximation of the true value θ_0. The second step of indirect inference based on simulations under (M) corrects for this bias.

11.5. Use-Based Inference (UBI) and Implicit Parameters

11.5.1. THE PRINCIPLE

When a model is well specified, then in general we assimilate the estimated distribution with the true underlying distribution. Then it can be used in the same way as the true distribution to answer different questions about prediction problems, optimal controls, etc. How can we solve such questions when the initial model is misspecified? The use of the estimated pseudo-true distribution in the same way as the true distribution may induce important sub-optimalities for all the applications related to prediction or control. An idea that has recently appeared in the literature (see Smith 1990: ch. 1 for application to an intertemporal optimization problem, and Gouriéroux and Laurent 1994 for an optimal hedging of a contingent claim) is that such misspecified models can be used to build parameterized classes of strategies—classes of prediction functions, parameterized sets of controls, etc.—and in this perspective the (misspecified) parameter no longer has to be determined by a general statistical procedure, but rather by using a criterion—prediction accuracy, tracking error—adapted to the application considered. This implies that the value of the parameter of interest depends on the practical use of the model. We will illustrate such an approach by considering pricing strategies of financial assets and the classical Black–Scholes formula (Black and Scholes 1973).

We want to model the joint evolution of the price of an underlying asset, denoted by S_t, of an instantaneous interest rate r_t, and of the prices of some contingent claims based on the underlying asset. To simplify, we assume that these derivative assets are European call options with strike K, and maturity τ. They deliver a cash flow equal to $\max(S_t - K, 0)$ at date $t + \tau$. Their prices at t are denoted by $P(t, \tau, K)$. The various prices are defined in continuous time.

The model is based upon the following assumptions.

ASSUMPTION 1. The instantaneous rate is deterministic and constant: $r_t = r$.

ASSUMPTION 2. The price of the underlying asset satisfies the stochastic differential equation:

$$dS_t = \mu S_t dt + \sigma S_t dW_t, \tag{30}$$

where (W_t) is a standard Brownian motion, and μ and σ are trend and volatility parameters, respectively.

ASSUMPTION 3. The prices of the derivative assets depend only on current and past values of S_t.

ASSUMPTION 4. The investor may trade continuously on the market, with no transaction costs, without liquidity constraints, and so on.

ASSUMPTION 5. There exists no arbitrage opportunity.

Under these assumptions, we deduce in a unique way optimal pricing or hedging strategies. It is established that the option price is

$$P(t, \tau, K) = g(S_t, r, t, \tau, K; \sigma), \tag{31}$$

where

$$g(S_t, r, t, \tau, K; \sigma) = S_t \left\{ \Phi\left[\frac{1}{\sigma\sqrt{\tau}} \log\frac{S_t}{K\exp - rt} + \frac{\sigma\sqrt{\tau}}{2} \right] \right.$$
$$\left. - \frac{K\exp - rt}{S_t} \Phi\left[\frac{1}{\sigma\sqrt{\tau}} \log\frac{S_t}{K\exp - rt} - \frac{\sigma\sqrt{\tau}}{2} \right] \right\},$$

and Φ is the c.d.f. of the standard normal. This is the classical Black–Scholes formula.

Let us now consider the hedging at data t_0 of a given option by a self-financed portfolio containing the riskless and risky assets in quantities $\delta_{0,t}$, $\delta_{1,t}$ respectively.

If the hedging horizon is H, we are looking for the sequence of allocations $\delta_t = (\delta_{0,t}, \delta_{1,t})$, $t \in (t_0, t_0 + H)$, such that δ_t is a function of past and current prices of the different assets (underlying asset, derivatives, interest rate), and which solves the intertemporal optimization problem

$$\begin{cases} \min_{\delta_t} \underset{t_0}{E} \, [P(t_0 + H, \tau, K) - \delta_{0,t_0+H} \, S_{0,t_0+H} - \delta_{1,t_0+H} \, S_{1,t_0+H}]^2, \\ \qquad\qquad\qquad\qquad \text{under the self-financing constraints.} \end{cases} \qquad (32)$$

Under Assumptions 1–5, the solution exists and is such that the allocation in risky asset is

$$\delta_{1,t} = \frac{\partial g}{\partial S_t} (S_t, r, t, \tau, K; \sigma). \qquad (33)$$

(The allocation in riskless asset is deduced from the budget constraint.)

When the model is well specified, there exist true values μ_0 and σ_0 of the parameters, which may be consistently estimated in different ways. For instance, we may

1. estimate the volatility by the maximum likelihood technique applied to the set of observations $S_1, \ldots, S_T$;
2. or calibrate σ from the pricing formula (31) in order to have the observed and theoretical option prices as close as possible; or
3. simulate different hedging strategies (33) corresponding to various values of σ, and retain the value providing the best hedging on the observation period.

The practical difficulty of these coherent approaches is that some of the Assumptions 1–5 are clearly not satisfied: the short-run interest rate is time-varying, the price of the underlying asset is conditionally heteroscedastic, the option prices may depend on some other factors—prices of other assets, trading volume, etc.; the investor can trade only at discrete dates. The different estimation methods above will lead to different results. Is it possible to use some of them, and, if so, which ones?

At this stage it is useful to note that the pricing formula (31) is often used in a dual form. It is solved with respect to σ in order to deduce the 'implied volatility':

$$\sigma_t^I = g^{-1}\{S_t, r, t, \tau, K; P(t, \tau, K)\}. \qquad (34)$$

If the model were well specified, this quantity would be independent of both the date and the option considered. In practice this is not the case, but the determination of σ_t^I remains interesting if we interpret it not as a volatility, but as an option price corrected for the cash flow effects, i.e. for the strike and maturity effects. This shows that, even under misspecification, formula (31) may keep some usefulness as soon as it is correctly interpreted.

In fact, the misspecified model has been used to construct classes of prediction formulas—$\{g[S_t, r_t, t, \tau, K; \sigma]; \sigma \in \mathcal{R}^+\}$ by replacing r by the observed

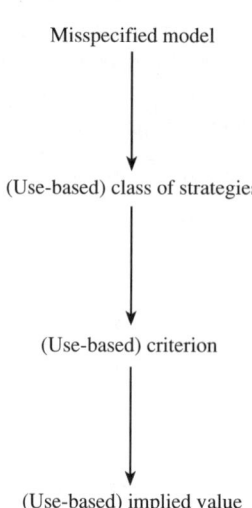

Misspecified model

(Use-based) class of strategies

(Use-based) criterion

(Use-based) implied value

Fig. 11.7. Use-based inference

short-run interest rate, or $\{g[S_t, r, t, \tau, K; \sigma], \sigma \in \mathcal{R}^+, r \in \mathcal{R}^+\}$ without this replacement.

If we are interested in the pricing of options with given strike K and maturity τ, we can use the previous classes to look for the best prediction of this form. For this purpose, we have to solve one of the following problems:

$$\min_{\sigma} \sum_{t=1}^{T} [P(t, \tau, K) - g(S_t, r_t, t, \tau, K; \sigma)]^2,$$

or

$$\min_{r,\sigma} \sum_{t=1}^{T} [P(t, \tau, K) - g(S_t, r, t, \tau, K; \sigma)]^2,$$

whose solutions tend (when T tends to infinity) to some implied (pseudo-true) values which depend on the strike and maturity: $\sigma^*(\tau, K)$ for the first problem, $r^{**}(\tau, K)$, $\sigma^{**}(\tau, K)$ for the second one. Therefore we see that in general there exist as many implied (pseudo-true) volatilities and implied (pseudo-true) interest rates as there are derivative assets to price, and that we have to choose the right implied values.

This approach, shown in Fig 11.7, may be imbedded in our general framework. Let us denote l_0 the true distribution, $\{l(y_t/\underline{y_{t-1}}; \theta), \theta \in \Theta\}$ the misspecified model, and ϕ the use-based criterion providing the parameterized class of strategies $\mathscr{C}$. In practice, this criterion is a theoretical measure of prediction, of hedging etc. At the estimation stage it is replaced by its empirical counterpart. The estimation criterion is of the kind $\sum_{t=1}^{T} \Psi(y_t, \underline{y_{t-1}}; \theta, \phi, \mathscr{C})$. It depends on both the use-based criterion and the class of strategies.

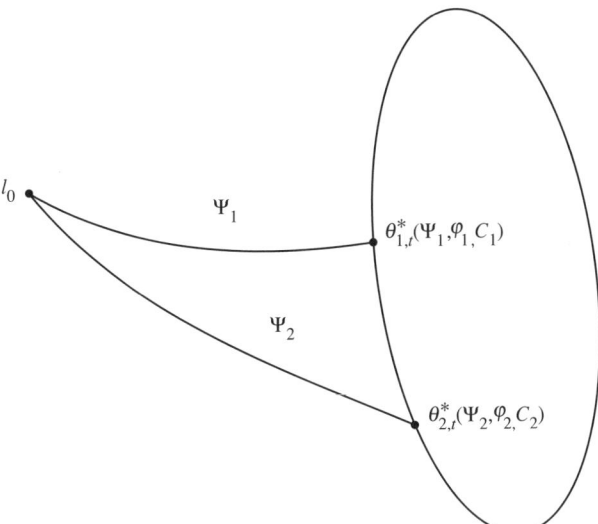

Fig. 11.8. Implicit (Pseudo-true) Values

The corresponding use-based estimator,

$$\hat{\theta}_T (\Psi;\ \phi,\ \mathcal{C}) = \arg \min_{\theta} \sum_{t=1}^{T} \Psi(y_t,\ \underline{y_{t-1}};\ \theta,\ \phi,\ \mathcal{C}), \qquad (35)$$

converges to the implied (pseudo-true) value solution of

$$\theta^* (\Psi;\ \phi,\ \mathcal{C},\ l_0) = \arg \min_{\theta} E_0\ \Psi(y_t,\ \underline{y_{t-1}};\ \theta,\ \phi,\ \mathcal{C}). \qquad (36)$$

The class of strategies strongly depends on the misspecified model from which it has been derived, and the final calibration criterion may be seen as a proximity measure between the initial model and the true distribution. To each specific problem—pricing of assets, hedging of contingent claims for financial applications, short or long-run prediction in dynamic macromodels, etc.—corresponds a specific proximity measure. When the initial model is well specified, the proximity between the model and the true distribution is equal to zero whatever the proximity measure is. This is no longer true under misspecification. The distance and the element of the model that is the closest to the true distribution change with the proximity measure. This point is illustrated in Fig. 11.8, where the isometric curves associated with the two different proximity measures are ellipsoids with different positionings.

It has to be noted that the encompassing theory described in Section 11.3.3 has been presented with a specific criterion, i.e. the Kullback–Leibler Information criterion, corresponding to the maximum likelihood technique. Implied and pseudo-true values coïncide in this case. If we are interested in a specific question, it is of course preferable to develop an encompassing theory with the corresponding criterion.

11.5.2. UPWARD APPROACH

In used-based inference (UBI), the upward approach generally does not consist in enlarging the initial misspecified model in order to be closer to the true distribution, but rather in enlarging directly the class of strategies in order to diminish the sub-optimality of the class. Let us come back to the pricing example. The price approximations deduced from Black–Scholes formula are: $g(S_t, r_t, t, \tau, K; \sigma)$, $\sigma \in \mathcal{R}^+$. We know that they do not take into account the conditional heteroscedasticity phenomena. Therefore it is natural to enlarge the previous class by considering for instance strategies of the kind

$$g(S_t, r_t, t, \tau, K; c(S_{t-1}/S_{t-2}; \theta)), \quad \theta \in \Theta,$$

where the volatility σ has been replaced by an implied stochastic volatility function of the lagged price ratio of the underlying asset. If we want to see whether it is useful to introduce the effect of S_{t-1}/S_{t-2} to determine its functional form, i.e. the set of parameterized functions to consider, we need some tools for testing the constancy of the implied (pseudo-true) parameter and the construction of residual plots oriented towards this parameter. Such tools have been introduced in Gouriéroux *et al.* (1990).

11.6. Maintenance of Models

The approaches of the previous sections have been described in a stationary framework, where the form l_0 of the true distribution is assumed to be time-invariant. If this condition is not satisfied, we have to adjust models and methods to this time deformation of l_0. We will consider the favourable case in which this modification arises sufficiently slowly for the stationarity assumption to be considered as valid on some sub-periods. Then at a given date t_0 we can look for a well specified model using available past data and a mixture of upward and downward approaches. If this research is correctly performed, we exhibit a model that is compatible with l_{0,t_0}:

$$l_{0,t_0}(y_{t_0}/\underline{y_{t_0-1}}) \in \{l(y_{t_0}/\underline{y_{t_0-1}}; \theta), \theta \in \Theta\}, \tag{37}$$

and an approximation of the true value, θ_{t_0}, defined by:

$$l_{0,t_0}(y_{t_0}/\underline{y_{t_0-1}}) = l(y_{t_0}/\underline{y_{t_0-1}}; \theta_{t_0}). \tag{38}$$

What will happen at future dates? Since the true distribution $l_{0,t}$ changes with time, and since the model has been assumed time-stable, we may reasonably guess that it will become misspecified. How can we ensure its maintenance? We have seen that under misspecification it was necessary to be precise about which uses of the model we are interested in, and to introduce the associated criteria. For illustration purposes, we consider two such criteria, $\Psi_1(\phi_1, \mathscr{C}_1; \theta)$, $\Psi_2(\phi_2, \mathscr{C}_2; \theta)$, and denote $\theta_{1t}^*(\Psi_{1t}, \phi_1, \mathscr{C}_1), \theta_{2t}^*(\Psi_{2t}, \phi_2, \mathscr{C}_2)$ the corresponding implied values. Then we can distinguish several steps in the maintenance of the model.

STEP 1. The true distribution is modified, but it remains closed to l_{0,t_0}, and the model is still well specified. In this case we continue to use the distribution estimated at t_0, for all kinds of applications.

STEP 2. The true distribution becomes significatively different from l_{0,t_0}, but the model is still well specified: $\exists \theta_t : l_{0,t}(y_t/\underline{y_{t-1}}) = l(y_t/\underline{y_{t-1}}; \theta_t)$. It is no longer possible to use the initially estimated distribution, but we may apply various techniques for regularly updating the value θ_t. Such methods are essentially numerical ones. For instance, we may partially update the value of the parameter by performing an iteration of a score algorithm, i.e. by computing

$$\hat{\theta}_t = \hat{\theta}_{t_0} - \left[\sum_{t=1}^{T} \frac{\partial^2 \log l(y_t/\underline{y_{t-1}}; \hat{\theta}_{t_0})}{\partial \theta \, \partial \theta'}\right]^{-1} \sum_{t=1}^{T} \frac{\partial \log l(y_t/\underline{y_{t-1}}; \hat{\theta}_{t_0})}{\partial \theta},$$

or by introducing models with time-varying coefficients and applying the Kalman filter. The true distribution is re-estimated at date t, and used for all kinds of applications:

$$\hat{\theta}_{1,t}^*(\Psi_1, \phi_1, \mathscr{C}_1) = \hat{\theta}_{2,t}^*(\Psi_2, \phi_2, \mathscr{C}_2), = \theta_t.$$

STEP 3. The true distribution is such that the initial model is misspecified, but the specification error is not too important. Such a situation may be detected by considering implied values with different parameters of interest, and by seeing that $\hat{\theta}_{1,t}^*(\Psi_1, \phi_1, \mathscr{C}_1)$ and $\hat{\theta}_{2,t}^*(\Psi_2, \phi_2, \mathscr{C}_2)$ become significantly different. If this effect is such that the loss on the performances of the model for the different applications is not too large, we will adjust the model only slightly depending on the application of interest; i.e., we will replace θ_t by a use-based estimation $\hat{\theta}_{j,t}^*(\Psi_j, \phi_j, \mathscr{C}_j)$.

STEP 4. When such an adjustment becomes insufficient, we can try to enlarge the corresponding classes of strategies to diminish the degree of sub-optimality, and re-estimate implied (pseudo-true) parameters with the criteria $\Psi_{j,t}(\phi_j, \tilde{\mathscr{C}}_j)$, where $\tilde{\mathscr{C}}_j$ are the new classes.

STEP 5. Finally, when the different classes are so modified that the coherence between the different kinds of applications is no longer ensured, it is necessary to perform a new building of a well specified model.

It is clear that these different steps—adjustment, partial modifications of the classes of strategies, complete re-estimation of a well specified model—imply various amounts of work, depending on the regularity of the uses of the model, and of the relative costs of the adjustment and partial modifications compared with the cost of a complete re-estimation.

The above simplified scheme of a model maintenance also shows that simple models will be often preferred, since they are easier to adjust, and that it may be important to keep in the model some explanatory variables which are not significant at date t_0, if they may become significant at future dates. Furthermore, all the adjustment operations have to be performed using performance criteria corresponding to the applications of interest, and not only general statistical criteria.

REFERENCES

Anderson, T. W. (1958), *An Introduction to Multivariate Statistical Analysis*. New York: John Wiley.

Black, F., and Scholes, M. (1973), 'The Pricing of Options and Corporate Liabilities', *Journal of Political Economy*, 81: 637–59.

Breusch, T., and Pagan, A. (1980), 'The Lagrange Multiplier Test and its Applications to Model Specification in Econometrics', *Review of Economic Studies*, 47: 239–54.

Chesher, A., and Irish, A. (1987), 'Residual Analysis in the Grouped and Censored Normal Linear Model', *Annals of Econometrics*, 34: 33–54.

Engle, R. (1982), 'A General Approach to Lagrange Multiplier Model Diagnostics', *Journal of Econometrics*, 20: 83–104.

—— and Granger, C. (1987), 'Co-integration and Error Correction: Representation, Estimation and Testing', *Econometrica*, 55: 255–76.

Gallant, R., and Tauchen, G. (1996), 'Which Moments to Match?' *Econometric Theory*, 12: 657–681.

Gouriéroux, C. and Laurent, J. P. (1994), 'Estimation of a Dynamic Hedge', CREST Discussion Paper.

—— and Monfort, A. (1993), 'Testing Non-Nested Hypotheses', *The Handbook of Econometrics*, Volume IV, 2585–637.

—— and —— (1995), 'Testing, Encompassing, and Simulating Dynamic Econometric Models', *Econometric Theory*, 11, 195–228.

—— and —— (1996), 'Simulation Based Econometric Methods', CORE Lectures, Oxford University Press.

—— and Peaucelle, I. (1992), 'Séries Codépendantes: Application à l'Hypothèse de Parité du Pouvoir d'Achat', *Actualité Economique*, 68, 283–304.

——, Monfort, A., and Trognon, A. (1983), 'Testing Nested or Non-Nested Hypotheses', *Journal of Econometrics*, 21, 83–115.

——, ——, and —— (1984), 'Pseudo-Maximum Likelihood Methods: Theory', *Econometrica*, 52, 681–700.

——, ——, Renault, E., and Trognon, A. (1987), 'Generalized Residuals', *Journal of Econometrics*, 34, 5–32.

—— —— , and Tenreiro, C. (1994), 'Kernel M-Estimators: Nonparametric Diagnostics for Structural Models', CEPREMAP Discussion Paper no. 9405.

——, ——, and Renault, E. (1995), 'Inference in Factor Models' in Maddala, Phillips, and Srinivasam (eds), *Advances in Econometrics and Qualitative Economics: Essays in Honour of Professor Rao*. Oxford: Basil Blackwell.

Govaerts, B., Hendry, D., and Richard, J. F. (1994), 'Encompassing in Stationary Linear Dynamic Models', European University Institute, Florence, Discussion Paper no. 9415.

Hansen, L. (1982), 'Large Sample Properties of the Generalized Method of Moments Estimators', *Econometrica*, 50, 1029–54.

Hendry, D. (1995), *Dynamic Econometrics*, Oxford: Oxford University Press.

—— and Richard, J. F. (1990), 'Recent Developments in the Theory of Encompassing' in B. Cornet and M. Tulkens (eds), *Contribution to Operations Research and Econometrics, the XXth Anniversary of CORE*, Cambridge, Mass.: MIT Press.

Jennrich, R. (1969), 'Asymptotic Properties of Nonlinear Least Squares Estimators', *Annals of Mathematical Statistics*, 40, 633–43.

Johansen, S. (1988), 'Statistical Analysis of Cointegration Vectors', *Journal of Economics Dynamics and Control*, 12, 231–54.

McCullagh, P. and Nelder, J. (1989), *Generalized Linear Models*, London: Chapman and Hall.

Malinvaud, E. (1970), 'The Consistency of Nonlinear Regressions', *Annals of Mathematical Statistics*, 41, 956–69.

Mizon, G. and Richard, G. (1986), 'The Encompassing Principle and its Application to Non-Nested Hypotheses', *Econometrica*, 54, 657–78.

Monfort, A. and Rabemananjara, T. (1990), 'From a VAR Model to a Structural Model with an Application to the Wage–Price Spiral', *Journal of Applied Econometrics*, 5, 203–28.

Newey, W. (1982), 'Maximum Likelihood Estimation of Misspecified Models', *Econometrica*, 50, 1–28.

—— and West, K. (1987), 'A Simple Positive Definite Heteroscedasticity and Autocorrelation Consistent Covariance Matrix', *Econometrica*, 55, 703–8.

Sargan, J. (1958), 'On the Estimation of Economic Relationships by Means of Instrumental Variables', *Econometrica*, 26, 393–415.

Silvey, S. (1959), 'The Lagrange Multiplier Test', *Annals of Mathematical Statistics*, 30, 389–407.

Smith, A. (1990), 'Three Essays on the Solution and Estimation of Dynamic Macroeconomic Models', Ph. D. thesis, Duke University.

—— (1993), 'Estimating Nonlinear Time Series Models Using Simulated Vector Autoregressions', *Journal of Applied Econometrics*, 8, 63–84.

Vuong, Q. (1989), 'Likelihood Ratio Tests for Model Selection and Non-Nested Hypotheses', *Econometrica*, 57, 307–34.

Wald, A. (1949), 'Note on the Consistency of the Maximum Likelihood Estimate', *Annals of Mathematical Statistics*, 20, 595–601.

White, H. (1980), 'A Heteroskedasticity-Consistent Covariance Matrix Estimator and a Direct Test for Heteroskedasticity', *Econometrica*, 48: 817–38.

—— (1982), 'Maximum Likelihood Estimation of Misspecified Models', *Econometrica*, 50: 1–28.

—— (1984), *Asymptotic Theory for Econometricians*. New York: Academic Press.

12

Short-Term Analysis of Macroeconomic Time Series

Agustín Maravall

12.1. Introduction

In this paper I shall be discussing the statistical treatment of short-term macroeconomic data. In particular, I shall focus on monthly time series of standard macroeconomic aggregates, such as monetary aggregates, consumer price indices, industrial production indices, export and import series, and employment series. The statistical treatment considered is that aimed at helping economic policy-makers in short-term control, and at facilitating the monitoring and interpretation of the economy by analysts in general. The purpose of the statistical treatment is to answer two basic questions, well summarized by P. G. Wodehouse when answering a question concerning his physical shape:

The day before yesterday, for instance, [the weighing machine in my bathroom] informed me—and I don't mind telling you, J. P., that it gave me something of a shock—that I weighed seventeen stone nine. I went without lunch and dined on a small biscuit and a stick of celery, and next day I was down to eleven stone one. This was most satisfactory and I was very pleased about it, but this morning I was up again to nineteen stone six, so I really don't know where I am or what the future holds. (Wodehouse 1981: 577)

The two separate—though related—questions are:

1. Where are we?
2. Where are we heading?

Of course, forecasting provides the answer to question 2. The answer to question 1 usually consists of an estimation of the present situation, free of seasonal variation; on occasion, variation judged transitory is also removed. Thus, seasonal adjustment and trend estimation are used to answer question 1. For monthly macroeconomic series, it is often the case that seasonal variation dominates the short-run variability of the series.

In the following sections I will briefly review the recent evolution of the statistical methodology used in this context, and will provide a (justified) forecast of how I would expect it to evolve over the next ten years. The discussion will address the evolution in terms of research and in terms of practical applications (such as, for example, official seasonal adjustment). While the former typically contains a lot of noise, practical applications lag research by several (sometimes many) years.

Whenever confronted with forecasting an event, one is bound to look first at the present and past history. I shall do that, and from the (critical) look my forecast will emerge in a straightforward and unexciting manner. The discussion centres on tools used for short-term analysis; at the end I present an example that illustrates the unreliability of these tools when our horizon is a long-term one.

12.2. Short-Term Forecasting

I shall start with a very brief mention of short-term forecasting in economics. Leaving aside judgemental (or 'expert') forecasting, in the remote past some deterministic models, for example models with linear trends and seasonal dummies, were used for short-term forecasting. This practice gave way to the use of *ad hoc* filters, which became popular in the 1950s and 1960s; examples are the exponentially weighted moving average method (Winters 1960; Cox 1961), and the discounted least squares method of Brown (1962). In the 1970s, the work of Box and Jenkins (1970) provoked a revolution in the field of applied forecasting; this revolution was further enhanced by another factor: the discovery by economic forecasters of the Kalman filter (see, e.g. Harrison and Stevens 1976). The Box–Jenkins approach offered a powerful, easy-to-learn and easy-to-apply methodology for short-term forecasting; the Kalman filter provided a rather convenient tool to apply and extend the methodology.

The outcome was a massive spread of statistical models (simple parametric stochastic processes) and in particular of the so-called autoregressive integrated moving average (ARIMA) model, and of its several extensions, such as intervention analysis and transfer function models (see Box and Tiao 1975; and Box and Jenkins 1970), and of the closely related structural time series models (see Harvey 1989). One can safely say that ARIMA models are used every day by thousands of practitioners. Some use is also made of multivariate versions of these models (see e.g. Litterman 1986), although multivariate extensions have often been frustrating. A good review of the economic applications of time-series models is contained, for example, in Mills (1990).

The point I wish to make at present is that, overall, stochastic-model-based forecasting has become a standard procedure. At present, two important directions of research are:

1. *multivariate extensions*, where the research on cointegration and common factors may lead to an important break (through a reduction in dimensionality and an improved model specification); see, for example, Gouriéroux (1992) and Hamilton (1994);
2. *nonlinear extensions*, such as the use of bilinear, ARCH, GARCH, stochastic parameter, Markov chain models, and so on (see, for example, Johansen 1996, and Tiao and Tsay 1989).

For the type of series considered, I would expect direction 1 eventually to play a very important role in applied short-term forecasting over the next decade. As for the future impact of direction 2, I doubt that in the next few years stochastic nonlinear models will become a standard tool for the average practitioner, working with monthly or quarterly series.

12.3. Unobserved Components Estimation and Seasonal Adjustment

Going back to question 1 of Section 12.1, we proceed to the problem of estimating the relevant underlying evolution of an economic variable, that is, to seasonal adjustment; we shall also consider some trend estimation issues. Two good references that describe the state of the art concerning seasonal adjustment over the last 20 years are Den Butter and Fase (1991) and Hylleberg (1992). As with forecasting, deterministic models were used in the distant past. At present, however, except for some isolated cases, official agencies producing monthly seasonally adjusted data do not remove seasonality with deterministic models.

It is widely accepted by practitioners that, typically, seasonality in macroeconomic series is of the moving type, for which the use of filters is appropriate. If x_t denotes the series of interest (perhaps in logs), n_t the seasonally adjusted series, and s_t the seasonal component, a standard procedure is to assume

$$x_t = n_t + s_t,$$

and to estimate s_t by

$$\hat{s}_t = C(B)x_t, \tag{1}$$

where B is the lag operator such that $B^k x_t = x_{t-k}$ (k integer), and $C(B)$ is the linear and symmetric filter,

$$C(B) = c_0 + c_1(B + F) + \ldots + c_r(B^r + F^r), \tag{2}$$

with $F = B^{-1}$. Of course, the filter $C(B)$ is designed to capture variability of the series in a (small) interval around each seasonal frequency. The seasonally adjusted series is, in turn, estimated by

$$\hat{n}_t = [1 - C(B)]x_t = A(B)x_t, \tag{3}$$

and $A(B)$ is also a centred, linear, and symmetric filter.

The symmetric and complete filters (1) and (3) cannot be used to estimate s_t or n_t when t is close to either end of the series. Specifically, at time T, when the available series is $(x_1, \ldots, x_T)$, estimation of s_t with (1) for $t < r$ requires unavailable starting values of x; analogously, estimation of s_t for $t > T - r$ requires future observations not yet available. Therefore, the centred and symmetric filter characterizes 'historical' estimates. For recent enough periods asymmetric filters have to be used, which yield preliminary estimators. As time passes and new

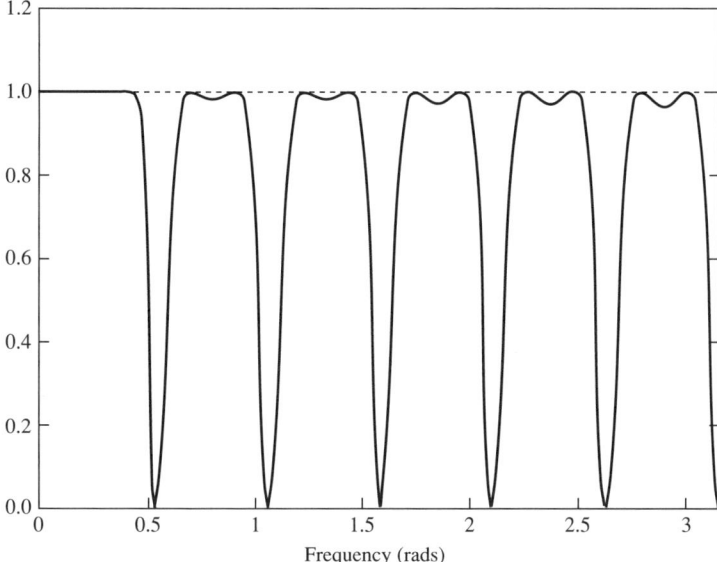

Fig. 12.1. X11: Transfer Function

observations become available, those preliminary estimators will be revised until the historical or final estimator is eventually obtained. We shall come back to this issue later.

In the same way that 1970 marks an important date for applied short-term forecasting (i.e., the year of publication of the book by Box and Jenkins), 1967 marks a crucial event in the area of seasonal adjustment. That event was the appearance of the program X11, developed by the US Bureau of the Census (see Shiskin *et al.* 1967). Except for some outlier treatment (which we shall ignore), X11 can be seen as a sequence of linear filters, and hence as a linear filter itself (see e.g. Hylleberg, 1986). For the discussion that follows, we use the parsimonious approximation to X11 (historical filter) of Burridge and Wallis (1984). Fig. 12.1 plots the transfer function (in the frequency domain) of the X11 monthly filter $A(B)$. This function represents, for each frequency, the proportion of the variability of x_t that is used to estimate the seasonally adjusted series. It is seen how the X11 filter passes the variation associated with all frequencies, except for some small intervals around the seasonal ones.

Over the next decade, X11 spread at an amazing speed, and many thousands of series came to be routinely adjusted with X11. It was an efficient and easy-to-use procedure that seemed to provide good results for many series (although the meaning of 'good' for seasonal adjustment is somewhat unclear). Yet, towards the end of the 1970s some awareness of X11 limitations started to develop. Those limitations were mostly associated with the rigidity of the X11 filter, i.e. with its *ad hoc*, relatively fixed structure ('fixed' includes the case in which a few fixed options may be available). It is to these limitations that I turn next.

12.4. Limitations of *Ad Hoc* Filtering

I shall provide simple illustrations of some major limitations of fixed *ad hoc* filters. For illustration we use X11 run by default

1. The danger of spurious adjustment is illustrated in Fig. 12.2. In a white-noise series, with spectrum that of part (*a*) in the figure, X11 will extract a seasonal component, with spectrum that of part (*b*). This spectrum is certaintly that of a seasonal component, but the series had no seasonality to start with.

2. In the previous white-noise series, trivially, the filter $A(B)$ used to season-ally adjust the series should simply be 1; at the other extreme, if the observed series has a spectrum as in part (*b*) of the figure, the filter to adjust the series seasonally should obviously be 0, since the series contains only seasonal vari-ation. The filter should thus depend on the characteristics of the series.

To illustrate the point, we use the well-known 'Airline model' of Box and Jenkins (1970: ch. 9). It is a model appropriate for monthly series displaying trend and seasonality. For series in logs, the model implies that the annual difference of the monthly rate of growth is a stationary process. The Airline model is, on the one hand, a model often encountered in practice; on the other hand, it provides an excellent reference example. The model is given by the equation

$$\nabla\nabla_{12}x_t = (1 - \theta_1 B)(1 - \theta_{12}B^{12})\, a_t + \mu, \tag{4}$$

where μ is a constant, a_t is a white-noise innovation (with variance V_a), $\nabla = 1 - B$, $\nabla_{12} = 1 - B^{12}$, and $-1 < \theta_1 < 1$, $0 < \theta_{12} < 1$. The series x_t, generated by (4), accepts a rather sensible decomposition into trend, seasonal, and irregular com-ponent (see Hillmer and Tiao 1982). As θ_1 approaches 1, model (4) tends towards the model

$$\nabla_{12} x_t = (1 - \theta_{12}B^{12})\, a_t + \mu_0 + \mu t,$$

with deterministic trend. Similarly, when θ_{12} becomes 1, the seasonal component becomes deterministic. Thus, the parameter $\theta_1(\theta_{12})$ may be interpreted as a measure of how close to deterministic the trend (seasonal) component is.

In the frequency domain, this 'closer to deterministic' behaviour of a com-ponent is associated with the width of the spectral peaks. Thus, for example, Fig. 12.3 displays the spectra of two series both following models of the type (4). The one with the continuous line contains more stochastic seasonal vari-ation, in accordance with the wider spectral peaks for the seasonal frequencies. The seasonal component in the series with spectrum given by the dotted line will be more stable, and hence closer to deterministic. Since the X11 seasonal adjust-ment filter displays holes of fixed width for the seasonal frequencies, it follows that X11 will underadjust when the width of the seasonal peak in the series

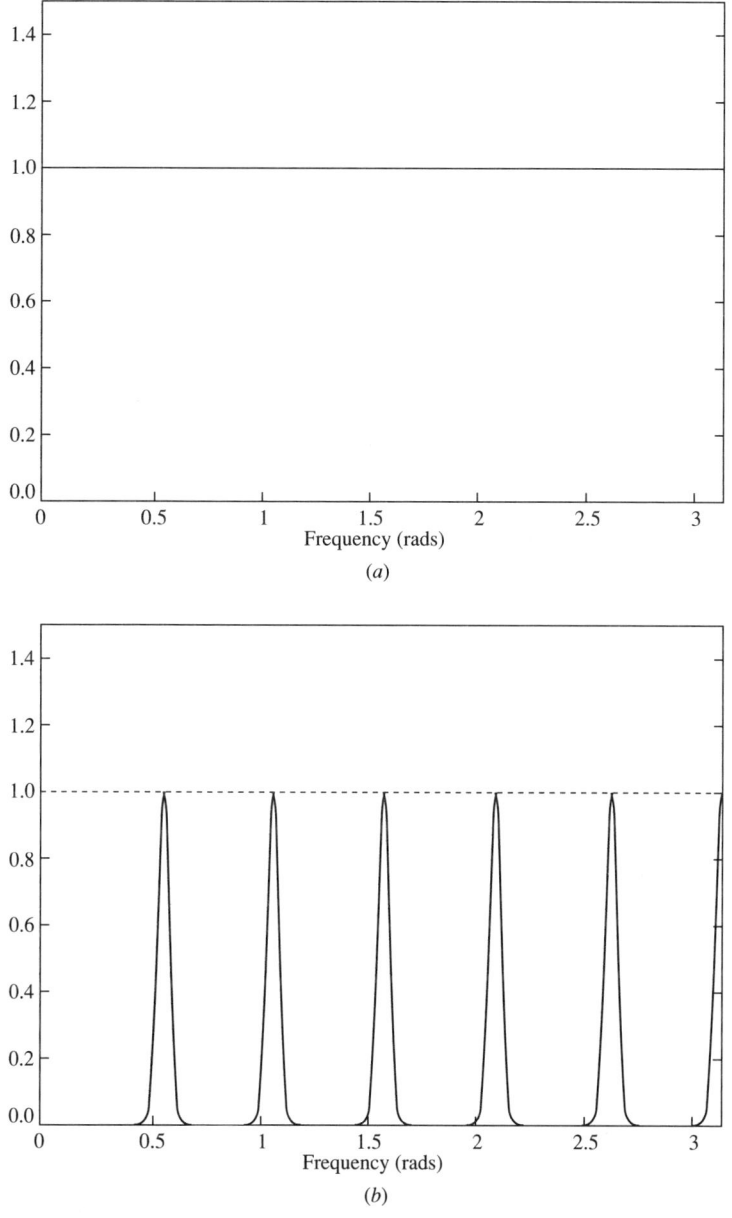

Fig. 12.2. (*a*) Spectrum: White-Noise Variable
(*b*) Spectrum: Seasonal Component in the White Noise (X11)

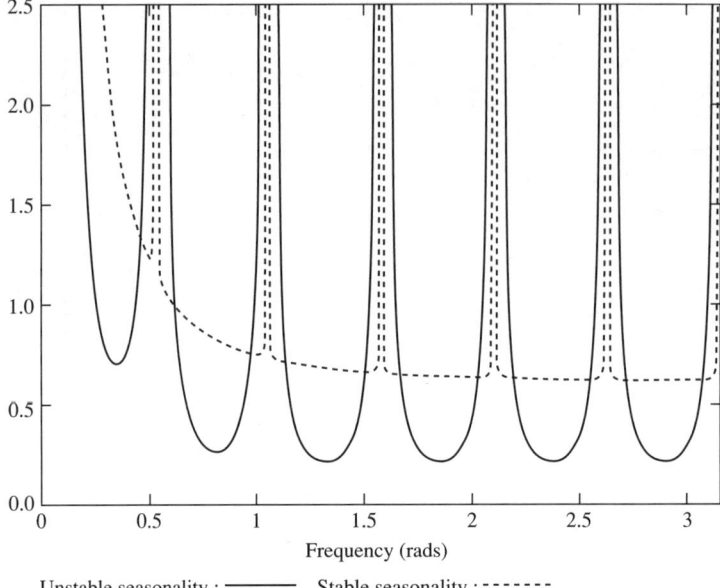

Frequency (rads)

Unstable seasonality : ———— Stable seasonality : - - - - - - -

Fig. 12.3. Spectra: Stable and Unstable Seasonality

spectrum is larger than that captured by the X11 filter. Fig. 12.4(*a*) illustrates this situation, and Fig. 12.4(*b*) displays the spectrum of the estimated seasonally adjusted series obtained in this case. The underadjustment is reflected in the two peaks that remain in the neighbourhood of each seasonal frequency: obviously, X11 has not removed all seasonal variation from the series.

On the other hand, X11 will overadjust (i.e. will remove too much variation from the series) when the width of the seasonal spectral peaks are narrower than those captured by X11. This effect is evidenced in Fig. 12.5: the holes in the seasonally adjusted series spectrum (part (*b*) of the figure) are now too wide.

3. Another limitation of X11 is the lack of a proper framework for detecting the cases in which its application is inappropriate. On the one hand, diagnostics are few and difficult to interpret. Moreover, when found inappropriate, there is no systematic procedure to overcome the inadequacies.

4. Even when appropriate, X11 does not contain the basis for proper inference. For example, what are the standard errors associated with the estimated seasonal factors? This limitation has important policy implications (see Bach *et al.* 1976; Moore *et al.* 1981). In short-term monetary control, if the monthly target for the rate of growth of M_1 (seasonally adjusted) is 10 per cent and actual growth for that month turns out to be 13 per cent, can we conclude that growth has been excessive and, as a consequence, raise short-term interest rates? Can

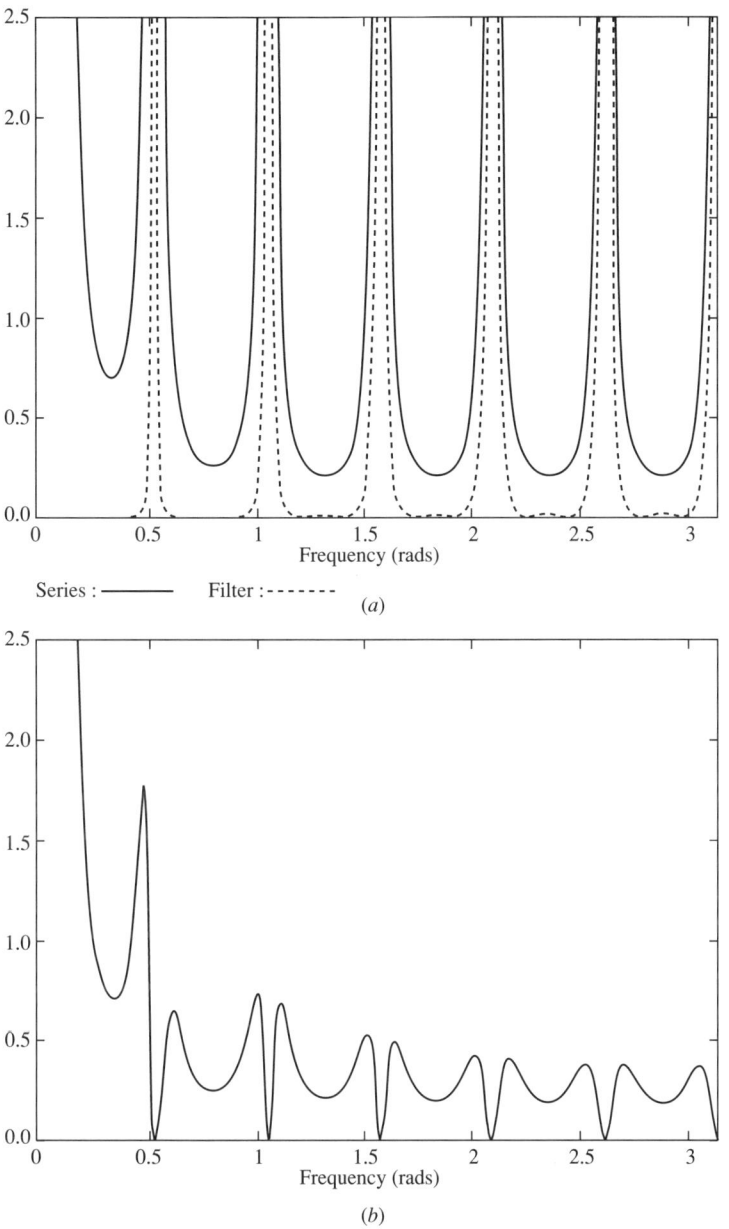

Fig. 12.4. (*a*) X11 Underadjustment: Series and Seasonal Filter
(*b*) X11 Underadjustment: Seasonally Adjusted Series

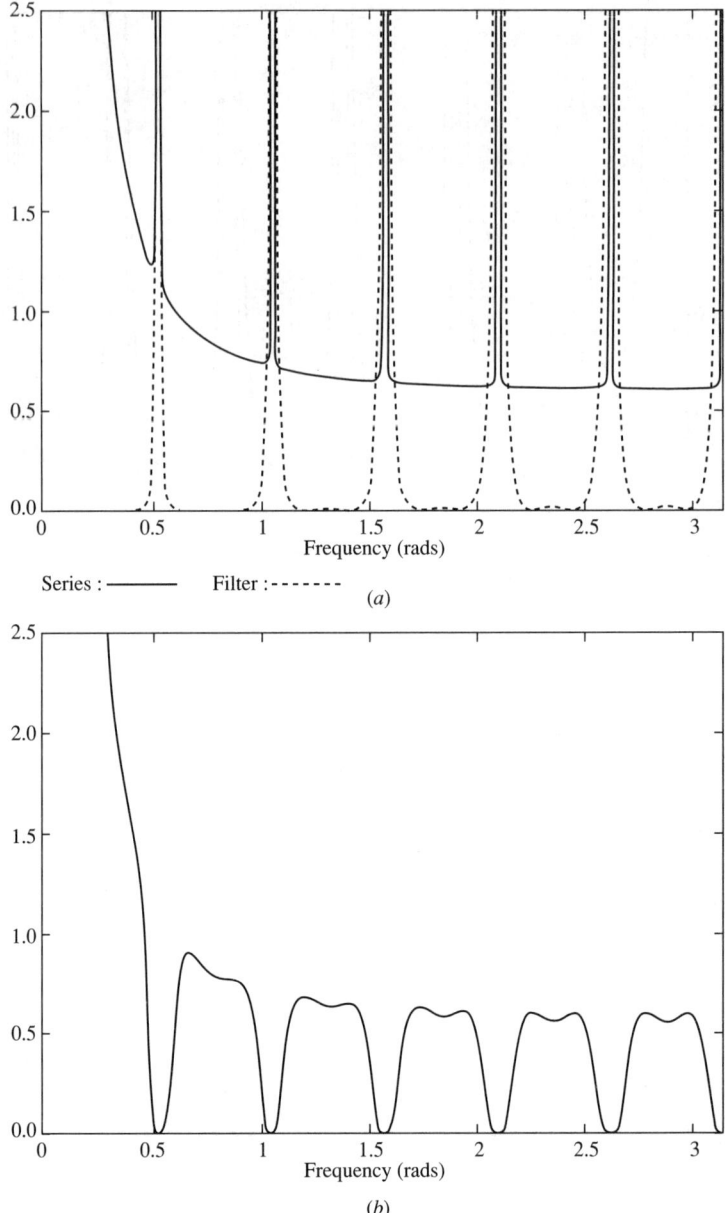

Fig. 12.5. (*a*) X11 Overadjustment: Series and Seasonal Filter
(*b*) X11 Overadjustment: Seasonally Adjusted Series

the 3 percentage point (p.p.) difference be attributed to the error implied by the estimation of the seasonally adjusted series? Similarly, when assessing the evolution of unemployment, if the series of total employment grows by 90,000 persons in a quarter, and the seasonal effect for that quarter is estimated as an increase of 50,000 persons, can we assume that the increase has been more than a pure seasonal effect?

5. In the same way that X11 does not provide answers to these questions, it does not allow us to compute optimal forecasts of the components. (Seasonal factors for the year ahead are simply computed by adding to this year factors one-half of the difference between them and the factors one year before. Of course, there is no measure of the uncertainty associated with these forecasts.)

6. Although X11 computes separate estimates of the trend, seasonal, and irregular components, their statistical properties are not known. Therefore, it is not possible to answer questions such as, for example, whether the trend or the seasonally adjusted series provide a more adequate signal of the relevant underlying evolution of the series (see Kenny and Durbin 1982; Moore *et al.* 1981; and Maravall and Pierce 1986).

To overcome some of those limitations, throughout the years X11 has been subject to modifications. In particular, the program X11 ARIMA, developed by Statistics Canada (see Dagum 1980), improved upon X11 in several ways. First, it incorporated several new elements for diagnosis. Perhaps more relevantly, it provided better estimators of the components at the end of the series. This was achieved by replacing the *ad hoc* X11 filters for the preliminary estimators with a procedure in which the series is extended with ARIMA forecasts, so that the filter $A(B)$ can be applied to the extended series (and hence to more recent periods). In fact, X11 ARIMA has replaced X11 in many standard applications.

At present, the US Bureau of the Census has just completed a new program for seasonal adjustment: X12 ARIMA (see Findley *et al.* 1998). The program follows the direction of X11 ARIMA, and incorporates some new sets of diagnostics and some new model-based features, having to do with the treatment of outliers and the estimation of special effects.

Be that as it may, practical applications (such as 'official' seasonal adjustment by agencies) lag with respect to research. So, let us now turn to the evolution of research during the last twenty years.

12.5. The Model-Based Approach

Towards the end of the 1970s and beginning of the 1980s, a new approach to the problem of estimating unobserved components in time series, and in particular to seasonal adjustment, was developed. The approach combined two elements: the use of simple parametric time-series models (mostly of the ARIMA type); and the use of signal extraction techniques. Although there were earlier attempts at using signal extraction on time-series models (see Nerlove *et al.* 1979), these attempts were of limited interest because they were restricted to stationary series, while economic series are typically non-stationary.

The model-based approach has taken two general directions. One is the so-called ARIMA-model-based methodology, and some relevant references are Burman (1980), Hillmer and Tiao (1982), Bell and Hillmer (1984), and Maravall and Pierce (1987). The second direction follows the so-called structural time-series methodology, and some important references are Engle (1978), Harvey and Todd (1983), and Gersch and Kitagawa (1983). We shall refer to them as the AMB and STS approaches, respectively. Both are closely related, and share the following basic structure (for a more complete description, see Maravall 1995).

The observed series $[x_t] = [x_1, \ldots, x_t]$ can be expressed as the sum of several orthogonal components,

$$x_t = \sum_i x_{it},$$

where each component x_{it} may be expressed as an ARIMA process (with Gaussian innovations). Thus, for example, the model for the trend, p_t, may be of the type

$$\nabla^2 p_t = \theta_p(B) \, a_{pt},$$

where $\theta_p(B)$ is a polynomial in B, and the model for the seasonal component, s_t, is often of the form (for monthly series):

$$(1 + B + \ldots + B^{11}) \, s_t = \theta_s(B) \, a_{st},$$

specifying that the sum of 12 consecutive seasonal components is a zero-mean stationary process (with 'small' variance). While the trend and seasonal components are typically non-stationary, the irregular component is a zero-mean stationary process, often simply white noise. Since the sum of ARIMA models yields an ARIMA model, the observed series x_t also follows an ARIMA model, say

$$\phi(B) \, x_t = \theta(B) \, a_t, \tag{5}$$

where $\phi(B)$ contains the stationary and non-stationary autoregressive roots.

Once the models are specified, the unobserved components are estimated as the minimum mean squared error (MMSE) estimator

$$\hat{x}_{it} = E(x_{it} \mid [x_t]), \tag{6}$$

and this conditional expectation is computed with signal extraction techniques.[1] The MMSE estimator (6) obtained in the model-based approach is also a linear filter, symmetric, centred, and convergent in the directions of both the past and

---

[1] This technique is a fairly general procedure that can be applied to a variety of statistical problems besides unobserved components estimation. In particular, forecasting can be seen as the particular case when $\hat{x}_{it}$ is the estimator of a future observation; another well-known application is interpolation of missing values.

the future. Thus, as was the case with filter (2), the filter applies to historical estimates, and the problem of preliminary estimation and revisions again reappears. The model-based approach offers an optimal solution: the observed series are extended with forecasts (and backcasts) as needed, and the symmetric and centred filter can then be applied to the extended series.[2]

The decomposition of x_t into unobserved components presents a basic identification problem. In general, the AMB and STS methods use somewhat different assumptions in order to reach identification; these different assumptions, of course, lead to differences in the specification of the component models. It is the case, however, that the STS trend and seasonal components can be expressed as the ones obtained from an AMB approach with superimposed orthogonal white noise (see Maravall 1985). Ultimately, the crucial assumption for identification of the components concerns the amount of variance assigned to the irregular; the AMB approach, in order to maximize the stability of the trend and seasonal components, maximizes the irregular component variance.

Besides these differences in the specification of the component models, there are some additional ones between the two approaches. The AMB method starts by specifying the model for the observed series, following standard Box–Jenkins techniques. From this aggregate model, the component models are then derived, and the conditional expectation (6) is obtained with the Wiener–Kolmogorov filter (see Whittle 1963; and Bell 1984). On the contrary, the STS method starts by directly specifying the models for the components, and uses the Kalman filter to compute the conditional expectation (6); see Harvey (1989).

A simple example can illustrate the basic differences between the two model-based approaches. Assume a non-seasonal series with possibly a unit root. The STS method would likely estimate the model

$$x_t = p_t + u_t, \tag{7a}$$

where p_t, the trend, follows the random walk model

$$\nabla p_t = b_t, \tag{7b}$$

and b_t is white noise, orthogonal to the white-noise irregular u_t. The parameters that have to be estimated are two, namely the variances $V(b_t)$ and $V(u_t)$.

That basic model implies that the observed series x_t follows an IMA(1, 1) model, say

$$\nabla x_t = (1 - \theta B) a_t. \tag{8}$$

A potential problem of the STS is that, since it does not include a prior identification stage, the model specified may be inappropriate. On the contrary, the AMB approach first identifies the model with standard ARIMA-identification tools. (There are indeed many available.) If, in the AMB approach, the model

---

[2] In terms of the observed values, the filter will be, of course, asymmetric; see Cleveland and Tiao (1976).

identified for the observed series turns out to be of the type (8), then the decomposition becomes

$$x_t = p_t^* + u_t^*, \tag{9a}$$

$$\nabla p_t^* = (1 + B)\, b_t^*, \tag{9b}$$

and b_t^* is white noise, orthogonal to the white-noise irregular u_t^*. The factor $(1 + B)$ in the MA part of (9b) implies that the spectrum of p_t^* is monotonically decreasing in the range $(0, \pi)$, with a zero at frequency π. It will be true that $V(u_t^*) > V(u_t)$, and, in fact, p_t can be expressed as

$$p_t = p_t^* + c_t,$$

where c_t is white noise, orthogonal to b_t^*, and with variance $[V(u_t^*) - V(u_t)]$.

The example illustrates some additional differences. It is straightforward to find, for example, that model (7), the STS specification, implies the constraint $\theta \geq 0$. (Otherwise the irregular has negative spectrum.) This constraint disappears in the AMB approach.

The parameters that have to be estimated in the STS approach are the variance of the innovations in the components, $V(u_t)$ and $V(b_t)$; in the AMB approach, the parameters to estimate are those of a standard ARIMA model. Of course, the STS approach has a parsimonious representation in terms of the component's models, and is likely to produce unparsimonious ARIMA expressions for the observed series. On the contrary, the AMB approach estimates a parsimonious ARIMA for the observed series, and the derived models for the components may well be unparsimonious. In both cases, estimation of the model is made by maximum likelihood. The component's estimators in the STS approach are obtained with the Kalman filter-smoother, while in the AMB approach the Wiener–Kolmogorov filter is used. If the former filter offers more programming flexibility, the Wiener–Kolmogorov is more informative for analytical purposes.

Be that as it may, despite the differences, both methods share the same basic structure of ARIMA components–ARIMA aggregate, where the components estimators are the expectations conditional on the available observations (their least-squares projections). Ultimately, both represent valid approaches. My (probably biased) view is that the AMB method, by using the data to identify the model, is less prone to misspecification. I find it reasonable, moreover, in the absence of additional information, to provide trend and seasonal components as smooth as possible, within the limits of the overall stochastic behaviour of the observed series. Further, the AMB method typically implies direct estimation of fewer parameters, and provides results that are quite robust and numerically stable. On the other hand, the state space–Kalman filter format in the STS methodology offers the advantage of its programming and computational simplicity and flexibility. In any case, both methods provide interesting and relatively powerful tools for unobserved components estimation in linear stochastic processes. It is worth noticing that many *ad hoc* procedures can be given a minimum

MSE-model-based interpretation for particular ARIMA models (see e.g. Cleveland and Tiao 1976; Burridge and Wallis 1984; and Watson 1986).

12.6. The Virtues of a Model-Based Method

The major advantage of a model-based method is that it provides a convenient framework for straightforward statistical analysis. To illustrate the point, I return to the six examples used when illustrating the limitations of *ad hoc* filtering is Section 12.4. As the model-based method, we use the program SEATS ('Signal Extraction in ARIMA Time Series; see Gomez and Maravall 1996), which enforces the AMB approach as in Burman (1980).

1. The danger of spurious adjustment is certainly attenuated: if a series is white-noise, it would be detected at the identification stage, and no seasonal adjustment would be performed.

2. The dangers of underadjustment (Fig. 12.4) and overadjustment (Fig. 12.5) are also greatly reduced. The parameters of the ARIMA model will adapt themselves to the width of the spectral peaks present in the series. Fig. 12.6 illustrates the seasonal adjustment (with the AMB method) of the series in Fig. 12.4: part (*a*) illustrates how the filter adapts itself to the seasonal spectral peaks, and part (*b*) shows how the spectrum of the estimated seasonally adjusted series shows no evidence now of underadjustment. AMB seasonal adjustment of the series with a very stable seasonal (the series of Fig. 12.5) is displayed in Fig. 12.7. The filter now captures a very narrow band, and the spectrum of the adjusted series estimator does not provide evidence of overadjustment.

3. To illustrate how the model-based approach can provide elements of diagnostics, we use an example from Maravall (1987). The example also illustrates how, when the diagnostic is negative, one can proceed in order to improve upon the results.

When adjusting with X11 the Spanish monthly series of insurance operations (a small component of the money supply), the program indicated that there was too much autocorrelation in the irregular estimator, $\hat{u}_t$. In fact, the lag $- 1$ autocorrelation of $\hat{u}_t$ was 0.42. This seems large, but what would be the correct value for X11? There is no proper answer to this question.

For a model-based method with a white-noise irregular component, u_t, the MMSE estimator $\hat{u}_t$ has the autocorrelation funcion (ACF) of the 'inverse' model of (5), that is of the model obtained by interchanging the AR and the MA polynomials. Hence, given the model for the observed series, the theoretical value of the ACF for $\hat{u}_t$ is easily obtained. For the model-based interpretation of X11 (for which u_t is white-noise), one finds $\rho_1(\hat{u}_t) = -0.2$ with a standard error of 0.1. Thus, a 95 per cent confidence interval for ρ_1 would be, approximately, $(-0.40, 0)$. Since the value obtained, 0.42, is far from the interval, in the model-based approach it is clear that there is indeed too much autocorrelation in the irregular.

A. Maravall

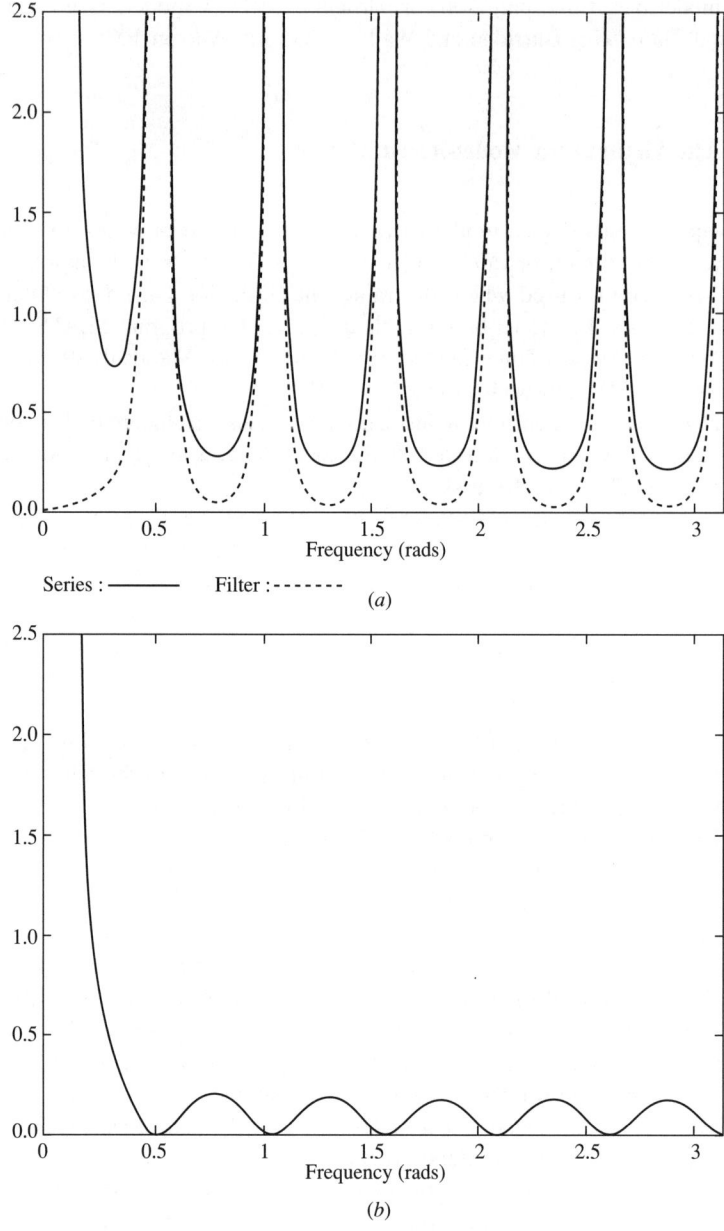

Fig. 12.6. (*a*) Unstable Seasonal: Series and AMB Seasonal Filter
(*b*) Unstable Seasonal: Seasonally Adjusted Series

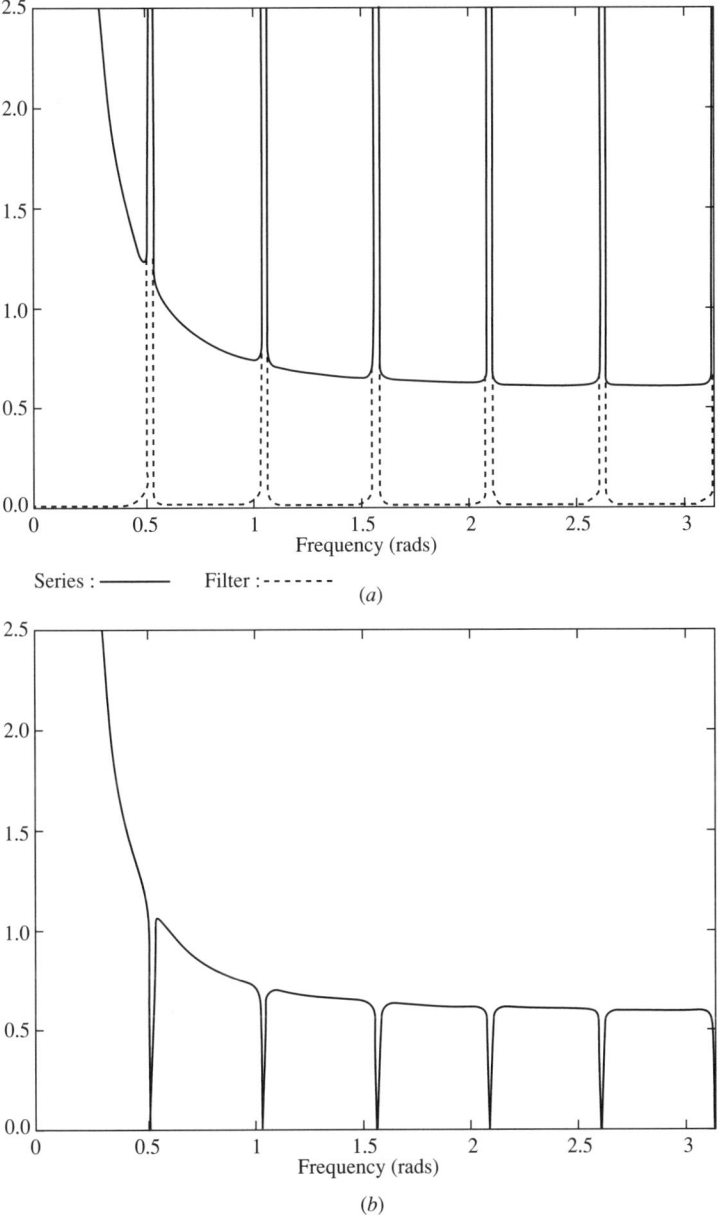

Series : ——————   Filter : - - - - - - -

(a)

(b)

Fig. 12.7. (*a*) Stable Seasonal: Series and Seasonal Filter
          (*b*) Stable Seasonal: Seasonally Adjusted Series

The relative large, positive autocorrelation in $\hat{u}_t$ seems to indicate underestimation of the trend, which, to some degree, contaminates the irregular. The ARIMA model for which X11 provides an MMSE filter contains the stationary transformation $\nabla\nabla_{12}$. Having had a negative diagnostic, back to the identification stage it was found that a model with the transformation $\nabla^2\nabla_{12}$, which allowed for a more stochastic trend, provided a better fit of the series. For this model, the theoretical value of $\rho_1(\hat{u}_t)$ was -0.83; AMB decomposition of the series with the new model specification yielded an irregular with $\hat{\rho}_1 = -0.82$, with the standard error (s.e.) = 0.05., perfectly in agreement with what should have been obtained.

Thus, the model-based approach offers a natural setup for carrying out diagnostics, and permits us to improve upon the results by applying the standard iterations (identification/estimation/diagnosis, and back to identification) of a model-building procedure.

4. As for the possibility of drawing inference, I mentioned the importance of measuring the errors associated with the estimated components.

Given the model, the estimator (6) contains two types of error. First, as mentioned in Section 12.3, when t is not far from the two ends of the series, a preliminary estimator will be obtained. Consider the case of concurrent estimation, that is the estimation of x_{it} when the last observation is x_t. As new observations become available, eventually the preliminary estimator will become the final one (i.e. the one that yields historical estimators). The difference between the preliminary and final estimator is the 'revision error'. The second type of error is the one contained in the final estimator, implied by the stochastic nature of the component. The revision error and the error in the final estimator are orthogonal (Pierce 1980).

With the model-based approach, it is straightforward to compute variances and autocorrelations of each type of error. Thus, in the examples used in point 4 of Section 12.4, the AMB method of SEATS yields the following answers. The standard error in the estimator of the monthly rate of growth of the seasonally adjusted Spanish monetary aggregate series is 1.95 percentage points of annualized growth. Thus, with a 95 per cent size we cannot reject the hypothesis that the measurement of 13 per cent growth is in agreement with the 10 per cent target. (If the size is reduced to 70 per cent, then the mea-sured growth becomes significantly different from the target.)

As for the quarterly series of Spanish employment, the standard error of the seasonal component estimator is equal to 19,000 persons. Thus, the 90,000 increase could be (barely) accepted as significantly more than the seasonal effect of 50,000.

5. The model-based approach provides MMSE forecasts of the components, as well as their associated standard errors. For example, for the Spanish monthly series of imports, the standard errors of the one- and twelve-periods-ahead forecasts for the original series, the seasonally adjusted series, and the trend are as follows (in percentages of the level):

No. of Periods ahead	Series	Seasonally adjusted series	Trend
1	11.6	11.0	5.4
12	14.9	14.6	11.0

The trend, thus, appears to be a considerably more precise forecasting tool.

The standard errors of the components provide answers to many problems of applied interest. For example, it is clear that optimal updating of preliminary seasonally adjusted data implies re-estimation whenever a new observation becomes available. This 'concurrent' adjustment implies a very large amount of work; in particular, it requires agencies producing data to change every month many series for many years. So, the overwhelming practice is to adjust once a year, and it is of interest to know how much precision is lost by this sub-optimal procedure. This can be easily computed, and, for the import series, moving from a once-a-year seasonal adjustment to a concurrent one decreases the root mean squared error (on average) by 10 per cent. Given real-life limitations, it would seem to me a case in which the improvement hardly justifies the effort.

6. In the previous point we compared the forecast errors of the trend and seasonally adjusted series. Since the two can be taken as alternative signals of the relevant underlying evolution of the series, it is of interest to look at a more complete comparison of their relative performances. Consider now the Spanish monthly series of exports. An Airline-type model fits the series well, although the series has a large forecast error variance. In terms of the components, this is associated with a large irregular component.

Starting with concurrent estimation (the case of most applied interest), the variances of the different types of error, expressed as fractions of the variance of a_t (the residuals of the ARIMA model), are as follows:

	Seasonally adjusted series	Trend
Revision error	0.073	0.084
Final estimation error	0.085	0.068
Total error	0.158	0.152

Therefore, the error contained in the concurrent estimator of the two signals is roughly equal. The error in the final estimator is smaller for the trend; in turn, the seasonally adjusted series is subject to smaller revisions.

In addition to the size of the full revision in the concurrent estimator, it is of interest to know how fast the estimator converges to the final value. After one year of additional data, for the trend component, 92 per cent of the revision standard deviation has been completed. The percentage drops to 28.8 per cent for the seasonally adjusted series. Thus, the trend estimator converges much faster to its final value.

Often, policy-makers or analysts are more interested in looking at rates of growth than at levels. Three of the most popular ones are the monthly rate of growth of the monthly series, r_1, the monthly rate of growth of a three-month moving average, r_3, and the annual rate of growth centred in the present month, r_{12} (that is, the growth over the last six months plus the forecasted growth over the next six months). For the export series, both r_1 and r_3 are annualized and the three rates are expressed in percentage points. The standard errors of the concurrent estimators of the three rates of growth are found to be:

	Series	Seasonally adjusted series	Trend
r_1	—	85.3	21.4
r_3	—	47.4	16.1
r_{12}	14.3	13.9	8.8

Thus, an attempt to follow the evolution of exports by looking at the monthly rate of growth of the seasonally adjusted series would be likely to induce a manic-depressive behaviour in policy-makers and analysts (similar to the one reported by Wodehouse).

Finally, the standard error of the one-period-ahead forecast of the series is 12.6 per cent of the level of the series. For the seasonally adjusted series, the corresponding forecast error becomes 11 per cent, and it drops to 4.5 per cent for the trend component.

From the previous results, it is clear that for the case of the export series (and a similar comment applies to the series of imports) the seasonally adjusted series provides a highly volatile and unstable signal, and the use of the trend in month-to-month monitoring seems certainly preferable.

12.7. The Next Ten Years

In the previous section I have tried to illustrate some of the advantages of a model-based approach in short-term analysis of macroeconomic data. In fact, the model-based approach can be a powerful tool, and it is gradually becoming available to the community of applied statisticians and economists. The speed of its diffusion, however, is damped by two basic problems. The first one is the inertia that characterizes beaurocratic institutions producing large amounts of economic data. (Old habits die hard!) The second is that, when dealing with many series, individual identification of the correct model for each series may seem, in practice, unfeasible.

This second limitation is, in my opinion, more apparent than real. There are already some automatic model identification procedures that can be enforced in an efficient and reliable manner (see e.g. Tsay and Tiao 1984, Beguin *et al.* 1980, and Gomez and Maravall 1998). They can also incorporate additional convenient features, such as automatic detection and correction for several types of outlier. In this way, they can be used routinely on large sets of series.[3]

My forecast for the next ten years will thus come as no surprise: model-based signal extraction with ARIMA-type models will increase its importance for practical applications, and will eventually replace the X11-based methodology (although this may take more than a decade). It is worth mentioning that the new Bureau of the Census program X12 (the successor to X11) contains a preadjustment program which is ARIMA-model-based, and hence represents a first move in the model-based direction. On the other side of the Atlantic, EUROSTAT is already using SEATS for routine adjustment of some of their series.

As for directions of new research, the extension of signal extraction to multivariate models seems to me a promising direction. I would expect to see multivariate models that incorporate the possibility that several series may share several components. This would permit a more efficient estimation of the components, and a more parsimonious multivariate model. Some preliminary steps in that direction can be found in Harvey *et al.* (1994), Fernandez-Macho *et al.* (1987) and Stock and Watson (1988). However, routine adjustment of hundreds of thousands of series will probably continue to be based on univariate filters for quite a few years.

Similarly to the case of forecasting, another obvious research direction is the extension of unobserved component models to nonlinear time series. It is the case, for example, that nonlinearity often affects seasonal frequencies, and hence should be taken into consideration when estimating seasonally adjusted series. Efforts in this direction are Kitagawa (1987), Harvey *et al.* (1992) and Fiorentini and Maravall (1996).

On a related, more practical and more important, issue, there is a forecast that I would really like to see realized: it concerns the practice of some data-producing agencies and companies of providing only seasonally adjusted data. We now know that seasonal adjustment, apart from the many problems pointed out by researchers (from Wallis 1974 to Ghysels and Perron 1993), seriously limits the usefulness of some of the most basic and important econometric tools. In particular, it forces us to work with non-invertible series, and hence autoregressive representations of the series, for example, are not appropriate (see Maravall 1995). By having to use the heavily distorted and distorting seasonally adjusted series, life for the economist is made unnecessarily difficult. The wish is thus that the damaging practice of making available only adjusted data will cease; the original, unadjusted data, should always be available.

---

[3] EUROSTAT (1996) presents the results of the automatic model identification procedure of the TRAMO program (see Gomez and Maravall 1996) for close to 15,000 series of economic indicators (all activities) in the 15 EU countries, USA, and Japan. They report that for 87% of the series the fit was good, for 11% it was reasonably acceptable, and for 2% only the fit was poor. They conclude that 'automatic modelization works much better than expected'.

To complete my statements about the future, I should add a last one, well known to any one who has been involved in actual forecasting: no matter what I may say, my forecast will most certainly be wrong.

12.8. Final Comment: Limitations of the Model-Based Approach

From the previous discussion, it would seem as if the use of a model-based approach is a panacea that will permit us to obtain proper answers to all questions. Yet this panacea is not a well-defined one. What do we really mean by a model? Ultimately the models we use are not properties of an objective reality that we manage to approximate, but figments of the researcher mind. In particular, the proper model to use can be defined only in terms of the problems one wishes to analyse. In this context, ARIMA models were devised for short-term analysis, yet they have been borrowed to deal with many other applications. We shall concentrate on one of these applications: the efforts by macroeconomists to measure the business cycle and analyse the behaviour of aggregate output. One of the directions of this research has been the attempt to measure the long-term effects of shocks to GNP and, in particular, to answer the question, does a unit innovation in GNP have a permanent effect on the level of GNP? This long-term effect of a unit innovation has been denoted 'persistence'. If $x_t = \log$ GNP follows the I(1) model,

$$\nabla x_t = \psi(B) a_t,$$

then the measure of persistence, m, can be defined as the effect of a unit innovation on the long-term forecast of x_t, or

$$m = \lim_{k \to \infty} (E_t x_{t+k} - E_{t-1} x_{t+k}) = \lim_{k \to \infty} \sum_{j=0}^{k} \psi_j = \psi(1), \tag{10}$$

since $a_t = 1$. Indeed, different values of m have been attributed to competing theories on the business cycle. Specifically, if $m > 1$, real factors, associated mostly with supply, would account for the business cycle; on the contrary, $m < 1$ would indicate that transitory, demand-type shocks play an important role in the generation of cycles. Whether the business cycle is driven by demand or by supply shocks has very different and important policy implications.

The standard procedure for estimating m has been to specify a model, then to fit it by a maximum likelihood (ML) or some least squares (LS) criteria, and then to use the parameter estimates for inference. We consider the quarterly series of US GNP.[4] For our purposes, a reasonable model is given by

$$\nabla x_t = (1 - \theta B) a_t + \mu, \tag{11}$$

---

[4] The series is the same as in Evans (1989): it consists of 144 observations.

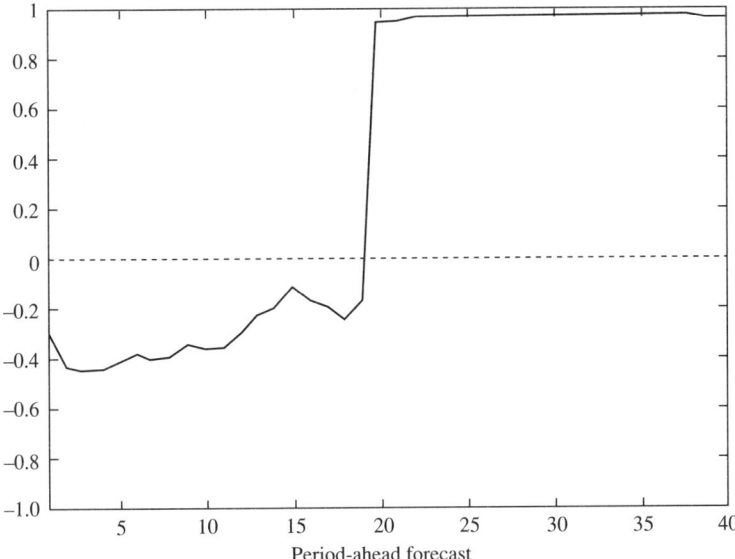

Fig. 12.8. Parameter Estimator as a Function of the Forecast Horizon

where μ is a constant. ML estimation yields $\hat{\theta} = -0.30$, and the residuals obtained seem to behave as white-noise. The measure of persistence becomes thus

$$\hat{m} = 1.30 \quad (\text{s.e.} = 0.08),$$

and hence it can be concluded that $m > 1$. This is in agreement with many univariate estimates of m found in the literature; see e.g. Campbell and Mankiw (1987).

Broadly, an ML or an LS criterion minimizes the sum of squares (SS) of the residuals a_t or, approximately, the SS of the one-period-ahead $(1 - \text{p.a.})$ forecast error. Why select the $1 - \text{p.a.}$ forecast? If our interest is the long-run, and this is certainly the case when measuring persistence, why not minimize a long-term forecast error? Since models are always simplifications which imply some degree of misspecification, it is a well-known fact that minimizing the SS of the $1 - \text{p.a.}$ forecast error may yield parameter estimates that differ substantially from those that minimize the SS of the $k - \text{p.a.}$ forecast (for k not close to 1). Some references are Gersch and Kitagawa (1983), Findley (1984), and Tiao and Xu (1992).

For our example, let $\hat{\theta}(k)$ denote the estimator that minimizes the SS of the (in-sample) $k - \text{p.a.}$ forecast errors. Fig. 12.8 displays $\hat{\theta}(k)$ as a function of k. For $k < 20$ periods, the estimator fluctuates between -0.2 and -0.4; then it jumps quickly to 0.94, and for $k \geq 20$ it remains basically unchanged around that value. Curiously enough, the sample information seems to discriminate two values for θ:

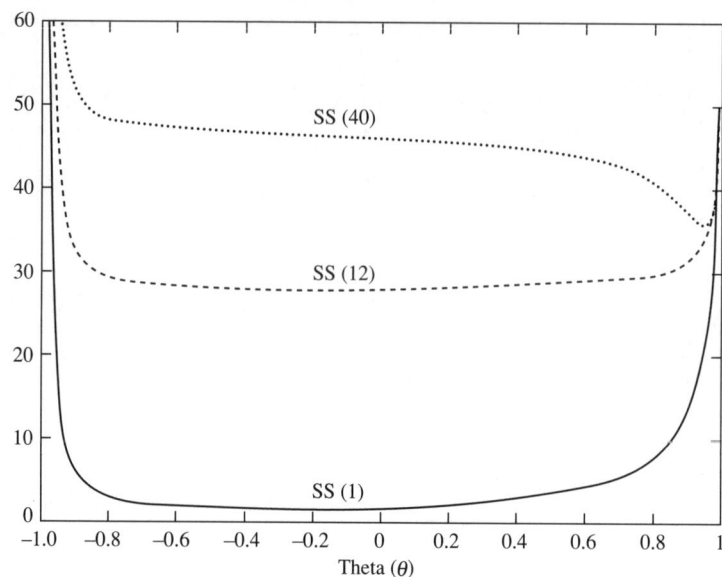

Fig. 12.9. Sum of Squares Function for Increasing the Forecasting Horizon

one for the short run (less than a five-year horizon) and one for the long run (more than a five-year horizon). A closer look at the behaviour of the SS function—Fig. 12.9—shows that for low values of k a minimum is found for a small, negative value of θ. Then, for the intermediate values $k = 10 - 20$, the SS function becomes very flat. As k becomes larger, the minimum for $\theta = 0.95$ becomes more and more pronounced. A similar behaviour of $\hat{\theta}(k)$ is obtained by Tiao and Xu (1992). This behaviour is, in fact, quite general. In Fabrizio (1995) the previous analysis is applied to the annual series of real GDP indices for 12 OECD countries in Maddison (1991). Again, they all display a roughly similar behaviour: $\hat{\theta}(k)$ is relatively low for k below some threshold, and $\hat{\theta}(k)$ becomes close to 1 for k above that threshold. Be that as it may, I find it intriguing that analysis of the data overwhelmingly produces this sharp and sudden distinction between short and long-term forecast.

If we compute the percentage increase in the MSE of the forecast from using the ML estimator instead of $\hat{\theta}(k)$, it is found that, for $k < 20$, that percentage is negligible (in line with the results in Weiss 1991, who considers values of $k \leq 4$). For $k = 24$, use of the ML estimator $\hat{\theta}(1)$ increases the MSE by 14 per cent; for $k = 32$, this percentage becomes 26 per cent, and for $k = 40$ it goes up to 31 per cent. Therefore, if our aim is the long-term forecast, it would seem quite inefficient to use as parameter $\hat{\theta}(1) = -0.30$: our MSE may deteriorate by more than 30 per cent.

It is easy to give an intuitive explanation for the behaviour of $\hat{\theta}(k)$. The good performance of ARIMA models is a result of their flexibility to adapt their

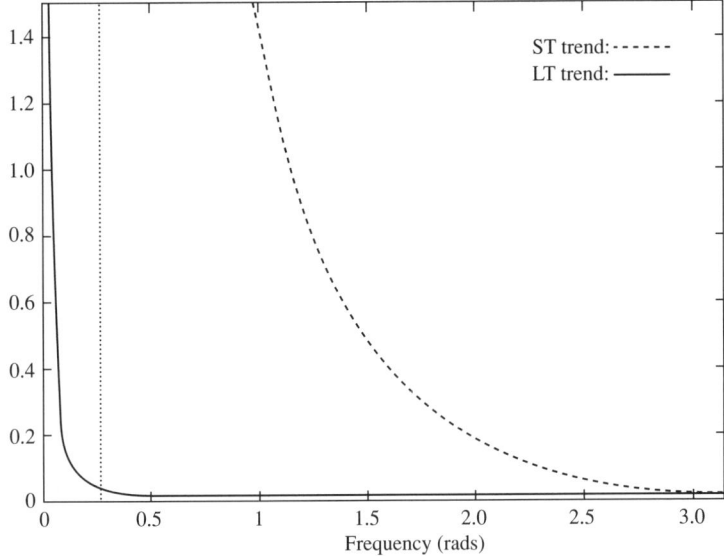

Fig. 12.10. Trend Spectrum: Short and Long-Term Models (five-year-period frequency)

forecast function to the short-run variability. Long-run extrapolation of this short-run flexibility will introduce too much noise in the long-term forecast.

Again, a look at the model components will prove helpful. The IMA(1, 1) model of (8) can be seen as the sum of a trend and an orthogonal white-noise component, where the variance of the noise component can take any value in the interval $(0, (1 + \theta)^2 V_a/4)$; see Box *et al.* (1978). In the trend-plus-noise decomposition of (8), the forecast of the series is the same as the forecast of the trend. The two models obtained by setting $\theta = -0.3$ and $\theta = 0.95$ will imply very different trend components. To compare them, for each of the two parameters, we select the decomposition of (8) that sets the variance of the noise equal to its maximum; this is the so-called canonical decomposition, and it maximizes the smoothness of the trend. For the two canonical decompositions corresponding to $\theta = -0.3$ and $\theta = 0.95$, the variances of the innovations in the trend component are $0.423 V_a$ and $0.001 V_a$, respectively. When $\theta = 0.95$, therefore, the trend contains very little stochastic variability. The two spectra are compared in Fig. 12.10. This comparison shows that the trend implied by the model that is optimal for long-term forecasting is very stable, and picks up only very small frequencies. This is a sensible result: when interested in short-term analysis, we look at the month-to-month or quarter-to-quarter forecasts. Thus, for example, the variability of the series associated in the spectrum with the frequency corresponding to a period of five years should be a part of the forecast and of the trend. However, if we are forecasting twenty years ahead, the variance of the series corresponding to a five-year cycle should not be considered, and hence should not be a part of the trend: in twenty years, the (damped) five-year cycle has practically disappeared. This is precisely what Fig. 12.10 tells us. When looking at the long run, only movements in the series associated with very large periods, i.e. very small frequencies, are of interest. Fig. 12.11 compares the two (short-term and long-term) trend estimates and the two associated estimates of the noise component. The short-run noise reflects the estimator of a white-noise variable; the long-run noise instead allows for larger effects, since over a long span of time they approximately cancel out.

If the measure of persistence, which attempts to measure the effect of a shock on the very long-term forecast, is based on the model optimal for long-term forecasting, then

$$\hat{m} = 1 - 0.95 = 0.05,$$

quite different from the measure obtained before, and certainly below one. Yet the point is not to claim that this result points towards a business cycle dominated by demand shocks. The way I read it, the conclusion is that the trend model obtained in the standard ML estimation–ARIMA specification approach makes sense only for relatively short-term analysis. It is with this type of analysis that I have here been concerned, and it seems to me that the short-term tools we use may not be appropriate for long-term inference.

REFERENCES

Bach, G. L., Cagan, P. D., Friedman, M., Hildreth, C. G., Modigliani, F., and Okun, A. (1976), *Improving the Monetary Aggregates: Report of the Advisory Committee on Monetary Statistics*. Washington, DC: Board of Governors of the Federal Reserve System.

Beguin, J. M., Gourieroux, C., and Monfort, A. (1980), 'Identification of a Mixed Auto-regressive-Moving Average Process: the Corner Method', in O. D. Anderson (ed.), *Time Series* (Proceedings of a March 1979 Conference). Amsterdam: North-Holland.

Bell, W. R. (1984), 'Signal Extraction for Nonstationary Time Series', *Annals of Statistics*, 12: 646–64.

—— and Hillmer, S. C. (1984), 'Issues Involved with the Seasonal Adjustment of Economic Time Series', *Journal of Business and Economic Statistics*, 2: 291–320.

Box, G. E. P., and Jenkins, G. M. (1970), *Time Series Analysis: Forecasting and Control*. San Francisco: Holden-Day.

—— and Tiao, G. C. (1975), 'Intervention Analysis with Applications to Economic and Environmental Problems', *Journal of the American Statistical Association*, 70: 71–9.

—— Hillmer, S. C., and Tiao, G. C. (1978), 'Analysis and Modeling of Seasonal Time Series', in A. Zellner (ed.), *Seasonal Analysis of Economic Time Series*. Washington, DC: US Department of Commerce, Bureau of the Census, 309–34.

Brown, R. G. (1962), *Smoothing, Forecasting and Prediction of Discrete Time Series*. Englewood Cliffs, NJ: Prentice-Hall.

Burman, J. P. (1980), 'Seasonal Adjustment by Signal Extraction', *Journal of the Royal Statistical Society* A, 143: 321–37.

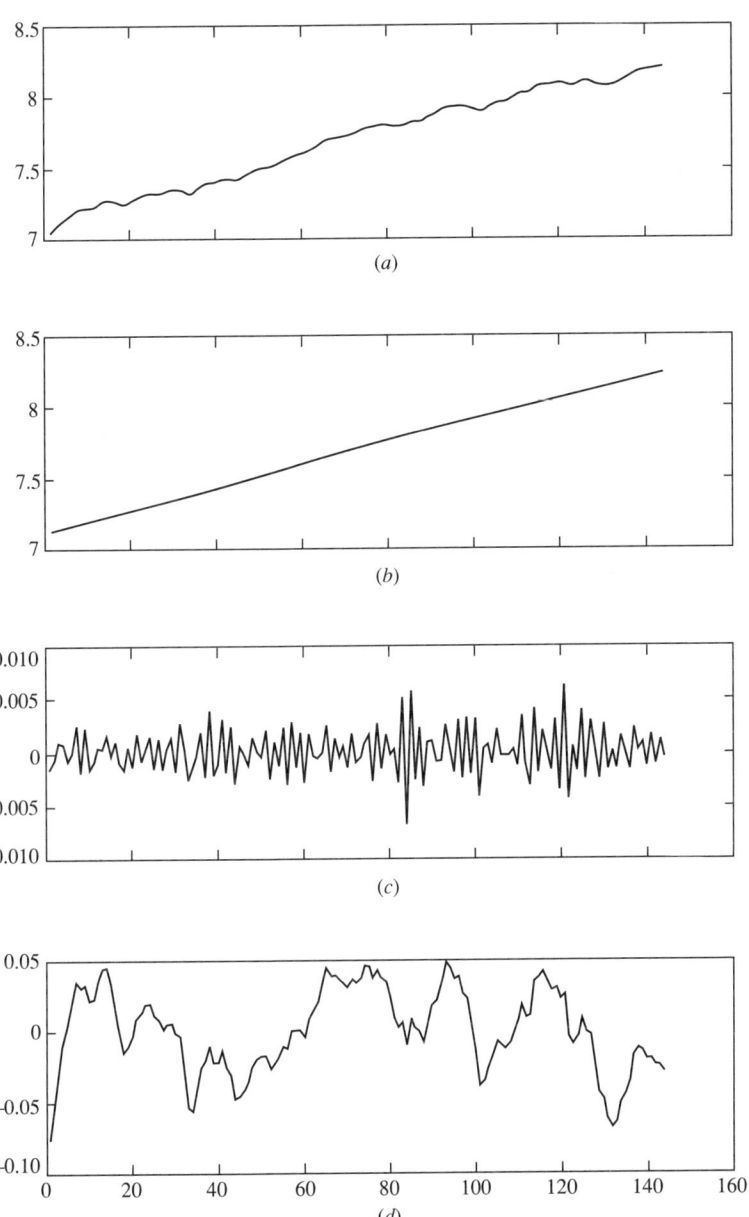

Fig. 12.11. (*a*) Short-run Trend
(*b*) Long-run Trend
(*c*) Short-run Noise
(*d*) Long-run Noise

Burridge, P., and Wallis, K. F. (1984), 'Unobserved Components Models for Seasonal Adjustment Filters', *Journal of Business and Economic Statistics*, 2: 350–9.

Campbell, J. Y., and Mankiw, N. G. (1987), 'Permanent and Transitory Components in Macro-economic Fluctuations', *American Economic Review Proceedings*, 1987: 111–17.

Cleveland, W. P., and Tiao, G. C. (1976), 'Decomposition of Seasonal Time Series: A Model for the X–11 Program', *Journal of the American Statistical Association*, 71: 581–7.

Cox, D. R. (1961), 'Prediction by Exponentially Weighted Moving Averages and Related Methods', *Journal of the Royal Statistical Society* B, 23: 414–22.

Dagum, E. B. (1980), 'The X11 ARIMA Seasonal Adjustment Method', Statistics Canada, Catalogue 12–564E.

Den Butter, F. A. G., and Fase, M. M. G. (1991), *Seasonal Adjustment as a Practical Problem*. Amsterdam: North-Holland.

Engle, R. F. (1978), 'Estimating Structural Models of Seasonality', in A. Zellner (ed.), *Seasonal Analysis of Economic Time Series*, Washington, DC: US Department of Commerce, Bureau of the Census, 281–97.

Evans, G. W. (1989), 'Output and Unemployment Dynamics in the United States: 1950–1985', *Journal of Applied Econometrics*, 4: 213–37.

Eurostat (1996), 'Is the ARIMA Model Adapted to Economic Time Series?' Presented at the Informal Group on Seasonal Adjustment, Eurostat/D3/SA/04.

Fabrizio, S. (1995), 'The Measurement of Persistence of Economic Shocks', Ph.D. Dissertation, Department of Economics, European University Institute.

Fernandez-Macho, F., Harvey, A. C., and Stock, J. H. (1987), 'Forecasting and Interpolation using Vector Autoregressions with Common Trends', *Annales d'Economie et de Statistique*, 6/7: 279–88.

Findley, D. F. (1984), 'On Some Ambiguities Associated with the Fitting of ARMA Models to Time Series', *Journal of Time Series Analysis*, 5: 217–27.

—— Monsell, B. C., Bell, W. R., Otto, M. C., and Chen, S. (1998), 'New Capabilities and Methods of the X12ARIMA Seasonal Adjustment Program', *Journal of Business and Economics Statistics*, 16, 127–52.

Fiorentini, G. and Maravall, A. (1996), 'Unobserved Components in Arch Models: An Application to Seasonal Adjustment', *Journal of Forecasting*, 15, 175–201.

Gersch, W., and Kitagawa, G. (1983), 'The Prediction of Time Series with Trends and Seasonalities', *Journal of Business and Economic Statistics*, 1: 253–64.

Ghysels, E., and Perron, P. (1983), 'The Effect of Seasonal Adjustment Filters on Tests for a Unit Root', *Journal of Econometrics*, 55: 57–98.

Gomez, V. and Maravall, A. (1998), 'Automatic Modeling Methods for Univariate Series', Working Paper 9808, Research Department, Bank of Spain.

—— and Maravall, A. (1996), 'Programs TRAMO (Time series Regression with Arima noise, Missing observations, and Outliers) and SEATS (Signal Extraction in Arima Time Series). Instructions for the User, Working Paper 9628, Servicio de Estudios, Banco de España.

Gouriéroux, C. (1992), *Modeles ARCH et Applications Financieres*, Paris: Económica.

Hamilton, J. D. (1994), *Time Series Analysis*, Princeton, NJ: Princeton University Press.

Harrison, P. J., and Stevens, C. F. (1976), 'Bayesian Forecasting', *Journal of the Royal Statistical Society* B, 38: 205–47.

Harvey, A. C. (1989), *Forecasting, Structural Time Series Models and the Kalman Filter*. Cambridge: Cambridge University Press.

—— and Todd, P. H. J. (1983), 'Forecasting Economic Time Series with Structural and Box–Jenkins Models: a Case Study', *Journal of Business and Economic Statistics*, 1: 299–306.

—— Ruiz, E., and Sentana, E. (1992), 'Unobserved Component Time Series Models with ARCH Disturbances', *Journal of Econometrics*, 52: 129–57.

——, ——, and Shephard, N. G. (1994), 'Multivariate Stochastic Variance Models', *Review of Economic Studies*, 61, 247–64.

Hillmer, S. C., and Tiao, G. C. (1982), 'An ARIMA-Model-Based Approach to Seasonal Adjustment', *Journal of the American Statistical Association*, 77: 63–70.

Hylleberg, S. (1986), *Seasonality in Regression*. New York: Academic Press.

—— (ed.) (1992), *Modeling Seasonality*. New York: Oxford University Press.

Johansen, S. (1996), *Likelihood Based Inference in Cointegrated Vector Autoregressive Models*, Oxford: Oxford University Press.

Kenny, P., and Durbin, J. (1982), 'Local Trend Estimation and Seasonal Adjustment of Economic and Social Time Series', *Journal of the Royal Statistical Society* A, 145: 1–28.

Kitagawa, G. (1987), 'Non-Gaussian State Space Modeling of Nonstationary Time Series', *Journal of the American Statistical Association*, 82: 1032–63.

Litterman, R. B. (1986), 'A Statistical Approach to Economic Forecasting', *Journal of Business and Economic Statistics*, 4: 1–5.

Maddison, A. (1991), *Dynamic Forces in Capitalist Development: a Long-Run Comparative View*. Oxford: Oxford University Press.

Maravall, A. (1985), 'On Structural Time Series Models and the Characterization of Compon-ents', *Journal of Business and Economic Statistics*, 3: 350–5.

—— (1987), 'On Minimum Mean Squared Error Estimation of the Noise in Unobserved Component Models', *Journal of Business and Economic Statistics*, 5: 115–20.

—— (1995), Unobserved Components in Economic Time Series, in H. Pesaran, P. Schmidt, and M. Wickens (eds.), *The Handbook of Applied Eco-nometrics*, i. Oxford: Basil Blackwell.

—— and Pierce, D. A. (1986), 'The Transmission of Data Noise into Policy Noise in US Monetary Control', *Econometrica*, 54: 961–79.

—— —— (1987), 'A Prototypical Seasonal Adjustment Model', *Journal of Time Series Analysis*, 8: 177–93.

Mills, T. C. (1990), *Time Series Techniques for Economists*. Cambridge: Cambridge University Press.

Moore, G. H., Box, G. E. P., Kaitz, H. B., Stephenson, J. A. and Zellner, A. (1981), *Seasonal Adjustment of the Monetary Aggregates: Report of the Committee of Experts on Seasonal Adjustment Techniques*. Washington, DC: Board of Governors of the Federal Reserve System.

Nerlove, M., Grether, D. M., and Carvalho, J. L. (1979), *Analysis of Economic Time Series: A Synthesis*. New York: Academic Press.

Pierce, D. A. (1980), 'Data Revisions in Moving Average Seasonal Adjustment Procedures', *Journal of Econometrics*, 14: 95–114.

Shiskin, J., Young, A. H., and Musgrave, J. C. (1967), 'The X11 Variant of the Census Method II Seasonal Adjustment Program', Washington, DC: Bureau of the Census, Technical Paper 15.

Stock, J. H., and Watson, M. W. (1988), 'Testing for Common Trends', *Journal of the American Statistical Association*, 83: 1097–1107.

Tiao, G. C. and Tsay, R. S. (1989), 'Model Specification in Multivariate Time Series', *Journal of the Royal Statistical Society B*, 51, 157–213.

—— and Xu, D. (1992), 'Robustness of MLE for Multi-Step Predictions: the Exponential Smoothing Case', Technical Report 117, Statistics Research Center, Graduate School of Business, University of Chicago.

Tsay, R. S., and Tiao, G. C. (1984), 'Consistent Estimates of Autoregressive Parameters and Extended Sample Autocorrelation Function for Stationary and Non-Stationary ARMA Models', *Journal of the American Statistical Association*, 79: 84–96.

Wallis, K. F. (1974), 'Seasonal Adjustment and Relations between Variables', *Journal of the American Statistical Association*, 69: 18–31.

Watson, M. W. (1986), 'Univariate Detrending Methods with Stochastic Trends', *Journal of Monetary Economics*, 18, 49–75.

Weiss, A. A. (1991), 'Multi-Step Estimation and Forecasting in Dynamic Models', *Journal of Econometrics*, 48: 135–49.

Whittle, P. (1963), *Prediction and Regulation by Linear Least-Square Methods*. London: English Universities Press.

Winters, P. R. (1960), 'Forecasting Sales by Exponentially Weighted Moving Averages', *Management Science*, 6: 324–42.

Wodehouse, P. G. (1981), *Wodehouse on Wodehouse*. London: Penguin Books.

Trends and Breaking Points of the Bayesian Econometric Literature

Luc Bauwens and Michel Lubrano

13.1. Introduction

During the last thirty years, Bayesian econometric literature has been occupied mainly with applying a Bayesian treatment to existing econometric models. The yardstick is given by the Drèze (1962) Northwestern University memorandum, which can be seen as the first step in a Bayesian counterpart to the research results of the Cowles Commission arrived at ten years before for the simultaneous equation model. This stream of research continued to encounter problems of calculability in these models. Bayesian inference relies on the evaluation of a posterior density, 'evaluation' meaning the computation of moments, fractiles, and eventually a graph of some marginal densities. This may be a formidable task if no analytical results are available, as in this case the posterior density has to be integrated numerically. Drèze (1977) noticed that for most linear models (regression, SURE, limited information, etc.) the posterior density has the form of a poly-*t* density which was proved to be easily integrable by semi-numerical algorithms (see Richard and Tompa 1980).

However, the analytical and numerical treatment of various kinds of models is not a self-contained aim. If a model is not correctly specified from the empirical point of view, the inference and prediction results given by the model will be useless. This idea, which seems to be trivial, did not produce interesting results before the beginning of the 1960s, in either the classical or the Bayesian framework. Testing procedures, reductions, and cuts in the likelihood function became the lot of a new literature. We can quote the works of Hendry and Richard (1982) and Haussman (1978) for the classical side, and of Leamer (1978), Florens and Mouchart (1985, 1989), and Aprahamian *et al.* (1991) for the Bayesian side.

One thing is worth noting. While in statistics test procedures have always been the main point of disagreement between the classical and Bayesian schools (a good discussion can be found in Lindley 1971, or in Berger 1985), in econometrics this did not seem to be the case; also, Bayesian econometricians were very happy when they could reproduce the classical results under a non-informative

Financial support from C.N.R.S. and F.N.R.S. is gratefully acknowledged.

prior. But this state of affairs resulted in a certain marginalization of Bayesian econometrics, and in a certain lack of interest in the Bayesian methods.

Things started to change fairly recently, and Bayesian methods have regained interest for two fields which are going to be the focus of this paper. The first field is controversial and concerns unit roots and cointegration. The second offers a fruitful convergence of interest between classical and Bayesian econometricians and is related to numerical methods based on Monte Carlo sampling. The aim of this paper is to review and discuss the results obtained in these two fields and to consider the research that could develop in these domains into the next millennium.

13.2. The Unit Roots Controversy in the Bayesian Literature

One of the main interests econometricians found in the unit root problem is that it is a very nice mathematical question. For a model as simple as

$$y_t = \rho y_{t-1} + \varepsilon_t, \tag{1}$$

the asymptotic distribution of the ordinary least squares (OLS) estimator of ρ is different in the stationary case ($\rho < 1$) and in the non-stationary case ($\rho = 1$). This difference is non-trivial, as we have

$$\sqrt{T}(\hat{\rho} - \rho) \xrightarrow{\mathcal{L}} N(0, 1 - \rho^2) \quad \text{if } \rho < 1 \tag{2}$$

$$T(\hat{\rho} - \rho) \Rightarrow \frac{1}{2} \frac{W(1)^2 - 1}{\int_0^1 W(r)^2 dr} \quad \text{if } \rho = 1 . \tag{3}$$

In the stationary case, the speed of convergence of the OLS estimator towards its true value is of the order of $\sqrt{T}$. In the non-stationary case the speed of convergence is much faster, as it is of the order of T but converges to a random quantity. In (3) $W(\cdot)$ denotes a standardized Wiener process. In (2) the asymptotic distribution is standard and symmetric; in (3) it is non-standard and skewed; moreover, adding, a constant term and/or a trend complicates the asymptotic distribution in a non-trivial way. The practical consequence is that, when one wants to test the null hypothesis of a unit root ($\rho = 1$), one has, first, to use special tables and, second, to use different tables when a constant and a trend are added.

13.2.1. COMPARING THE BAYESIAN AND THE CLASSICAL TREATMENT OF UNIT ROOTS

For a Bayesian econometrician or statistician, once the sample is observed, it is fixed and non-random and the sole source of uncertainty is the parameter. If the ε_t are $IN(0, 1)$, $\hat{\rho}$ is a sufficient statistic and the likelihood function $l(\hat{\rho}|\rho)$ has the form of a normal density for ρ, with mean $\hat{\rho}$, and variance $1/\Sigma y_{t-1}^2$. If $\varphi(\rho)$ denotes the prior density of ρ, then the product

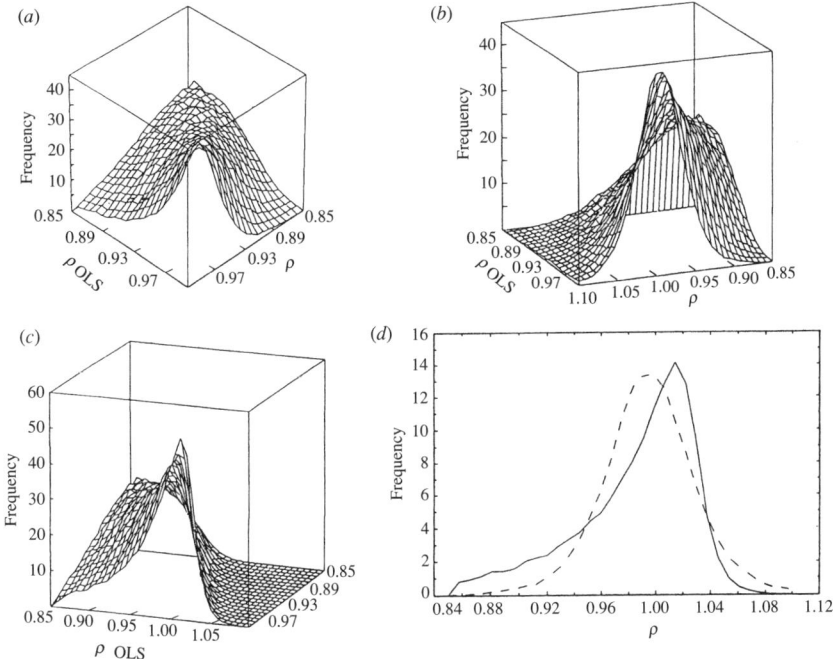

Fig. 13.1. (*a*) Surface sliced to one
(*b*) View of ρ along ρ OLS = 1
(*c*) View of ρ OLS along ρ = 1
(*d*) Distribution of ρ OLS and posterior of ρ

$$l(\hat{\rho}, \rho) = l(\hat{\rho} \mid \rho) \, \varphi(\rho) \qquad (4)$$

represents the joint density of the OLS estimator $\hat{\rho}$ and the parameter ρ. The prior density can be chosen non-informative with

$$\varphi(\rho) \propto 1.$$

The function $l(\hat{\rho}, \rho)$ is a very convenient tool for comparing the Bayesian and the classical approach of the unit roots in a Monte Carlo experiment. For a fixed value of ρ, we can simulate the small sample distribution of $\hat{\rho}$. For a chosen $\hat{\rho}$, we obtain the corresponding posterior density of ρ. Sims and Uhlig (1991) have designed the following experiment to compare Bayesian and classical results. By Monte Carlo simulation they build a grid over ρ and $\hat{\rho}$. The values of ρ are chosen along a grid of thirty-three points on the ordered interval [0.85, 1.10]. For each point of this interval, a vector y_t of size $T = 50$ is generated according to the DGP (data generating process) $y_t = \rho y_{t-1} + \varepsilon_t$ and the corresponding $\hat{\rho}$ computed. With 50,000 replications and zero initial condition, one can obtain a good approximation of the graph of the bivariate density of $(\hat{\rho}, \rho)$. This bivariate graph is shown from different angles in Fig. 13.1.

- Part (a) represents the bivariate density of $(\hat{\rho}, \rho)$ when both axes are restrained to the range [0.85, 1.00] as the complete graph is dominated by explosive values.
- Part (b) shows the same bivariate density sliced at $\hat{\rho} = 1$.
- Part (c) operates the same cut but at $\rho = 1$.
- Part (d) gives two conditional densities extracted from the previous graphs: the continuous line is $p(\hat{\rho} \mid \rho = 1)$, the classical small-sample distribution of the OLS estimator under the null, and the segmented line is $\varphi(\rho \mid \hat{\rho} = 1)$, the Bayesian posterior density of ρ for a sample containing a unit root.

The remarkable fact is that the Bayesian posterior density of ρ is symmetric around $\hat{\rho}$ while the classical small-sample distribution of $\hat{\rho}$ is skewed to the left. When the uncertainty comes from the sample for fixed ρ, the distribution is non-standard. In Bayesian analysis, uncertainty comes from the parameter for a fixed sample and the posterior density of ρ is the same as in the usual static regression model. In conclusion, Sims and Uhlig (1991) recommend that in testing for unit roots one should consider not special tables, but rather the usual student tables.

13.2.2. A FLAT PRIOR OR A JEFFREYS PRIOR?

This is the first significant case of classical and Bayesian results totally differing under a flat prior. This discrepancy led to an increase of interest in Bayesian methods, which have recently gained some favours in econometric meetings. The discussion can be articulated around two points: the prior density on ρ, and the model that is used to test for a unit root.

For Phillips (1991), this apparent contradiction comes solely from the prior. Bayesian results favour the stationary hypothesis because the flat prior on ρ is very informative in favour of the stationary case. In dynamic models, the flat prior and the Jeffreys prior on the location parameter ρ do not coincide. The Jeffreys prior goes at speed T (the sample size) to infinity, when ρ goes beyond the value one. The prior derived by Phillips for the simple model above and zero initial condition is

$$\varphi(\rho) \propto \left[\frac{1}{1-\rho^2} \left(T - \frac{1-\rho^{2T}}{1-\rho^2} \right) \right]^{1/2}. \tag{5}$$

A graph of this prior is given in Fig. 13.2. An extensive discussion about the use of this type of prior in dynamic models is found in the final issue of the 1991 *Journal of Applied Econometrics*.

Let us summarize the controversy.

1. For Sims and Uhlig (1991) and their followers, the sample has to be considered as fixed (likelihood principle); prior ignorance is modelled with a flat prior (which respects the minimum entropy principle). Consequently there is no difference between a static and a dynamic model; the posterior density of ρ is symmetric and standard.

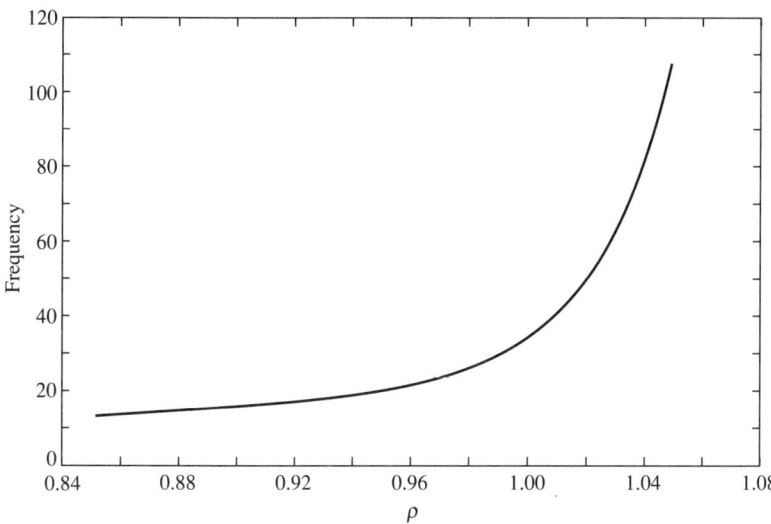

Fig. 13.2. Jeffreys prior on ρ for $T = 50$

2. Phillips's point of view is of course different: in dynamic models the rate of accumulation of information is different in the stationary and the non-stationary cases (as shown above); if one wants to be really non-informative, one has to take into account this fact as the Jeffreys prior does; and with the Jeffreys prior, classical and Bayesian results are reasonably similar.
3. The problem is that a lot of authors do not like the Jeffreys prior in this context; see the discussion in the special issue of the *Journal of Applied Econometrics* 1991, mentioned above.

The idea that we shall promote in the following sections is that it is possible to find a Bayesian inference procedure that gives results that are not so different from the classical results when one uses a flat prior. This inference procedure relies on the use of a differently parameterized model. The following sections promote the use of this model. In Section 13.3 we show that initial conditions are essential for testing for unit roots. This result has its classical counterpart in two not very well known papers by Pierre Perron. In Section 13.4 we show how this model equipped with a flat prior gives results that are more different from those provided by the traditional linear model plus its flat prior than from those produced by the Phillips prior.

13.3. Initial Conditions are Essential for Testing for Unit Roots

In a stationary process, the effect of initial conditions vanishes as time goes on as the decomposition of the simple model, $y_t = \rho y_{t-1} + \varepsilon_t$, gives

$$y_t = \rho^t y_0 + \sum_{l=1}^{t-1} \rho^l \varepsilon_{t-1}.$$

On the contrary, when $\rho = 1$, the initial level of the series has a permanent effect on the current level. This simple fact partially explains why there is a discontinuity in the classical asymptotic theory between the stationary and the nonstationary case. In a series of two papers, Perron (1991a, b) has tried to bridge this gap. Perron's approach requires the explicit consideration of the initial conditions of the process. We shall now present a model for a time series with a possible unit root, which has many nice characteristics.

13.3.1. AR MODELLING OF A TIME SERIES WITH A POSSIBLE UNIT ROOT

The model we shall consider in this paper has the following form:

$$A(L)(y_t - \mu - \delta t) = \varepsilon_t, \tag{6}$$

where μ is the intercept of the deterministic trend and δ its slope. The lag polynomial $A(L)$ is

$$A(L) = 1 - \alpha_1 L - \alpha_2 L^2 - \ldots - \alpha_p L^p.$$

We can easily factorize this polynomial in order to make apparent a possible unit root. For the simple case $p = 1$, we have

$$A(L) = 1 - \rho L = (1 - L) + (1 - \rho)L.$$

So the model becomes

$$\Delta y_t = \delta + (\rho - 1)[y_{t-1} - \mu - \delta(t - 1)] + \varepsilon_t. \tag{7}$$

Under a unit root, the constant term μ and the trend term $\delta(t - 1)$ disappear. They are replaced by a simple drift δ. This illustrates the fact that with a unit root the trend intercept is not defined. This apparent difficulty has very nice consequences. Under the null of a unit root and the alternative of stationarity, the series y_t has the same order of magnitude. This model has been used by Schotman and van Dijk (1991) and by Lubrano (1995). It imposes a common factor between the series y_t and its deterministic part $\mu + \delta t$. We shall call it the common factor model.

Many authors such as De Jong and Whiteman (1989, 1991) or Phillips (1991) use on the contrary a linear model with no common factor:

$$y_t = \rho y_{t-1} + \beta_0 + \beta_1 t + \varepsilon_t. \tag{8}$$

In this way it is easy to verify that y_t is $O(T)$ under the alternative of stationarity and $O(T^2)$ under the null of a unit root. Moreover, β_0 is defined whatever the value of ρ.

13.3.2 DIFFERENT HYPOTHESES FOR THE INITIAL CONDITIONS

Initial conditions are found by considering the model at time $t = 0$:

$$y_0 = (\mu + \delta \cdot 0 + u_0) \tag{9}$$

Two cases can be considered corresponding to two different hypotheses made on u_0. In one case the process starts at time $t = 0$ with

$$u_0 \sim N(0, \sigma^2),$$

so

$$p(y_0 | \mu, \sigma^2) = f_N(y_0 | \mu, \sigma^2), \tag{10}$$

as in Zivot (1992). In the other case it starts in the infinite past and is stationary until the period 0, so that

$$(1 - \rho L)u_0 = \varepsilon_0,$$

$$\varepsilon_0 \sim N(0, \sigma^2),$$

$$p(y_0 | \mu, \sigma^2, \rho) = f_N(y_0 | \mu, \sigma^2(1 - \rho^2)). \tag{11}$$

When writing the likelihood function, we can consider the initial conditions as fixed and work with

$$L(y | y_0, \theta) \propto \sigma^{-T} \exp -\frac{1}{2\sigma^2} \left(\sum_{t=1}^{T} e_t^2 \right), \tag{12}$$

with $e_t = y_t - \rho y_{t-1} - (1 - \rho)(\mu + \delta t) - \rho \delta$; or we may consider the complete likelihood function, defined by

$$L(y_0, y | \theta) = L(y | y_0, \theta) p(y_0 | \theta). \tag{13}$$

Zellner (1971: 88) shows that in the general stationary case it is of no importance to consider (12) or (13). What we shall show next is that in the unit root case the choice between (12) and (13) is of prime importance. With a non-informative prior, the posterior density of ρ is unbounded at $\rho = 1$ when computed with (12); it is bounded and well defined at $\rho = 1$ when computed with (13). The prior we shall use is a flat prior for δ, log (σ^2), and ρ:

$$\varphi(\mu, \delta, \sigma^2, \rho) = \varphi(\mu, \delta | \sigma^2)\varphi(\sigma^2) \varphi(\rho) \propto 1/\sigma^2. \tag{14}$$

Let us now show these two results.

13.3.3. AN UNBOUNDED POSTERIOR FOR ρ

Let us consider the conditional likelihood (12) and multiply it by the prior (14). The posterior density of all the parameters θ is proportional to this product. The marginal posterior density of ρ is now fairly easy to derive and is proportional to the constant of integration of the marginalized likelihood function of the model. (See Lubrano (1992) for detailed calculus.)

$$\tilde{\varphi}(\rho \mid y, y_0) \propto [\tilde{s}_*(\rho)]^{-T/2} \left| \tilde{M}_*(\rho) \right|^{-1/2}, \qquad (15)$$

with

$$\tilde{M}_*(\rho) = \begin{bmatrix} T(1-\rho)^2 & \sum_{t=1}^{T}(1-\rho)^2 t + T(1-\rho)\rho \\ \sum_{t=1}^{T}(1-\rho)^2 t + T(1-\rho)\rho & \sum_{t=1}^{T}[(1-\rho)t+\rho]^2 \end{bmatrix}, \qquad (16a)$$

$$\beta_*(\rho) = M_*^{-1}(\rho) \begin{bmatrix} \sum_{t=1}^{T}(y_t - \rho y_{t-1}) \\ \sum_{t=1}^{T} t(y_t - \rho y_{t-1}) \end{bmatrix}, \qquad (16b)$$

$$s_*(\rho) = \sum_{t=1}^{T}(y_t - \rho y_{t-1})^2 - \beta_*'(\rho) M_*(\rho) \beta_*(\rho) \qquad (16c)$$

The posterior (15) is unbounded under the null, as is shown in the next theorem. So it cannot be used for testing the unit root.

THEOREM 1. The marginal posterior density of ρ (15), computed under a flat prior $\varphi(\rho) \propto 1$, is unbounded for $\rho = 1$.

Proof. let us compute the limit of each member of (15):

$$\lim_{\rho \to 1} \left| \tilde{M}_*(\rho) \right|^{-1/2} = \begin{vmatrix} 0 & 0 \\ 0 & T \end{vmatrix}^{-1/2},$$

$\lim_{\rho \to 1}[\tilde{s}_*(\rho)]^{-T/2}$ is finite as it is a residual sum of squares.

Consequently

$$\lim_{\rho \to 1} \tilde{\phi}(\rho \mid y, y_0) = \infty$$

Zellner (1971: 89) remarked in a note that, when there is a constant term in a model with autocorrelated errors, the posterior density of ρ is not defined for $\rho = 1$; but he did not pursue the argument.

13.3.4. A BOUNDED POSTERIOR DENSITY FOR ρ

Let us now write the full expression of the joint likelihood function (13). It is convenient to introduce the generic notation $q_{\upsilon}(1 - \rho^2)$ which is equal to 1 in the case of (10) and to $(1 - \rho^2)$ in the case of (11). The definition of $q_{\upsilon}(1 - \rho^2)$ will be extended in the sequel to another interesting case. The generic joint likelihood function with a random initial condition is

$$L(y_0, y \mid \theta) = L(y \mid y_0, \theta) p(y_0 \mid \theta)$$

$$\propto \sqrt{q_{\upsilon}(1 - \rho^2)} \, \sigma^{-(T+1)} \exp -\frac{1}{2\sigma^2} \left[q_{\upsilon}(1 - \rho^2)(y_0 - \mu)^2 + \sum_{t=1}^{T} e_t^2 \right]. \quad (17)$$

In the first case (10), for $\rho = 1$ the likelihood function identifies μ as the initial level of the process and δ as the mean growth rate of y_t. In the second case (11), for $\rho = 1$ the likelihood function is zero.

Let us now derive the marginal posterior density of ρ using the same prior as in the previous paragraph. We have

$$\varphi(\rho \mid y, y_0) \propto [s_*(\rho)]^{-T/2} \mid M_*(\rho) \mid^{-1/2} q_{\upsilon}(1 - \rho^2)^{1/2}, \quad (18)$$

with

$$M_*(\rho) = \begin{bmatrix} T(1 - \rho)^2 + q_{\upsilon}(1 - \rho^2) & \sum_{t=1}^{T}(1 - \rho)^2 t + T(1 - \rho)\rho \\ \sum_{t=1}^{T}(1 - \rho)^2 t + T(1 - \rho)\rho & \sum_{t=1}^{T}[(1 - \rho)t + \rho]^2 \end{bmatrix} \quad (19a)$$

$$\beta_*(\rho) = M_*^{-1}(\rho) \begin{bmatrix} \sum_{t=1}^{T}(y_t - \rho y_{t-1}) + y_0 q_{\upsilon}(1 - \rho^2) \\ \sum_{t=1}^{T} t(y_t - \rho y_{t-1}) \end{bmatrix} \quad (19b)$$

$$s_*(\rho) = \sum_{t=1}^{T}(y_t - \rho y_{t-1})^2 + y_0^2 q_{\upsilon}(1 - \rho^2) - \beta_*'(\rho) M_*(\rho) \beta_*(\rho). \quad (19c)$$

The posterior (18) is now bounded as shown in the following theorem.

THEOREM 2. The marginal posterior density of ρ given in (18) is bounded at $\rho = 1$ when computed under a flat prior.

Proof. the result is the same whether there is a trend or not. In order to simplify the presentation, we shall take $\delta = 0$. Under (11), we have

$$\lim_{\rho \to 1} \varphi(\rho \mid y, y_0) \propto [\Delta y' \Delta y]^{-T/2}$$

since

$$\lim_{\rho \to 1} M_*(\rho)^{-1/2} q_\upsilon (1-\rho^2)^{1/2} = \lim_{\rho \to 1} \frac{(1-\rho^2)^{1/2}}{[T(1-\rho)^2 + (1-\rho^2)]^{1/2}} = 1$$

and

$$\lim_{\rho \to 1} s_*(\rho) = \Delta y' \Delta y.$$

Under (10), the limit of $\varphi(\rho \mid y, y_0)$ is also finite but slightly different, since

$$\lim_{\rho \to 1} M_*(\rho)^{-1/2} q_\upsilon (1-\rho^2)^{1/2} = \lim_{\rho \to 1} \frac{1}{(T(1-\rho)^2 + 1)^{1/2}} = 1$$

$$\lim_{\rho \to 1} s_*(\rho) = \Delta y' \Delta y + y_0^2 - (i' \Delta y + y_0)^2,$$

where i is a $(T \times 1)$ vector of ones.

Remark. The hypothesis of a random initial condition such as (10) or (11) is strictly equivalent to the use of a prior density on μ as μ and y_0 enter in a symmetric way in the likelihood function. We are then in a model with an informative prior on $(\mu \mid \rho, \sigma^2)$ and a fixed initial condition. Schotman and van Dijk (1991, 1993) retain this interpretation.

13.3.5. WHICH POSTERIOR TO USE

Whatever method we use for testing the unit root, the posterior density of ρ has to be well defined at $\rho = 1$. This is very easy to see if we use posterior odds. With a flat prior on ρ, defined as

$$\varphi(\rho) \propto 1/(1-a) \quad \text{if } \rho \in [a, 1], \tag{20}$$

where a is a positive number defining the prior range of ρ, the posterior odds for $\rho = 1$ are defined by

$$K_0 = \varphi(\rho = 1 \mid y)(1-a). \tag{21}$$

Of course, the value of a has to be sample-dependent. If $\varphi(\rho = 1 \mid y)$ is unbounded, the posterior odds will always favour the null.

Let us examine the question on an artificial sample. In Fig. 13.3 we have graphed the posterior of ρ for various hypotheses on the initial conditions and for a particular drawing of a random walk. The first graph (*a*) gives the particular random walk that has been used together with its ADF test computed with a constant term and no trend. With a value of −2.11 we have an intermediate case. The 10 per cent critical value is −2.57. So we cannot reject the unit root, but we

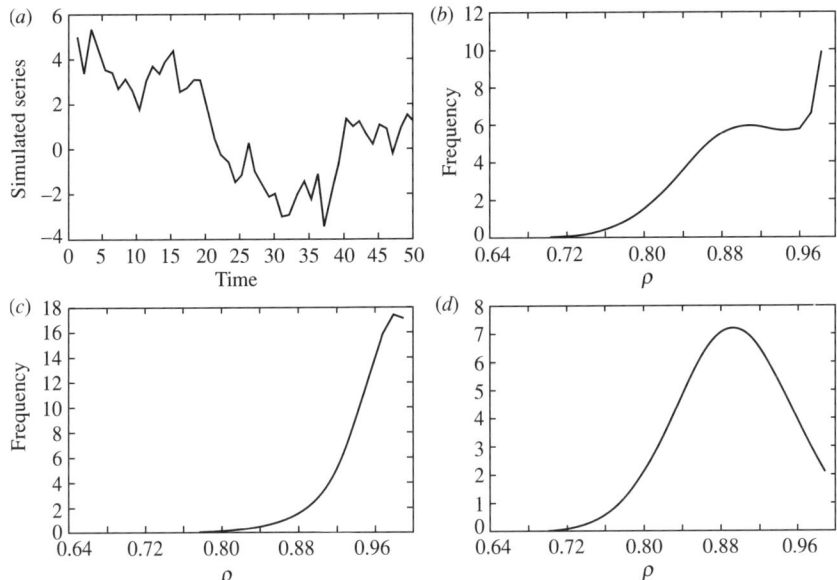

Fig. 13.3. (a) $\Delta y_t = \varepsilon$; $y_0 = 5$; ADF $= -2.11$
(b) Var $(u_0) = 0$
(c) Var $(u_0) = \sigma^2$
(d) Var $(u_0) = \sigma^2/(1 - \rho^2)$

are not very far from rejecting it. The second graph (b) shows the unbounded posterior (15) which corresponds to fixed initial conditions. The third graph (c) shows the bounded posterior (18) with initial conditions (10), and on the graph (d) is displayed the case with initial conditions (11). With a prior range of ρ that covers most of the density, we have a posterior odds of $17 \times 0.2 = 3.40$ with (10) and a posterior odds of $1.5 \times 0.3 = 0.45$ with (11). This example shows that initial conditions (10) (which were used by Zivot 1992) give a weight to the unit root that is too important. We shall prefer (11), which gives more balanced results. Equation (11) has been used by Schotman and van Dijk (1991) and by Lubrano (1995).

13.4. The Flat Prior is not Culprit

As stressed in Section 13.2, one part of the debate concerns the type of prior to be used on ρ. For Phillips (1991), a flat prior with the linear model introduces a bias towards stationarity. The Jeffreys prior compensates for this deficiency. In this section we want to challenge this opinion and show that our common factor model (6) equipped with a simple flat prior gives 'better' results than the linear model of Phillips with a Jeffreys prior.

What do we mean by better? Phillips (1991) provides a Monte Carlo experiment in which he shows how his model departs from the linear model with a flat prior and favours more often the unit root. Our point is that the common factor model with a flat prior can depart even more from the linear model with a flat prior than can the one used by Phillips. Instead of showing this on a Monte Carlo experiment, which may be very costly, we shall show it on two empirical applications concerning testing for a unit root in exchange rate series and in real GNP series.

13.4.1. COMPARING POSTERIOR DENSITIES

How can we compare posterior densities? We shall use the concept of ϕ-divergence. We recall that the ϕ-divergence between two densities f and g is defined by:

$$D_\phi = \int \phi(f(\rho)/g(\rho))g(\rho)\,d\rho$$

For $\phi(x) = (\sqrt{x} - 1)^2$ we get the square of the Hellinger distance. We get the negative entropy for $\phi(x) = x\log x$ and the χ^2 distance for $\phi(x) = (x - 1)^2$. We shall compute these distances in the empirical application using the Hellinger distance, which is

$$D_H = 2(1 - \int \sqrt{f(\rho)\cdot g(\rho)}\,d\rho).$$

Let us now specify some points of notation. We shall distinguish between the different posterior densities with subscripts according to the following conventions:

- $\varphi_{LF}(\rho\,|\,y, y_0)$: linear model with a flat prior
- $\varphi_{LJ}(\rho\,|\,y, y_0)$: linear model with a Jeffreys prior
- $\varphi_{CF}(\rho\,|\,y, y_0)$: common factor model with a flat prior using (11)

We expect that the distance between $\varphi_{LF}(\rho\,|\,y, y_0)$ and $\varphi_{LJ}(\rho\,|\,y, y_0)$ is certainly as big as the distance between $\varphi_{LF}(\rho\,|\,y, y_0)$ and $\varphi_{CF}(\rho\,|\,y, y_0)$ when measured with an appropriate ϕ-divergence.

13.4.2. SOME TECHNICAL POINTS

We first have to give an expression for the posterior density of ρ in the linear model (8) when the prior for ρ is Jeffreys with (5). With a fixed initial condition y_0 (which will be put equal to zero in what follows), the likelihood function is quite simple:

$$L(y\,|\,\rho, \beta_0, \beta_1, y_0) \propto \sigma^{-T} \exp\left(-\frac{1}{2\sigma^2} \sum_{t=1}^{T} (y_t - \rho y_{t-1} - \beta_0 - \beta_1 t)^2\right).$$

A flat prior is given by

$$\varphi_F(\rho, \beta_0, \beta_1) \propto 1,$$

whereas a simplified version of the Phillips prior is given in (5) and noted $\varphi_J(\rho)$.[1] The Jeffreys prior introduces a non-linearity in ρ. The posterior density of ρ, $\varphi_{LJ}(\rho \,|\, y, y_0)$, is obtained as the integrating constants depending on ρ of the kernel $\kappa(\cdot)$ of the conditional posterior density of $\beta' = (\beta_0, \beta_1)$:

$$\varphi_{LJ}(\rho \,|\, y, y_0) \propto \varphi_J(\rho) \int \kappa(\beta \,|\, \rho, y) \, d\beta.$$

If we assume a flat prior on (β_0, β_1) and log (σ^2), the marginal posterior on ρ, $\varphi_{LJ}(\rho \,|\, y, y_0)$ has the following shape:

$$\varphi_{LJ}(\rho \,|\, y, y_0) \propto [\tilde{s}_*(\rho)]^{-1/2} \varphi_J(\rho),$$

with

$$\tilde{s}_*(\rho) = \sum_{t=1}^{T} (y_t - \rho y_{t-1})^2 - \beta'_*(\rho) M_* \beta_*(\rho)$$

$$M_* = \begin{bmatrix} T & T(T+1)/2 \\ T(T+1)/2 & T(T+1)(2T+1)/6 \end{bmatrix}$$

$$\beta_*(\rho) = M_*^{-1} \cdot \begin{bmatrix} \displaystyle\sum_{t=1}^{T} (y_t - \rho y_{t-1}) \\ \displaystyle\sum_{t=1}^{T} t(y_t - \rho y_{t-1}) \end{bmatrix}.$$

In order to test for a unit root, Phillips does not use the posterior odds approach, but computes the posterior probability $\Pr(\rho \geq 1 \,|\, y)$. This posterior probability is defined only if the range of ρ is not constrained to be $[-1, 1]$. However, in our model (6), with initial conditions like (11), the range of ρ is implicitly truncated to $[-1, 1]$, which is also equivalent to defining q_υ as max $[1 - \rho^2), 0]$. In order to allow for comparisons between the two methods, we shall widen slightly the range of truncation and smooth the max operator as in Lubrano (1995), using a smooth transition function defined by

$$q_\upsilon(1 - \rho^2) = \begin{cases} 0 & \text{if } |\rho| < \sqrt{1 + \upsilon} \\ (1 - \rho^2 + \upsilon)^2/4\upsilon & \text{if } \sqrt{1 - \upsilon} \leq |\rho| \leq \sqrt{1 + \upsilon} \\ 1 - \rho^2 & \text{if } |\rho| < \sqrt{1 - \upsilon}. \end{cases}$$

---

[1] A Jeffreys prior is derived from the log-likelihood function and is equal to the square root of the determinant of the information matrix. The resulting prior given in Phillips (1991) for the model with a constant and a trend is rather complicated. It is a variation of the Jeffreys's prior obtained in the simple case where $\beta_0 = \beta_1 = 0$, but it puts more weight on the stationary case. So we shall prefer the simple expression given in (5) and derived with a zero initial condition.

Table 13.1.[a]

	$\hat{\rho}$	ADF	p	$E(\rho\|y)$	s.d.$(\rho\|y)$	$\Pr(\rho \geq 1\|y)$	D_H
FR/WG	0.950	−2.18	1	0.955	0.023	0.024	0.87
				0.970	0.037	0.200	0.95
FR/US	0.982	−1.33	1	0.985	0.013	0.135	0.87
				0.992	0.018	0.318	0.93
JP/US	0.983	−1.22	1	1.005	0.007	0.729	1.34
				0.995	0.019	0.369	0.95

[a] First lines: $\varphi_{CF}(\rho\|y)$; second lines: $\varphi_{LJ}(\rho\|y)$.

The range of truncation of ρ is then widened to $[-\sqrt{1 + \upsilon}, -\sqrt{1 + \upsilon}]$, where υ is an arbitrary small number. $\Pr(\rho \geq 1\|y)$ can now be computed without difficulty and is not empirically sensitive to the choice of υ.

13.4.3. ANALYSING REAL EXCHANGE RATES AND REAL GNP

We shall end this *tour d'horizon* of Bayesian unit roots by two empirical applications. The first one comes from Schotman and van Dijk (1991) and is about real exchange rates. If the purchasing power parity theory is verified by the data, then real exchange rates do have a mean; otherwise, they follow a random walk. We have selected three series, corresponding to the real exchange rate between France and West Germany (*FR/WG*), France and USA (*FR/US*), and Japan and USA (*JP/US*). The data cover the period 1973(01)–1988(06) on a monthly basis, which makes a total of 186 observations (see Table 13.1). The model is analysed with a constant term, no trend, and no extra lag to cope for remaining residual autocorrelation ($p = 1$), as in the original paper.

A classical Dickey–Fuller test leads us to conclude that there is a unit root in each series. With a Bayesian approach based on the nonlinear common factor model using a posterior confidence interval of 0.95 per cent, there is no unit root in the first series, possibly one in the second, and definitely one in the last series (results given in the first line of each row of Table 13.1). For a 5 per cent probability level, the linear model with a Jeffreys prior gives slightly different results, as is indicated in the second line of each row of the table. The posterior expectation of ρ is not very different between the two models, but the standard deviation is much larger for the linear Jeffreys model. It has a tendency to produce greater posterior probabilities for non-stationarity, except for the last series. The posterior expectation of ρ is also slightly larger with the linear Jeffreys model, except in the last case. The last column gives the square of the Hellinger distance between each of the two models and the linear model with a flat prior. For the two first cases these distances are similar, with a slight advantage going

Table 13.2.[a]

	$\hat{\rho}$	ADF	p	$E(\rho\mid y)$	s.d.$(\rho\mid y)$	$\Pr(\rho \geq 1\mid y)$	D_H
USA	0.686	−2.343	4	0.863	0.117	0.124	1.12
				0.770	0.205	0.133	0.92
FRA	1.021	0.431	4	0.987	0.051	0.208	1.09
				1.062	0.055	0.879	0.96
JAP	0.905	−2.035	5	0.933	0.034	0.004	0.96
				0.914	0.046	0.033	0.87

[a] First line: $\phi_{CF}(\rho\mid y)$; second line: $\phi_{LJ}(\rho\mid y)$.

to the Phillips model. For the last case, it is the common factor model that departs the most from the linear-flat model. So in a way our bet is won.

The second empirical application comes from Schotman and van Dijk (1993) and concerns real GNP (Table 13.2). The purpose is to determine the nature of its trend: deterministic or stochastic. Here annual GNP data for USA, France, and Japan covering the period 1948–87 are chosen. The model includes a constant term, a trend, and $(p - 1)$ lags to cope for remaining autocorrelation. With a classical ADF test, there is a unit root in every series. The Bayesian answer is of course more subtle. There is a unit root in the first two series, but not in the last one. But the two methods give the same results. However, as is indicated by the value of D_H, the distance between the common factor model and the simple linear model is greater than the distance between the Phillips model and the simple linear model. So we have won our bet.

These two empirical examples confirm our initial feelings. The 'right' Bayesian model for testing for unit roots is the common factor model with a flat prior, and not the linear model with a Jeffreys prior. A Jeffreys prior corrects the bias towards stationarity induced by the linear model a bit but not totally, and at the cost of an increased dispersion in many cases.

13.5. Numerical Methods and Gibbs Sampling

We have seen that inference using non-stationary data led to a major dispute between classical and Bayesian econometricians. The field of numerical methods, on the contrary, could lead to a fruitful cooperation. Numerical integration is usually mandatory in the Bayesian approach, and, as is emphasized below, Bayesian econometricians have made major contributions in this domain. Certain econometric models (survival models, disequilibrium models, etc.) lead to likelihood functions that contain integrals, sometimes of a high dimension. In fact, this is the case every time one has to deal with latent variables or unobserved components. So classical econometricians may have to use numerical integration for computing those likelihood functions.[2]

13.5.1. HISTORICAL BACKGROUND

Bayesian computations require mainly integration techniques. With a few exceptions, the integration needs to be done by numerical methods. In the early stages of the development of Bayesian econometrics, numerical integration was a big challenge, even in a univariate case. Researchers devoted some efforts to circumventing the need for numerical integration by looking for prior densities that combined with the likelihood sufficiently to provide a posterior with known properties (moments, univariate marginals, etc.), but this was not always possible or acceptable (if the prior was too restrictive, as in the simultaneous equation model (SEM)) (Rothenberg 1963; Drèze 1962). In the early 1970s, with better computers and more software developments, numerical integration in a small dimension (three at most) became quite feasible routinely (see e.g. Zellner 1971, and the development of the Bayesian Regression Program (BRP) at CORE: Bauwens *et al.* 1981). But for the treatment of the SEM we were still confined to the case of two equations, as illustrated in the thesis of Richard (1973).

Then a big revolution started in Bayesian computations with the introduction in econometrics of Monte Carlo integration by Kloek and van Dijk (1978), because this technique allows us to integrate in a large dimension. It is remarkable that this breakthrough was due to Bayesian econometricians rather than to statisticians; it reflects the use of rather complex models with many parameters (like the SEM) in econometrics.

The technique of Monte Carlo integration (especially importance sampling) was applied with some success to the SEM (Bauwens 1984; van Dijk 1984; Steel 1987) and to other models (e.g. Lubrano 1985; Geweke 1989). However, it has some limitations: it requires the construction of a density that is a 'good enough' approximation of the posterior density and that belongs to a class of densities amenable to direct simulation. This may not be easy to achieve routinely. More recently, another class of methods of Monte Carlo integration was introduced in statistics and later in econometrics: Markov chain sampling methods, which simulate dependent samples, contrary to direct or importance sampling, which simulate independent samples—see e.g. Tierney (1994).

We shall describe briefly one particular case, the Gibbs sampler, that seems very useful for a lot of econometric models (Section 13.6.2). We shall discuss briefly its application to the regression model with autocorrelated errors in Section 13.6.3, since this model can be used for univariate cointegration analysis (see Section 13.3.2).

---

[2] See e.g. Laroque and Salanie (1989) for an implementation of Monte Carlo integration in an example of multimarket disequilibrium models.

13.5.2. GIBBS SAMPLING

The idea under Gibbs sampling is quite simple. A multivariate density $p(\theta)$ is too complicated to allow for a direct simulation. Let us consider a partition of θ into (θ'_1, θ'_2). It may be easy to make random drawings from the conditionals $p(\theta_1|\theta_2)$ and $p(\theta_2|\theta_1)$. The trick is of course to find the interesting partition of θ. A Gibbs sampling is a rule that allows us to pass from $2 \times N$ conditional drawings to N drawings $\{\theta^{(n)}\}_1^N$ of the joint density $p(\theta)$. Starting from an arbitrary initial vector $\theta_2^{(0)}$ in the support of θ_2, the first drawing $\theta_1^{(1)}$ is obtained from $p(\theta_1|\theta_2^{(0)})$ which in turn is used to generate $\theta_2^{(1)}$. In two calculations, we have obtained a drawing of $p(\theta)$. The operation is continued until N.

In the general case, we may consider more complicated partitions of θ. The problem is then described as follows.

ASSUMPTION 1. There exists a partition of θ into $(\theta'_1 \ \theta'_2, \ldots, \theta'_k)'$ for some integer k satisfying $2 \le k \le m$ such that the conditional densities $p(\theta_1|\theta_{1c})$, where θ_{1c} is obtained by dropping θ_i from θ, are strictly positive and can be directly simulated for all i and θ_{ic}.

DEFINITION 1. A *Gibbs sample* is defined as a sequence $\{\theta^{(n)}\}_1^N$ generated as

$$\theta_1^{(n+1)} \sim p(\theta_1|\theta_{1c}^{(n)})$$
$$\theta_2^{(n+1)} \sim p(\theta_2|\theta_1^{(n+1)}, \theta_3^{(n)} \ldots \theta_k^{(n)})$$

. . .

$$\theta_k^{(n+1)} \sim p(\theta_k|\theta_{kc}^{(n+1)}),$$

starting from an arbitrary initial vector $\theta_{1c}^{(0)}$ in the support of θ_{1c}.

A Gibbs sample is not in general a sequence of independent draws. It can be shown (see e.g. Tierney 1994), using the theory of Markov chains, that the Markov chain $\{\theta^{(n)}\}_1^N$ is ergodic with stationary density $p(\theta)$; i.e., for large N the sequence of generated values can be considered as a sample (though not independent) drawn from $p(\theta)$. Furthermore, to estimate $E[f(\theta)]$, one can use the simple average $\sum_1^N f(\theta^{(n)})/N$, which is strongly consistent and even asymptotically normal under a supplementary condition (see Tierney 1994).

For practical implementation, several problems have to be solved. First, one has to choose a value of N, i.e. to decide if convergence of the sample means to the population means is achieved; examining the stability of the estimates for increasing values of N provides a simple check. Second, one may have the freedom to choose k, i.e. to decide how to partition θ. Intuitively, it seems more efficient to choose k as small as possible: if $k = 1$ is possible, Gibbs sampling reduces to direct sampling from $p(\theta)$, which is of course the best Monte Carlo method (possibly using antithetic acceleration). Moreover, for given k, it would be ideal to partition θ in mutually independent components $\theta_1, \theta_2, \ldots, \theta_k$, since again Gibbs sampling reduces to direct sampling. If this is not possible, one can at least try to go in this direction.

13.5.3. APPLICATION TO THE REGRESSION MODEL WITH AUTOCORRELATED ERRORS

This model was introduced in Section 13.3 as a convenient model for analysing unit roots and cointegration. Let us refer to formulae (6). The equation can also be written as

$$A(L)y_t = A(L)x'_t\beta + \varepsilon_t.$$

Conditionally on α, the vector of parameters in $A(L)$, this model is linear in β. And conditionally on β, the model is linear in α. Consequently the conditional posterior density of β is a Student density, and the conditional posterior density of α is also a Student, provided we stay in a natural conjugate framework. Student random drawings are very easy to obtain. Integration by Gibbs sampling should be very easy.

In order to put some flesh on these statements, let us define two alternative reparameterizations of the model:

$$y_t(\alpha) = x'_t(\alpha)\beta + \varepsilon_t, \tag{22}$$

with

$$y_t(\alpha) = A(L)y_t, \quad x_t(\alpha) = A(L)x_t, \tag{23}$$

which gives a model linear in $\beta\,|\,\alpha$, and

$$y_t(\beta) = z'_t(\beta)\alpha + \varepsilon_t, \tag{24}$$

with

$$y_t(\beta) = y_t - x'_t\beta, \quad z'_t(\beta) = (y_{t-1}(\beta), \dots, y_{t-p}(\beta)). \tag{25}$$

which gives a model linear in $\alpha\,|\,\beta$. Let us now define a non-informative prior on the parameters

$$\varphi(\beta, \alpha, \sigma^2) \propto 1/\sigma^2. \tag{26}$$

The two conditional posterior densities are

$$\varphi(\beta\,|\,\alpha, y) = f_t(\beta\,|\,\beta_*(\alpha), M_*(\alpha), s_*(\alpha), T-k), \tag{27}$$

$$\varphi(\alpha\,|\,\beta, y) = f_t(\alpha\,|\,\alpha_*(\beta), M_*(\beta), s_*(\beta), T-p). \tag{28}$$

These are obtained by simple application of natural conjugate formulae, and the hyperparameters are:

$$\begin{cases} M_*(\alpha) = X'(\alpha)X(\alpha) \\ \beta_*(\alpha) = M_*^{-1}(\alpha)\,X'(\alpha)\,y(\alpha) \\ s_*(\alpha) = y'(\alpha)\,y(\alpha) - \beta'_*(\alpha)\,M_*(\alpha)\,\beta_*(\alpha), \end{cases} \tag{29}$$

and

$$\begin{cases} M_*(\beta) = Z'(\beta)Z(\beta) \\ \alpha_*(\beta) = M_*^{-1}(\beta)Z'(\beta)y(\beta) \\ s_*(\beta) = y'(\beta)y(\beta) - \beta_*(\beta)M_*(\beta)\beta_*(\beta), \end{cases} \quad (30)$$

where y, X, and Z denote the vector and matrix of stacked observations of the corresponding variable.

Gibbs sampling in this model may be very powerful, as we have to partition the parameters into just two groups. Moreover, random drawings from a Student density are very simple to obtain. However, the symmetric treatment of α and β imposes either that we are non-informative or that we stick to the natural conjugate framework. But the interpretation of α is different from that of β. For instance, when $p = 1$, a stability condition is that $\alpha < 1$. We may want to impose this condition with the prior. This is not possible with a normal prior, except by truncation, but it raises the issue of the effect of truncation on Gibbs sampling. In a unit root testing problem, we may wish to use a special prior for α such as the Phillips prior. In both examples, the conditional posterior $\varphi(\alpha|\beta, y)$ is no longer a Student density. So, at least for $p = 1$, the classical numerical integration by a product rule may still be of a great interest. However, for $p \geq 3$ Gibbs sampling recovers its interest, as for those dimensions product rules are no longer feasible.

13.6. Bayesian Inference in a Cointegrated VAR System

In this section we proceed with the application of Gibbs sampling to a more complex case, which is Bayesian inference in cointegrated vector autoregressive (CVAR) systems *à la* Johansen (1988, 1991). We assume that the number v of cointegrating vectors is known a priori, or has been selected, for example by Johansen's LR test (Johansen 1991). We start by presenting the class of models and its parameterization, in order to discuss an identification problem. We then give the form of the posterior density of the cointegrating vectors and discuss its numerical integration for a particular class of identifying restrictions. Finally, we give an empirical illustration. This section is based on a paper of Bauwens and Lubrano (1996).

13.6.1. CVAR SYSTEMS AND IDENTIFICATION RESTRICTIONS

Let x_t denote an $I(1)$ vector of n random variables among which there are v cointegrating linear relations $\beta'x_t$, β being a $n \times v$ (with $v < n$) matrix of unknown parameters. The CVAR system, assumed to represent an admissible reduction of the DGP, is parameterized in the error correction form:

$$\Delta x_t = \psi D_t + \sum_{i=1}^{p-1} \Pi_i \Delta x_{t-i} + \alpha\beta' x_{t-1} + v_t, \quad t = 1, 2, \ldots, T, \tag{31}$$

where D_t is a vector of m deterministic components (constant and dummy variables), and the errors v_t are assumed $IN(0, \Omega)$. The matrices ψ ($n \times m$), Π_i ($n \times n$), and $\Omega(n \times n$, PDS) contain nuisance parameters, and could be subject to linear restrictions. Whether in a ML or in a Bayesian setup, linear restrictions on ψ or Π_i complicate considerably the computations except in special cases (such as identical restrictions in all the equations). The parameters of interest are the cointegrating vectors (the columns of β) and their weights (contained in α).

The hypothesis of cointegration is reflected in (31) by the parameterization of the $n \times n$ matrix of coefficients of x_{t-1}, say Π, *of reduced rank v*, as $\alpha\beta'$, where α is $n \times v$ like β'. Both α and β are also of rank v. This raises immediately a problem of identification. The matrix Π is obviously identified, but it has only $n^2 - (n - v)^2 = 2nv - v^2$ free elements. The matrices α and β must be subject to a total of v^2 restrictions since they have a total of $2nv$ elements. There are obviously many ways to do this.

The usual classical solution is to normalize the cointegrating vectors by $\hat{\beta}'S\hat{\beta} = I_v$, where S is sample-dependent and $\hat{\beta}$ is the ML estimate of β, and to choose the cointegrating vectors that yield error correction terms having the maximum correlation with Δx_t (see Johansen and Juselius 1992). These restrictions are intrinsic to the estimation method (maximum canonical correlation) and cannot be used in a Bayesian approach. We have instead to rely on linear parametric restrictions. We can choose the required v^2 restrictions on the matrix of cointegrating vectors β or on the matrix of adjustment coefficients α (or on both).

The easiest case is to impose v^2 linear restrictions on β and to leave α unrestricted. Let us indicate the v cointegrating vectors by β_i. Linear restrictions on β_i may be formalized by an $s_i \times n$ matrix R_1 of known constants such that:

$$R_i\beta_i = 0, \quad (i = 1, \ldots, v). \tag{32}$$

The resulting β_i is identified if the rank of R_1 is greater than or equal to v (including normalization). (See Johansen and Juselius (1992) for more details.) In this paper we investigate only the particular case where β is constrained by

$$\beta = (-I_v, \beta_*) \tag{33}$$

where β_* is $v \times (n - v)$ and unrestricted. (See e.g. Kleibergen and van Dijk (1994) for another type of implementation of the CVAR model.) This type of restriction has an economic meaning if the long-run solution ($\beta' x_t = 0$) is interpreted as a system of equilibrium conditions forming an incomplete simultaneous equation model (in structural form). Then the restriction of having $-I_v$ in β is a way of getting v reduced-form equations for the first v variables y_t of x_t, given the remaining variables z_t; the long-run solution can then be written as $y_t = \beta_* z_t$. The general case of linear restrictions such as (32) is detailed in Bauwens and Lubrano (1996). Note that this approach, which consists in leaving α unrestricted and imposing restrictions only on β, is compatible with the classical two-step modelling approach detailed, for instance, in Hendry and Mizon (1993), where the cointegrating vectors are estimated first and a simultaneous equation model (for the differenced variables) is specified in a second step, conditionally on the estimation of β.

The key to a Bayesian analysis of (31) (as well as to ML estimation) is to notice that (31) is linear in its parameters conditionally on β. One can then use the standard results on the Bayesian analysis of multivariate regression models (see e.g. Zellner 1971: ch. 8; or Drèze and Richard 1983: s. 4). To do this, we write (31) for the T observations in the condensed matrix format:

$$Y = X\Gamma + Z\beta\alpha' + V := \tilde{W}B + V. \tag{34}$$

The tth row of $Y(T \times n)$, $X(T \times k)$, $Z(T \times n)$, and V $(T \times n)$ is given by $\Delta x'_t$, $(D'_t\Delta x'_{t-1}, \ldots, \Delta x'_{t-p+1})$, x'_{t-1}, and v'_t, respectively. $\Gamma(k \times n)$ is obtained by stacking ψ and the Π_i; hence $k = m + n(p - 1)$. Finally, $B = (\Gamma' \alpha)'$, and $\tilde{W} = (X \tilde{Z})$, with $\tilde{Z} = Z\beta$. (The tilde is used on top of some matrices to indicate that they depend on β.) Therefrom, the likelihood function is (D stands for data)

$$L(\beta, B, \Omega \mid D) \propto |\Omega|^{-T/2} \exp\left[-\frac{1}{2}\mathrm{tr}\Omega^{-1}(Y - \tilde{W}B)'(Y - \tilde{W}B)\right]. \tag{35}$$

In principle, any prior density $\varphi(\beta)$ on the elements of β can be used, since the computation of the posterior density and moments of β needs to be performed numerically. For the other parameters, we do not bother about defining informative prior densities. We must keep in mind that any kind of prior other than non-informative or natural conjugate introduces an overwhelming computational burden. So our prior is the usual non-informative prior of B and Ω in a multivariate regression model times a prior on β:

$$\varphi(\beta, B, \Omega) \propto |\Omega|^{-(n+1)/2} \varphi(\beta) \tag{36}$$

13.6.2. POSTERIOR DENSITIES

As we have said, conditionally on β, the system (34) is a traditional multivariate regression model. If B and Ω are unrestricted, the posterior density of these parameters is completely characterized by a conditional inverted Wishart (IW) density and a marginal matrix–Student (MT) density:

$$\Omega \mid B, \beta, D \sim IW[(Y - \tilde{W}B)'(Y - \tilde{W}B), T] \tag{37}$$

$$B \mid \beta, D \sim MT(\tilde{B}, \tilde{S}, \tilde{W}'\tilde{W}, T - k - v), \tag{38}$$

where $\tilde{B} = (\tilde{W}'\tilde{W})^{-1}\tilde{W}'Y$ and $\tilde{S} = (Y - \tilde{W}\tilde{B})'(Y - \tilde{W}\tilde{B})$. For details, refer to Drèze and Richard (1983) or to Zellner (1971).

The next theorem gives the form of the marginal posterior density of β_* in (33). The proof is given in Bauwens and Lubrano (1996).

THEOREM 3. For the model defined by (33), (34), and (35) and the prior (36) with $\varphi(\beta) \propto 1$, the marginal posterior density of the $(n - v) \times v$ matrix β_* is a 1–1 poly-matrix-t density defined by

$$\varphi(\beta_* \mid D) \propto \left| Q_0 + (\beta_* - b_0)' H_0 (\beta_* - b_0) \right|^{l_0}$$
$$\times \left| Q_1 + (\beta_* - b_1)' H_1 (\beta_* - b_1) \right|^{-l_1}, \qquad (39)$$

where

$$l_0 = (T - k - v - n)/2,$$
$$l_1 = (T - k - v)/2,$$

and where $Q.$, $b.$, and $H.$ (where $\cdot$ stands for 0 or 1) are defined by

$$W. = \begin{pmatrix} W_v^{\cdot} & W_{*v}^{\cdot} \\ W_{v*}^{\cdot} & W_*^{\cdot} \end{pmatrix} = \begin{pmatrix} Q. + b.'H.b. & -H.b. \\ -b.H. & H. \end{pmatrix},$$

after a partition of $W.$ along its first v rows and columns. The matrices W_0 and W_1 are defined as

$$W_0 = Z' M_X Z, \quad M_X = I_T - X(X'X)^{-1} X'$$
$$W_1 = Z' M_X [I_T - Y(Y' M_X Y)^{-1} Y'] M_X Z.$$

A 1–1 poly matrix-t density is proportional to the ratio of two matrix-t densities, like a 1–1 poly-t is proportional to the ratio of two Student densities. If there is a single cointegrating vector ($v = 1$), the posterior density is a 1–1 poly-t density which can be evaluated by the algorithms of Richard and Tompa (1980) included in the Bayesian Regression Program (Bauwens *et al.* 1981). Notice that, because of the difference between the exponents l_1 and l_0, the posterior density (39) is integrable but has no moments of order 1 or higher (even in large samples). This is the Bayesian counterpart of the Phillips result (1994) that the ML estimator of β has a finite sample distribution with no finite moments. The existence of posterior moments can be obtained by using an informative prior on β, or by truncating the posterior distribution to a finite range. From a Bayesian viewpoint, the lack of existing moments is not a problem: the posterior density of any element of β can be characterized by its median, interquartile range, plot, etc. To ensure the existence of posterior moments, one can use an informative prior or truncate the posterior to a finite region.

Poly-matrix-t densities arise as posterior densities of some econometric models (see Drèze 1976; Drèze and Richard 1983; Zellner *et al.* 1988; Bauwens and van Dijk 1990). Their moments or marginal densities are not known analytically, but some conditional densities are easily obtained.

THEOREM 4. If $\beta_* = (\beta_1, \ldots, \beta_v)$ has the density (39), and if β_{ic} is β_* without its ith column, $\varphi(\beta_i \mid \beta_{ic}, D)$ is a 1–1 poly-t density.

Table 13.3.

Null	Alternative	Max stat.	90% crit. val.	Trace stat.	90% crit val.
$r = 0$	$r \geq 1$	14.69	18.59	27.32	26.79
$r \leq 1$	$r \geq 2$	7.25	12.07	12.63	13.33
$r \leq 2$	$r = 3$	5.38	2.69	5.38	2.69

Proof. It suffices to apply to the two factors of the right-hand side of (39), which are kernels of matrix-*t* densities, the property that the marginal density of a column of a matricvariate-*t* random matrix is a Student density; see e.g. Drèze and Richard (1983: 589). The parameters of the two quadratic forms in β_1 appearing in the kernel of $\varphi(\beta_1 | \beta_{1c}, D)$ are obtained by applying formula (A34) of Drèze and Richard (1983).

Since an algorithm is available for generating random draws of a 1–1 poly-*t* density (see Bauwens and Richard 1985), Gibbs sampling can in principle be applied to compute posterior marginal densities of elements of β (but not moments, as they do not exist). Since the algorithm of Bauwens and Richard is rather computer-intensive, it remains an open question to determine whether Gibbs sampling may be useful in practice for integrating poly-matrix-*t* densities; some experiments have to be performed before answering this question. A comparison with importance sampling is also on our research agenda.

13.6.3. THE BELGIAN MONEY DEMAND EQUATION

As an empirical illustration, we use three variables which characterize the Belgian money demand equation and are regrouped in x_t following the notations of model (31):

$$x_t = (m_t, y_t, r_t)',$$

where m_t is the log of deflated money stock (M1), y_t is the log of deflated disposable income of households, and r_r is log $(1 + R_t)$, R_t being the interest rate on three-month Treasury certificates. We have annual data for Belgium over the period 1953–82 a period during which the variables are all trending.

Let us first analyse the data by maximum likelihood with two lags in the VAR. The trace statistics indicate that there is one cointegrating vector at 90 per cent, but with the maximum eigenvalue statistics there is no cointegration (see Table 13.3). The unique cointegrating vector, normalized for m_t, seems reasonable (see Table 13.4), and the adjustment vectors, given in the second line of Table 13.4, indicate a rather slow speed of adjustment. A χ^2 test would accept a unit income elasticity with a *P*-value of 0.63, but would reject the nullity of the coefficient of r_t with a *P*-value of 0.018.

Table 13.4.

m_t	y_t	r_t
−1.00	0.94	−3.83
−0.16	−0.10	0.19

Table 13.5.

	Post mode	Median	First decile	Last decile
β_y	0.88	0.92	0.69	1.29
β_r	−3.32	−3.63	−7.95	−0.75

Let us now turn to the Bayesian analysis of those data under a diffuse prior. As there is a single cointegrating vector, the posterior density of β is a simple poly-t density. With $p = 2$, and as the data are trending, our model is written with the intercept outside the cointegrating space:

$$\Delta x_t = \mu + \beta \Delta x_{t-1} + \alpha \beta' x_{t-1} + v_t,$$

where $\alpha = (\alpha_m \ \alpha_y \ \alpha_r)'$, $\beta' = (-1 \ \beta_y \ \beta_r)$, and μ is the vector of the three intercepts. The two marginal densities of β_y and β_r have no moment and thus display very long and flat tails. But we can compute their mode, median, and first and last decile as shown in Table 13.5. These results are not very different from the classical ones, but they allow for some more precise qualification of the inference process.

Finally, we can compute the posterior odds of the two hypotheses analysed in the classical part, which are $\beta_y = 1$ and $\beta_r = 0$. With a flat prior on the truncated range covered by the first and last deciles, the two posterior odds are, respectively, 2.83 and 0.003, which correspond to $\Pr(\beta_y = 1 | X) = 0.74$ an $\Pr(\beta_r = 0 | X) = 0.003$.

13.7. Conclusion

We stated a very ambitious aim for this paper in the introduction: to describe what will happen between now and 2002 in two fields of Bayesian econometrics. The experiment first proposed by Sims and Uhlig (1991) gives a good account of the distance that may exist between a classical approach and a Bayesian approach to the unit root question. But the model they use is the simplest one. We have shown that, with a richer and carefully specified model, one could get results that, if they are still different from the classical ones, are no longer so opposed. But one (provocative) question is worth asking: within ten years, who will care about unit roots, from either a classical or a Bayesian point of view? The question of cointegration seems deeper and more amenable to future intensive work (see e.g. Lubrano 1992). Cointegration is deeply related to model specification and model search. A Bayesian approach is very motivating as it gives small-sample results and allows for sensitivity analysis in a domain where the lack of long series is recurrent. When the sample is not very informative, one has to provide extra (prior) information and to give indications of the sensitivity of the results to the hypothesis. The computational burden associated with Bayesian cointegration is high, and Gibbs sampling may prove valuable in the future.

Enthusiasm about this method is enormous in the profession. We have attempted to exercise caution in the text to indicate for each case its apparent limitations. The least we can say is that we need empirical experience. And the future will provide much of that.

REFERENCES

Aprahamian, F., Lubrano, M., and Marimoutou, V. (1991), 'A Bayesian Approach to Misspecification Tests', Document de Travail GREQE, no. 91–A–17.

Bauwens, L. (1984), *Bayesian Full Information Analysis of Simultaneous Equation Models Using Integration by Monte Carlo*. Berlin: Springer-Verlag.

—— and Lubrano, M. (1996), 'Identification Restrictions and Posterior Densities in Co-integrated VAR Models', in T. B. Fomby and R. Carter Hill (eds), *Advances in Econometrics, Vol. 11, Part B: Bayesian Methods Applied to Time Series Data*, JAI Press.

—— and Richard, J. F. (1985), 'A 1–1 Poly-*t* Random Variable Generator with Application to Monte Carlo Integration', *Journal of Econometrics*, 29: 19–46.

—— and van Dijk, H. K. (1990), 'Bayesian Limited Information Analysis Revisited', in J. J. Gabszewicz *et al.* (eds.), *Economic Decision Making: Games, Econometrics and Optimization*. Amsterdam: North–Holland.

—— Bulteau, J. P., Gille, P., Longree, L., Lubrano, M., and Tompa, H. (1981), *Bayesian Regression Program (BRP) User's Manual*, CORE Computing Report 81–A–01. Louvain-la-Neuve: CORE.

Berger, J. O. (1985), *Statistical Decision Theory and Bayesian Analysis*. Berlin: Springer-Verlag.

De Jong, D. N., and Whiteman, C. H. (1989), 'Trends and Cycles as Unobserved Components in US Real GNP: a Bayesian Perspective', *Proceedings of the American Statistical Association*,

—— —— (1991), 'Reconsidering Trends and Random Walks in Macroeconomic Time Series', *Journal of Monetary Economics*, 28: 221–4.

Drèze, J. H. (1962), 'The Bayesian Approach to Simultaneous Equation Estimation', ONR Research Memorandum 67, The Technological Institute, Northwestern University.

—— (1976), 'Bayesian Limited Information Analysis of the Simultaneous Equations Model', *Econometrica*, 44: 1045–75.

—— (1977), 'Bayesian Regression Analysis Using Poly-*t* Densities', *Journal of Econometrics*, 6: 329–54.

—— and Richard, J. F. (1983), 'Bayesian Analysis of Simultaneous Equation Systems', in Z. Griliches and M. D. Intriligator (eds.), *Handbook of Econometrics*. Amsterdam: North-Holland.

Engle, R. F., and Granger, C. W. J. (1987), 'Co-Integration and Error Correction: Representation, Estimation and Testing', *Econometrica*, 55: 251–76.

Florens, J. P., and Mouchart, M. (1985), 'Conditioning in Dynamic Models', *Journal of Time Series Analysis*, 53: 15–35.

—— —— (1989), 'Bayesian Specification Tests', in B. Cornet and H. Tulkens (eds.), *Contributions to Operations Research and Economics*, Proceedings of the CORE XXth Anniversary Symposium. Cambridge, Mass.: MIT Press.

Geweke, J. (1989), 'Bayesian Inference in Econometric Models Using Monte Carlo Integration', *Econometrica*, 57: 1317–39.

Haussman, J. (1978), 'Specification Tests in Econometrics', *Econometrica*, 46: 1251–71.

Hendry, D. F., and Mizon, G. E. (1993), 'Evaluating Dynamic Econometric Models by Encompassing the VAR', in P. C. B. Phillips (ed.), *Models, Methods and Applications of Econometrics*. Oxford: Basil Blackwell.

—— and Richard, J. F. (1982), 'On the Formulation of Empirical Models in Dynamic Econometrics', *Journal of Econometrics*, 20: 3–33.

Johansen, S. (1988), 'Statistical Analysis of Cointegration Vectors', *Journal of Economic Dynamics and Control*, 12: 231–54.

—— (1991), 'Estimation and Hypothesis Testing of Cointegration Vectors in Gaussian Autoregressive Models', *Econometrica*, 59: 1551–80.

—— and Juselius, K. (1992), 'Identification of the Long Run and Short Run Structure: an Application to the ISLM Model', mimeo, Copenhagen.

Kleibergen, F., and van Dijk, H. K. (1994), 'On the Shape of the Likelihood/Posterior in Cointegration Models', *Econometric Theory*, 10(3–4), 514–51.

Kloek, T., and van Dijk, H. K. (1978), 'Bayesian Estimates of Equation Systems Parameters: an Application of Integration by Monte Carlo', *Econometrica*, 46: 1–19.

Laroque, G., and Salanie, B. (1989), 'Estimation of Multimarket Fix-Price Models: an Application of Pseudo Maximum Likelihood Methods', *Econometrica*, 57: 831–60.

Leamer, E. (1978), *Specification Searches: Ad Hoc Inference with non Experimental Data*. New York: John Wiley.

Lindley, D. (1971), *Bayesian Statistics: a Review*. Philadelphia: SIAM.

Lubrano, M. (1985), 'Bayesian Analysis of Switching Regression Models', *Journal of Econometrics*, 29: 69–95.

—— (1995), 'Testing for Unit Roots in a Bayesian Framework', *Journal of Econometrics*, 69: 81–109.

—— (1992), 'Bayesian Tests for Single Equation Cointegration in the Case of Structural Breaks', UCSD Discussion Paper, 92–10.

Perron, P. (1991*a*), 'A Continuous Time Approximation to the Unstable First-Order Autoregressive Process: the Case without an Intercept', *Econometrica*, 59, 211–36.

—— (1991*b*), 'A Continuous Time Approximation to the Stationary First-Order Autoregressive Model'. *Econometric Theory*, 7, 236–52.

Phillips, P. C. B. (1991), 'To Criticize the Critics: an Objective Bayesian Analysis of Stochastic Trends', *Journal of Applied Econometrics*, 6: 333–64.

—— (1994), 'Some Exact Distribution Theory for Maximum Likelihood Estimators of Cointegrating Coefficients in Error Correction Models', *Econometrica*, 62: 73–94.

Richard, J. F. (1973), *Posterior and Predictive Densities for Simultaneous Equation Models*. Berlin: Springer-Verlag.

—— and Tompa, H. (1980), 'On the Evaluation of Poly-*t* Density Functions', *Journal of Econometrics*, 12: 335–51.

Rothenberg, T. (1963), 'A Bayesian Analysis of Simultaneous Equation Systems', Econometric Institute Report, no. 6315, Erasmus University, Rotterdam.

Schotman, P. C., and van Dijk, H. K. (1991), 'A Bayesian Analysis of the Unit Root in Real Exchange Rates', *Journal of Econometrics*, 49: 195–238.

―――― (1993), 'Posterior Analysis of Possibly. Integrated Time Series with an Application to Real GNP', in P. Caines, J. Geweke, and M. Taggu (eds.), *New Directions in Time Series Analysis*, IMA Volume in Mathematics and its Applications. Berlin: Springer Verlag.

Sims, C., and Uhlig, H. (1991), 'Understanding Unit Rooters: a Helicopter Tour', *Econometrica*, 59: 1591–9.

Steel, M. (1987), 'A Bayesian Analysis of Multivariate Exogeneity: a Monte Carlo Approach', Unpublished Ph.D. dissertation. CORE, Louvain-la-Neuve.

Tierney, L. (1994), 'Markov Chains for Exploring Posterior Distributions (with discussion)', *Annals of Statistics*, 22: 1701–62.

van Dijk, H. K. (1984), 'Posterior Analysis of Econometric Models Using Monte Carlo Integration', unpublished Ph.D. dissertation, Erasmus University, Rotterdam.

Zellner, A. (1971), *An Introduction to Bayesian Inference in Econometrics*. New York: John Wiley.

―――― Bauwens, L., and van Dijk, H. K. (1988), 'Bayesian Specification Analysis and Estimation of Simultaneous Equation Models using Monte Carlo Methods', *Journal of Econometrics*, 38: 39–72.

Zivot, E. (1992), 'A Bayesian Analysis of the Unit Root Hypothesis within an Unobserved Components Model', Working Paper, Wellesley College.

14

Microeconometrics: The Large Data Set Revolution

Richard Blundell

14.1. Overview

The need for familiarity with microeconometric techniques in applied economics has arisen as a result of the increasing use of large individual-level data sources in the analysis of economic behaviour. This reflects not only the growing availability of such data, but also our increasing ability, as applied economists, to utilize micro-level data sources effectively on microcomputers. Whether it be the study of household behaviour or the study of firms' behaviour, analysis based at the 'individual' level is persuasive. It avoids the problem of aggregation bias and also identifies the factors that lead to a different distribution and usage of resources across households and firms. However, in microeconometrics distinct issues relating to endogenous selection, censoring, and individual heterogeneity have to be faced. Indeed, it may often be difficult to draw useful inferences from cross-section data alone, especially where history-dependence or state-dependence is important. Longitudinal data or panel data, which follow individual economic agents through time, can be utilized so as to avoid some of these drawbacks. In addition, panel data combine the attractive features of time-series analysis with individual-level behaviour.

There seem to be at least five distinct developments in microeconometrics that are likely to shape the way in which routine empirical analysis will be conducted in the future. The first is the use of non-parametric techniques to describe economic relationships. The second is the use of 'difference of differences' estimation, especially in relation to the analysis of natural experiments. The third is the semi-parametric analysis of sample selection models or, more generally, models that combine discrete and continuous variables. Fourth, there are the developments of efficient estimation methods for panel data models, which allow for correlated heterogeneity and predetermined regressors that have arisen out of the poor performance of the 'standard' GMM estimators in economic panel data. Finally, there is the estimation of nonlinear discrete data models on panel data that allow for correlated heterogeneity and predetermined regressors.

Many standard microeconometric estimators are typically not robust to changes in what may be termed 'incidental' assumptions. For example, a normal distribution for preference errors and measurement errors may not be central to the economic hypothesis under investigation, but may well be critical for consistent estimation of its parameters using commonly available econometric techniques. In general, since many microeconometric models are rendered necessarily nonlinear through selectivity or censoring, stochastic assumptions become critically important. As a result, the focus of many recent developments in microeconometrics has been on weakening the reliance on parametric distributions and on utilizing semi- or non-parametric estimators (see e.g. Heckman 1990; Horowitz 1993; Manski 1975, 1989, 1990; Newey *et al.* 1990; Powell 1994). These developments are important, but they have not yet become common practice in applied econometrics. There does now exist a well developed battery of easily implementable diagnostic tests which will provide some indication of model reliability (see e.g. Blundell 1987, and Davidson and MacKinnon 1993).

The past ten years have shown how microeconometric models are fragile to changes in 'non-vital' parts of specification. The next ten years will see the application and introduction of more robust methods based on very large data sets. Accurate inference on individual data requires large data sets. Individual behaviour at the household or firm level is most often dominated by unobserved heterogeneity, and drawing inferences on the impact of variables of economic policy interest requires the careful analysis of large samples. What is presented here is a personal and relatively non-technical view of the five new developments mentioned above with an eye on empirical application.

14.2. Non-parametric Data Analysis

The obsession with linearity in empirical economic analysis clearly does not stem from any strong prior of economic theory. Non-parametric regression analysis seems to provide a compelling alternative to linear regression, allowing the data to determine the 'local' shape of the conditional mean relationship (see Blundell and Duncan 1998). Suppose the relationship of interest is given by

$$y = g(x) + \varepsilon, \tag{1}$$

where ε is defined such that $E(\varepsilon \mid x) = 0$. For example, in Engel curve analysis y would represent the expenditure or expenditure share on some good or group of goods and x would represent total disposable income or the total budget.

Engel curve analysis provides a particularly useful illustration of the advantages of non-parametric regression and will be used as a running illustration throughout this section. It has been at the centre of applied microeconomic research since the early studies of Working (1943) and Leser (1963) uncovered the stability of the expenditure share–log income specification for food expenditures. Recently attention has focused on Engel curves, which have a greater variety of curvature than is permitted by the Working–Leser form underlying the translog and 'almost ideal' models of Jorgenson *et al.* (1975; see also Jorgenson and Lau 1975) and Deaton and Muellbauer (1980a, b), respectively. This reflects growing evidence from a series of empirical studies suggesting that quadratic logarithmic income terms are required for certain expenditure share equations (see e.g. Atkinson et al. 1990; Banks, Blundell and Lewbel 1997); Bierens and Pott-Buter 1990; Härdle and Jerison 1988; Lewbel 1991; and Blundell et al. 1993). Non-parametric regression analysis avoids the imposition of any parametric assumptions on the conditional mean function $g(x)$. It can be used in a graphical or a classical hypothesis-testing framework to evaluate a particular parametric form.

Typically, x is univariate, as in the Engel curve example, although higher-order relationships are easily estimated using standard non-parametric regression techniques. Clearly, in order to use a data-driven method for the determination of the local shape of $g(x)$, there must be sufficient density of x. In sparse regions of the x density, prior assumptions on $g(x)$ are inevitable. Moreover, as I will document below, introducing measurement error or endogeneity in x is not straightforward and explains the continuing use of parametric forms for $g(x)$ in simultaneous or measurement error systems.

14.2.1. KERNEL ESTIMATION

The emphasis in this section will be on kernel regression, although nearest-neighbour, series, and spline techniques are now all commonly available alternative techniques (see Härdle 1990 for a comprehensive review). The aim of kernel regression will be to replace $g(x)$ by a local estimator of the conditional mean,

$$E(y|x) = \int yf(y|x)\mathrm{d}y, \tag{2}$$

where $f(y|x)$ is the conditional density of y. Noting that $f(y|x) = f(x, y)/f(x)$ and $f(x) = \int f(y, x)\mathrm{d}y$, we can rewrite (2) as

$$E(y|x) = \frac{\int yf(y, x)\mathrm{d}y}{\int f(y, x)\mathrm{d}y}, \tag{3}$$

and the objective will be to replace the numerator and denominator in (3) with estimators based on locally weighted averages.

The denominator in (3) is simply $f(x)$ and the kernel density estimator is given by

$$\hat{f}(x) = \frac{1}{nh}\sum_{j=1}^{n}K((x_j - x)/h), \tag{4}$$

where $K((x_j - x)/h)$ is the kernel function evaluated at x and h is the bandwidth or smoothing parameter. Typical choices for the kernel function include the Gaussian, in which $K(\kappa) = \sqrt{2\pi}\exp(-\kappa^2/2)$, and the Epanechnikov, in which $K(\kappa) = 3/4(1 - \kappa^2)^2 I(|\kappa| \leq 1)$ where $I(\cdot)$ is the unit indicator function. Notice that the Epanechnikov kernel truncates the points local to x when calculating $\hat{g}(x)$

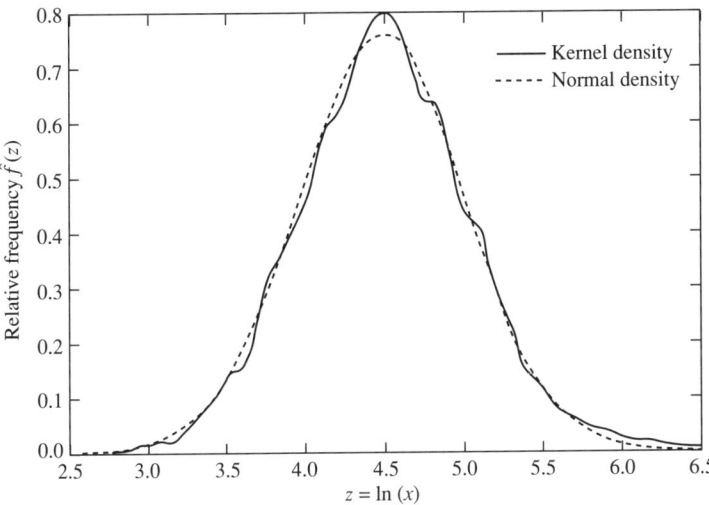

Fig. 14.1. The Normality of Log Expenditure

whereas the normal kernel uses all observations in the calculation of the conditional mean at each point. As a consequence, it is common to truncate the normal kernel so as to reduce the computational burden. In each case the kernel function is symmetric, is continuously differentiable, and integrates to unity. A useful discussion of other kernel functions is given in Härdle and Linton (1995).

For an illustration of kernel density estimation, we can turn to the total budget variable in our Engel curve analysis. This is typically transformed by the log transformation as total outlay is often supposed to have a normal cross-section distribution. To illustrate the power of the kernel method, Fig. 14.1 presents the (Gaussian) kernel density estimation using a group of around 1,000 households from the UK Family Expenditure Survey (FES). These are married couples with no children, so as to keep a reasonable degree of homogeneity in the demographic structure. The results are striking. It is difficult to distinguish the non-parametric density from the fitted normal curve which is also shown. This 'graphical' method of assessing the parametric specification seems particularly appealing and will be developed further below. Statistics based on a goodness-of-fit measure are also now available and will be discussed below.

By analogy with (4), the kernel estimator of (3) is

$$\hat{g}(x) = \frac{1}{nh} \frac{\sum_{j=1}^{n} y_j K((x_j - x)/h)}{\hat{f}(x)}. \tag{5}$$

Figs. 14.2 and 14.3 present kernel regressions for the Engel curves of two commodity groups in the FES. Although the linear logarithmic formulation appears

R. Blundell

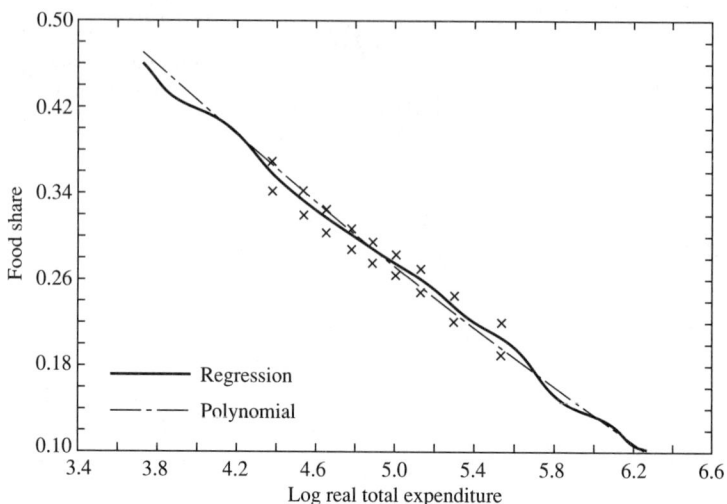

Fig. 14.2. Engel Curves for Food, Married Couples Only, 1980–1982

Source: Banks *et al.* (1997)

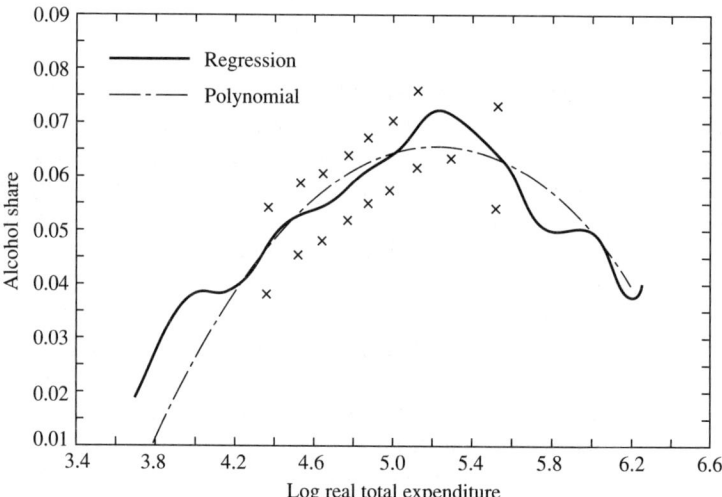

Fig. 14.3. Engel Curves for Alcohol, Married Couples Only, 1980–1982

Source: Banks *et al.* (1997)

to provide a reasonable approximation for the food share curve, for alcohol distinct nonlinear behaviour is evident. These pictures are drawn from the Banks *et al.* (1997) study, which presents kernel regressions that indicate stability in the overall patterns across time.

14.2.2. CHOICE OF BANDWIDTH

Choice of bandwidth parameter h is clearly not independent of the kernel function chosen; however, the relationship between bandwidths in each case is proportional, and a useful list of bandwidth 'exchange rates' is given in the Härdle–Linton (1995) paper. The most popular method for choosing the bandwidth parameter minimizes an approximation to the mean integrated squared error (MISE) using a cross-validation statistic. This statistic is simply the following weighted sum of squared deviations of y_j from its conditional mean seen as a function of h:

$$CV(h) = \frac{1}{n} \sum_{j=1}^{n} w(x_j)[y_j - \hat{g}_{h,j}(x_j)]^2. \tag{6}$$

The conditional mean $\hat{g}_{h,j}(x_j) = n^{-1} \sum_{i \neq j} w_{hi}(x_j)$, however, is calculated by leaving out the jth observation.

The CV method involves a costly computation, and certain rules of thumb can be used to come pretty close to the cross-validated choice of h. If the density of x is truly normal, for example, then the optimal MISE choice for h in estimating the density $f(x)$ is given by $1.06\sigma_x n^{-1/5}$ (see Silverman 1986). This does not translate directly to the regression function, but, as we will see below in the kernel regression example, the method of choosing a bandwidth that is proportional to $\sigma_x n^{-1/5}$ often provides a useful rule of thumb. The overall shape of Figs. 14.2 and 14.3 is little effected by variations in the choice of kernel or smoothing parameter. Fig. 14.4 investigates the sensitivity of the alcohol Engel curve to variations in the bandwidth.

An attractive addition to this method of choosing the bandwidth is to allow the bandwidth to vary with the density of x. In the application below, this is shown to smooth out 'wiggles' very effectively in areas where the density of x is sparse. If we let

$$\lambda_i = \left(\frac{\hat{f}(x_i)}{\eta} \right)^{-\rho}, \quad 0 \leq \rho \leq 1,$$

with the normalization factor η given by

$$\ln \eta = \frac{\sum_j \ln f(x_j)}{n},$$

then the *adaptive kernel* estimator takes the form

R. Blundell

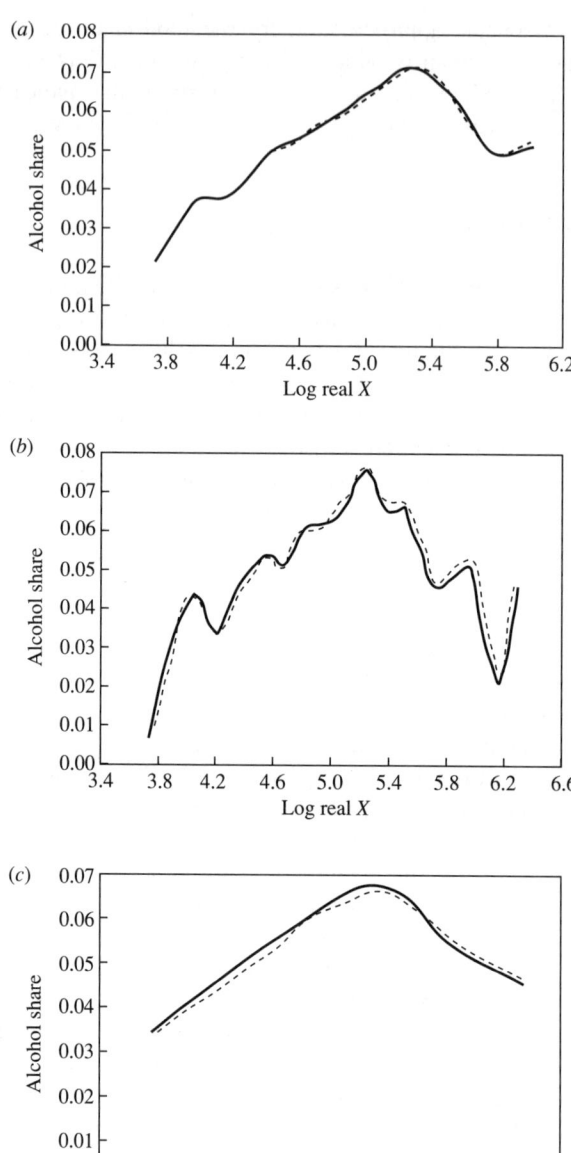

Fig. 14.4. 'Bandwidth' Sensitivity: Alcohol Share Engel Curve Gaussion Kernel regression

Based on Family Expenditure Survey 1980–1982
(*a*) CV $h(0.1057)$
(*b*) 'Small' $h(0.0708)$; $p = 0.6$
(*c*) 'Large' $h(0.2361)$; $p = 2.0$
$h = 1.06\sigma n^{-1/5} = 0.1245$

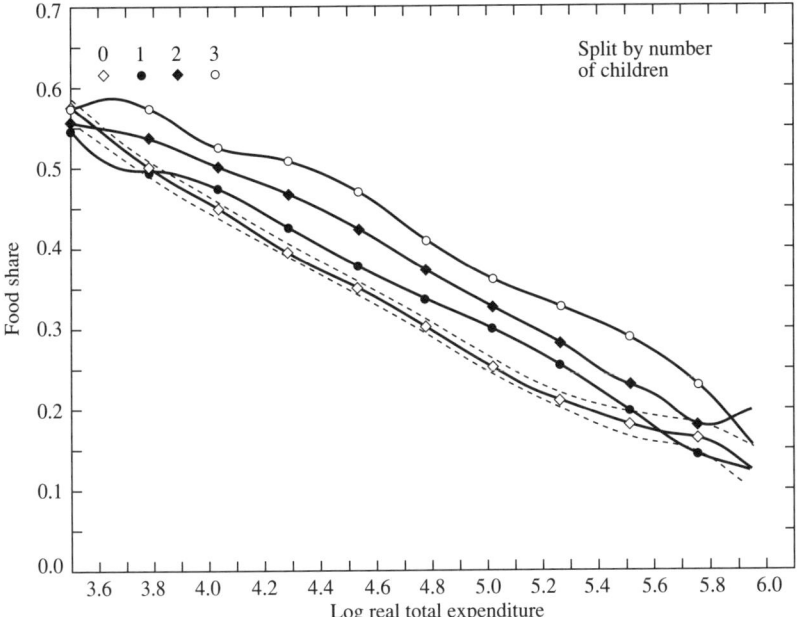

Fig. 14.5. Shifts in Engel Curves for Food

$$\hat{f}^A(x) = \frac{1}{n}\sum_{j=1}^{n}\frac{1}{h\lambda_j}K((x_j - x)/\lambda_j h) \tag{7}$$

for the density estimator with a corresponding form for the conditional mean.

Figs. 14.5 and 14.6 give an example of the usefulness of the adaptive kernel. Fig. 14.5 presents the kernel regression lines for the food Engel curve across four different household types split according to the number of children. Fig. 14.6 is the same but with the adaptive kernel. Notice how the 'wiggles' in the Engel curves that appear at the edges of the x distribution are essentially ironed out by adaptive estimation.

14.2.3. INFERENCE IN NON-PARAMETRIC REGRESSION

Inference in non-parametric regression can take place in a number of ways. Perhaps the most obvious, and the one at the frontier of current research activity, is to use the non-parametric regression to test a parametric null. Recent work by Ait-Sahalia *et al.* (1994) is particularly notable. Letting $\hat{g}(x_i)$ be the non-parametric estimate of the regression curve and $\delta(x_i, \hat{\beta})$ some parametric estimate, they derive $\sqrt{n}$ asymptotically normal statistics for this comparison based on a simple squared error goodness-of-fit statistic,

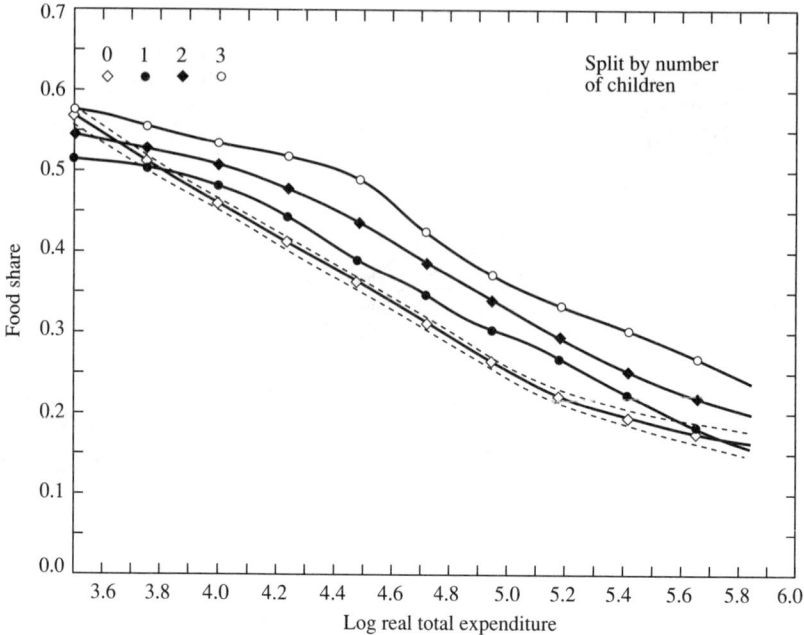

Fig. 14.6. Adaptive Kernel Technique

$$\hat{\Gamma} = \frac{1}{n} \sum_{i=1}^{n} [\hat{g}(x_i) - \delta(x_i, \beta)]^2 w(\hat{f}(x_i)), \tag{8}$$

a linear transformation of which is shown to have a limiting normal distribution with mean zero and estimable variance. In the empirical analysis that follows, I take a more graphical approach to inference. As non-parametric regression analysis is a largely graphical method, this seems an appropriate method of drawing inferences.

To do this, we need to be able to place a confidence band around the estimated regression curve. A simple way to do this is to choose k fixed points in the x distribution—say the decile points. If we denote $\sigma^2(x)$ as the conditional variance of x, then under certain regularity conditions (see Härdle 1990), the ratio statistic

$$\left\{ (nh)^{1/2} \left(\frac{\hat{g}_h(x_j) - g_h(x_j)}{\sigma^2(x) c_K / f(x_j)^{1/2}} \right) \right\}_{j=1}^{k} \rightarrow^{L} N(b, 1), \tag{9}$$

where c_K is a kernel-specific constant ($= \int K^2(u)\,du$) and b is a non-disappearing bias. Ignoring this bias, we can use this result to place pointwise confidence intervals around the estimated non-parametric regression curve.

As an illustration, it is interesting to focus on a comparison of the non-parametric metric Engel curve estimates in Figs. 14.2 and 14.3 with the simple second-order polynomial fit given by the dashed line in those figures. Some guide to the reliability of this approximation can be drawn from the pointwise confidence intervals (evaluated at the second to ninth decile points) also shown in the

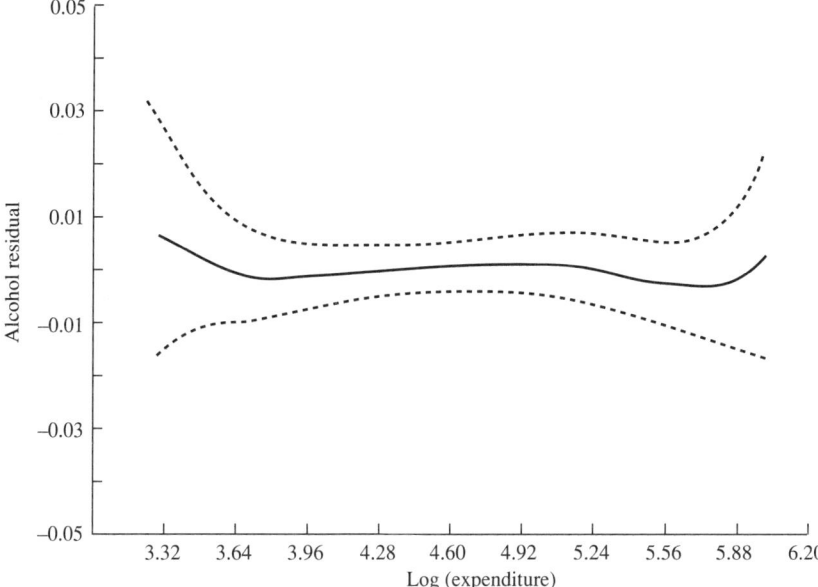

Fig. 14.7. Quadratic Specification

figures. It is only where the data are sparse and the confidence bands relatively wide that the paths diverge.

This can be examined more closely by a residual based analysis. In Fig. 14.7 a non-parametric regression curve is presented between the residuals from the parametric quadratic regression curve and the log total expenditure—the x_i variable in the above kernel regressions. A well specified parametric model should display a line through zero. This is seen to be pretty much the case for our quadratic logarithmic Engel curve for alcohol shares.

It will often be useful to consider extensions of (1) that include a parametric part. In the Engel curve analysis below it may be useful to add a set of demographic characteristics to the conditional mean specification. For example, we may wish to estimate

$$y = g(x) + z'\gamma + \varepsilon \tag{10}$$

in which $z'\gamma$ represents a linear index in terms of observable regressors z and unknown parameters γ. This model is typically labelled *semi-parametric* and it is often the case that γ is the parameter of interest and an estimator of γ is required that is robust to a general form for $g(x)$. Following Robinson (1988), a simple transformation of the model can be used to yield an estimator for γ. Taking expectations of (10) conditional on x and subtracting from (10) yields

$$y - E(y|x) = (z - E(z|x))'\gamma + \varepsilon. \tag{11}$$

Replacing $E(y|x)$ and $E(z|x)$ by their non-parametric counterparts yields a simple $\sqrt{n}$ consistent least squares estimator for γ. Blundell, Duncan and Pendakur

(1998) give a comprehensive review of alternative methods of introducing demographic variables in the semiparametric analysis of consumer demand.

14.3. Difference in Differences and Natural Experiments

The 'difference in differences' approach has gained considerable popularity recently and its simplicity will probably make its popularity enduring among empirical economists. It is most usefully applied when there is a specific regressor that relates directly to a policy instrument of interest, for example a tax rate, a training programme, a minimum wage regulation, or a host of other policy variables of direct interest. The idea is to use repeated data, either from a cross-section or a panel, and to compare (at least) two groups, one of which has experienced a specific policy change while the other has experienced a similar environment but with no change in the policy variable. The comparison group is essentially supposed to mimic a control group in experimental terminology.

By aggregating over individuals in each group and comparing group means, issues relating to individual heterogeneity can be effectively removed while separation of the change in the regressor of interest from other contemporaneous changes in the economic and social environment can be abstracted from by use of the comparison group. It should be clear that the relationship of 'difference of differences' estimation and the use of natural experiments is very close indeed. The requirements for consistent estimation of the parameter of interest in each case are identical.

Although attractive, the 'difference in differences' approach relies on strong assumptions.[1] These relate in an obvious fashion to the correlation of unobservables with the policy change of interest. To see the issues involved, consider the regression model

$$y_{it} = \alpha + \beta x_{it} + \zeta_{it} + k_i m_t. \tag{12}$$

In (12), $E(\zeta_{it} | x_{it}) \neq 0$ and $k_i m_t$, is the effect of a *common* (taste or productivity) shock in period t as it affects the ith individual. Suppose a discrete grouping variable G_{it} is available such that $E(\zeta_{it} | G_{it} = S, t = \tau) = a(S)$, which is fixed over time, and $E(k_i m_t | G_{it} = S, t = \tau) = m_\tau$. Suppose G_{it} is just a binary indicator. Then the 'difference of differences' estimator is analogous to a simple extension of the Wald estimator with observations before and after a policy reform:

$$\tilde{\beta} = \frac{\Delta \bar{y}_t^C - \Delta \bar{y}_t^T}{\Delta \bar{x}_t^C - \Delta \bar{x}_t^T}, \tag{13}$$

where Δ is the difference operator, and $\Delta \bar{y}_t^I$ denotes the change in average y_{it} for each group $I (I = T, C)$.

The averaging over individuals eliminates all idiosyncratic heterogeneity apart from a group-specific effect, the differences over time eliminate the group-specific effect, and the differences across groups eliminate the effect of

---

[1] See Blundell, Duncan, and Meghir (1998) for a detailed analysis of the assumptions underlying the difference in differences approach.

common shocks. The basic assumption underlying this estimator is that the sample we are considering is not endogenously selected, or at least the factors affecting selection into the sample are constant over time and have the same effect over time. Moreover, a grouping instrument is required with the property described above.[2] Essentially, this instrument splits up the sample into a 'control group' and a 'treatment group'. (See Heckman and Robb (1985) for a detailed description of these issues.) Angrist (1991) discusses the use of optimally weighted Wald estimators and their relationship to instrumental variable estimators and applies them to the analysis of labour supply using US data.

This type of estimator was used recently by Eissa (1994) to evaluate the effects of the US 1986 tax reform on married women's labour supply. In her study she used as a treatment group (T) the women in the 99th percentile of the income distribution and for the control group (C) the women in the 75th percentile of the income distribution.

To see the issues involved, consider the labour supply and tax reform model above where for notational simplicity we have removed the 'other income' term,

$$h_{it} = \alpha + \beta \ln w_{it} + \zeta_{it} + k_i m_t, \tag{15}$$

where h_{it} is hours of work, and w_{it} the marginal wage rate. In (15) $E(\zeta_{it}|\ln w_{it}) \neq 0$, and $k_i m_t$ is the effect of a *common* (taste) shock in period t as it affects the ith individual. The difference in differences estimator, with observations before and after a reform, is given by

$$\tilde{\beta} = \frac{\Delta \bar{h}_t^C - \Delta \bar{h}_t^T}{\Delta \ln \bar{w}_t^C - \Delta \ln \bar{w}_t^T}, \tag{16}$$

where Δ is the difference operator and $\Delta \bar{h}_t^I$ denotes the change in average hours of work for group $I(I = T, C)$.

In the context of tax reform, we would like to compare the relative experiences of taxpayers affected by the reforms and non-taxpayers, who are not. The underlying difficulty with this is that taxpayer status is itself endogenous. This is a problem of self-selection which has to be dealt with in conjunction with self-selection into employment. In the absence of time effects, we can group across taxpayers and non-taxpayers, thus controlling for endogenous taxpayer status. Ignoring this problem can induce large biases. An illustration of these biases is given in the Blundell *et al.* (1998) paper. Table 14.1 gives the results of the 'difference of differences' estimator using taxpayer *v.* non-taxpayer groups in the UK over the 1980s. The strongly negative coefficient is easily explained by the growing number of newly working women paying tax and working just a little above the tax threshold. This changes the composition of the taxpaying group before and after the reform. The mean of hours in the taxpaying group actually falls.

---

[2] Identification also requires that

$$E(\Delta x_{it}|G_{it} = C, t = \tau) - E(\Delta x_{it}|G_{it} = T, t = \tau) \neq 0, \tag{14}$$

i.e. that the change in the average x for the 'treatment' and 'control' groups are different.

R. Blundell

Table 14.1. Difference of Differences' Estimator, No Correction for Selection

Wage elasticities of labour supply at the mean

Women with children		No children	
No income effect	Income effect	No income effect	Income effect
−0.39	−0.40	−0.50	−0.49
(0.031)	(0.036)	(0.034)	(0.040)

To correct for these composition effects in the presence of time effects, Blundell *et al.* (1998) exploit the differential growth of wages and participation (and other income) between different education and date-of-birth (cohort) groups in the UK. The fastest increases in the returns to education, for example, have been found among younger cohorts as the labour demand for skilled workers has increased and that for less skilled workers has declined markedly (see Gosling *et al.*, 1994). Hence the proportion of high-wage individuals has been increasing faster among the group of educated individuals, which (as a result) contains an increasing proportion of taxpayers relative to the other groups. Assuming that the effect of education and age on preferences is stable over time provides sufficient restriction to identify the model using this information. The basic idea is to compare the relative experiences of these different groups over time and to see whether the different time path of their after-tax wages has led to a different time path of hours of work. The results, given in Table 14.2, are striking. All

Table 14.2. Labour Supply Elasticities at the Mean, with Correction for Self-Selection[a]

Group	Uncompensated		Compensated income			
	wage		wage			
(a) Without time effects						
Child aged 0–2	0.127	(0.048)	0.167	(0.062)	−0.061	(0.044)
Child aged 3–5	0.206	(0.057)	0.253	(0.064)	−0.098	(0.044)
Child aged 5–10	0.093	(0.040)	0.104	(0.052)	−0.022	(0.043)
Child aged 11+	0.094	(0.033)	0.137	(0.047)	−0.072	(0.034)
No children	0.095	(0.018)	0.112	(0.028)	−0.014	(0.015)
(b) With time effects						
Child aged 0–2	0.022	(0.055)	0.063	(0.068)	−0.064	(0.043)
Child aged 3–5	0.095	(0.061)	0.144	(0.068)	−0.101	(0.044)
Child aged 5–10	−0.044	(0.045)	0.008	(0.056)	−0.024	(0.043)
Child aged 11+	0.012	(0.038)	0.056	(0.051)	−0.073	(0.034)
No children	0.031	(0.023)	0.050	(0.032)	−0.014	(0.015)

[a] Standard errors in parentheses.

compensated labour supply elasticities are now positive, effectively reversing the implausible 'difference in differences' results.

14.4. Discrete Data and Self-Selection

Microeconomic data very often display a mixture of continuous and discrete properties. Hours of work, for example, summarize the continuous supply of hours and discrete participation. Investment decisions require a discrete location choice and a continuous level of expenditure at the chosen location. In general, econometric models for this type of data can be best summarized through the definition of two latent processes that generate the continuous and discrete components of observed process through a simple nonlinear observation rule. Typically, the underlying processes are assumed to have a (linear) parametric conditional mean, so that we can write

$$y_{1i}^* = \beta_1' x_{1i} + u_{1i} \tag{17}$$

and

$$y_{2i}^* = \beta_2' x_{2i} + u_{2i}, \tag{18}$$

with an observation rule given by

$$y_{1i} = g(y_{1i}^*, y_{2i}^*). \tag{19}$$

The categorization of the standard models is now straightforward. The simple probit or logit models of discrete choice have

$$y_{1i} = 1(y_{1i}^* > 0), \tag{20}$$

where $1(\cdot)$ is the unit indicator function. In these models u_{1i} has a standard normal or logistic distribution. Semi-parametric extensions described below maintain the 'linear index' formulation but relax the distributional assumptions on u_{1i}. The linear index assumption restricts the distribution of u_{1i} to depend on x_{1i} only through the linear index $\beta_1' x_{1i}$.

The Tobit model makes use of the continuous information on y_{1i} but keeps to the univariate formulation, so that the observation rule becomes

$$y_{1i} = y_{1i}^* 1(y_{1i}^* > 0) \tag{21}$$

and $u_{1i} \sim N(0, \sigma_1^2)$. Clearly, it allows the scale parameter σ_1^2 to be identified, but at the cost of observing y_{1i}^* when it is positive.

The restriction between the discrete and continuous components in the Tobit model make it particularly attractive for semi-parametric estimation but also make it less reasonable for many economic applications. The selectivity model (see Heckman 1979, 1990) relaxes this restriction, so that

$$y_{1i} = y_{1i}^* 1(y_{2i}^* > 0), \tag{22}$$

in which u_{1i} and u_{2i} are assumed normally distributed with correlation ρ and unit variance for u_{1i}. An alternative two-index characterization of the censored data model is given by the double-hurdle specification (see Cragg 1971), in which

$$y_{1i} = y_{1i}^* 1(y_{1i}^* > (0), y_{2i}^* > 0), \tag{23}$$

so that to obtain continuous observations on y_{1i} two hurdles need to be passed. For example, to obtain employment a reservation wage condition needs to be passed and an acceptable job offer has to be found (as in Blundell *et al.* 1987).

The aim of semi-parametric analysis in this area has been to maintain the linear index assumption and relax the distributional assumptions on u_{1i} and u_{2i}. The linear index assumption typically means that $\sqrt{n}$ consistent estimators for β_1 and β_2 can be found. Many of these estimators exploit the structure of the likelihood of each of these models, so it is worth writing down the form of the likelihood in each case.

For an independently drawn random sample,[3] the discrete choice model has a likelihood of the from

$$L_P(\beta_1, \theta) = \prod_{i=1}^{n} [F(\beta_1' x_{1i} \mid x_{1i}, \theta)]^{D_{1i}} [1 - F(\beta_1' x_{1i} \mid x_{1i}, \theta)]^{1-D_{1i}}, \tag{24}$$

where $F(\beta_1' x_{1i} \mid x_{1i}, \theta) = \Pr[y_{1i}^* > 0 \mid x_{1i}, \theta]$, θ are the parameters on which the of u_{1i} depends and $D_{1i} = 1(y_{1i}^* > 0)$. In the normal i.i.d. model $\theta = \sigma_1^2$, β_1 and since β_1 is estimated only up to scale, the presence of θ can be ignored by normalizing $\sigma_1^2 = 1$.

For our discussion of the semi-parametric estimation of this model, it will be useful to note that

$$E(D_{1i} \mid x_{1i}, \theta) = F_1(\beta_1' x_{1i} \mid x_{1i}, \theta),$$

so that it will be natural to replace $F_1(\cdot)$ by the non-parametric estimator of the conditional mean of D_{1i} given the linear index $\beta_1' x_{1i}$.

In general, incorrect specification of F or the mean function $\beta_1' x_{1i}$ will cause the maximum likelihood estimators of β_1 and θ to be inconsistent (see e.g. Amemiya 1985 and Ruud 1983 for some exceptions). This result provides a strong motivation for non-parametric and semi-parametric estimation.

The Tobit model identifies the scale of y_{1i}^* and has likelihood

$$L_T = \prod_{i=1}^{n} [f_1(\beta_1' x_{1i}, \sigma_1^2)]^{D_{1i}} \left[1 - F_1\left(\frac{\beta_1' x_{1i}}{\sigma_1}\right) \right]^{1-D_{1i}}, \tag{25}$$

[3] Exogenous statification, that is where the design is conditioned on the x variates, does not alter any of the discussion below (see e.g. Pudney 1989). Even for choice-based samples, an appropriately weighted adaption of the estimators can achieve $\sqrt{n}$ consistency.

where $f_1(\beta_1' x_{1i}, \sigma_1^2)$ is the density of y_{1i}^* evaluated at conditional mean $\beta_1' x_{1i}$ with variance σ_1^2. For generalizations of the normal distribution, $f_1(\cdot)$ will depend on additional moments or parameters of the distribution, and so, strictly speaking, the likelihood, the density f_1, and the distribution function F_1 should depend on θ as in the discrete choice likelihood (24).

The selectivity model has the likelihood

$$L_S = \prod_{i=1}^{n} [f_{12}(\beta_1' x_{1i}, \beta_2' x_{2i}, \sigma_1^2, \rho) F_2(\beta_2' x_{2i})]^{D_{2i}} [1 - F_2(\beta_2' x_{2i})]^{1-D_{2i}}, \quad (26)$$

where f_{12} is the conditional density function for y_{1i}^*, given y_{2i}^*, $D_{2i} = 1(y_{2i}^* > 0)$, and $F_2(\beta_2' x_{2i}) = E(D_{2i} | \beta_2' x_{2i})$. Notice that the discrete participation decision identifies β_2, which immediately gives rise to a two-step estimator in which the discrete choice estimator is used to estimate β_2, and a conditional (quasi-) likelihood method is used to estimate β_1, σ_1, and ρ. When $\rho = 0$, then the selectivity likelihood reduces to the product of a standard normal likelihood on $D_{2i} = 1$ and a discrete choice likelihood,

$$L_S^{\rho=0} = \prod_{i \in y_{2i}^* > 0} [f_1(\beta_1' x_{1i}, \sigma_1^2)]^{D_{2i}} \prod_{i=1}^{n} [F_2(\beta_2' x_{2i})]^{D_{2i}} [1 - F_2(\beta_2' x_{2i})]^{1-D_{2i}}, \quad (27)$$

in which case the least squares estimation of β_1 is $\sqrt{n}$ consistent and efficient.

The two-step estimator for the selectivity model is attributable, in the joint normal specification, to Heckman (1979). It is typically termed the Heckman estimator and lies behind most of the semi-parametric estimators for the selectivity model. To see its amenability to semi-parametric techniques, notice that the conditional mean of y_{1i}^*, given $\beta_1' x_{1i}$ and $y_{2i}^* > 0$, is

$$E(y_{1i}^* | \beta_1' x_{1i}, y_{2i}^* > 0) = \beta_1' x_{1i} + h(\beta_2' x_{2i}),$$

which, given $\beta_2' x_{2i}$, is precisely the form in the semi-parametric model (10). Given a first-round estimator for $\beta_2' x_{2i}$, estimation can follow the Robinson method described in Section 14.2. This will be outlined in more detail below, where series as well as kernel estimators are suggested for the non-parametric components.

In the joint normal model, the selectivity correction has a well known form:

$$h(\beta_2' x_{2i}) = \sigma_{12} \lambda_i,$$

where

$$\lambda_i = \frac{\phi(\beta_2' x_{2i})}{\Phi(\beta_2' x_{2i})} \quad (28)$$

is the ratio of standard normal density to distribution functions that enter the mean of a truncated normal (see e.g. Heckman 1979). The 'inverse Mills ratio' (28) provides a specific parametric representation of $h(\cdot)$ in terms of the linear index $\beta_2' x_{2i}$ and provides complete parametric identification of β_1 at the second step. In general, non-parametric identification will require independent variation in $\beta_2' x_{2i}$ over that in $\beta_1' x_{1i}$. This is achieved through an additional continuous variate in x_{2i}. Even then, identification of the intercept term in β_1 typically requires a limiting argument in which $\lim_{\beta_2' x_{2i} \to \infty} h(\beta_2' x_{2i}) \to 0$. Notice that the Tobit model assumption implies that

$$E(y_{1i}^* | \beta_1' x_{1i}, y_{1i}^* > 0) = \beta_1' x_{1i} + h(\beta_1' x_{1i}), \tag{29}$$

so that precisely the same index determines participation as determines the unconditional mean of y_{1i}^*, and non-parametric identification is more easily achieved.[4] In general, unless an additional variate can be found that determines participation but not the unconditional mean of y_{1i}^*, identification of the selectivity model is achieved purely from parametric functional form assumptions.

The final model for censored data considered here is the double-hurdle model. This can be seen as more straightforward generalization of the Tobit model, with likelihood

$$L_{DH} = \prod_{i=1}^{n} [f_{12}(\beta_1' x_{1i}, \beta_2' x_{2i}, \sigma_1^2, \rho) F_2(\beta_2' x_{2i})]^{D_{2i}}$$
$$\left[1 - F_{12}\left(\frac{\beta_1' x_{1i}}{\sigma_1}, \beta_2' x_{2i}, \rho\right) F_2(\beta_2' x_{2i})\right]^{1-D_{2i}}, \tag{30}$$

where $D_{2i} = 1(y_{1i}^* > 0, y_{2i}^* > 0)$. When $\rho = 0$, the two hurdles are independent and the double-hurdle likelihood reduces to

$$L_{DH}^{\rho=0} = \prod_{i=1}^{n} [f_1(\beta_1' x_{1i}, \sigma_1^2) F_2(\beta_2' x_{2i})]^{D_{2i}}$$
$$\left[1 - F_1\left(\frac{\beta_1' x_{1i}}{\sigma_1}\right) F_2(\beta_2' x_{2i})\right]^{1-D_{2i}}, \tag{31}$$

and when $F_2(\beta_2' x_{2i}) = 1$ for all i, then $L_{DH} = L_T$, the Tobit likelihood.

14.4.1. SEMI-PARAMETRIC ESTIMATION IN THE BINARY CHOICE MODEL

To begin the discussion, I will assume that we have the discrete binary choice framework with the linear index assumption, so that the probability of $y_{1i}^* > 0$ depends on x_{1i} solely through the linear index $\beta_1' x_{1i}$, so that $\Pr[y_{1i}^* > 0 | x_{1i}] = F_1(\beta_1' x_{1i})$. Suppose now that the index is known and define the scalar variable $z_i \equiv \beta_1' x_{1i}$. We can write

$$E(D_{1i} | z_i) = F_1(z_i), \tag{32}$$

so that $F_1(z)$ can be estimated by kernel regression methods of Section 14.2. This is essentially the proposal of Härdle and Stoker (1989), and is carefully discussed in the excellent lecture notes of Stoker (1991).

---

[4] The EM algorithm for the Tobit model is based around (29).

Estimation of β_1 first requires a discussion of identification. The linear index assumption is clearly important, but it is obvious that the intercept term in β_1 will not be identified and, as is the case in all binary choice models, β_1 is identifiable only up to scale. Identification has been investigated by Ichimura (1987), Klein and Spady (1993), and Manski (1988). Notice that the linear index assumption limits the form of heteroscedasticity. Quantile independence is an alternative assumption used by Manski (1985) to identify β_1 in the binary choice setup allowing arbitrary heteroscedasticity.

In the linear index case, Powell *et al.* (1989) develop the average derivative estimator based on an idea by Stoker (1986). Their suggestion is to use the following relationship for the density weighted average derivative:

$$\int f_x^2 \frac{\partial F_1(\beta_1' x_1)}{\partial x_1} \, dx = -2E\left[y_1 \frac{\partial f_x}{\partial x} \right],$$

replacing the unknown f_x with a kernel estimator. They show that this estimator of the derivative, which estimates the β_1 up to scale and sign, is $\sqrt{n}$ consistent and asymptotically normally distributed.

Ichimura (1987) suggested the direct replacement of $F_1(\beta_1' x_1)$ by a kernel estimator within a least squares algorithm for estimating β_1. This relaxes the assumption of continuously distributed x_1 which is required by the average derivative approach. The Ichimura estimator is simply

$$\hat{\beta}_1 = \arg\min_{\beta_1} \left[n^{-1} \sum_{i=1}^n (y_{1i} - \hat{F}_1^{(h)}(\beta_1' x_1))^2 \right], \tag{33}$$

where $\hat{F}_1^{(h)}(\beta_1' x_1)$ is the kernel estimator of $F_1(z_1)$ for bandwidth h. Ichimura also shows $\sqrt{n}$ consistency and asymptotic normality for $\hat{\beta}_1$. A related quasi-likelihood approach has been suggested by Klein and Spady (1993) in which β_1 is estimated by

$$\hat{\beta}_1 = \arg\min_{\beta_1} \left[-n^{-1} \sum_{i=1}^n \tau_i y_{1i} \ln \hat{F}_1(\beta_1' x_1) + (1 - y_{1i}) \ln(1 - \hat{F}_1(\beta_1' x_1)) \right], \tag{34}$$

where τ_i is a trimming function that downweights observations near the boundary of the support of $\beta_1' x_1$. Given β_1, the estimator for $\hat{F}_1(\beta_1' x_1)$ that Klein and Spady propose makes ingenious use the sample proportion of $y_{1i}^* > 0$ and the kernel density at $\beta_1' x_1$, rather than using the kernel regression estimator of the conditional mean of $y_{1i} | x_{1i}$. They show asymptotic normality and show that the outer product of gradients of the quasi-likelihood is a consistent estimator of the variance–covariance matrix.

Under quantile independence, Manski (1975, 1985) has developed a maximum score estimator which essentially chooses the β_1 that maximizes the prediction of $y_{1i} = 1$ when $\beta_1' x_1 \geq 0$. It is given by

$$\arg\max_{\beta_1}\left[n^{-1}\sum_{i=1}^{n}(2D_{1i}-1)1(\beta_1'x_1\geq 0)\right].$$

$\sqrt{n}$ consistency is not possible under quantile independence, and this estimator converges in distribution at a rate $n^{-1/3}$. Manski and Thompson (1986) propose the use of a bootstrap estimator for the standard errors. However, Horowitz (1992) shows that smoothing the score function can considerably improve the behaviour of this estimator, although he still recommends the use of the bootstrap.

The important work of Matzkin (1992) considers the identification of the binary choice model without the finite parameter or linear index assumption on $E(y_{1i}^*|x_{1i})$. Further details of this and the other estimators are given in the excellent surveys by Horowitz (1993) and Powell (1994).

14.4.2. SEMI-PARAMETRIC ESTIMATION IN THE TOBIT MODEL

The Tobit model is particularly open to semi-parametric estimation since the rule for observing $y_{1i}^* > 0$ is identical to the rule that generates y_{1i}^* itself. If this is taken together with a symmetry assumption on the distribution of the unobservables, then a simple symmetric trimming estimator proposed by Powell (1986a) can be used to estimate β_1 consistently, although a strong assumption of symmetry, it should be pointed out, allows for heteroscedasticity. If we write the Tobit model as

$$y_{1i}^* = x_{1i}'\beta_1 + u_{1i},$$

with

$$y_{1i} = y_{1i}^* 1(y_{1i}^* > 0),$$

then the observable model can be expressed

$$y_{1i} = x_{1i}'\beta_1 + u_{1i}^*, \tag{35}$$

in which

$$u_{1i}^* = \max\{u_{1i}, -x_{1i}'\beta_1\}.$$

The asymmetric censoring of the error terms can be seen to produce the bias in least squares estimation of (35). Symmetric trimming simply trims the upper tail of y_{1i} according to $y_{1i} \geq 2x_{1i}'\beta_1$. The conditional mean of the resulting trimmed dependent variable is zero, and so standard least squares is consistent. However, estimation requires an algorithm since β_1 in the trimming function is unknown. Of course, if a poor initial estimate of β_1 is chosen, then much data will be lost since there is no information in observations with $x_{1i}'\beta_1 \leq 0$. In the Monte Carlo simulations reported in Powell (1986a), the cost of relaxing the normality assumption was clear, with standard errors nearly three times the size even for quite large sample sizes, once again pointing to the need for very large data sets for the relaxation of parametric assumptions.

Powell (1986b) has also suggested the use of a censored-least-absolute-deviations (CLAD) estimator for the Tobit model. Assuming that the conditional median of u_{1i} is zero, the median of y_{1i} is given by $y_{1i} = x'_{1i}\beta_1 1(x'_{1i}\beta_1 > 0)$. The CLAD estimator minimizes the absolute distance of y_{1i} from its median; that is,

$$\hat{\beta}_1 = \arg\min_{\beta_1} \left[\sum_{i=1}^{n} \left| y_{1i} - x'_{1i}\beta_1 1(x'_{1i}\beta_1 > 0) \right| \right]. \tag{36}$$

Powell is able to show the consistency and asymptotic normality of this estimator. Honoré (1993) has recently extended this style of estimation to the censored panel data case.

14.4.3. SEMI-PARAMETRIC ESTIMATION IN THE SELECTIVITY MODEL

The Tobit model is equivalent to assuming a corner solution on non-participation. In economic terms, this rules out fixed costs or constraints in the process determining participation. In many examples this has been shown to be an unreasonably strong assumption, and nowhere more so than in the labour force participation and hours model. Fixed costs (and search costs) invalidate the Tobit assumption, and the papers of Cogan (1981) and Mroz (1987) make the importance of this abundantly clear.

The identification of the selectivity model often relies heavily on the parametric distributional assumptions about the joint distribution of u_{1i} and u_{2i} in (22). Without these assumptions, identification requires the inclusion of a variable in x_{2i} that is not in x_{1i}. In the fixed costs story, for example, this would typically require observing the money (or time) costs directly. This is clearly a tall order, especially for those individually who do not participate and therefore do not pay the fixed costs.

Given such an exclusion restriction, semi-parametric estimation can proceed in a fairly straightforward manner. As we observed above, the conditional mean of y_{1i}^*, given $\beta'_1 x_{1i}$ and $y_{2i}^* > 0$, is

$$E(y_{1i}^* \mid \beta'_1 x_{1i}, y_{2i}^* > 0) = \beta'_1 x_{1i} + h(\beta'_2 x_{2i}), \tag{37}$$

which, given $\beta'_2 x_{2i}$, is precisely the form in the semi-parametric model (10). A first-round estimator for $\beta'_2 x_{2i}$ can be derived form the discussion of semi-parametric estimation in the binary choice model above. As was pointed out there, the constant term is not identified and β_{2i} will be identified only up to scale and sign. However, to estimate the slope parameters in β_1, one can follow the Robinson method described in Section 14.2. This essentially eliminates the $h(\beta'_2 x_{2i})$ term according to (11) and is developed in Powell (1994).

The issue is really how to approximate $h(\beta_2' x_{2i})$. Ichimura and Lee (1990) suggest a kernel regression approach. Newey (1988) suggests a series approximation. The Newey suggestion essentially amounts to estimating

$$y_{1i} = x_{1i}' \beta_1 + \sum_{j=1}^{J} \eta_j \rho_j \left(\hat{\beta}_2' x_{2i} \right) + \zeta_i, \tag{38}$$

in which the $\rho(\beta_2' x_{2i})$ terms are given by known basis functions. These are typically polynomial functions of the generalized residuals from the probit discrete choice model, i.e. the Heckman selection correction terms (28). These techniques are explored in a useful application to the Mroz (1987) labour supply model by Newey *et al.* (1990). They find that, with the sample sizes used in the Mroz application, the semi-parametric methods suffer from a precision problem but do not appear to change the results of the parametric two-step Heckman estimator to any great extent.

14.5. Improving the Precision of Estimating Dynamic Panel Data Models

In dynamic panel data models, where there is a reasonably large autoregressive parameter and the number of time-series observations is moderately small, the linear generalized methods of moments (GMM) estimator of Anderson and Hsiao (1982), Holtz-Eakin *et al.* (1988), and Arellano and Bond (1991), obtained after first differencing, has been found to be poorly behaved. Lagged levels of the series provide weak instruments for first differences in this case. Nonlinear moment conditions, developed in Ahn and Schmidt (1995), which could be expected to improve this behaviour, are available for these models but have not been widely adopted in practice. Blundell and Bond (1997) consider alternative estimators that are designed to improve the properties of the standard first-differenced GMM estimator and are conveniently linear; they show that relatively mild restrictions on the initial conditions process can be used both to simplify the nonlinear moment conditions and to increase precision. The resulting linear estimator uses lagged *differences* of y_{it} as instruments for equations in levels, in addition to lagged *levels* of y_{it} as instruments for equations in first differences. Monte Carlo simulations of this linear system estimator and asymptotic variance calculations show that this offers dramatic efficiency gains in the situations where the basic first-differenced GMM estimator performs poorly.

In models with regressors x_{it}, the precise set of moment conditions available will depend on assumptions made about the correlation between x_{it} and u_{it}. To exploit the additional moment conditions, an additional requirement is that $E(\Delta x_{it}' \eta_i) = 0$, which is clearly weaker than requiring the levels of x_{it} to be uncorrelated with the individual effects. This is precisely the case considered in Arellano and Bover (1995). Together with the restriction on the initial conditions process, this allows the use of both lagged Δy_{it} and lagged Δx_{it} as instruments in levels equations. Stricter exogeneity restrictions on the x_{it} will allow the use of further instruments, as detailed in Arellano and Bond (1991), Ahn and Schmidt (1995), and Arellano and Bover (1995).

The gain in precision that results from exploiting the initial condition information is shown to increase for higher values of the autoregressive parameter and as the number of time series observations gets smaller. For short panels, a large downward bias is found and a very low precision for the standard first-differenced estimator. The initial condition information exploited in our system estimators not only greatly improves the precision but also greatly reduces the finite sample bias in this case. It is also observed that, while the finite sample bias of the differenced estimator is generally downwards (in the direction of OLS in first differences), the much smaller finite sample bias of the system estimator is generally upwards (in the direction of OLS levels).

In the next subsection I briefly review the standard moment conditions for the autoregressive error components model in the framework of Anderson and Hsiao (1981*a*, *b*), Holtz-Eakin *et al.* (1988), Arellano and Bond (1991), and Ahn and Schmidt (1995). I then consider restrictions on the initial condition process that render lagged values of Δy_{it} valid as instruments for the levels equations. The resulting estimator is equivalent to that recently proposed by Arellano and Bover (1995).

14.5.1. THE STANDARD GMM ESTIMATOR

Consider an AR(1) model with unobserved individual-specific effects

$$y_{it} = \alpha y_{i,t-1} + \eta_i + v_{it} \tag{39}$$

for $i = 1, \ldots, N$ and $t = 2, \ldots, T$, where $\eta_i + v_{it} = u_{it}$ is the usual 'fixed effects' decomposition of the error term; N is large and T is fixed.[5] Since our focus is on the role of initial conditions, we will assume, for most of our discussion, that η_i and v_{it} have the familiar error-components structure in which

$$E(\eta_i) = 0, \; E(v_{it}) = 0, \; E(v_{it}\eta_i) = 0,$$

$$\text{for } i = 1, \ldots, N \text{ and } t = 2, \ldots, T \tag{40}$$

and

$$E(v_{it}v_{is}) = 0 \quad \text{for } i = 1, \ldots, N \text{ and } \forall t \neq s. \tag{41}$$

In addition, there is the standard assumption concerning the initial conditions y_{i1} (see e.g. Ahn and Schmidt 1995):

$$E(y_{i1}v_{it}) = 0 \quad \text{for } i = 1, \ldots, N \text{ and } t = 2, \ldots, T. \tag{42}$$

---

[5] All of the estimators discussed below and their properties extend in an obvious fashion to higher-order autoregressive models.

Conditions (40), (41), and (42) imply moment restrictions that are sufficient to (identify and) estimate α. However, we may also wish to incorporate the homoscedasticity restrictions

$$E(v_{it}^2) = \sigma_v^2, \quad E(\eta_i^2) = \sigma_\eta^2 \quad \text{for } i = 1, \ldots, N \text{ and } t = 2, \ldots, T, \quad (43)$$

so that

$$E(u_i u_i') = \Omega = \sigma_\eta^2 J_{T-1} + \sigma_v^2 I_{T-1}.$$

where $u_i' = (u_{i2}, \ldots, u_{iT})$ and J_{T-1} is the $(T-1) \times (T-1)$ unit matrix and I_{T-1} the $(T-1) \times (T-1)$ identity matrix.

In the absence of any further restrictions on the process generating the initial conditions, the autoregressive error components model (39)–(43) implies the following orthogonality conditions:

$$E(y_{i,t-s} \Delta v_{it}) = 0 \quad \text{for } t = 3, \ldots, T \text{ and } s \geq 2, \quad (44)$$

$$E(y_{i,t-2} \Delta v_{i,t-1} - y_{i,t-1} \Delta v_{it}) = 0 \quad \text{for } t = 4, \ldots, T, \quad (45)$$

which are linear in the α parameter. Although these moment conditions can be expressed in alternative ways, the organization of (44) and (45) will prove useful in what follows. The $0.5(T-1)(T-2)$ orthogonality conditions in (44) simply reflect the assumed absence of serial correlation in the time-varying disturbances v_{it}, together with the restriction (42). The $T-3$ conditions in (45) depend on the homoscedasticity through time of v_{it}.

The moment restrictions in (44) and (45) can be expressed more compactly as

$$E(Z_i' \bar{u}_i) = 0,$$

where Z_i is the $(T-2) \times m$ matrix given by (omitting the i subscripts)

$$Z_i = \begin{bmatrix} y_1 & y_2 & 0 & 0 & 0 & \ldots & 0 & 0 & \ldots & 0 \\ 0 & -y_3 & y_1 & y_2 & y_3 & \ldots & 0 & 0 & \ldots & 0 \\ \ldots & \ldots & \ldots & \ldots & \ldots & \ldots & \ldots & & \ldots & \ldots & \ldots \\ 0 & 0 & 0 & 0 & 0 & \ldots & -y_{T-1} & y_1 & \ldots & y_{T-2} \end{bmatrix},$$

$\bar{u}_i$ is the $(T-2)$ vector $(\Delta v_{i3}, \Delta v_{i4}, \ldots, \Delta v_{iT})'$, and $m = 0.5(T-1)(T-2) + (T-3)$.

The generalized method of moments estimator based on these moment conditions minimizes the quadratic distance $(\bar{u}' ZA_N Z' \bar{u})$ for some metric A_N, where Z' is the $m \times N(T-2)$ matrix $(Z_1', Z_2', \ldots, Z_N')$ and $\bar{u}$ is the $N(T-2)$ vector $(\bar{u}_1', \bar{u}_2', \ldots, \bar{u}_N')'$. This gives the GMM estimator for α as

$$\hat{\alpha} = (\bar{y}_{-1}' ZA_N Z' \bar{y}_{-1})^{-1} \bar{y}_{-1}' ZA_N Z \bar{y},$$

where $\bar{y}_i$ is the $(T-2)$ vector $(\Delta y_{i3}, \Delta y_{i4}, \ldots, \Delta y_{iT})'$.

Alternative choices for the weights A_N give rise to a set of GMM estimators based on the moment conditions in (44) and (45), all of which are consistent for large N and finite T, but which differ in their asymptotic efficiency. In general, the optimal weights are given by

$$A_N = \left(N^{-1} \sum_{i=1}^{N} Z_i' \hat{\mathbf{u}}_i \hat{\mathbf{u}}_i' Z_i \right)^{-1},$$

where $\hat{\mathbf{u}}_i$ are residuals from an initial consistent estimator. This is typically referred to as the *two-step* GMM estimator[6] (see e.g. Arellano and Bond 1991). In the absence of any additional knowledge about the process for the initial conditions, this estimator is asymptotically efficient in the class of estimators based on the linear moment conditions (44) and (45) (see Hansen 1982).

In a recent contribution, Crepon *et al.* (1993) have noted that the autoregressive error components model implies a further $(T - 1)$ linear moment conditions which are given by

$$E(u_{it}) = 0 \quad \text{for } t = 2, \ldots, T. \tag{46}$$

This implies that the $(T - 1)$ time dummies could be used as instruments for the equations in levels.

Whether these extra moment conditions (46) will be helpful in estimating α depends crucially on the nature of the initial conditions. In the stationary model, we also have

$$E(y_{it}) = 0 \quad \text{for } t = 1, \ldots, T.$$

In this case the use of time dummies as instruments would not be informative. However, for other 'start-up' processes it might be (for example if $y_{i1} = k_i$ with $E(k_i) \neq 0$).

Finally, a number of authors have suggested using the additional $T - 3$ non-linear moment conditions (see Ahn and Schmidt 1995: eq. (4)):

$$E(u_{it} \Delta u_{i,t-1}) = 0 \quad \text{for } t = 4, 5, \ldots, T, \tag{47}$$

---

[6] As a choice of A_N to yield the initial consistent estimator, we consider

$$A_N = \left(N^{-1} \sum_{i=1}^{N} Z_i' H Z_i \right)^{-1}$$

where H is the $(T - 2) \times (T - 2)$ matrix given by

$$H = \begin{pmatrix} 2 & -1 & 0 & \ldots & 0 \\ -1 & 2 & -1 & \ldots & 0 \\ 0 & -1 & 2 & \ldots & 0 \\ \ldots & \ldots & \ldots & \ldots & \ldots \\ 0 & 0 & 0 & \ldots & 2 \end{pmatrix},$$

which can be calculated in one step. Note that, when the v_{it} are i.i.d., the one-step and two-step estimators are asymptotically equivalent in this model.

which could be expected to improve efficiency and clearly are implied by (41) and (42). These conditions relate directly to the absence of serial correlation in v_{it} and do not require homoscedasticity. Under homoscedasticity, Ahn and Schmidt (1995: eq. (11b)) show the existence of an additional nonlinear moment condition,

$$E(\bar{u}_i \Delta u_{i3}) = 0 \quad \text{where } \bar{u}_i = \frac{1}{T-1} \sum_{t=2}^{T} u_{it}. \tag{48}$$

These nonlinear moments are likely to be particularly informative in the case where α is close to unity.

14.5.2. INITIAL CONDITION INFORMATION

Following Blundell and Bond (1997), consider an additional but in many cases relatively mild restriction on the initial conditions process which allows the use of additional linear moment conditions for the levels equations in the GMM framework. This allows the use of lagged differences of y_{it} as instruments in the levels equations. These additional moment conditions are likely to be important in practice when α is close to unity, since lagged values in the differenced equations will be weak instruments in this case. Very conveniently, these linear moment conditions also imply the nonlinear conditions (47), from which it follows that the optimal GMM estimator can be implemented as a linear GMM estimator under this restriction.[7]

In contrast to the nonlinear moment restrictions (47), Blundell and Bond (1997) consider the following $T - 3$ linear moment conditions:

$$E(u_{it} \Delta y_{i,t-1}) = 0 \quad \text{for } t = 4, 5, \ldots, T. \tag{49}$$

The use of lagged differences as possible instruments for equations in levels was proposed by Arellano and Bover (1995). Clearly, (49) does not imply (47). However, notice that, since Δy_{i2} is observed, there is an additional restriction available, namely

$$E(u_{i3} \Delta y_{i2}) = 0. \tag{50}$$

Note also that the validity of this extra moment condition depends on a restriction on the initial condition process generating y_{i1}. Condition (50) has two important implications. First, combining (50) with the model for periods $2, \ldots,$ T set out in (39)–(42) implies the validity of the linear moment restrictions in

---

[7] In this section we focus on moment conditions that remain valid under heteroscedasticity. Ahn and Schmidt (1995: eq. (12b)) have shown that the homoscedasticity restrictions (45) and (46) can be replaced by a set of $T - 2$ linear moment conditions under the restriction (50) specified below.

(49).[8] Second, combining (49) and (50) implies the nonlinear restrictions in (47), and renders these redundant for estimation.

For $\alpha < 1$, we write y_{i1} as[9]

$$y_{i1} = \frac{\eta_i}{1 - \alpha} + u_{i1}. \tag{51}$$

The model specifies a convergent level for y_{it} from $t = 2$ onwards for each individual, and u_{i1} is simply the initial deviation from this convergent level. Necessary conditions for (50) are then

$$E(u_{i1}\eta_i) = E(u_{i1}v_{i3}) = 0 \quad \text{for } i = 1, \ldots, N. \tag{52}$$

The key requirement therefore is that the initial *deviations* from $\eta_i/(1 - \alpha)$ are not correlated with the *level* of $\eta_i/(1 - \alpha)$ itself.

This condition is clearly satisfied in the fully stationary model, where u_{i1} will be the infinite weighted sum $\sum_{s=-1}^{\infty}(\alpha^{s+1}v_{i,-s})$. However, stationarity is not necessary for the validity of the extra linear moment conditions in (50) and (49). Condition (52) imposes no restriction on the variance of u_{i1}, and any entry period 'disequilibrium' from $\eta_i/(1 - \alpha)$ that is randomly distributed across agents will preserve condition (50). Other departures from stationarity such as $y_{i1} = k \; \forall \; i$ or $y_{i1} \sim$ i.i.d. $(0, \sigma_{y_1}^2)$ will violate (52), however, so this requirement is not trivial.

Calculation of the GMM estimators based on conditions (49) and (50) requires a stacked system comprising $(T - 2)$ equations in first differences and the $(T - 2)$ equations in levels corresponding to periods $3, \ldots, T$, for which instruments are observed. The instrument matrix for this system can be written

$$Z_i^+ = \begin{bmatrix} Z_i & 0 & 0 & \ldots & 0 \\ 0 & \Delta y_{i2} & 0 & \ldots & 0 \\ 0 & 0 & \Delta y_{i3} & \ldots & 0 \\ \ldots & \ldots & \ldots & \ldots & 0 \\ 0 & 0 & 0 & \ldots & \Delta y_{i,T-1} \end{bmatrix}, \tag{53}$$

where Z_i is as defined above.

This linear GMM estimator based on the system of both differenced and levels equations exploits the additional restriction in (50), and therefore is asymptotically strictly more efficient than the nonlinear GMM estimator exploiting (47) if this restriction is valid.

---

[8] Since the model implies

$$\Delta y_{it} = \alpha^{t-2}\Delta y_{i2} + \sum_{s=0}^{t-3} \alpha^s \Delta v_{i,t-s} \quad \text{for } t = 3, 4, \ldots, T.$$

[9] Blundell and Bond (1995) also consider the case where $\alpha = 1$.

14.5.3. SOME EXPERIMENTAL EVIDENCE

Blundell and Bond report the results of a Monte Carlo study which investigates the finite-sample behaviour of the standard first-differenced GMM estimator, the conditional GLS estimator, and the GMM estimator that exploits the additional restriction (50) on the initial condition process. I now document the improvement in precision and finite sample performance that may result from the use of these alternative estimators. This is found to be particularly important when the autoregressive parameter α is high and when the number of time-series observations is small.

In all experiments, the series y_{it} was generated as

$$y_{it} = \alpha y_{i,t-1} + \eta_i + v_{it}$$

for $i = 1, 2, \ldots, N$, and $t = 2, 3, \ldots, T$, where $\eta_i \sim$ i.i.d. $N(0, 1)$ and $v_{it} \sim$ i.i.d. $N(0, 1)$. The initial conditions y_{i1} were generated from a model of the form

$$y_{i1} = k + \delta\eta_i + u_{i1},$$

where $u_{i1} \sim$ i.i.d. $N(0, \sigma_{u1}^2)$. New values for the initial observations are drawn in each of the replications.

Table 14.3 summarizes the gains in precision in a range of experiments when the two-step GMM estimator based on the stacked system of levels and differenced equations is compared with the standard two-step GMM estimator based on differenced equations alone. This is shown as the ratio of the empirical variance of the differenced estimator in our simulation experiments to the empirical variance of the system estimator. This is reported for a range of sample sizes and values of the autoregressive parameter α. In each case, the design of the initial conditions process is chosen to satisfy stationarity, so the linear moment conditions (49) and (50) are valid for the equations in levels.

Column (1) of table 14.3 reports results for the case of $T = 4$. For high values of the autoregressive parameter α we find dramatic efficiency gains compared with the basic first-differenced GMM estimator. Lagged levels of the series provide weak instruments for first differences in these cases. Not surprisingly, therefore, the gain in precision that results from exploiting the initial condition information decreases for lower values of α.

Column (2) of the table reports results for the case of $T = 11$. Again, we find big efficiency improvements for high values of α. However, comparing columns (1) and (2), we find that, for a given value of α, the gain from exploiting the initial conditions tends to decrease as the number of time-series observations gets larger.

We can compare these simulation results with ratios of the corresponding (large N) asymptotic variances. For $T = 4$ and $\alpha = 0.8$ the asymptotic variance ratio is 13.45, and for $\alpha = 0.9$ it is 49.51; these are close to the Monte Carlo results found in Table 14.3, column (1), for $N = 500$. These asymptotic results for

Table 14.3. Efficiency Gains

$$y_{i1} = \frac{\eta_i}{1-\alpha} + u_{i1}; \ u_{i1} \sim \text{i.i.d. } N(0, v_1)$$

v_1 is chosen such that $var(y_{i1}) = var(y_{it})$ for $t = 2, \ldots, T$

N	α	(1) T = 4 var(GMM−DIF)/var(GMM−SYS)	(2) T = 11 var(GMM−DIF)/var(GMM−SYS)
100	0.0	1.93	1.12
	0.3	2.52	1.28
	0.5	4.25	1.59
	0.8	43.27	6.99
	0.9	36.80	60.90
200	0.0	2.19	1.08
	0.3	3.31	1.18
	0.5	5.41	1.28
	0.8	34.02	2.69
	0.9	30.62	23.13
500	0.0	1.51	1.42
	0.3	1.91	1.75
	0.5	2.68	2.16
	0.8	12.21	3.36
	0.9	58.60	10.98

Source: Blundell and Bond (1997).

our GMM estimator can also be compared with results reported by Ahn and Schmidt (1995) for the GMM estimator that exploits the nonlinear moment conditions (47) but not the linear conditions (49) and (50). For $T = 4$ and with $\alpha = 0.8$ and $\alpha = 0.9$, Ahn and Schmidt (1995) report asymptotic variance ratios of 2.42 and 2.54 respectively. This comparison indicates that, exploiting the extra initial conditions information, (50) can, when valid, result in a dramatic improvement in precision at low values of T.

In table 14.4 we further investigate the finite sample performance of these GMM estimators. For low values of T and high values of α, we find both a huge downward bias and very low precision for the standard first-differenced estimator, even when $N = 500$. The initial condition information exploited in our system estimator not only greatly improves the precision but also greatly reduces the finite sample bias in this case. We can also observe that, while the finite sample bias of the differenced estimator is generally downwards (in the direction of OLS in first differences), the finite sample bias of the system estimator is generally upwards (in the direction of OLS levels). However, the advantages of

Table 14.4. Two-Step GMM Estimators underlying Table 14.3

α	DIF		SYS	
	Mean	(s. d.)	Mean	(s. d.)
$T = 4$, $N = 100$				
0.5	0.4489	(0.2561)	0.5212	(0.1242)
0.9	0.1919	(0.8007)	0.9614	(0.1320)
$T = 4$, $N = 500$				
0.5	0.4863	(0.1042)	0.5026	(0.0636)
0.9	0.5917	(0.6897)	0.9092	(0.0901)
$T = 11$, $N = 100$				
0.5	0.4712	(0.0630)	0.5797	(0.0499)
0.9	0.6530	(0.1636)	0.9763	(0.0210)
$T = 11$, $N = 500$				
0.5	0.4967	(0.0272)	0.5038	(0.0185)
0.9	0.8214	(0.0279)	0.9303	(0.0220)

Source: Blundell and Bond (1995).

exploiting the additional moment conditions when α is high in the results of these simulations are clearly more efficient than nonlinear GMM in this case.

14.6. Nonlinear Panel Data Models

In many economic applications to panel data, the variable of interest is discrete. In this section I will concentrate on count data processes, for example the number of job applications, visits to the doctor, patent applications, or technological innovations made in a period of time. It is often the case that the process under study is inherently dynamic, so that the history of the count process itself is an important determinant of current outcomes. Like other panel data applications, it is also likely that unobservable fixed effects induce persistently different counts across individuals or firms. Distinguishing between dynamics and individual fixed effects is made difficult in panel data by the correlation between the error process and the lagged dependent variable generated by the presence of individual fixed effects. In linear models a number of generalized method of moments (GMM) estimators can be used to estimate the parameters of a dynamic fixed-effects model. In count data models, where a natural nonlinearity is produced by the positive and discrete nature of the data, these methods are not directly applicable, and the presence of both fixed effects and dynamics is particularly difficult to deal with.

In Blundell and Windmeijer (1995), the properties of several dynamic models for count data are examined and a linear feedback model (LFM) for panel data applications is proposed. In the LFM the expectation of an integer-dependent variable —the count variable—is modelled linearly in the history of the count process. This is based on the integer valued autoregressive (INAR) process, which has its foundations in the generalization of the Poisson model to the ARMA case developed by Al-Osh and Alzaid (1987), Alzaid and Al-Osh (1993), and Brännäs (1994).

The standard estimator for count data models with fixed effects is the conditional likelihood estimator proposed by Hausman *et al.* (1984). This is shown to be equivalent to a moment estimator that replaces the fixed effect with the ratio of within-group means. However, this estimator is not consistent for the parameters of interest if the regressors are weakly exogenous or predetermined, which is clearly the case with a lagged dependent variable. From the work of Chamberlain (1992, 1993) and Wooldridge (1997), quasi-differencing GMM estimators for the dynamic model specifications are considered that are analogous to those for dynamic linear panel data models. Blundell and Windmeijer (1995) develop a moment estimator that draws on the conditional likelihood approach but replaces the fixed effect by the ratio of *pre-sample* means. This *mean scaling* estimator is specifically designed to exploit additional pre-sample information that is available in the patents data described below. This method also controls for weakly exogenous or predetermined regressors and correlated fixed effects. While this estimator is not consistent for short panels, Monte Carlo evidence presented in that paper shows considerable improvement in mean squared error and precision in situations where the GMM estimator performs poorly.

14.6.1. THE COUNT DATA MODEL

Let y_{it} denote the discrete count variable to be explained for subject i, $i = 1, \ldots,$ N, at time t, $t = 1, \ldots, T$; and let x_{it} denote a vector of explanatory variables. Throughout, the series y_i and x_i are assumed to be weakly stationary. The static exponential – or log-link – model of the form

$$E(y_{it} \mid x_{it}) = \exp(x_{it}'\beta) \tag{54}$$

is commonly used for count data.[10] An important feature in panel data applications is unobserved heterogeneity or individual fixed effects. For count data models, these effects are generally modelled multiplicatively as

$$E(y_{it} \mid x_{it}, v_i) = \mu_{it} v_i, \tag{55}$$

where $\mu_{it} = \exp(x_{it}'\beta)$, and in which v_i is a permanent scaling factor for the individual specific mean. Alternatively, writing $v_i \equiv e^{\eta_i}$, this model may be expressed in the more commonly recognized additive form[11]

---

[10] See Gouriéroux *et al.* (1984), McCullagh and Nelder (1989), and Cameron and Trivedi (1986) for good general discussions of these models.

[11] Notice that these are different from the negative binomial model in which a term like η_i is included with a gamma distribution. In the panel data model presented here, the η_i are the *same* across time for each individual, whereas in the negative binomial model they are independent random draws in each time period and therefore are not *fixed* effects.

$$E(y_{it}|x_{it}, \eta_i) = \exp(x_{it}'\beta + \eta_i).\tag{56}$$

Several estimators for β have been proposed that allow for individual effects that may be correlated with the regressors. Hausman *et al.* (1984) use the conditional maximum likelihood method, conditioning on the sufficient statistic for η_i, viz. $\sum_t y_{it}$. This method mimics the fixed-effects logit approach of Chamberlain (1984) and, as is the case for the logit model, provides consistent estimates of β for finite T only when the explanatory variables x_{it} are *strictly* exogenous.[12] Blundell and Windmeijer (1995) provide an interpretation of the conditional maximum likelihood estimator as a mean scaling estimator in which the fixed effect is measured by the ratio of within-group means of y_{it} to $\exp(x_{it}'\beta)$. This is derived for the standard fixed-effects count data model with strictly exogenous regressors and can be thought of as the multiplicative equivalent of the within-groups estimator in the standard error components panel data framework (see Hsiao 1986).

14.6.2. STRICT EXOGENEITY

Consider the case where the x_{it} are strictly exogenous, which is defined in terms of the conditional mean by

$$E(y_{it}|x_{it}) = E(y_{it}|x_{iT}, \ldots, x_{i1}).\tag{57}$$

To derive the conditional likelihood, suppose that y_{it} is distributed as a Poisson random variable with mean

$$E(y_{it}|x_{it}, v_i) = \mu_{it}v_i,\tag{58}$$

where $\mu_{it} = \exp(x_{it}'\beta)$. This implicitly defines a regression model

$$y_{it} = \mu_{it}v_i + u_{it},\tag{59}$$

in which $E(u_{it}|x_{it}, v_i) = 0$. The log-likelihood function, conditional on $\sum_t y_{it}$, is given (see Hausman *et al.* 1984: 919) by

$$L = \sum_{i=1}^{N}\sum_{t=1}^{T}\Gamma(y_{it}+1) - \sum_{i=1}^{N}\sum_{t=1}^{T}y_{it}\log\left[\sum_{s=1}^{T}\exp(-(x_{it}-x_{is})'\beta)\right].\tag{60}$$

Alternatively, define the *mean scaling* model as

$$y_{it} = \exp(x_{it}'\beta)\frac{\bar{y}_i}{\bar{\mu}_i} + u_{it}^*,\tag{61}$$

where the ratio of the within group means, $\bar{y}_i = T^{-1}\sum_t y_{it}$ and $\bar{\mu}_i = T^{-1}\sum_t \mu_{it}$, is used to measure v_i. The conditional maximum likelihood estimator and a moment estimator for the mean scaling model are equivalent, as shown in Blundell and Windmeijer (1995).

---

[12] For difinitions of exogeneity see Engle *et al.* (1983).

The conditional likelihood approach is therefore equivalent to replacing v_i by the ratio of within-group means $\bar{y}_i/\bar{\mu}_i$. Further, $u_{it}^* = u_{it} - \exp(x_{it}'\beta)(\bar{u}_i/\bar{\mu}_i)$, which under strict exogeneity of x_{it} satisfies $E(u_{it}^*|x_{it}, \bar{\mu}_i) = 0$. Since by definition $\sum_{t=1}^{T} u_{it}^* = 0$, condition (60) can be conveniently rewritten as

$$\sum_{i=1}^{N}\sum_{t=1}^{T}(x_{it} - \bar{x}_i)u_{it}^* = 0. \tag{62}$$

14.6.3. WEAK EXOGENEITY

In economic applications, it is commonly the case that the regressors do not satisfy the condition of strict exogeneity. With weakly exogenous or predetermined regressors, condition (57) does not hold and therefore thee estimator of β that solves the sample moment condition (62) is no longer consistent, since x_{it} is now correlated with u_{it}^* through $\bar{u}_i$. This result is analogous to the inconsistency result for the within-groups estimator for linear panel data models with predetermined regressors in short panels (see Nickell 1981).

In this section two alternative methods are developed for estimating models in which some of the variables in x_{it} are weakly exogenous with respect to β, or are predetermined. The first considers a quasi-differencing moment condition that removes the individual effect. This estimation strategy, following from the work of Chamberlain (1992) and Wooldridge (1997), is an attempt to mimic the standard GMM panel data estimators of Holtz-Eakin *et al.* (1988) and Arellano and Bond (1991) outlined in Section 14.5 above. As in the standard panel data case, these methods, although consistent in the presence of weakly exogenous or predetermined regressors, have the drawback of eliminating the levels information in the model and can behave quite poorly in moderately sized samples when the explanatory variables are highly autoregressive.

The second approach considered draws on the conditional likelihood or within-groups approach by looking for statistics that can be used to measure the fixed effect. However, in contrast to estimators that condition on within-sample means, it exploits the availability of a long history of pre-sample information of the dependent variable. The ratio of pre-sample means, rather than within-sample means, is used to proxy the fixed effect. This is used in the work on modelling technological innovations in Blundell, Griffith, and van Reenan (1995), in which the firm fixed effect was interpreted as an *entry stock* variable measured using the long pre-sample series on innovations for each firm.

14.6.4. GMM ESTIMATORS

Mirroring the discussions in Section 14.5 concerning standard GMM estimators for *linear* panel data models with weakly exogenous regressors, Chamberlain (1992) and Wooldridge (1997) have proposed transformations that eliminate the fixed effect from the multiplicative model and lead to orthogonality conditions that can be used for consistent estimation. For the count regression model (58), the transformation that Chamberlain proposed is

$$S_{it} = y_{it+1} \frac{\mu_{it}}{\mu_{it+1}} - y_{it}$$

$$= u_{it+1} \frac{\mu_{it}}{\mu_{it+1}} - u_{it}. \tag{63}$$

Define a set of instruments z_{it} such that

$$E(u_{it} \mid v_i, z_{i1}, \ldots, z_{it}) = 0. \tag{64}$$

Then the conditional mean of S_{it} is given by

$$E(s_{it} \mid z_{i1}, \ldots, z_{it}) = E_{v|z}(E(s_{it} \mid v_i, z_{i1}, \ldots, z_{it})) = 0, \tag{65}$$

using the law of iterated expectations. This provides an orthogonality condition that can be used consistently to estimate the model parameters β by the GMM estimation technique (see Hansen 1982; Ogaki 1993). This estimator minimizes

$$\left(\frac{1}{N} \sum_{i=1}^{N} s_i' Z_i \right) W_N^{-1} \left(\frac{1}{N} \sum_{i=1}^{N} Z_i' s_i \right),$$

where Z_i is the matrix of instruments and W_N is a weight matrix. The optimal weight matrix is given by

$$W_N = \sum_{i=1}^{N} Z_i' \tilde{s}_i \tilde{s}_i' Z_i,$$

where $\tilde{s}_i$ is some initial (first-round) estimate. When a just identifying set of instruments is used, the GMM estimator solves the sample moment condition

$$\sum_{i=1}^{N} \sum_{t=1}^{T-1} z_{it} s_{it} = -\sum_{i=1}^{N} \sum_{t=1}^{T-1} z_{it} \left(y_{it} - \exp(x_{it}'\beta) \frac{y_{it}+1}{\mu_{it}+1} \right) = 0. \tag{66}$$

Introducing dynamics into models of the form (55) can be problematic, since the conditional mean is required to remain positive. Inclusion of functions of the lagged dependent variable in the exponential function can lead to explosive series or to problems with transforming zero values. Three dynamic specifications are considered in Blundell and Windmeijer (1995): the multiplicative distributed lag model; the multiplicative feedback model, in which the natural logarithm of the lagged dependent variable enters directly into the exponential mean function and zero values are replaced by an arbitrary (estimated) constant; and the linear feedback model, which is based on the integer-valued autoregressive model, in which the lagged dependent variable enters linearly in the conditional mean.

14.7. Concluding Comments

Whether it be the study of household behaviour or the study of firms' behaviour, empirical economic analysis based on the 'individual' level is persuasive. It avoids the problem of aggregation bias as well as identifying the factors that lead to a different distribution and usage of resources across households and firms. However, in microeconometrics distinct issues relating to endogenous selection, censoring, and individual heterogeneity have to be faced. Indeed, it may often be difficult to draw useful inferences from cross-section data alone, especially where history dependence or state dependence is important. Longitudinal data or panel data, which follow individual economic agents through time, can be utilized so as to avoid some of these drawbacks. In addition, panel data combine the attractive features of time-series analysis with individual-level behaviour.

This paper has not set out to be a forecasting exercise of what will happen in microeconometrics over the next ten years. It is a biased and subjective view of some of what is likely to dominate discussion in applied microeconomics. I have not focused on theoretical developments. There are many omissions, and the idea has been to characterize what is likely to be the trend in the next ten years by picking on certain specific issues.

As I see it, there are certain 'big' developments, these being the use of non-parametric and semi-parametric techniques, the use of quasi-experimental techniques, nonlinear panel data models with heterogeneity, and dynamic panel data models in general. It is around these that I have set out my view of where the important innovations lie. In each case there are many drawbacks that I have downplayed and many developments that I have omitted.

REFERENCES

Ahn, S. C., and Schmidt, P. (1995), 'Efficient estimation of models for dynamic panel data', *Journal of Econometrics*, 68: 5–28.

Ait-Sahalia, Y., Bickel, P. J., and Stoker, T. M. (1994), 'Goodness-of-Fit Tests for Regression Using Kernel Methods', Mimeo, MIT, November.

Al-Osh, M. A., and Alzaid, A. A. (1987), 'First-Order Integer Valued Autoregressive (INAR(1)) Process', *Journal of Time Series Analysis*, 8: 261–75.

Alzaid, A. A., and Al-Osh, M. A. (1993), 'Some Autoregressive Moving Average Processes with Generalised Poisson Marginal Distributions', *Annals of the Institute of Mathematical Statistics*, 45: 223–32.

Amemiya, T. (1973), 'Regression Analysis when the Dependent Variable is Truncated Normal', *Econometrica*, 1193–1205.

—— (19), 'Tobit Models: A Survey', *Journal of Economic Literature*, 1984.

—— (1985), 'Advanced Econometrics', Basil Blackwell Ltd. Oxford.

Anderson, T. W., and Hsaio, C. (1981a), 'Formulation and Estimation of Dynamic Models using Panel Data', Journal of Econometrics, 18: 570–606.

Anderson, T. W., and Hsaio, C. (1981*b*), 'Estimation of Dynamic Models with Error Components', *Journal of the American Statistical Association*, 76: 598–606.

Angrist, J. (1991), Grouped Data Estimation and Testing in Simple Labor Supply Models, Journal of Econometrics, 47: 243–65.

Arellano, M., and Bond, S. R. (1991), 'Some tests of specification for panel data: Monte Carlo evidence and an application to employment equations', *Review of Economic Studies*, 58: 277–97.

—— and Bover, O. (1995), 'Another look at the instrumental-variable estimation of error-components models', *Journal of Econometrics*, 68: 29–52.

Atkinson, A. B., Gomulka, J., and Stern, N. H. (1990), 'Spending on Alcohol: Evidence from the Family Expenditure Survey 1970–1983', *Economic Journal*, 100: 808–827.

Baltagi, B. (1995), *Econometric Analysis of Panel Data*. Chichester: John Wiley.

Banks, J., Blundell, R., and Lewbel, A. (1997), 'Quadratic Engel Curves, Indirect Tax Reform and Welfare', *Review of Economics and Statistics*, 79(4), 527–39.

Bhagarva, A., and Sargan, J. D. (1983), 'Estimating Dynamic Random Effects Models from Panel Data Covering Short Time Periods', *Econometrica*, 51: 1635–59.

Bierens, H. J., and Pott-Buter, H. A. (1990), 'Specification of Household Engel Curves by Nonparametric Regression', *Econometric Reviews*, 9: 123–84.

Blundell, R. W. (ed.) (1987) 'Specification Testing in Limited and Discrete Dependent Variable Models', *Journal of Econometrics*, 34.

—— (1988), 'Consumer Behaviour: Theory and Empirical Evidence', *Economic Journal*, 98: 16–65.

Blundell, R. and Bond, S. (1997), 'Initial Conditions and Moment Conditions in Dynamic Panel Data Models', UCL Discussion Paper no. 97-07, forthcoming in *Journal of Econometrics*.

—— and Duncan, A. (1998), 'Kernel Regression in Empirical Microeconomics', *Journal of Human Resources*, Symposium on 'Recent Methods for Empirical Microeconomics', May.

—— and Smith, R. J. (1989), 'Estimation in a Class of Simultaneous Equation Limited Dependent Variable Models', *Review of Economic Studies*, 56: 37–58.

—— —— (1991), 'Initial Conditions and Efficient Estimation in Dynamic Panel Data Models', *Annales d'Economie at de Statistique*, 20/21: 109–23.

—— and Walker, I. (1986), 'A Life-Cycle Consistent Empirical Model of Family Labour Supply using Cross-Section Data', *Review of Economic Studies*, 53: 539–58.

—— Ham, J., and Meghir, C. (1987), 'Unemployment and Female Labour Supply', *Economic Journal*, 97: 44–64.

—— Pashardes, P., and Weber, G. (1993), 'What Do We Learn about Consumer Demand Patterns from Micro Data?' *American Economic Review*, 83: 570–97.

—— Griffith, R., and van Reenen, J. (1995), 'Dynamic Count Data Models of Technological Innovation', *Economic Journal*.

——, ——, and Windmeijer, F. (1995), 'Individual Effects and Dynamics in Panel Data Count Models', IFS Working Paper 95/11, October.

——, ——, and Meghir, C. (1998), 'Estimating Labour Supply Responses Using Tax Reforms', *Econometrica*, July.

——, ——, and Pendakur, K. (1998), 'Semiparametric Estimation and Consumer Demand', forthcoming in *Journal of Applied Econometrics*, Symposium on Semiparametric Estimation, October.

——, Ham, J., and Meghir, C. (1987), 'Unemployment and Female Labour Supply', *Economic Journal*, 97, 44–64.

Brännäs, K. (1994), 'Estimation and Testing in Integer Valued AR(1) Models', Umeå Economic Studies Paper no. 335, Department of Economics, University of Umeå, February.

Cameron, A., and Trivedi, P. (1986), 'Econometric Models Based on Count Data: Comparisons and Applications of Some Estimators and Tests', *Journal of Applied Econometrics*, 1: 29–53.

Chamberlain, G. (1984), 'Panel Data', in Z. Griliches, and M. Intrilligator (eds.), *Handbook of Econometrics*. Amsterdam: North-Holland.

—— (1986), 'Asymptotic Efficiency in Semi-parametric Models with Censoring', *Journal of Econometrics*, 32: 189–218.

—— (1987), 'Asymptotic Efficiency in Estimation with Conditional Moment Restrictions', *Journal of Econometrics*, 34: 305–34.

—— (1992), 'Comment: Sequential Moment Restrictions in Panel Data', *Journal of Business and Economic Statistics*, 10: 20–6.

—— (1993), 'Feedback in Panel Data Models', mimeo, Econometric Society Summer Meeting, Boston, June.

Chesher, A. D. (1984), 'Testing for Neglected Heterogeneity', *Econometrica*, 52: 865–72.

Cogan, J. F. (1981), 'Fixed Costs and Labor Supply', *Econometrica*, 49: 945–64.

Coslett, S. R. (1981), 'Efficient Estimation of Discrete Choice Models', in C. F. Manski and D. McFadden (eds.), *Structural Analysis of Discrete Data with Econometric Applications*. Cambridge, Mass.: MIT Press, 51–111.

Cragg, J. G. (1971), 'Some Statistical Models for Limited Dependent Variables with Applications to the Demand for Durable Goods', *Econometrica*, 39, 829–44.

Crepon, B., Kramarz, F., and Trognon, A. (1993), 'Parameter of Interest, Nuisance Parameter and Othogonality Conditions: an Application to Autoregressive Error Components Models', CREST Working Paper no. 9335, July.

Davidson, R., and MacKinnon, J. G. (1993), *Estimation and Inference in Econometrics*. Oxford: Oxford University Press.

Deaton, A. S. (1985), 'Panel Data from Time Series of Cross Sections', *Journal of Econometrics*, 30: 109–26.

—— and Muellbauer, J. (1980a), 'An Almost Ideal Demand System', *American Economic Review*, 70: 312–26.

—— (1980b), *Economics and Consumer Behaviour*. Cambridge: Cambridge University Press.

Duncan, A. S., and Jones, A. S. (1992), 'NP-REG: an Interactive Package for Kernel Density Estimation and Non-Parametric Regression', IFS Working Paper W92/07.

Eissa, N. (1994), 'Taxation and Labor Supply of Married Women: the Tax Reform Act of 1986 as a Natural Experiment', mimeo, Department of Economics, University of Berkeley.

Engle, R. F., Hendry, D. F., and Richard, J. F. (1983), 'Exogeneity', *Econometrica*, 51: 277–304.

Gallant, R., and Nychka, D. (1987), 'Semi-Nonparametric Maximum Likelihood Estimation', *Econometrica*, 55: 363–90.

Goldberger, A. S. (1981), 'Linear Regression after Selection', *Journal of Econometrics*.

Gorman, W. M. (1981), 'Some Engel Curves', in A. S. Deaton (ed.), *Essays in the Theory and Measurement of Consumer Behaviour*. Cambridge: Cambridge University Press.

Gosling, A., Machin, S., and Meghir, C. (1994), 'The Changing Distribution of Male Wages in the UK 1966–1992', IFS Discussion Paper 94/13.

Gourieroux, C., Monfort, A., Renault, E., and Trognon, A. (1987), 'Generalised Residuals', *Journal of Econometrics*, 34: 5–32.

—— Monfort, A., and Trognon, A. (1984), 'Pseudo Maximum Likelihood Methods: Applications to Poisson Models', *Econometrica*, 52: 701–20.

Hall, A. (1993), 'Some Aspects of Generalized Method of Moments Estimation', in G. S. Maddala, C. R. Rao, and H. D. Vinod (eds.), 'Econometrics', *Handbook of Statistics*, xi. Amsterdam: North-Holland.

Hall, B., Griliches, Z., and Hausman, J. (1986), 'Patents and R and D: Is There a Lag?' *International Economic Review*, 27: 265–83.

Hansen, L. P. (1982), 'Large Sample Properties of Generalised Method of Moment Estimators', *Econometrica*, 50: 1029–54.

Hansen, L. P. and Singleton, K. J. (1982), 'Generalised Instrumental Variable Estimation of Non-Linear Rational Expectations Models', *Econometrica*, 50: 1269–86.

Härdle W. (1990), *Applied Nonparametric Regression*. Cambridge: Cambridge University Press.

—— and Jerison, M. (1988), 'The Evolution of Engel Curves over time', Discussion Paper no. A-178.SFB 303, University of Bonn.

—— and Linton, O. (1995), 'Nonparametric Regression Analysis', in R. F. Engle and D. McFadden, *Handbook of Econometrics*, iv. Amsterdam: North-Holland.

—— Hall, B., and Griliches, Z. (1984), 'Econometric Models for Count Data and an Application to the Patents–R&D Relationship', *Econometrica*, 52: 909–38.

—— Newey, W. K., Ichimura, H., and Powell, J. L. (1991), 'Identification and Estimation of Polynomial Errors in Variables Models', *Journal of Econometrics*, 50: 273–96.

—— —— and Powell, J. L. (1995), 'Nonlinear Errors in Variables: Estimation of Some Engel Curves', *Journal of Econometrics*, 65: 205–34.

Heckman, J. J. (1978), 'Dummy Endogenous Variables in a Simultaneous Equation System', *Econometrica*, 46: 931–60.

—— (1979), 'Sample Selection Bias as a Specification Error', *Econometrica*, 47: 153–61.

—— (1990), 'Varieties of Selection Bias', *American Economic Review*, 80: 313–18.

—— and Robb, R. (1985), 'Alternative Methods for Evaluating the Impact of Interventions', in Heckman and Singer (eds.), *Longitudidal Analysis of Labor Market Data*, Econometric Society Monograph 10. Cambridge: Cambridge University Press.

Holz-Eakin, D., Newey, W., and Rosen, H. S. (1988), 'Estimating Vector Autoregressions with Panel Data', *Econometrica*, 56: 1371–96.

Honoré, B. E. (1993), 'Orthogonality Conditions for Tobit Models with Fixed Effects and Lagged Dependent Variables', *Journal of Econometrics*, 59, 35–61.

Horowitz, J. L. (1992), 'A Smoothed Maximum Score Estimator for the Binary Response Model', *Econometrica*, 60: 505–31.

—— (1993), 'Semiparametric and Nonparametric Estimation of Quantile Response Models', in G. S. Maddala, C. R. Rau, and H. D. Vinod (eds.), *Handbook of Statistics*, xi. Amsterdam: North-Holland, 45–72.

Hsiao, C. (1986), *Analysis of Panel Data*, Econometric Society Monographs. Cambridge: Cambridge University Press.

Ichimura, H. (1987), PhD, MIT.

Ichimura, I. (1993), 'Semiparametric Least Squares Estimation of Single Index Models', *Journal of Econometrics*, 58, 71–120.

—— and Lee, L. F. (1990), 'Semi-parametric Least Squares Estimation of Multiple Index Models: Single Equation Estimation', in W. A. Barnett *et al.* (eds.), *Nonparametric and Semiparametric Estimation Methods in Econometrics and Statistics*. Cambridge: Cambridge University Press.

Jorgenson, D. W., and Lau, L. J. (1975), 'The Structure of Consumer Preferences', *Annals of Social and Economic Measurement*, 4: 49–101.

—— —— (1979), 'The Integrability of Consumer Demand Functions', *European Economic Review*, 12: 115–47.

—— Christensen, L. R., and Lau, L. J. (1975), 'Transcendental Logarithmic Utility Functions', *American Economic Review*, 65: 367–83.

—— Lau, L. J., and Stoker, T. M. (1980), 'Welfare Comparison and Exact Aggregation', *American Economic Review*, 70: 268–72.

Klein, R. and Spady, R. (1993), 'An Efficient Semiparametric Estimator for Binary Response Models', *Econometrica*, 61, 387–422.

Lee, L. F. (1984), 'Tests for the Bivariate Normal Distribution in Econometric Models with Selectivity', *Econometrica*, 52: 843–64.

Leser, C. E. V. (1963), 'Forms of Engel Functions', *Econometrica*, 31, 694–703.

Lewbel, A. (1991), 'The Rank of Demand Systems: Theory and Nonparametric Estimation', *Econometrica*, 59, 711–30.

Maddala, G. S. (1986), *Limited Dependent and Qualitative Variables in Econometrics*. Cambridge: Cambridge University Press.

Manski, C. F. (1975), 'Maximum Score Estimation of the Stochastic Utility Model of Choice', *Journal of Econometrics*, 3: 205–28.

—— (1985), 'Semiparametric Analysis of Discrete Response: Asymptotic Properties of the Maximum Score Estimator', *Journal of Econometrics*, 27: 313–33.

—— (1988), 'Identification of Binary Response Models', *Journal of American Statistical Association*, 83: 729–38.

—— (1989), 'Anatomy of the Selection Problem', *Journal of Human Resources*, 24: 343–60.

—— (1990), 'Nonparametric Bounds on Treatment Effects', *American Economic Review*, 80: 319–23.

—— and Thompson, T. S. (1986), 'Operational Characteristics of Maximum Score Estimation', *Journal of Econometrics*, 32: 65–108.

Matzkin, R. L. (1992), 'Nonparametric and Distribution-Free Estimation of the Binary Threshold Crossing and Binary Choice Models', *Econometrica*, 60: 239–70.

McCullagh, P., and Nelder, J. A. (1989), *Generalized Linear Models*, Monographs on Statistics and Applied Probability, 37. London: Chapman and Hall.

McFadden, D. (1973), 'Conditional Logit Analysis of Qualitative Choice Behaviour', in P. Zarembka (ed.), *Frontiers in Econometrics*. New York: Academic Press.

—— (1975), 'Comments on "Estimation of a Stochastic Model of Reproduction: An Econometric Approach" ', in N. Terleckyji (ed.), *Household Production and Consumption*. New York: National Bureau of Economic Research.

—— (1976), 'Quantal Choice Analysis: a Survey', *Annals of Economic and Social Measurement*, 5.

—— (1981), 'Econometric Models of Probabilistic Choice', in C. F. Manski and D. McFadden (eds.), *Structural Analysis of Discrete Data with Econometric Applications*. Cambridge, Mass.: MIT Press.

—— (1982), 'Qualitative Response Models', in W. Hildenbrand (ed.), *Econometrics*, Econometric Society Monograph, Cambridge.

—— (1987), 'What do Microeconometricians Really Do?' *Proceedings of the American Statistical Association*, Business Statistics Section.

—— (1989), 'A Method of Simulated Moments in Estimation of Multinomial Probits without Numerical Integration', *Econometrica*.

—— and Hausman, J. (1984), 'A Specification Test for the Multinomial Logit Model', *Econometrica*.

—— Newey, W. K., and McFadden, D. (1995), 'Large Sample Estimation and Hypothesis Testing', in R. F. Engle and D. McFadden (eds.), *Handbook of Econometrics*, iv. Amsterdam: North-Holland.

McKenzie, E. (1988), 'Some ARMA Models for Dependent Sequences of Poisson Counts', *Advances in Applied Probability*, 20: 822–35.

Mroz, T. A. (1987), 'The Sensitivity of an Empirical Model of Married Women's Hours of Work to Economic and Statistical Assumptions', *Econometrica*, 55: 765–800.

Newey, W. K. (1988), 'Two Step Series Estimation of Sample Selection Models', mimeo, MIT.

—— Powell, J. L., and Walker, J. R. (1990), 'Semiparametric Estimation of Selection Models: Some Empirical Results', *American Economic Review*, 80: 324–8.

Nickell, S. J. (1981), 'Biases in Dynamic Models with Fixed Effects', *Econometrica*, 49: 1417–26.

Ogaki, M. (1993), 'Generalized Method of Moments: Econometric Applications', in G. S. Maddala, C. R. Rao, and H. D. Vinod (eds.), 'Econometrics', *Handbook of Statistics*, xi. Amsterdam: North-Halland.

Powell, J. L. (1984), 'Least Absolute Deviations Estimation for the Censored Regression Model', *Journal of Econometrics*, 25: 303–25.

—— (1986*a*), 'Symmetrically Trimmed Least Squares Estimation for Tobit Models', *Econometrica*, 54: 1435–60.

—— (1986*b*), 'Censored Regression Quantiles', *Journal of Econometrics*, 32: 143–55.

—— (1994), 'Estimation of Semi-Parametric Models', in R. F. Engle and D. McFadden (eds.), *Handbook of Econometics*, iv. Amsterdam: Elsevier. 1994.

—— Stock, J., and Stoker, T. (1989), 'Semiparametric Estimation of Index Coefficeients', *Econometrica*, 57: 1403–30.

Pudney, S. (1989), *Modelling Individual Choice: the Econometrics of Corners, Kinks and Holes*. Oxford: Basil Blackwell.

Robinson, P. M. (1988), 'Root N-Consistent Semiparametric Regression', *Econometrica*, 56, 931–54.

Ruud, P. (1983), 'Consistent Estimation of Limited Dependent Variable Models Despite Misspecification of Distribution', *Journal of Econometrics*, 32: 157–87.

Shephard, N. (1994), 'Autoregressive Time Series Models Based on the Exponential Family', mimeo, Nuffield College, Oxford.

Silverman, B. W. (1986), *Density Estimation for Statistics and Data Analysis*. London: Chapman and Hall.

Smith, R. J., and Blundell, R. W. (1986), 'An Exogeneity Test for the Simultaneous Equation Tobit Model', *Econometrica*, 54: 679–85.

Stoker, T. M. (1986), 'Consistent Estimation of Scaled Coefficients', *Econometrica*, 54: 1461–81.

—— (1991), *Lectures in Semiparametric Econometrics*, CORE Lecture Series. Louvain-la-Neuve: CORE Foundation.

White, H. (1980), 'A Heteroskedasticity-Consistent Covariance Matrix Estimator and a Direct Test of Heteroskedasticity', *Econometrica*, 48: 817–38.

Wooldridge, J. (1997), 'Multiplicative Panel Data Models without the Strict Exogeneity Assumption', *Econometric Theory*, 13(5), 667–78.

Working, H. (1943), 'Statistical Laws of Family Expenditure', *Journal of the American Statistical Association*, 38, 43–56.

Zeger, S. L., and Qaqish, B. (1988), 'Markov Regression Models for Time Series: a Quasi-Likelihood Approach', *Biometrics*, 44: 1019–31.

Index